Gnosticism:
From Nag Hammadi
to the Gospel of Judas

David Brakke, Ph.D.

THE
GREAT
COURSES

PUBLISHED BY:

THE GREAT COURSES
Corporate Headquarters
4840 Westfields Boulevard, Suite 500
Chantilly, Virginia 20151-2299
Phone: 1-800-832-2412
Fax: 703-378-3819
www.thegreatcourses.com

David Brakke, Ph.D.
Joe R. Engle Chair in the History of
Christianity and Professor of History
The Ohio State University

Professor David Brakke is the Joe R. Engle Chair in the History of Christianity and Professor of History at The Ohio State University, where he has taught since 2012. After receiving his B.A. in English with highest distinction from the University of Virginia, he received his M.Div. from Harvard Divinity School and his Ph.D. in Religious Studies from Yale University. He taught for 19 years (from 1993 to 2012) in the Department of Religious Studies at Indiana University, where he was department chair for 5 years.

Professor Brakke has published extensively on the history and literature of ancient Christianity, especially Egyptian Christianity, early monasticism, the formation of the biblical canon, and Gnosticism. He has edited and translated several ancient works that survive in Coptic and Syriac. He is currently a member of an international team of scholars producing the first unified critical edition and translation of the works of the monk Shenoute of Atripe (348–465), the greatest native writer of Coptic. Professor Brakke is also preparing a revised edition of Bentley Layton's *The Gnostic Scriptures*.

At Indiana University, the professor received recognition for his teaching and research, including the Outstanding Junior Faculty Award. He has held several important fellowships, including ones from the National Endowment for the Humanities and the Alexander von Humboldt Foundation. He has held visiting positions at Concordia College, the University of Chicago, and Williams College.

Professor Brakke is the author of *Athanasius and the Politics of Asceticism*; *Demons and the Making of the Monk: Spiritual Combat in Early Christianity*; *The Gnostics: Myth, Ritual, and Diversity in Early Christianity*; and *Introduction to Christianity*, with Mary Jo Weaver. He has coedited six

i

volumes of scholarly essays and contributed nearly 40 articles to professional journals and volumes. From 2005 to 2015, he served as editor of the *Journal of Early Christian Studies*. ∎

Table of Contents

Table of Contents

Table of Contents

Gnosticism:
From Nag Hammadi to the Gospel of Judas

Scope:

Gnosticism is one of the most fascinating and perplexing phenomena in Western religious history. At its heart was *gnōsis*—direct knowledge of God—expressed in complicated myths. Yet Gnosticism itself often escapes our knowledge. Was it the first great Christian heresy? A new world religion? Or an invention of alarmed Christian leaders and modern scholars? How did it influence other religions? And why did its mythology appeal to so many people? Above all, what does *Gnosticism* mean?

During the last 75 years, previously lost Gnostic writings have reappeared, from the codices found near Nag Hammadi in Egypt in 1945 to the Gospel of Judas, first published in 2006. These texts have given scholars new insights into the diversity of Gnosticism. This course uses these new writings to explore the myths, rituals, and teachings of the first Gnostics and the other movements that used mythology to seek knowledge of God. Gnostics, Valentinians, Manichaeans, and others offered profound answers to the deep questions of human existence, especially the problem of evil. And "orthodox" Christianity developed partially in direct response to these groups.

In this course, we'll discover the diversity of early Christianity, beginning with the so-called Gnostic school of thought, which flourished in the Roman Empire during the 2nd and 3rd centuries A.D. In such works as the Secret Book According to John and the Gospel of Judas, the Gnostics combined the book of Genesis with Jewish, Platonist, and Christian traditions to create a strange but beautiful myth that explained how this universe came into being through an ignorant and malevolent lower god. The Gnostics offered salvation from ignorance and fate through knowledge of a higher God, who sent Jesus, and they claimed that people could have mystical contact with that God now. The Christian teacher Valentinus and his disciples revised the original Gnostic myth to make it even more Christ centered, and they invited Christians to a deeper understanding of the Christian scriptures, sacraments, and doctrines. The Valentinian school existed alongside of, and in competition with, "orthodox" Christianity for centuries. The Gospel According to Thomas did not share the Gnostic myth, but it did teach that to know one's self is to know God, that is, the Jesus who is within you and who you are.

From these core groups within Gnosticism, we'll follow the paths of *gnōsis*, myth making, and new revelations through the ancient Mediterranean world into the Middle Ages and to the present day. We'll meet Mani, who founded a worldwide religion, Manichaeism, that left its traces in the thought of one of Catholic Christianity's heroes, Saint Augustine. And we'll encounter Plotinus and the Neoplatonists, the followers of the Greco-Egyptian god Hermes Trismegistus, the Cathars of medieval Europe, and the Mandaeans, who continue to follow a myth much like that of the Gnostics. We'll follow Paul to the tenth heaven and learn secret teachings of Jesus from Mary Magdalene. And we'll see how "orthodox" Christians, such as Irenaeus of Lyon and Origen of Alexandria, invented the idea of heresy and their Christian doctrines in opposition to the Gnostics and Valentinians. The course concludes with the revival of Gnostic themes in the 20th century in pop culture and new religious movements.

By studying movements that were condemned as heretical and lost, we will gain new understanding of why orthodox Christianity developed as it did, and we will encounter alternative religious paths in the Western tradition—paths to *gnōsis*.■

Rediscovering *Gnōsis*
Lecture 1

In this course, we will study a set of religious texts, persons, and groups that date mostly to the Roman Empire in the first four centuries A.D. We will find that these texts and the people who wrote them were diverse in their teachings and lifestyles. But they all share an interest in knowledge—*gnōsis*, in Greek—and they all suffered rejection and condemnation from what eventually became orthodox Catholic Christianity. The movements that scholars have called Gnosticism may have been labeled heretical, but they were profound and compelling attempts to speak to the human condition of evil and suffering, and they exerted a strong influence on the history of Western religions.

Defining Terms

- The English word *Gnosticism* was invented by an English scholar in the 17th century, but he based it on the Greek word *gnōsis*, meaning personal, direct, and immediate knowledge. The ancient Gnostics claimed to have *gnōsis* of God.

- The adjective and noun *Gnostic* comes from the Greek word *gnōstikos*, which meant "having to do with *gnōsis*" or "supplying *gnōsis*." A *gnōstikos* science, in other words, provides higher knowledge, as opposed to practical knowledge.

- Later philosophical writers continued to use the term *gnōstikos* to refer to fields of study or aspects of the human intellect. However, around the year 180 A.D., a Christian leader named Irenaeus revealed that certain Christians were using the term *gnōstikos* to refer to themselves. This is the first time in history that we know of people being called gnostic. Clearly, these self-proclaimed Gnostics were highlighting their special relationship to *gnōsis*.

Common Gnostic Ideas

- Irenaeus was a fierce critic of the Gnostics; the persons and groups that he condemned had some key ideas in common, although they did not teach all the same things.

- First, they believed that the material universe in which we live is seriously flawed—even a mistake, something that God did not intend. The Gnostics and others had a profound sense of the imperfection that surrounds us and oppresses us—the disease, suffering, and death in the world. Such a world simply cannot be our true home; it cannot be where we are meant to live forever.

Plato invented the adjective *gnōstikos* to describe fields of study and parts of the human intellect that are related to *gnōsis*—"knowledge."

- Thus, the Gnostics and others concluded, as a second point of commonality, that the god who created this universe cannot be the highest, ultimate God. Instead, he must be a lower, inferior god—perhaps even a demonic or hostile god. The Gnostics offered *gnōsis* of the true God, a God who is entirely spiritual, serene, and unchanging; a God worthy of our devotion and worship; a God that most human beings have not known.

  ○ This is an important point of conflict between the Gnostics and other Christians. The Gnostics claimed that the God in the book of Genesis is not the real God but a lower, inferior god.

  ○ We will see that this idea was not as different from what other Jews and Christians believed as we might think, but the Gnostics and groups like them emphasized the inferiority of the God of the Jewish Bible or the Old Testament to a degree that disturbed their opponents.

- Third, Gnostic movements tended to stress that we have our origin in the spiritual world of the highest God. That is, our true selves are not our bodies and sometimes not even our souls; these substances come from the lower universe and are not eternal. Instead, our true selves are our intellect or spirit, which originated in the spiritual realm and will return there. A large part of the *gnōsis* that Gnostics offered was knowledge of our true selves.

- Finally, Gnostic movements tended to communicate their ideas in elaborate myths that told who God is, how the universe came to be, what the original human beings were like, and what will happen in the future. These myths drew on a variety of religious and philosophical traditions, including the Jewish Bible, the works of Plato, and even pagan mythology.

The Nag Hammadi Codices

- Studying the Gnostics and other so-called heretical groups like them is difficult because so few sources survive. For centuries, historians had to rely on the writings of Irenaeus and other opponents of the Gnostics for information about them. Obviously, this information is useful but problematic. The *heresiologists* (writers who catalogue heretical groups) did not seek to present an objective account of heresies in order to help later historians. Instead, their goal was to expose the false nature of the heretical teachings.

- For this reason, historians were excited when, during the 19th and 20th centuries, manuscripts of Gnostic works and other heretical writings were discovered in Egypt. The most spectacular of these findings was the discovery of the Nag Hammadi codices, 13 ancient manuscripts found in 1945. The fact that these manuscripts are codices rather than scrolls was the first clue that their original owners were probably Christians.

- The codices were found by Muhammad 'Ali al-Samman, an Egyptian peasant who was digging for fertilizer in the cliffs across the Nile River from the town of Nag Hammadi. Ultimately, the manuscripts were given to a local priest, who sent one to Cairo to be appraised.
  - Scholars quickly recognized that the Nag Hammadi codices are written in Coptic, which is the last phase of the ancient Egyptian language. Christians themselves invented written Coptic in the 3rd century in order to translate the Bible into Egyptian.

  - Although the texts in the Nag Hammadi codices are written in Coptic, they were originally composed in Greek. The manuscripts we have today were probably copied sometime between 350 and 450 A.D., but some of the original texts may be about 200 years older.

- The Dead Sea Scrolls, which were discovered around the same time as the Nag Hammadi codices, were associated with a specific Jewish community. But the owners of the Nag Hammadi manuscripts remain unknown. Although the codices are sometimes referred to as the Nag Hammadi library, we don't know whether they constituted an intentional collection owned by a single person or institution. In fact, as many as 14 different scribes copied these manuscripts, and the texts are written in several dialects of Coptic. It's possible, then, that the books originally belonged to several people and were only brought together at a later time.

Contents of the Codices
- The Nag Hammadi codices contain a total of 52 texts, but some of these are different versions of the same work. Thus, there are actually 46 separate works or, as scholars call them, *tractates*. These works vary widely in character.

- Most of the tractates can be considered Jewish or Christian because they make use of the Old Testament, or Hebrew Bible; the New Testament; and other Jewish and Christian literature. Such biblical characters as Adam and Eve or Jesus and the apostles appear in nearly all of them. But other tractates do not come originally from Jews or Christians. For example, there is a fragment of the *Republic*, written by Plato centuries before Christ!

- Many of the treatises are apocalypses or revelations. These are books in which a divine figure, such as Jesus, or a legendary human being, such as Adam, reveals future events, secrets of the cosmos, or spiritual teachings to a chosen person or group. For example, in the Gnostic text known as the Revelation of Adam, Adam reveals to his son Seth the story of creation and foretells many events in the future.

- Other types of literature found in the Nag Hammadi codices include theological treatises, sermons, hymns, and philosophical letters. In addition, several tractates are called "gospels," although none of them resembles the gospels in the New Testament, which tell the story of Jesus's ministry and emphasize his passion and death. The Gospel According to Thomas from Nag Hammadi, for instance, presents a collection of Jesus's sayings, somewhat like the biblical book of Proverbs.

Religious Traditions in the Codices

- Since the Nag Hammadi codices were discovered and translated, scholars have identified four religious groups or traditions represented in the texts. The first of these is the Gnostics or Gnostic school of thought that Irenaeus wrote about in 180 A.D.
  - Irenaeus described the myth that the Gnostics taught, and it's precisely the same myth found in the Secret Book According to John from Nag Hammadi.

  - This myth is expressed in at least 11 other tractates, including the Revelation of Adam, the Reality of the Rulers, and the Holy Book of the Great Invisible Spirit.

- A second set of works in the codices comes from the Valentinian school of Christianity. Irenaeus tells us of an influential Christian teacher named Valentinus (d. c. 175 A.D.), who adapted the Gnostic myth in creating his own system of thought.

○ Valentinian theologians devoted considerable attention to such traditional Christian topics as sin and salvation, the resurrection of the dead, and the sacraments.

○ Valentinian works found at Nag Hammadi include the Treatise on Resurrection and the Gospel According to Philip, among others. Some scholars argue that Valentinus himself is the author of the famous—and anonymous—Gospel of Truth.

• A third group of Nag Hammadi writings grants special authority to the apostle Didymus Judas Thomas, credited in Christian tradition with bringing Christianity to Mesopotamia and India. We see this special authority given to Thomas in the Gospel According Thomas and the Book of Thomas the Contender. Thomas theology emphasized the divine origin of the soul, its fall from perfection into the body and the material world, and its ability to return to its origin through the reunion with its true self.

• The fourth group of writings consists of three tractates from Codex VI: the Discourse on the Eighth and Ninth, the Prayer of Thanksgiving, and an excerpt from the Perfect Discourse, also known as Asclepius.
   ○ Although both the Prayer of Thanksgiving and Asclepius were known before the Nag Hammadi discovery, the Discourse on the Eighth and Ninth is a new addition to the corpus of what scholars call *Hermetic literature*, or *Hermeticism*.

   ○ These writings belong to a body of ancient literature that centers on the god Hermes; they may have originated in religious and philosophical circles that were active in Greco-Roman times and late ancient Egypt. In these texts, the divine revealer is "thrice-great Hermes," or Hermes Trismegistus, a composite of the Egyptian god Thoth and the Greek god Hermes.

• After we have examined these movements and others, we will need to ask a basic question: Do they all make up a single thing called

Gnosticism, or is Gnosticism itself an invention of ancient church leaders and modern scholars?

Suggested Reading

Layton, *The Gnostic Scriptures*, general introduction.

Lewis, *Introduction to "Gnosticism."*

Meyer, *The Gnostic Discoveries*, chapters 1–2.

———, ed., *The Nag Hammadi Scriptures*, introduction.

Questions to Consider

1. Give some additional examples of the difference between ordinary knowledge and *gnōsis*.

2. It's hard to determine who might have owned the Nag Hammadi codices because all we have are the books themselves. Consider your own personal library: What might a later historian think about you based solely on the books you own?

Rediscovering *Gnōsis*
Lecture 1—Transcript

One day in 1945, an Egyptian peasant named Muhammad 'Ali al-Samman went out to dig for fertilizer, and he started a revolution in how we understand the history of religions in the ancient world. Ali was digging in the cliffs across the Nile River from the town of Nag Hammadi. While he was digging, he came upon a large earthenware jar with manuscripts inside. Those manuscripts opened the door to an entire religious world that we once knew only dimly. That world is the religious movements that we call "Gnosticism."

In this course, we're going to study a set of religious texts, persons, and groups that date mostly to the Roman Empire in the first four centuries A.D. We will find that these texts and the people who wrote them are very diverse in their teachings and lifestyles. But they all share an interest in knowledge—in Greek, *gnōsis*. And they all suffered rejection and condemnation from what eventually became orthodox Catholic Christianity. They are all, as the bishops and priests of the Church would say, heretics.

The movements that scholars have called "Gnosticism" may have been labeled heretical, but they were profound and compelling attempts to speak to the human condition of evil and suffering. We'll want to understand the messages of hope and salvation that they offered to ancient people.

And these movements are important because they exerted a strong influence on the history of Western religions. Orthodox Christianity became what it is in part in response to these teachings of *gnōsis*. The Gnostics and other religious teachers offered advanced knowledge of religious truth, they produced complicated myths to explain God and the origin of this world, and they sought mystic union with the divine. These themes of advanced knowledge, myth-making, and mystical union have persisted, not only in Christianity, but also in Judaism and Islam.

To begin, I want to explain what words like *gnōsis*, "Gnostic," and "Gnosticism" mean and give you a sense of the general features of the religious movements that we call Gnosticism: What were their distinctive ideas? Why did these ideas appeal to ancient people? And why did the teachings of the Gnostics alarm other Christian leaders? I also want to explain the importance of the manuscripts that Muhammad 'Ali al-Samman found near Nag Hammadi—and why much of what I will discuss in this course we didn't even know just 70 years ago.

The English word *Gnosticism* was invented by an English scholar in the 17th century, but he based it on the Greek word *gnōsis*. As I said, *gnōsis* in ancient Greek means knowledge, but not just any kind of knowledge—it refers to personal, direct, immediate knowledge. For example, if I told you that I know a lot about the city of London, you would expect that I know where it is located, what its history is, how it is laid out, and so on, but you might not think that I have necessarily been to London personally. I could have acquired this knowledge through books, television programs, or web sites.

But if I were to say to you, "I know London," that's something different. In that case, I'm saying that I've been to London. I've walked its streets, talked to its inhabitants, eaten in its restaurants, and so on. This kind of knowledge is immediate, direct, and personal—and it's hard to put into words. I might say about another person, "Yes, I know Susan," and I could probably describe Susan and her life in some detail. But I probably would not be able to explain to you fully in words my knowledge of Susan—you really have to get to know Susan yourself if you want to really know Susan. And you really have to go to London yourself if you really want to know London. That's the kind of knowledge *gnōsis* is.

What the ancient Gnostics said is that they have and they can offer to others *gnōsis* of God—direct, immediate, personal knowledge of God. Now this claim—that they have and supply *gnōsis* of God—did not make the Gnostics unique in the ancient world. Many other religious teachers and groups said the same thing, including other Christians who are now considered orthodox. What set the Gnostics apart was their use of the term *gnostic* to describe themselves and the content of the *gnōsis* or knowledge that they offered.

The adjective and noun *Gnostic* comes from the Greek word *gnōstikos*, which meant "having to do with *gnōsis*" or "supplying *gnōsis*." The great philosopher Plato, who died around 347 B.C., invented the adjective *gnōstikos* to describe fields of study and parts of the human intellect that have to do with *gnōsis*. Fields of study that are *gnōstikos*, Plato said, don't give you practical knowledge, knowledge that you can use directly to accomplish things, like carpentry or baking. Instead, a *gnōstikos* science provides knowledge that's simply knowledge, higher knowledge that may make you wiser or more virtuous, but doesn't really give you a skill—for example, higher forms of mathematics.

Later philosophical writers who admired Plato continued to use the term *gnōstikos*, but always to refer to fields of study or to aspects of the human intellect. It was a highly technical word, one that scholars would use—not one that most ordinary people would ever use.

But around the year 180 A.D., a Christian leader and writer named Irenaeus revealed that certain Christians were using the term *gnōstikos* to refer to themselves. They were the Gnostics, and they formed a group called the Gnostic School of Thought. This is the first time in history that we know of people being called gnostic. Clearly these self-proclaimed Gnostics were highlighting their special relationship to *gnōsis*. A lot of people and groups claimed to offer *gnōsis* of God—including Irenaeus—but these folks made *gnōsis* the defining feature of their religious identity.

In the coming lectures we'll learn a lot more about Irenaeus, who was a leader of Christians in Lyons, in France. That's because Irenaeus's writings constitute our earliest and most detailed source for the teachings of the Gnostics and other groups that modern people call Gnosticism. The Gnostics were among the many groups of Christians during Irenaeus's day. But Irenaeus was a fierce critic of the Gnostics and these other groups. According to him, the Gnostics did not offer true *gnōsis* of God. Rather, their teachings provided "*gnōsis*, falsely so-called!

That brings us to the second distinctive feature of the Gnostics and the other movements of ancient Gnosticism—the content of the religious knowledge that they offered. We're going to see that the persons and groups that Irenaeus condemned did not teach all the same things, but there are some key ideas that they all had in common.

First, they believed that the material universe in which we live is seriously flawed—even a mistake, something that God did not really intend. The Gnostics and others had a profound sense of the imperfection that surrounds us and oppresses us. This is a world of disease, suffering, and death. Rich and powerful people dominate and enslave those who are weaker and more vulnerable. This world simply cannot be our true home. It cannot be where we are meant to live forever.

And so the Gnostics and others concluded, second, that the god who created this universe cannot be the highest, ultimate God. Instead, he must be a lower, inferior god—perhaps even a demonic or hostile god. The Gnostics offered *gnōsis* of the true God, a God who is entirely spiritual and serene and unchanging, a God truly worthy of our devotion and worship; a God that most human beings have not known.

This is an important point of conflict between the Gnostics and other Christians, for the Gnostics claimed that the God that you meet in the book of Genesis—the God who created the universe, the God who made Adam and Eve, the God who destroyed the world with a flood and saved Noah—that God is not the real God, but a lower, inferior god. We'll see that this idea was not as different from what other Jews and Christians believed as we might think at first, but the Gnostics and groups like them emphasized the inferiority of the God of the Jewish Bible or the Old Testament to a degree that disturbed their opponents.

Third, the movements that we call Gnosticism tend to stress that we have our origin in the spiritual world of the highest God. That is, our true selves are not the bodies that we have, and sometimes not even our souls—these substances come from this lower universe and are not eternal. Instead, our true selves are our intellect or spirit, which originated in the spiritual realm and will return there. The problem is is that most of us don't know this—I think that my body and its needs for food, sleep, sex, and so on are what's important. I mistakenly think that this world is my true home. I'm ignorant of my true self, alienated from who I really am. So a big part of the *gnōsis* that Gnostics offered was knowledge of one's own self—an end to my self-alienation.

Finally, the movements that we call Gnosticism tended to communicate their ideas in elaborate myths: sacred stories that told who God is, how the universe came to be, what the original human beings were like, and what will happen in the future. These myths drew upon a variety of religious and philosophical traditions. We'll see that the Jewish Bible, especially Genesis, was the major source for the themes and characters in Gnostic myth. But the Gnostics also looked to the works of Plato and sometimes even to pagan mythology for their ideas.

The myths that we will study usually strike modern readers as strange and complicated—and that's because they are. We will meet characters that may be familiar to you from the Bible and Christianity, such as Adam and Eve, their son Seth, Noah, Jesus, and even God's Wisdom. But we will also meet divine beings that are unique to Gnostic mythology. Some of these have abstract philosophical names, like Forethought or the Divine Self-Originate, but others have obscure proper names like Ialdabaōth, Barbēlō, and Ēlēlēth. There are even some new human characters, like Nōrea, the sister of Seth.

We'll explore the complexity of the myths told by the Gnostics and others, like the Manichaeans, but we will try to look behind that complexity to see the appeal of these stories. In fact, I think that the complexity of the myths was part of their appeal. Some of it must have been simply entertaining, just as people today might find a complicated fantasy novel with lots of characters fun to read. But at a deeper level, I think that ancient people might have expected that *gnōsis* of the true God, wisdom that has been hidden for ages, would be difficult and not simple. Mastering a complex myth, understanding its characters and its themes, might have given people a sense of their own intelligence and religious wisdom. I really do know something important, a Gnostic probably thought!

Studying the Gnostics and other so-called heretical groups like them is difficult because so few sources survive. This is a general problem with studying anything having to do with the ancient world. Even beloved and important works from major authors have been lost or survive in very few copies because it was up to medieval and Byzantine monks to copy them by hand over centuries. In the case of Gnostic and other so-called heretical works, the problem is more acute. Monks just stopped copying these texts; no one wanted to read them, and sometimes you could get in trouble for reproducing them.

For centuries, then, historians had to rely on the writings of Irenaeus and other opponents of the Gnostics for information about them. We call writers like Irenaeus *heresiologists* because their works catalogue heretical groups and summarize their teachings. Obviously, this is useful information, but it is very problematic. The heresiologists did not want to present an objective or neutral account of these heresies in order to help later historians. No, their goal was to expose the false nature of the heretical teachings and to denigrate them as much as possible.

Imagine, then, how excited historians were when, during the 19th and 20th centuries, manuscripts of Gnostic works and other heretical writings were discovered. All of these new texts were discovered in Egypt because Egypt's dry climate means that books that are buried or hidden away can survive for centuries. The most spectacular and important of these new findings was the discovery of the Nag Hammadi codices.

The Nag Hammadi codices are 13 ancient manuscripts that were discovered in 1945 in Egypt, across the Nile River from the town of Nag Hammadi. But what are "codices"? Well, "codices" is the plural for "codex." And a codex is a type of ancient manuscript. It's formatted like a modern book, with individual pages, written on the back and front, which are then sewn together and placed inside a cover.

The codex was a major innovation in antiquity. Most ancient manuscripts were scrolls. These were long, single sheets of papyrus. A scribe would write on one side of the scroll—from the top to the bottom—and then roll and unroll it when he wanted to use it. Although this style of writing was quite ancient, I'm sure you can imagine that it was also impractical and cumbersome.

Starting in the 100s A.D., however, the early Christians began using the codex for their manuscripts. Some scholars speculate that early Christians changed to the codex because codices made it easier for them to quickly find passages in the Bible. In any case, the fact that the Nag Hammadi manuscripts are codices and not scrolls is our first clue that their original owners were probably Christians.

So, how did the Nag Hammadi codices get into the possession of scholars? Muhammad 'Ali al-Samman, the peasant who found the codices, could not read them, but Ali believed that they might be worth something so he brought the books home. And according to the report, his mother actually used some of the pages to start a fire in her oven! Of course, we historians of early Christianity just shudder when we hear that little detail.

Ali and his brother wound up getting involved in a violent feud with another family, and so he gave the codices to a local Christian priest for safekeeping. While they were in his possession, the priest showed the manuscripts to a friend, who realized that they might be valuable. From here, the priest sent one of the manuscripts to Cairo to be appraised. And with this kind of exposure, antiquities dealers soon became aware of the existence of the codices. Ali and other peasants who got hold of one or more of the manuscripts did get some money for the books, but not much. Eventually they all ended up in the Coptic Museum in Cairo, where they're still kept today.

After the codices were discovered, scholars had to figure out what they were. What language were they written in? What texts did they contain? When were these texts composed—and by whom?

Scholars quickly recognized that the Nag Hammadi codices are written in Coptic, which is the last phase of the ancient Egyptian language. Coptic uses the Greek alphabet and a few extra letters to spell Egyptian words. Christians themselves invented written Coptic in the 3rd century so that they could translate the Bible into Egyptian.

But while the texts in the Nag Hammadi codices were written in Coptic, they weren't originally composed in Coptic. Like the books of the New Testament, they were all originally written in Greek. Only later were they translated into Coptic.

So when we read works from Nag Hammadi in Coptic, we're actually reading ancient Coptic translations of originally Greek texts. But because Coptic had a smaller vocabulary than Greek, sometimes the Coptic translator simply borrowed the Greek word for his translation. And that borrowing helps scholars reconstruct what the Greek wording in the original might have been.

We believe that the manuscripts—as we have them—were copied sometime between 350 and 450 A.D. Why do we believe this? Well, the persons who made the covers for the codices used scraps of discarded papyrus to make a stiff backing for the leather covers. It turns out that some of these scraps have dates on them, and the latest date is 348 A.D. So we know that the books must have been made sometime after that date.

Of course, this doesn't mean that the texts in the codices themselves were originally composed after 348. Because we're dealing with copies of translations, the original Greek texts may have been written much earlier. As we'll see, scholars believe that many of the texts come from the 2nd and 3rd centuries, which would make some of the Greek originals about 200 years older than the translated collection.

Now, we don't know who owned these codices or why. Here the discovery of the Nag Hammadi codices differs greatly from the discovery of the famous Dead Sea Scrolls, a discovery that occurred about the same time.

Archaeologists have uncovered evidence for a large community that lived around where the Dead Sea Scrolls were deposited. Archaeological remains and clues in the texts themselves have enabled scholars to identify the community that produced the Dead Sea Scrolls as most likely the Jewish sect of the Essenes.

In contrast, however, there are no remains of a community where the Nag Hammadi codices were found. There was an ancient Christian monastery not too far away, but there's no indication in the codices that they came from this or any other monastery. So here, scholars can only guess as to who produced and owned the codices. We do know that nicely copied manuscripts with leather covers were expensive, so the owners may have been wealthy, educated individuals, or they could have been a group, like a monastic community.

People sometimes refer to the codices as the Nag Hammadi Library, but we don't know whether they actually did make up a library, that is, an intentional collection owned by a single person or institution. As a matter of fact, as many as 14 different scribes copied these manuscripts, and the texts are written in several different dialects of Coptic. So it's possible that the books originally belonged to several people and were only brought together at a later time, perhaps just before they were buried. We don't know when or why the codices were placed in the jar and buried in the desert sand. Egypt's climate is so dry that manuscripts buried in this way can last for many centuries.

As you may know, other Coptic texts appeared before the Nag Hammadi discovery in 1945, and some have been discovered since then. The most famous recent discovery of this kind is a codex that contains the Gospel of Judas. But the Nag Hammadi discovery was revolutionary for scholars and historians.

OK, so that's what we know and don't know about the language, dates, and original owners of the Nag Hammadi codices. What about the writings themselves? The contents of the codices are highly diverse, and they provide a good introduction to the different groups and kinds of texts that we will be looking at in this course.

The Nag Hammadi codices contain a total of 52 texts, but some of these are different versions of the same work. So, there are actually 46 separate works or, as scholars call them, *tractates*. These works vary widely in their character.

Most of the tractates can be considered Jewish or Christian because they make use of the Old Testament or Hebrew Bible, the New Testament, or other Jewish and Christian literature. Such biblical characters as Adam and Eve or Jesus and the apostles appear in nearly all of them. But other tractates do not come originally from Jews or Christians. For example, there is a fragment of the *Republic*, written by Plato centuries before Christ!

Many of the treatises are apocalypses or revelations. These are books in which a divine figure like Jesus, or a legendary human being like Adam, reveals future events, secrets of the cosmos, or spiritual teachings to a chosen person or group. For example, in the Apocalypse or Revelation of Adam, Adam reveals to his son Seth the story of creation and foretells many events in the future. Or in the Secret Book of James, Jesus appears to his disciples after his resurrection and gives secret teachings to a small group of insiders.

The apocalypse or revelation is the most frequent type of literature found in the Nag Hammadi codices. But there are also other types of literature, such as theological treatises, sermons, hymns, philosophical letters, and other kinds of writings. And several tractates are called "gospels," but none of them resemble the gospels in the New Testament. The four New Testament gospels tell the story of Jesus's ministry and emphasize his passion and death.

But the Gospel According to Thomas from Nag Hammadi, for instance, presents a collection of Jesus's sayings, somewhat like the biblical book of Proverbs. It does not give any narrative description of Jesus's life or death. In fact, if you had only the Gospel of Thomas, you wouldn't know that Jesus had even been crucified! Likewise, the Gospel of Truth is not a story about Jesus. Rather, it's a sermon about how Jesus brought knowledge of the truth to human beings.

So the tractates have different literary forms. They also represent different theological views. All of the works may have appealed to the later collector or collectors in the 4th or 5th century, but they were composed within diverse—even opposed—religious communities as early as the 1st century.

Since the Nag Hammadi codices were discovered, edited, and translated, scholars have been working to identify the religious groups and theological perspectives that the works represent. So far, a consensus of scholars has identified four religious groups or traditions represented in the literature from the Nag Hammadi manuscripts.

First, we believe that one group is the Gnostics or Gnostic school of thought that Irenaeus wrote about in the year 180 A.D. Irenaeus described the myth that the Gnostics taught, and it's precisely this same myth that we find in the Secret Book According to John from Nag Hammadi. This myth is expressed in at least eleven other tractates. Among these works are the Revelation of

Adam, the Reality of the Rulers, and the Holy Book of the Great Invisible Spirit. These texts differ in some details, but they all share the same basic myth or sacred story that the Gnostics told.

This discovery was very exciting, because—thanks to Nag Hammadi—we now have texts that come directly from the so-called Gnostic heretics themselves! We will spend the next seven lectures exploring the myth and rituals of the Gnostic school of thought.

But the Gnostics are only one of the groups represented in the Nag Hammadi codices. A second set of works comes from the Valentinian school of Christianity. Once again, it's Irenaeus who fills in the details for us. He says that an influential Christian teacher named Valentinus adapted the Gnostic myth in creating his own system of thought.

Valentinus died around the year 175, and, in the decades following his death, Christian theologians following and teaching in his tradition formed study groups of interested Christians. This was alongside and sometimes in direct competition with other established Christian churches. We will explore in some detail the myth and teachings of Valentinian Christians.

Valentinian theologians devoted considerable attention to such traditional Christian topics as sin and salvation, the resurrection of the dead, and the sacraments. Valentinian works found at Nag Hammadi include the Treatise on Resurrection and the Gospel According to Philip, among others. Some scholars argue that Valentinus himself is the author of the famous—and anonymous—Gospel of Truth, and he certainly seems to be an ideal candidate.

The Valentinian school of Christianity lasted from the middle of the 2nd century into the 4th century, and it represented an important Christian theological tradition. But after Christianity became the favored religion of the Roman Empire, the Valentinians were condemned as heretics. Valentinus and the Valentinians will be an important part of the course, with four lectures devoted just to them.

In addition to the Gnostic school of thought and the Valentinian Christians, a third group of Nag Hammadi writings grants special authority to the apostle Didymus Judas Thomas. Christian tradition credits Thomas with bringing Christianity to Mesopotamia and India, and it sometimes even identifies him as Jesus's twin brother!

We see this special authority given to Thomas in the Gospel According Thomas and the Book of Thomas the Contender. And as it turns out, these two works share literary and theological connections with a third work called the Acts of Thomas. This text survives in Greek and Syriac, but it was not found at Nag Hammadi. Taken together, some scholars consider these works evidence for a "Thomas Christianity," similar to the community of Christians affiliated with St. Paul.

Thomas theology emphasized the divine origin of the soul, its fall from perfection into the body and the material world, and how it can return to its origin through the reunion with its true self.

We will devote two lectures to the Gospel According to Thomas. We'll see that, although it's often referred to as the most prominent of the "Gnostic gospels," the Gospel of Thomas lacks evidence of the kind of elaborate myth found in the Gnostic works, so scholars are increasingly reluctant to refer to it as being "Gnostic."

A fourth and final group of writings is perhaps the strangest to our ears. It consists of three tractates from Codex VI—the Discourse on the Eighth and Ninth, the Prayer of Thanksgiving, and an excerpt from the Perfect Discourse, also known as Asclepius.

While both the Prayer of Thanksgiving and Asclepius were known before the Nag Hammadi discovery, the Discourse on the Eighth and Ninth is a new addition to the corpus of what scholars call "Hermetic literature," or Hermeticism.

These writings belong to a body of ancient literature that centers around the god Hermes; and they may have originated in religious and philosophical circles that were active in Greco-Roman and late ancient Egypt. In these texts, the divine revealer is "thrice-great Hermes" or Hermes Trismegistus. This mythic figure is a composite of the native Egyptian god Thoth and the Greek god Hermes.

Hermeticism is one variety of non-Christian *gnōsis* that we will learn about. Others include Neoplatonism, Manichaeism, and Mandaeism. And after we have examined many of these movements, we will need to ask the most basic question of all: Do they all make up a single thing called *Gnosticism*, or is Gnosticism itself just an invention of ancient church leaders and modern scholars?

But first, let's learn what we can about the original Gnostics, the first people we know of who developed a myth of *gnōsis*. In the next lecture I'll say more about what Irenaeus tells us about the Gnostics, and we'll see how they fit into the great diversity of Christianity in the 2nd and 3rd centuries.

Who Were the Gnostics?
Lecture 2

For centuries, scholars interested in the Gnostics or Valentinians had to rely on Irenaeus of Lyon, a bishop of the late 2nd century. Irenaeus was an enemy of the Gnostics, whom he called heretics. Although he's not an objective source of information about Gnosticism, Irenaeus still gives us some important insights. First, his writings reveal that Christianity was quite diverse in its first few centuries. Second, Irenaeus gives us some basic information about the Gnostics: He tells us what they taught, and even more important, he gives us clues about what they wrote. In this lecture, we'll look closely at Irenaeus and see what we can take away from him about the Gnostics.

Irenaeus of Lyon
- In the late 170s, Irenaeus became the leader of a small group of Christians in Lyon, which was a major city in the Roman province of Gaul (modern-day France). Most of the Christians in Lyon were Greek-speaking immigrants and were distrusted by the majority population. In fact, at the time Irenaeus became their leader, the Christians of Lyon had just endured a horrifying persecution. When he became bishop, Irenaeus sought to rebuild the confidence of the Christian community in Lyon and somehow to attract new followers.

- But Irenaeus was not the only Christian leader in Lyon. Other teachers of Christianity offered messages that conflicted with what Irenaeus taught. Irenaeus claimed that these other Christian teachers taught false knowledge and should not be called Christians—"followers of Christ"—but Valentinians—"followers of Valentinus." They were not members of the one true Christian church but members of multiple deceptive schools of thought—or heresies.

- Irenaeus took it upon himself not only to stop Christians in Lyon from following these other teachers but also to help other Christian leaders throughout the world combat them. He wrote a massive work known as *Against the Heresies*, in which he described false versions of Christianity to enable his readers to recognize these false teachings when they encountered them.

Diversity in Early Christianity

- Irenaeus claimed that a single true Christianity originated with Jesus and the apostles. In his view, other groups, such as the Gnostics, may have claimed to be Christians, but they were false deviations from the one true Christianity. Irenaeus claimed to represent orthodox Christianity, and all competing Christians were heretics.

- For a long time, scholars tended to believe Irenaeus. That is, they thought that a single, unified Christianity had been born in the 1st century and this original Christianity could be found in the New Testament. Later on, some teachers, such as the Gnostics and Valentinus, diverged from mainstream Christianity. These days, however, most historians do not agree with this picture. They believe that Christianity was diverse from the very beginning.

- We can see this diversity already in the New Testament. The earliest Christian sources that we have are the letters of Paul, all of which are believed to come from the 50s A.D., about 20 years after the death of Jesus. Paul's letters reveal disagreement among the earliest Christians. One particular issue occurs multiple times in Paul's letters: How should Gentiles be included in salvation? The argument about this question shows us that even the first apostles did not always agree about the basics of the Christian faith.
  - Some of the apostles argued that to become fully righteous and be saved, Gentiles needed to believe in Jesus as God's Son and to give up their paganism by becoming Jews. That is, Gentile believers must undergo circumcision (if they were male) and observe the Jewish Law by keeping a kosher diet and so on.

  - Paul violently disagreed with this position. In his view, Gentiles needed only to have faith in Jesus to be righteous. Certainly, this meant giving up their pagan gods and living moral lives, but they did not have to get circumcised and follow the Law. God had given the Law to the Jews for them to follow until the Messiah came. But now that he had come, Gentiles may be included in salvation simply by having faith in Christ.

- In contrast to Irenaeus's claims, we can see that even the original apostles did not agree on a single Christian message. In fact, they disagreed about a basic question: How are people to be saved— by faith in Christ alone or by faith in Christ and following the Jewish Law?

Marcion

- Disagreement on the question of inclusion of Gentiles and whether they should follow the Jewish Law persisted among Christians for decades. One Christian teacher, Marcion, argued that Christians should not use the Jewish Bible at all.

- Marcion was a Christian teacher in Rome in the 140s who concluded that Paul's gospel of faith in Christ was opposed to the Jewish Bible's teaching of circumcision and following the Law. In his view, Jesus and Paul preached a message of forgiveness and love—the New Testament—but the Bible preached a message of retribution and punishment—the Old Testament.
  - Marcion argued that Jesus could not be the Son of the Old Testament God. Instead, the Father of Jesus Christ must be some other God, a God that was unknown until Jesus revealed him. Jesus came to rescue people from the punishments inflicted on them by the overly righteous God of the Old Testament.

  - Marcion said that the Old Testament should no longer be read as scripture by Christians. Instead, they should use only the letters of Paul and a gospel about Jesus.

- Paul himself certainly would have disagreed with Marcion, but we can see how Marcion's message could develop from Paul's. Because Paul often contrasted faith in Christ with following the Law, Marcion concluded that Christianity should be completely separate from Judaism and everything Jewish, including the Old Testament.

- Many other Christians in Rome argued that Marcion was a heretic who taught false Christianity. Thus, Marcion began forming churches outside of Rome. Eventually, a network of Christian churches devoted to Marcion's teachings spread throughout the Roman Empire and lasted for centuries.

- The story of Marcion illustrates two important points.
  - First, we have seen that Christians were diverse and often in disagreement and that some Christians, such as Marcion, were called heretics by others. But notice that there was no enforcement of the declaration of Marcion as a heretic. Christians in the 2nd century had no worldwide structure to impose standard teachings and practices.

  - Second, it's not correct to say, as Irenaeus would, that Marcion deviated from an original Christian truth. Rather, Marcion's distinctive view of how Christians should relate to the Old Testament and Jewish Law reflects longstanding diversity on this question.

Irenaeus on the Gnostics
- As we said, Irenaeus wrote *Against the Heresies* to help other Christian leaders recognize the teachings of so-called heretics and refute them. Certainly, Irenaeus disparages the teachers and groups he describes, but he is nonetheless careful to lay out their teachings in some detail. Thus, we can gain several insights into the Gnostics from Irenaeus.

- Primarily, Irenaeus tells us that the Gnostics taught a myth that explains who God is, how the world we live in came into being, how sin and death entered the world, and how God is acting to save people. According to Irenaeus, this myth presented a complicated picture of God.

- The Gnostic God, he says, consisted of several aspects or divine emanations from God, called *aeons*. The myth also told about the creation of this world by revising and restating the stories in the biblical book of Genesis. Finally, the Gnostics said that Jesus came into this world to save people and will gather the souls of the saved at the end of time.

- The most striking feature of the Gnostic myth as Irenaeus tells it is that the God of Genesis is a divine being who is lower than the ultimate God and is arrogant, ignorant, and evil. He is hostile to human beings because human beings have a share of the divine spirit that belongs to the higher God. The real name of the god who created this world is Ialdabaōth—a spiritual being who runs this universe like a tyrant.

In the Gnostic myth, the serpent that persuades Adam and Eve to eat from the tree of knowledge may not be leading them into sin but helping them to gain true spiritual knowledge.

- This idea—that the God of Genesis is actually a malevolent cosmic ruler—has important implications for how Gnostics understand the rest of the Genesis story.
  - If this god is hostile to human beings, then when he commands Adam and Eve not to eat from the tree of knowledge of good and evil, he is preventing them from knowing spiritual truth.

  - When Adam and Eve eat from the tree, they gain *gnōsis*, knowledge of the true God. As human beings continue to seek true spiritual knowledge, Ialdabaōth grows jealous of their devotion to the higher God and causes a flood to wipe out humanity. Fortunately, the higher God saves Noah and his family from Ialdabaōth's evil plot.

○ Finally, human beings later begin to lose the knowledge that Adam and Eve gained when they ate from the tree. But the higher God sends Jesus to restore this lost *gnōsis* and rescue them from Ialdabaōth and his fellow rulers.

● Obviously, the Gnostic myth was a direct challenge to how Irenaeus saw God and Jesus, but we can draw two conclusions from his report.
○ First, the Gnostics were concerned about aspects of the God of Genesis that did not seem godlike. For example, would a perfect god change his mind about the creation of human beings and cause a flood to wipe out nearly all of them? The Gnostics concluded that the god who did this must not be the ultimate, perfect God but something lower and imperfect.

○ Second, we have seen that Christians disagreed about the role that the Jewish Bible should play in their religion. When Paul said that salvation was based on faith in Christ and not on following the Law, he opened the door to Christians like Marcion, who concluded that the Jewish Bible was no longer relevant to Christians. The Gnostics took a different approach: The Bible is relevant, but it's not quite accurate. It tells the story of salvation, but we need to understand that the god it honors is not the true God.

Suggested Reading

Brakke, *The Gnostics*, chapters 2–3.

Ehrman, *Lost Christianities*.

Layton, *The Gnostic Scriptures*, "The Gnostics According to St. Irenaeus of Lyon" and "Other Gnostic Teachings According to St. Irenaeus of Lyon."

Räisänen, "Marcion."

1. Why did the Jewish Law pose a problem for early Christians?

2. According to Irenaeus, what are the main features of Gnostic teaching?

Who Were the Gnostics?
Lecture 2—Transcript

In the first lecture we saw that, after the Nag Hammadi codices were discovered, scholars were able to identify some of the ancient religious groups that had produced the texts that they contained. Above all, many of the writings seemed to come from Christians known as Gnostics or Valentinians. How did historians know this? What information about Gnostics and Valentinians did scholars have before the Nag Hammadi discovery?

For centuries, scholars interested in these heretical groups had to rely on Irenaeus of Lyons, a bishop of the late 2nd century. Irenaeus was an enemy of the Gnostics, whom he called heretics. So he's not exactly a trustworthy source for getting objective information about Gnostics. Still, we can learn some very important things from the writings of Irenaeus—even after the discovery at Nag Hammadi. First, they reveal that Christianity was very diverse in the first few centuries, and there was no worldwide structure that could control this diversity. Second, Irenaeus gives us some basic information about the Gnostics: He tells us what they taught and, even more important, he gives us clues about what they wrote, including the famous Gospel of Judas. First, let's learn more about Irenaeus and the challenges that he faced.

In the late 170s, Irenaeus became the leader of a small group of Christians in Lyons. Lyons was a major city in the Roman province of Gaul, modern-day France, where most educated people spoke and wrote in Latin. But Irenaeus was a Greek-speaker: he had immigrated to Lyons from his home in Asia Minor, modern-day Turkey. After spending some time in Rome, Irenaeus had settled in Lyons. Most of the other Christians in Lyons were also Greek-speaking immigrants from the eastern part of the Roman Empire. They had probably moved to Western Europe to seek better jobs. But now they were a small group of foreigners in a city that distrusted them.

In fact, when Irenaeus became their leader or, as we call him today, their bishop, the Christians in Lyons had just endured a horrifying persecution. We know about this persecution because the surviving Christians described it in a letter to their friends and fellow Christians back home in Asia Minor.

At first, people in Lyons discriminated against them by not letting them use the public baths or do business in their shops. Then Christians were attacked by groups of thugs. Finally, they were accused of being traitors to the Roman state because they refused to worship the gods of Rome. They were given the choice of renouncing Christianity and sacrificing to the gods or dying in the arena as the victims of wild animals or professional gladiators.

The persecution was devastating. The most active and faithful members of the small group were executed after prolonged torture. Others gave up and agreed to worship the Roman gods. Worst of all, their elderly bishop Pothinus was killed. Then the persecution subsided.

So when Irenaeus succeeded Pothinus as the group's bishop, he had a lot of work to do. The group's leading members had been killed, and others had given up their Christian faith. The survivors were understandably shaken and uncertain about their future. Irenaeus needed to rebuild their confidence, and also he wanted somehow to attract new followers to a group that had been seen as dangerous to the community.

But these were not the only problems the new bishop faced. Irenaeus was not the only Christian leader in Lyons. Other teachers of Christianity offered people their own messages of salvation through Jesus Christ—messages that conflicted with what Irenaeus taught. According to Irenaeus, what these teachers said to his followers sounded like what Irenaeus taught. That is, they also talked about God the Father, Jesus his Son, sin and salvation, the Bible, and the resurrection of the dead. But Irenaeus complained that, when you learned what these teachers meant by these teachings, it was not at all the same. He claimed that these other Christian teachers were not really Christians at all. Instead, they taught false knowledge—false *gnōsis*—and they should not be called Christians—"followers of Christ"—but Valentinians—"followers of Valentinus." They are not members of the one true Christian church, but members of a multitude of deceptive schools of thought—or heresies.

Irenaeus felt that it was urgent that he defend his flock against these rival Christian teachers. In the Gospel of Matthew, Jesus warns his followers against false prophets. "They come to you in sheep's clothing," Jesus says, "but inwardly they are ferocious wolves." According to Irenaeus, that's what Valentinian Christian teachers were—the "wolves in sheep's clothing" that Jesus had predicted. On one level, Irenaeus's personal authority was at stake. There weren't many Christians in Lyons—or anywhere else, for that matter. So if Christians followed after these other leaders, who would follow Irenaeus?

But even more important for Irenaeus, salvation was at stake. He sincerely believed that Christians who followed the true message of Jesus would enjoy eternal life in heaven after Jesus returned to judge the world. Everyone else would be damned to hell. In his view the damned would include not only pagans and other non-believers, but also false Christians. If Christians followed these Valentinian teachers, they would lose their salvation and spend eternity in the torment of hell.

For these reasons Irenaeus took it upon himself not only to stop Christians in Lyons from following these other Christians, but also to help other Christian leaders like him throughout the world combat them as well. He wrote a massive work entitled *Detection and Overthrow of Gnōsis, Falsely So-Called*, which is also known more simply as *Against the Heresies*. In this book, Irenaeus described all the false versions of Christianity that he knew about so that his readers could recognize these false teachings when they encountered them. It was like a catalogue of all the brands of Christianity that were circulating in the Roman Empire.

In Irenaeus's view, however, only the Christianity that he and bishops like him taught was the true Christianity—that is, true *gnōsis* or knowledge of God. All the others were false distortions of the single true Christianity that Jesus and the apostles had taught.

Later in the course we'll study Irenaeus's own theology more closely and we'll learn how he developed a distinctive vision of Christianity to combat that of the Gnostics and Valentinians. But today I want to use Irenaeus's work to do two things. First, I'll question his picture of Christianity as existing in one true Church—that is, his Church—and ask how these other versions of Christianity came to be. That is, were the Gnostics really heretical offshoots of true Christianity? And second, we want to find out what Irenaeus tells us about the Gnostics and learn how he can help us to identify previously lost Gnostic writings.

As I have said, Irenaeus claimed that a single true Christianity originated with Jesus and the apostles. Other groups, like the Gnostics, may have claimed to be Christian, but they were really false deviations from the one true Christianity. That is, Irenaeus claimed to represent orthodox Christianity, and all his competing Christians were heretics.

For a long time, scholars tended to believe Irenaeus. That is, historians followed Irenaeus in believing that a single unified Christianity was born in the 1st century, and they thought that this single original Christianity could be found in the writings of the New Testament. Later on, some teachers, like the Gnostics and Valentinus, diverged from mainstream Christianity. Even if they would not call these other Christians "heretics," historians treated them like aberrations, strange and exotic offshoots of basic Christianity.

These days, however, most historians do not agree with this picture. We believe that Christianity was diverse from the very beginning. There probably was no golden age when all Christians agreed about everything—if there was, maybe it lasted a few days. Instead, people responded to the ministry of Jesus in a variety of ways, and sometimes they came into conflict over their views.

We can see this diversity already in the New Testament. The earliest Christian sources that we have are the letters of Paul, all of which we believe come from the 50s in the 1st century. Now Jesus was crucified probably around the year 30, so Paul's letters give us a snapshot of Christianity about 20 years or so after Jesus. Do we find in Paul's letters what Irenaeus claims there was? That is, was there a single Christian message taught by all the apostles? In brief, no.

Paul's letters reveal that the earliest Christians disagreed about many things, including some of the basic ideas of Christianity, like what the resurrection of the dead would mean. One particular issue occurs multiple times in Paul's letters: How should Gentiles (non-Jews) be included in salvation? The argument about this question can show us how even the first apostles did not always agree about the basics of the Christian faith.

Like most other early Christians, Paul believed that it would not be long before the world as he knew it would come to an end. Jesus had preached that a new kingdom of God was coming and that people should repent and prepare for the final judgment. The Roman rulers found this message frightening—they did not want their empire to be replaced by a kingdom of God—and so they executed Jesus as the false King of the Jews. But after his death Jesus appeared to people, including Paul, and these appearances convinced them that God had raised Jesus from the dead. For Jews like Paul, this was a sign that the kingdom of God was very near and that Jesus was God's messiah or anointed one, the leader who would bring this kingdom.

Paul told his followers that Jesus would return soon and bring the current world order to an end. God would liberate faithful Jews from Roman rule and establish a new order of justice and peace—the kingdom of God. This kingdom would not be in heaven, but it would be this world, miraculously transformed. The dead would be resurrected, and everyone would be judged. God's elect or chosen ones would live forever in God's kingdom, while unbelievers and sinners would perish in eternal punishment.

These ideas of a coming kingdom of God, a messiah, a resurrection, and a judgment were common among ancient Jews. They looked forward to a time when they would no longer be ruled by foreign powers like the Romans and when God would fulfill the promises of salvation that he made to Abraham and Moses and King David. For example, you can find these ideas in books of the Hebrew Bible, like Daniel, and in the Dead Sea Scrolls, which a group of Jews wrote in the centuries before Jesus and Paul.

What was unique about the message of the first Christians, who were also Jews, was that Jesus was that messiah. Jesus, however, did not fit the traditional view of the Messiah. He did not liberate the Jews from the Romans and establish a kingdom. Rather, he was executed as a common criminal. So early Jesus believers like Peter and James did not succeed in converting many of their fellow Jews. Paul himself had rejected the idea of Jesus as the Messiah—until Jesus himself appeared to Paul and charged Paul to bring his message not to other Jews, but to non-Jews, to Gentiles.

This idea—including Gentiles in the kingdom of God—was also traditional in Jewish thinking about what they called "the day of the Lord." Biblical books like Isaiah and Zechariah taught that on the day of the Lord righteous Gentiles would give up their worship of idols and turn to the God of Israel. And so they would be saved, along with faithful Jews. Paul believed that Jesus the Messiah had commissioned him to bring this message to Gentiles: they should give up their pagan gods, worship the God of Israel, and find salvation in the coming kingdom.

But this raised the question of how Gentiles would be made righteous and so worthy of salvation. And here's where the early Christians disagreed. Some of the apostles argued that, to become fully righteous and be saved, Gentiles need to believe in Jesus as God's Son and they must give up their paganism by becoming Jews. That is, Gentile believers must undergo circumcision, if they are male, and observe the Jewish Law by keeping a kosher diet and so on. After all, God made his promises to the descendants of Abraham, all of whom are supposed to be circumcised, if they are men.

Paul violently disagreed with this position. In his view, Gentiles needed only to have faith in Jesus to be righteous. Certainly this meant giving up their pagan gods and their living a moral life, but they did not have to get circumcised and follow the Law. God had given the Law to the Jews for them to follow until the Messiah came. But now that he has come, Gentiles may be included in salvation simply by having faith in Christ.

Let's notice a couple things about this. First, this was a question that divided the original apostles. It's clear from Paul's writings that such apostles as Peter and James were originally on the pro-circumcision side of the question. At a meeting with Paul and his allies in Jerusalem, Peter and James agreed that Paul should continue to preach to Gentiles and let them become Christians without being circumcised. But even this agreement did not bring full unity because later on Paul and Peter had another big fight about whether Jewish Christians and Gentile Christians could share the same non-kosher foods.

So, in contrast to Irenaeus's claims, we see that the original apostles did not agree on a single Christian message. In fact, they disagreed about a very basic question: how are people to be saved—by faith in Christ alone or by faith in Christ and following the Jewish Law?

Second, we must conclude that Jesus gave his followers no guidance on this matter. According to the Gospels, Jesus limited his preaching to his fellow Jews in Galilee and Judea. He is quoted as saying that his mission was only to the lost sheep of the house of Israel. Jesus did not lay out any plan for a Christian church that would include both Jews and Gentiles. So, again, in contrast to Irenaeus's claims, Jesus did not give true Christian teaching to his apostles, who then passed it on to his Church. Instead, the earliest Christians had to figure out a lot of what they should believe—and they came up with different answers!

In this case, there was no "original" or "orthodox" Christian doctrine from which other Christians diverged. Instead, Christians disagreed from the beginning. Not only this, but disagreement on this issue persisted for decades. Different Christian groups took different approaches to the question of including Gentiles and how they should follow the Jewish Law. Some Christians continued to require that all believers get circumcised, follow a kosher diet, and observe other parts of the Law. Some even wrote books that depicted Paul as a false Christian apostle inspired by Satan.

Other Christians agreed that Gentile believers did not have to get circumcised, but they felt that Paul's rejection of the Law had gone too far. There are examples of this position in the New Testament itself. The Gospel of Matthew has Jesus state that he did not come to abolish the Law and the prophets, but to fulfill them. Not a single thing of the Law is to be abolished, and Jesus condemns anyone who teaches Christians to break any of the Law's commandments. Likewise, the Letter of James insists that faith is not enough for salvation; Christians must also perform works to gain their salvation.

Many Christians, of course, followed Paul's view. Gentile believers did not have to be circumcised, and Christians did not need to keep kosher and follow other regulations found in the Bible, like those dealing with worship in the Temple. But this position raised the question of what role the Jewish

Bible and its Law should then play in Christianity? What should Christians do with the Law if they don't need to follow its rules about diet, priests, and sacrifices? One Christian teacher argued that Christians should not use the Jewish Bible at all.

Marcion was a Christian teacher in Rome in the 140s. He concluded that Paul's gospel of faith in Christ was opposed to the Jewish Bible's teaching of circumcision and following the Law. In his view, Jesus and Paul preached a message of forgiveness and love—the New Testament—but the Bible preached a message of retribution and punishment—the Old Testament. Marcion argued that Jesus could not be the Son of the Old Testament God. Instead, the Father of Jesus Christ must be some other God, a God that was unknown until Jesus revealed him. Jesus came to rescue people from the punishments inflicted on them by the overly righteous God of the Old Testament.

Marcion said that the Old Testament, the Jewish Bible, should no longer be read as Scripture by Christians. Instead, they should use only the letters of Paul and a gospel about Jesus. Now Paul himself certainly would have disagreed with Marcion. Paul believed that the Jewish Bible paved the way for Jesus. If you read the Bible properly, Paul said, you would see that it points to Jesus. But I think we can see how Marcion's message could develop from Paul's. Because Paul often contrasted faith in Christ with following the Law, Marcion concluded that Christianity should be completely separate from Judaism and everything Jewish, including the Old Testament.

Marcion developed a group of Christians devoted to his teachings in Rome. He tried to persuade other Christian groups in Rome to follow his views, but they refused. They argued that Marcion was not a true Christian, but a heretic who taught false Christianity. So Marcion cut off his relations with other Christians and began forming churches in cities other than Rome. Eventually a network of Christian churches devoted to Marcion's teachings spread throughout the Roman Empire and lasted for centuries.

The story of Marcion illustrates a couple things. First, we have seen that Christians were diverse and disagreed about things and that some Christians, like Marcion, were called heretics by other Christians. But notice that there is no way for anyone to enforce the declaration of Marcion as a heretic.

Christians in the 2nd century had no worldwide structure to make sure that everyone taught and practiced the same things. So Marcion could just go on doing what he wanted, and only in hindsight do we see that his Christian movement would not prevail in the long run.

Second, it's not right to say, as Irenaeus would, that Marcion deviated from an original Christian truth. Rather, Marcion's distinctive view of how Christians should relate to the Old Testament and Jewish Law reflects long-standing diversity on this question, which goes back to the days of Paul. This is an important point to remember as we think about the Gnostics. We cannot trace the Gnostics as a separate movement back to the earliest years of Christianity; but their distinctive views, like those of Marcion, have roots in the period of the apostles.

If Irenaeus was wrong about the Gnostics, Marcion, and other so-called heretics deviating from an original Christian orthodoxy, is there anything we can learn from him about the Gnostics? Indeed there is—quite a lot, in fact. Let's remember that Irenaeus wrote his big book *Against the Heresies* precisely to help other Christian leaders to recognize the teachings of the so-called heretics and refute them. Certainly Irenaeus disparages the teachers and groups he describes, and he accuses them of being immoral as well as theologically stupid. Nonetheless, he is careful to lay out their teachings in some detail, and when we can use other sources to check on what Irenaeus says, he usually appears to be pretty accurate.

This is what Irenaeus tells us about the Gnostics. He calls them "the Gnostic school of thought," and he calls individual members *Gnostics*—in Greek *Gnōstikoi*. By calling the group a "school of thought," Irenaeus uses the same Greek term that comes to mean *heresy—hairesis*. Later in the course we will discuss in more detail how Irenaeus helped to create the concept of heresy, but now let's notice that by labeling the Gnostics a school of thought or *hairesis*, Irenaeus indicates that they were some sort of group, but it is not clear how close-knit they were. Some schools of thought in antiquity were small, tight groups, like religious sects. But others were more loose and disorganized, more intellectual movements, like Freudian psychology or neo-conservatives today. We'll have to look at Gnostic literature for signs of how organized a group they might have been.

We also don't know where the Gnostic school of thought originated. It spread all over the Mediterranean world, but where did it start? Without any positive evidence, most historians guess that it was Alexandria in Egypt. Alexandria was one of the ancient world's most cosmopolitan cities, and it had a large community of philosophers and religious teachers, including many Jews. As we'll see, some of the ideas we find in Gnostic myth are similar to those of Philo, a prominent Jewish intellectual who lived in Alexandria during the 1st century. Alexandria would have provided an excellent environment for a movement like the Gnostics to begin and grow.

Irenaeus says that the teachings of the Gnostics influenced Valentinus, the leader of the Christian theological movement that he found so threatening. We will want to check that claim out as well when we study Valentinus. But mostly Irenaeus tells us that the Gnostics taught a myth, a sacred story that explains who God is, how the world we live in came into being, how sin and death entered the world, and how God is acting to save people.

According to Irenaeus, this myth presented a very complicated picture of God. The Gnostic God, he says, consisted of several aspects or divine emanations from God, called *aeons*. The myth also told about the creation of this world by revising and restating the stories in the biblical book of Genesis. The Gnostics claimed to base their teachings not only on Genesis, but also on the other books of the Jewish Bible. Finally, the Gnostics said that Jesus came into this world to save people and he will gather the souls of the saved at the end of time.

The most striking feature of the Gnostic myth as Irenaeus tells it is that the God of Genesis, the god who created the world and Adam and Eve, is not the real God. Instead, the God of Genesis is a divine being lower than the truly ultimate God, and lower even than the aspects or aeons of that truly ultimate God. Not only this, but the God of Genesis, the creator of this world, is arrogant, ignorant, and evil. He is hostile to human beings because human beings have a share of the divine spirit that belongs to the higher, ultimate God. The real name of the god who created this world is Ialdabaōth, and the myth calls him a ruler—a spiritual being who runs this universe like a tyrant. He was the chief ruler of an entire set of malevolent beings who exert power over us and this world.

This idea—that the God of Genesis is actually a malevolent cosmic ruler named Ialdabaōth—has important implications for how the Gnostics understand the rest of the Genesis story. If this god is hostile to human beings, then when he commands Adam and Eve not to eat from the tree of knowledge of good and evil, this is not a good thing to help the human beings, but a bad thing, to prevent them from knowing spiritual truth. The serpent that persuades Adam and Eve to eat from the tree may not be leading them into sin, but helping them to gain true spiritual knowledge. When Adam and Eve eat from the tree, they gain *gnōsis*, knowledge of the true higher God, and they realize that the god who created them is not really the true God. As human beings continue to seek true spiritual knowledge, Ialdabaōth grows jealous of their devotion to the higher God. And this is why he causes a flood to wipe out the human beings who refused to worship him. Fortunately, the higher God saves Noah and his family from Ialdabaōth's evil plot.

And finally, human beings later begin to lose the knowledge that Adam and Eve gained when they ate from the tree. But the higher God sends Jesus to restore this lost *gnōsis* and rescue them from Ialdabaōth and his fellow rulers.

You can see why Irenaeus found the Gnostic myth so disturbing. Irenaeus and Christians like him worshiped the God of Genesis as the father of Jesus Christ. They saw the serpent in the Garden of Eden as an evil tempter, who led human beings away from the true God. The flood was God's just punishment of sinful human beings, not the wicked act of a jealous Ialdabaōth. The Gnostic myth was a direct challenge to how Irenaeus saw God and Jesus.

For centuries, Irenaeus's narrative was the only account of the Gnostic myth that scholars had. They wondered why Gnostics would believe such things and what religious purpose such a myth could serve. Without the words of the Gnostics themselves it was hard to tell. But we can see two things, even from Irenaeus's hostile report.

First, the Gnostics worried about aspects of the God of Genesis that did not seem very god-like. According to Genesis, God walks and talks in an earthly garden. Is that something a spiritual God who created everything would do? This God asks Adam, "Where are you?" Shouldn't God know everything, including where Adam is? This God changes his mind about the creation of human beings and causes a flood to wipe out nearly all of them. Does a perfect God change his mind and indiscriminately kill numerous people? The Gnostics concluded from this that this God must not be the ultimate, perfect God, but something lower and imperfect.

Second, we have seen that Christians disagreed about the role that the Jewish Bible should play in their religion. When Paul said that salvation was based on faith in Christ and not on following the Law, he opened the door to Christians like Marcion, who concluded that the Jewish Bible was no longer relevant to Christians. The Gnostics took a different approach: the Bible is relevant, but it's not quite accurate. It tells the story of salvation, but you need to understand that the God it honors is not the true God.

Part of the Gnostic myth that Irenaeus tells matches precisely the myth that is found in one of the texts from Nag Hammadi, the Secret Book According to John. So we now know that the Secret Book comes from the Gnostics. And Irenaeus tells us the name of another text that the Gnostics produced— the Gospel of Judas. The Gospel of Judas also came from the Gnostics.

So if we want to know what the Gnostics themselves believed and how they told their myth, we can read these two works: the Secret Book According to John and the Gospel of Judas. And that's what we'll do in our next few lectures.

God in Gnostic Myth
Lecture 3

T he Secret Book According to John is the most important Gnostic writing that survives today. We know it's Gnostic because a major part of it matches what Irenaeus tells us the Gnostics taught. It's important because it tells the entire Gnostic myth, starting with God and the creation of this world and ending with the coming of the Savior and the salvation of humanity. Scholars believe that the book was written sometime between 100 and 150 A.D., which makes it the oldest surviving Christian work of any kind that gives a complete and comprehensive narrative of salvation. In this lecture, we'll explore the Gnostic conception of God found in this work.

The Secret Book as an Apocalypse

- The Secret Book According to John presents itself as a revelation from the Savior to the disciple and apostle John.
  - When the text opens, the crucifixion and resurrection of Jesus have already happened, and the disciple John is on his way to the Temple in Jerusalem, when he meets a Pharisee. The Pharisee tells John that Jesus has misled him and turned him away from the true traditions of his ancestors, the Jews. This encounter upsets John, who begins to question his beliefs.

  - At this point, the heavens open, and the Savior appears to John. The Savior strangely takes three forms—a child, a young person, and an elderly person. The Savior then begins a long speech to John, which takes up the remainder of the book.

  - When the Savior finishes his revelation, he instructs John to write it down and keep it safe. The Savior then disappears, and John goes off to tell the disciples what the Savior has revealed to him.

- The Secret Book, then, is an apocalypse—a revelation from a divine figure to a human being. Jews and Christians wrote many such revelations in the centuries before and after Jesus.
  - These revelations were an important way for people to communicate new religious insights. Their authors recorded their insights in the form of a revelation from God to an authoritative human figure from the past. Often, the divine revealer tells the human being to keep the revelation secret until the proper time. The revelations usually explain events in the present and predict what will happen in the future.

  - Like other revelations, the Secret Book According to John portrays the current world order as dominated by evil rulers who oppress human beings and work to prevent them from achieving their full spiritual potential. But the book offers the hope that through the Savior, God will soon overthrow these rulers and bring his people to salvation. In this respect, the Secret Book is similar to other Jewish and Christian works of its time.

  - But the Secret Book is also different from other Jewish and Christian revelations. Unlike the book of Revelation, it is not symbolic, and it focuses more on the past than the future. It details the story of the creation of humanity, and it devotes a great deal of attention to simply describing God. According to the Gnostic author, people can find hope and salvation not by knowing what will happen in the future but by understanding better who God is and how the world we live in came to be.

The Gnostic God

- The best way to envision the Gnostic God is to think of him as a vast intellect—a mind—similar to, but much greater than, our minds. Like an intellect, God is complex, full of thoughts called *aeons* and constantly active and creative. Just as we find peace when our minds are still and quiet, so, too, God is perfectly still and quiet, even as he is active and creative. Further, just as we can never fully know another person's intellect, so, too, God is ultimately unknowable to human beings.

- This is where the revelation of the Savior to John begins—with God's ultimate unknowability. The Savior calls this ultimate unknowable God the Invisible Spirit or the Invisible Virgin Spirit. This Spirit is unlimited, unfathomable, ineffable, immeasurable, and incorruptible. It should not even be called divine because it is beyond our concept of divinity. It is complete silence and complete rest.

In the Secret Book According to John, the Savoir lays out the complicated Gnostic picture of God to the apostle John.

- If the Invisible Spirit were all there is to God, we would never know God. In fact, we would not exist because the Invisible Spirit would just be—eternally at rest. But again, God is like an intellect; thus, the Invisible Spirit thinks, and its thinking produces a first thought, called Forethought (see **Figure 1**). Forethought is the Invisible Spirit's thought about itself.

  ○ Forethought is the first aeon that comes forth from the Invisible Spirit, and it's the highest level of God that we can possibly hope to know. The Gnostics believed that human beings, like God's thoughts, ultimately came from Forethought and would return to Forethought.

  ○ The Secret Book also gives Forethought another name, the Barbēlō, which has no equivalent in English.

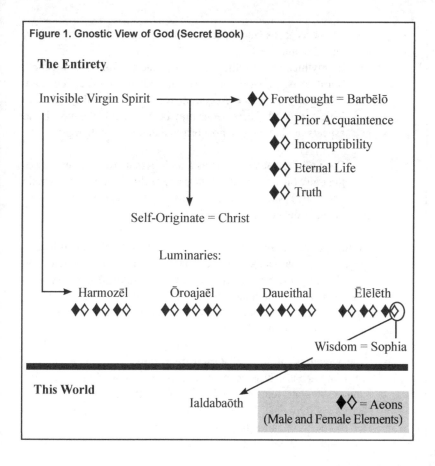

Figure 1. Gnostic View of God (Secret Book)

The Entirety

Invisible Virgin Spirit ⟶ ♦◇ Forethought = Barbēlō

♦◇ Prior Acquaintance

♦◇ Incorruptibility

♦◇ Eternal Life

♦◇ Truth

Self-Originate = Christ

Luminaries:

Harmozēl Ōroajaēl Daueithal Ēlēlēth
♦◇ ♦◇ ♦◇   ♦◇ ♦◇ ♦◇   ♦◇ ♦◇ ♦◇   ♦◇ ♦◇ ♦◇

Wisdom = Sophia

This World

Ialdabaōth   ♦◇ = Aeons
                        (Male and Female Elements)

- With these two aspects of God, the Invisible Spirit and Forethought, we can start to think of God not only as a person but as something like a place or realm, populated by God's thoughts, the aeons. When the Gnostics think of God as a collection of aeons or eternal beings, they call God the Entirety, that is, the total of all spiritual reality, which is God.

- Of course, once God starts thinking and produces Forethought, many other thoughts emerge. The Barbēlō is called the womb of the

45

Entirety because, as God's Forethought, it begins the multiplication of God's thoughts.

- o In mythical terms, the Barbēlō requests from the Invisible Spirit to be given eternal realms, and in response, four new aeons appear: Prior Acquaintance, Incorruptibility, Eternal Life, and Truth. These aeons may be considered the most basic aspects of God, God's most original and central thoughts.

- o Each of these aeons exists as a male-female pair that expresses the unity of two aspects of the same reality. Which aeon is male and which is female is determined by the gender of the aeon's name in the Greek language.

- At this point, the Invisible Spirit gazes at the Barbēlō, and this gaze begets in the Barbēlō a luminous spark, which becomes a new aeon called the Divine Self-Originate; in Greek, this is Autogenēs, who is also called the Anointed One, or Christ. The Gnostics think of the Invisible Spirit, the Barbēlō, and the Self-Originate as something like a nuclear family: Father, Mother, and Son.

- The begetting of the Self-Originate results in the emanation of yet more aeons. These aeons exist in four groups of three, and the four groups are led by four beings called the Luminaries, named Harmozēl, Ōroaiaēl, Daueithai, and Ēlēlēth. The 12 aeons that are led by the Luminaries have abstract names that indicate aspects of God, such as Word, Perception, Intelligence, Peace, and Wisdom.

Creation of the World

- According to the Secret Book, our world came into being when the harmony and stability of the Entirety were disturbed. Wisdom, the lowest aeon, desired to think her own thought, apart from the will of the Invisible Spirit and without the consent of her consort. Her thinking produced another divine being, but because she acted on her own, the being she produced was imperfect and ugly.

- Wisdom was mortified by what she had done. She called her ugly divine being Ialdabaōth and cast it outside the Entirety. Outside that realm was formless matter, which Ialdabaōth used to make this universe. Because Ialdabaōth had come from the Entirety, he had a dim memory of what the spiritual world is like and formed this universe as a kind of replica of it. But because of his ignorance and the imperfection of matter, the universe we live is like the spiritual world but flawed—full of corruption and decay.

- Ialdabaōth, however, was quite impressed with what he had done. He proclaimed, "I am a jealous god. There is no other god apart from me." Ialdabaōth's delusion disturbed his mother, Wisdom, who realized that he had taken power from her and now ignorantly believed that he was the ultimate God. Wisdom began to move about in her distress, disturbing the rest and harmony of the Entirety.

Origins of Gnostic Ideas

- As we've seen, the Gnostics believed that the ultimate God was remote and could not be fully known, that we can know and understand only lower aspects or manifestations of God, and that this universe was created by an inferior god as a poor copy of the spiritual world.

- The Gnostic view of God was not particularly strange in its ancient context. In fact, it was similar to ideas found in other philosophical works of the time that were indebted to Plato. In one of his most popular works, the *Timaeus*, Plato described how a god named the Demiurge or Craftsman created the universe in which we live as a material copy of an ideal spiritual world made up of eternal ideas.

- Other Jews and Christians also accepted these ideas. For example, Philo was a Jewish philosopher who lived in Alexandria in Egypt in the 1st century A.D. The ultimate God, Philo said, is simply being itself and beyond our direct knowledge.
  - Further, the ultimate God did not create the world directly. Rather, he did so through a lower aspect of God or a divine meditating principle, which Philo called God's Word (Greek: *logos*).

o   The Gospel of John in the New Testament has similar ideas. According to John, it is the Word of God that became human in Jesus Christ, not the ultimate God, the Father.

- What stands out about the Gnostics in this context is the fact that their craftsman god is the ignorant and evil Ialdabaōth, not a positive god, as in Plato, Philo, and the New Testament. As suggested in the last lecture, the Gnostics most likely concluded that the creator God of Genesis is ignorant and malicious for two reasons.

    o   First, the God of Genesis at times acts in ways that suggest ignorance and malice. In such stories as Noah and the flood, God destroys numerous people. The Gnostics probably saw these actions as unworthy of a good God.

    o   Second, there were tendencies in the Christian tradition to see the Old Testament in a negative light. Paul, for example, contrasted faith in Christ with obedience to the Jewish Law: Christians should follow faith, not the Law.

    o   Thus, building on the Platonist philosophy of the time and on Christian ambivalence about the Jewish tradition, the Gnostics concluded that it was the inferior deity Ialdabaōth who created this world, not the pure and perfect Invisible Spirit.

Suggested Reading

Brakke, *The Gnostics*, chapter 3.

King, *The Secret Revelation of John*.

Layton, *The Gnostic Scriptures*, "The Secret Book According to John."

Meyer, ed., *The Nag Hammadi Scriptures*, "The Secret Book of John."

Questions to Consider

1. What would you say is the dominant element in the Gnostic idea of God—the Bible or Platonism?

2. Does the "error" of Wisdom suggest that ultimately the Gnostics' God is imperfect?

God in Gnostic Myth
Lecture 3—Transcript

The Secret Book According to John—or Apocryphon of John—is the most important Gnostic writing that survives today. We know it's Gnostic because a major part of it matches what Irenaeus tells us the Gnostics taught. It's important because it tells the entire Gnostic myth, starting with God and the creation of this world, and ending with the coming of the Savior and the salvation of humanity. It seems to have been very influential in the ancient world because four copies of it survive—all Coptic translations of the original Greek. And these four copies show that the Secret Book was revised and updated more than once, even as its basic myth remained the same.

But the importance of the Secret Book According to John goes even beyond this. We know that it comes from the middle of the 2nd century because Irenaeus knew its myth around the year 180. Unfortunately, we have no idea who the author was. The book claims to describe a revelation from God to the apostle John, but scholars don't believe this. Instead, they think that the book was written sometime between 100 and 150. This means that the Secret Book is the oldest surviving Christian work of any kind that gives a complete and comprehensive narrative of salvation. It's the earliest grand vision of Christianity that we know of.

Because of the length and importance of this work, I'm going to talk about it in this lecture and the following one. First I'll explore the conception of God we see in this Gnostic book. According to the Gnostics, God is a complex intellect, consisting of numerous aspects or dimensions called *aeons*. The true God may be complicated, but he is perfect and serene. Not so the God who created this world—he is imperfect and angry. The God who created this world is something of a mistake, and so our universe is tragically flawed. That's why we need salvation from the true God.

The Secret Book According to John presents itself as a revelation from the Savior to the disciple and apostle John. When the text opens, the crucifixion and resurrection of Jesus have already happened, and the disciple John is on his way to the Temple in Jerusalem when he meets a Pharisee. The Pharisees were an important group of teachers in 1st-century Judaism. They appear often in the Gospels as opponents of Jesus. So it's no surprise to find a Pharisee criticizing Jesus in the Secret Book. The Pharisee tells John that Jesus has misled him and turned him away from the true traditions of his ancestors, the Jews. His encounter with the Pharisee upsets John, who begins to ask questions: Who was Jesus really? Who is his Father? What's the place where Jesus has gone and where his followers will go? And so on.

It's then that the heavens open, a light begins to shine, and the Savior appears to John. The Savior strangely takes three forms—as a child, a young person, and an elderly person—and these three forms morph from one to another. So there's only one Savior, but he appears in three ways. The Savior then begins a long speech to John, which takes up the remainder of the book. Only a few times does John interrupt the Savior and ask questions.

When the Savior finishes his long revelation, he instructs John to write down what he told him and keep it safe. He curses anyone who tries to sell this revealed knowledge, whether for money, food, or anything else. The Savior then disappears, and John goes off to tell his disciples what the Savior had revealed to him.

The Secret Book, then is an apocalypse—a revelation from a divine figure to a human being. Jews and Christians wrote many such revelations in the centuries before and after Jesus. Some of these ended up in the Bible—the book of Daniel in the Old Testament is a good example, and the Revelation to John in the New Testament as well. Others did not end up in the Bible, such as the multiple books of Enoch, or the Revelations of Adam and Paul, and of course, our Secret Book According to John.

These revelations are not all the same in their literary structure, but they were all an important way for people to communicate new religious insights. Some of them probably originated in visionary experiences that the authors had. All of the authors surely believed that through study and contemplation they had gained some new information from God. They wrote this new information in a revelation from God to an authoritative human figure from the past—such as the prophet Daniel, or Moses, or as in our case, the apostle John. And often the divine revealer tells the human being to keep the revelation secret until the proper time. This explains why, say, Moses or Enoch received this revelation many, many years ago, but we are only reading it now.

And we are usually reading it now because these revelations explain things that are happening now and what's going to happen in the future. They often say that the world we know is going to come to an end soon and will be replaced by a new kingdom of God. That's the message of Daniel in the Old Testament and the book of Revelation in the New Testament. This was good news to Jews and later Christians who lived in a world ruled by the pagan Romans— and, they believe, ultimately ruled by the devil. These divine revelations gave them the good news that the present world order of injustice and sin would soon be replaced by a new kingdom of justice and righteousness.

And that's the message of the Secret Book According to John as well. Like these other revelations, it portrays the current world order as dominated by evil rulers who oppress human beings and work to prevent them from achieving their full spiritual potential. But it offers the hope, that through the Savior who came in Jesus, God will soon overthrow these rulers and bring his people to salvation. In this respect, the Secret Book is traditional and similar to other Jewish and Christian works of its time. It brings revelation from God of truths that people don't know but which will bring them hope and salvation.

But the Secret Book According to John is also very different from other Jewish and Christian revelations. Most of these other books, like Revelation in the New Testament, concentrate on the future, what has not yet happened, and they give their message in highly symbolic visions that are hard to understand. According to the author of Revelation, people will find hope and salvation when they understand God's plan for the future and how it's starting to come true now. Throughout the ages, therefore, people have tried to figure out what the visions in Revelation mean and how they apply to present and future events.

In contrast, the Savior's revelation to John in the Secret Book may be complicated, but it's not symbolic. And it focuses less on the future and more on the past. It goes over in close detail the story of the creation of humanity and the Garden of Eden in Genesis. And it devotes a great deal of attention simply to describing God, and how the creator of this world came to be. According to this Gnostic author, people find can find hope and salvation not by knowing what's going to happen in the future, but by understanding better who God is and how the world we live in came to be. If you want to know God, be a better person, and find salvation, the Secret Book says you need to understand that you come from a God higher than the one you now know, and that the world in which we live is not how it should be.

So who is this God that we came from, according to the Secret Book? The best way to think about the Gnostic God is to think about him as a vast intellect—a mind—similar to but much greater and more, well, intellectual than our minds. And so just as our intellects are complex—full of thoughts and constantly active and creative—so, too, God is complex—full of thoughts called *aeons* and constantly active and creative. And just as we find peace when our mind is still and quiet, so, too, God is perfectly still and quiet, even as he is active and creative.

And even more, we can never fully know another person's intellect; no matter how much I love and become familiar with another person, there will always be a part of this person's mind that I cannot know. You could say that I can never fully know even my own intellect. In the same way, God is ultimately unknowable to human beings. There is a part of God—or better, the very heart of God—it's unknowable, beyond our capacity to understand.

And that's where the revelation of the Savior to John begins—with God's ultimate unknowability. He calls this ultimate unknowable God the Invisible Spirit—or sometimes the Invisible Virgin Spirit. The Invisible Spirit really cannot be talked about at all, and yet the Savior says a lot about it. It's completely one, but otherwise it transcends anything we can say. It's unlimited, unfathomable, ineffable, immeasurable, incorruptible. It really even should not be called divine because it is beyond our concept of divinity. It's complete silence and complete rest.

Now I have been using the neuter pronoun *it* to refer to the Invisible Spirit, and that's right because the Invisible Spirit is certainly beyond any idea of gender; it's neither male nor female. But the Gnostics can also refer to the

Invisible Spirit as a father, and perhaps less specifically as a parent. We'll see that at certain points the Invisible Spirit acts in ways that seem typical of a male being. So I'll keep referring to the Invisible Spirit as *it*, but the Gnostics were not completely gender-neutral in their thinking about it.

If the Invisible Spirit were all there is to God, we would never know God. In fact, we would not exist at all because the Invisible Spirit would just be—eternally at rest. But again, God is like an intellect, and so the Invisible Spirit thinks, and its thinking produces something—a thought, indeed, a first thought, a thought that comes before every other thought. The Invisible Spirit's first thought is Forethought, the thought that precedes all other thoughts. Forethought is the image of the Invisible Spirit because what did the Invisible Spirit have to think about except itself? So Forethought is the Invisible Spirit, just once removed, or slightly less, the Invisible Spirit's thought about itself.

Now the ancient Greek word that I'm translating as Forethought is *Pronoia*. In some translations of Gnostic and Valentinian texts, you'll find words like *Pronoia* left in Greek when they are working as proper names. So this first aeon is called *Pronoia* in many translations. But my policy is to translate such Greek terms into English when there is an English equivalent, and so I'll call *Pronoia* by its English name, Forethought.

Forethought is the first aeon that comes forth from the Invisible Spirit. And it's the highest level of God that we can possibly hope to know. The Gnostics believed that human beings, like God's thoughts, ultimately come from Forethought and will return to Forethought. In this life, we'll see later, human beings may experience fleeting moments in which they gain *gnōsis* or knowledge of Forethought. That's what this myth is ultimately really about—how we can gain *gnōsis* of God through Forethought.

The name of this aeon, Forethought, makes sense because it communicates well the status of this aeon as the thought that comes before all other thoughts. But the Secret Book gives Forethought another name as well, Barbēlō, which has no equivalent in English. The Barbēlō aeon is one of the most distinctive features of Gnostic myth. When you see the Barbēlō in an ancient text, you are almost certainly dealing with Gnostics. Believe it or not, scholars don't know where this name comes from. Historians have proposed various theories, but none has persuaded most people. For now at least, this will remain one of the mysteries of the Gnostics.

Now that we have two aspects of God, the Invisible Spirit and Forethought, or the Barbēlō, we can start to think of God not only as a person, but something like a place, or a realm, or space, populated by God's thoughts, the aeons. When the Gnostics think of God as a collection of aeons or eternal beings, they call God "The Entirety," that is, the total of all spiritual reality, which is God. And once God gets thinking and produces Forethought, you can bet that lots of other thoughts are going to emerge. And they do!

The Barbēlō is called the womb of the Entirety because, as God's Forethought, the Barbēlō begins the multiplication of God's thoughts. In mythical terms, the Barbēlō requests from the Invisible Spirit to be given eternal realms, and in response, four new aeons appear: Prior Acquaintance, Incorruptibility, Eternal Life, and Truth. These aeons may be considered the most basic aspects of God, God's most original and central thoughts. From one perspective, they are distinct from Forethought, the Barbēlō, and so we now have five aeons. But from another perspective, they are the same as Forethought, contained within Forethought, so the Barbēlō is itself a quintet or set of five aeons.

And from yet another perspective, there are now ten aeons because we learn that each aeon exists in a pair. The Gnostics think of the Entirety as stable and serene because each aeon has another aeon that completes it. They compare this pairing of aeons to the complementary natures of male and female in humanity. And so they imagine these aeons in male-female pairs that express the unity of two aspects of the same reality. Which aeon is male and which is female is determined by the gender of the aeon's name in the Greek language. So, for example, the Greek word for Prior Acquaintance is *prognōsis*, which is a feminine noun, and so it's considered female. Its consort is Intellect, which in Greek is *nous*, a masculine noun, and so Intellect is male. This male-female distinction will become important in a few moments.

So now we have a godhead or an Entirety made up of ten aeons, which are somehow also five, and somehow also just one. If this seems complicated, that's because it is. Again, consider your own mind and how you think. Your intellect is full of different thoughts, and yet your mind is still one. Sometimes you might say to someone, "My thoughts about this are complicated." And indeed they are. And thus so is God, in whose image your intellect exists.

At this point the Invisible Spirit gazes at the Barbēlō, and this gaze begets in the Barbēlō a luminous spark, which becomes a new aeon called the Divine Self-Originate—in Greek *Autogenēs*—who is also called the anointed one, or Christ. The Self-Originate or Christ comes into being in a way different from the other aeons. While aeons like Eternal Life and Truth simply appeared when the Barbēlō requested them, the Self-Originate comes into being from an act that looks something like sexual intercourse—as the Invisible Spirit gazes at the Barbēlō and begets the Self-Originate from the Barbēlō.

So the Gnostics think of the Invisible Spirit, the Barbēlō, and the Self-Originate as something like a nuclear family—as father, mother, and son. This trinity, so to speak, lies at the heart of the Gnostic idea of God. This may explain why the Savior takes three forms when he appears to John.

Just as the appearance of the Barbēlō resulted in the emanation of ten aeons, so, too, the begetting of the Self-Originate, or Christ, results in the emanation of twelve more aeons. These aeons exist in four groups of three. These four groups are led by four beings called the Luminaries. The names of the Luminaries are, like that of the Barbēlō, obscure. They are Harmozēl, Ōroaiaēl, Daueithai, and Ēlēlēth. These four luminaries are said to stand before or to attend the Self-Originate. They are, we might say, the Self-Originate's entourage.

The Self-Originate and his four attendant Luminaries with their distinctive names are another important feature of Gnostic myth. When you see these characters in a text, you are almost certainly reading a work of the Gnostics. The four Luminaries together provide the basic organization for this part of the Entirety. There are two aspects to this.

First, as we have seen, they are in charge of four sets of three aeons, making a total of twelve. These twelve aeons have abstract names that indicate aspects of God, such as Word, Perception, Intelligence, and Peace. The last aeon named is Wisdom—*Sophia*. Wisdom will have an important role to the play in the myth.

Second, the four Luminaries also contain within them divine archetypes or patterns of significant human beings or groups of human beings. The four divine archetypes are Adam, his son Seth, the posterity of Seth, and then repentant human beings. We'll learn in our next lecture why these particular human beings and groups are important. But here we might wonder why there are divine archetypes or patterns of human beings within God at all.

The answer is in Genesis, where God is said to create human beings "in our image." Genesis says that human beings were created in God's image. What does that mean? Jews and Christians have answered this question in different ways throughout the ages. For the Gnostics, it meant that archetypes or patterns of human beings exist eternally within God, settled in the four Luminaries.

We now have the Gnostic picture of God completely laid out. God consists of a multiplicity of thoughts or aeons, organized around the central trinity of the Invisible Spirit, the Barbēlō, and the Self-Originate or Christ, along with the four Luminaries. As complicated as the Gnostic God is, the Entirety has unity and stability because all the aeons are aspects of the Invisible Spirit and because all the aeons exist in harmonious, male-female pairs.

How does our world relate to this spiritual realm of the Entirety? Where did our world and we ourselves come from? Our world came into being when the harmony and stability of the Entirety were disturbed. What happened was, Wisdom, the lowest aeon—the aeon farthest from the Invisible Spirit, so to speak—desired to think her own thought, apart from the will of the Invisible Spirit, and without the consent of her consort. Wisdom is considered female because her Greek name, *Sophia*, is a feminine noun. The female Wisdom wanted to think a thought without the cooperation of her male consort.

On the one hand, Wisdom is an aeon of God, and so she possesses divine power. This means that her thinking had to be productive. It would produce another divine being. On the other hand, because Wisdom acted on her own, without her consort, the divine being she produced was imperfect, ugly, misshapen. Amazingly, therefore, the divine intellect made a mistake, and a bad thought was produced—an error.

Wisdom was mortified and embarrassed by what she had done, and so she cast her ugly thought outside the Entirety, so that the other divine beings would not see it. She called her mistaken, ugly divine being *Ialdabaōth*. The name Ialdabaōth probably comes from Aramaic and means something like "Begetter of Armies"—we will see that Ialdabaōth creates for himself a multitude of angels or heavenly rulers. Ialdabaōth has other names as well, most importantly, Saklas. It's Ialdabaōth who is the God of the book of Genesis, and Ialdabaōth is the God who created the universe in which we live.

Outside the realm of the Entirety was formless matter, and Ialdabaōth used that to make this universe. Ialdabaōth could do this because, when his mother Wisdom cast him out of the Entirety, he took with him the great power of the Entirety. Because Ialdabaōth had this divine power and had come from the Entirety, he had a dim memory of what the spiritual world is like. He formed this universe as a kind of replica of the spiritual world. So, for example, he made himself a bunch of fellow rulers, just as the Invisible Spirit has his aeons.

This universe is not a very good copy of the spiritual world, however, because, of course, Ialdabaōth is not a perfect divine being, but a spiritual error, a mistake. His ignorance and the imperfection of matter mean that the universe in which we live is like the spiritual world, but it's flawed and full of corruption and decay.

Ialdabaōth, however, was quite impressed with what he had done. Looking at his creation and all his assisting rulers, he proclaimed, "I am a jealous god. There is no other god apart from me." This arrogant and clearly mistaken statement combines things that the God of Israel says in the books of Exodus, Deuteronomy, and Isaiah. Ialdabaōth's delusion disturbed his mother Wisdom: She realized that he had taken power from her and that he now ignorantly believed that he was himself the ultimate God. Wisdom began to move about in her distress, disturbing the rest and harmony of the Entirety.

In the next lecture we will see how human beings get created and what Wisdom does to correct her error and make up for the lack of power that she has caused. But let's first stop here and ask about the origins of these ideas. The Gnostics believed that the ultimate God was remote and could not be fully known, that we can know and understand only lower aspects or manifestations of God, and that this universe was created by an inferior god as a poor copy of the spiritual world. Were these new ideas? Where did they come from?

The Gnostic view of God was not particularly strange in their ancient context. In fact, it was similar to ideas found in other philosophical works of the time that were indebted to Plato. The great philosopher Plato died in the middle of the 300s B.C., some 400 years before the Gnostics. But many philosophers, including Jews and Christians as well as pagans, continued to look to Plato for inspiration.

In one of his most popular works, the *Timaeus*, Plato had described how a god named the Demiurge or Craftsman created the universe in which we live by making it as a material copy of an ideal spiritual world made up of eternal ideas. The craftsman god makes other lower gods to help him as he makes this world as good a copy of the spiritual world as it can be. You can already see that the Gnostics' Ialdabaōth works like Plato's craftsman god by creating his fellow rulers, and then making this universe as an imperfect copy of the spiritual Entirety.

Did Plato think that there was a god higher than the craftsman, just as the Gnostics thought that the Invisible Spirit was a higher god than Ialdabaōth? Plato himself is not very clear on this point, but later readers of Plato agreed that there must be such a higher god. For one thing, the craftsman god in Plato's *Timaeus* makes this material world as a copy of the spiritual world. If that's true, who made the spiritual world? Platonist philosophers figured that some higher God must have done so. Moreover, in another of his works Plato spoke of a God he called The One, who was beyond description and even beyond normal existence. The craftsman god does not seem much like The One, so again, most people concluded that Plato must have taught that there is an ultimate God, higher than the craftsman god, whom we don't really know. That God is obviously much like the Gnostics' Invisible Virgin Spirit.

As I said, other Jews and Christians also accepted these ideas. For example, Philo was a Jewish philosopher who lived in Alexandria in Egypt in the 1st century A.D. He believed that Plato and the Jewish Bible must have been saying the same thing. The ultimate God, Philo said, is simply being itself and beyond our direct knowledge. This ultimate God did not create the world directly. Rather, he did so through a lower aspect of God or a divine meditating principle, which Philo called God's Word, or in Greek, God's *logos*. Through the Word, or Logos, God created the world as we read in Genesis. The Word created this world, just as Plato said, as a copy of a spiritual world in the mind of God. Philo taught that God has other divine powers as well, such as Wisdom.

The Gospel of John in the New Testament has similar ideas. It starts out, "In the beginning was the Word"—Logos—"And the Word was with God, and the Word was God. All things were made through him," that is, through the Word. According to the Gospel of John, it's this Word of God that became human in Jesus Christ, not the ultimate God, the Father. Likewise, Paul in his letters calls Christ the Wisdom of God.

So both the Jewish philosopher Philo and the Christian Gospel of John agreed that it's too simple to say that there's just one God. Rather, there's an ultimate God the Father, who has divine powers, including Wisdom and Word. It's one of these divine powers who actually created the universe in which we live.

In this context, what stands out about Gnostics is how many aspects and powers they attributed to God—like Philo, Paul, and the Gospel of John, they have God's Word and God's Wisdom, but they have also the Barbēlō, the Self-Originate, the four Luminaries, and so on. But even more striking is that the craftsman god of the Gnostics is the ignorant and evil Ialdabaōth, not a positive god as in Plato and these other Jews and Christians. Why is that, and what does it mean?

As I suggest in the last lecture, the Gnostics most likely concluded that the Creator God of Genesis is not just inferior to the higher God, but also ignorant and malicious for two reasons. First, the God of Genesis at times acts in ways that suggest ignorance and malice. In the Garden of Eden he asks Adam where he is, and in stories like Noah and the flood and Sodom and Gomorrah, God destroys numerous people. The Gnostics probably saw these actions as unworthy of a good God.

Second, there were tendencies in the Christian tradition to see the Old Testament in a negative light. Paul, you will remember, contrasted faith in Christ with obedience to the Jewish Law. Christians should follow faith, not the Law. Consider also the Gospel of John, which spoke of the Word of God as the creator of this world. That Gospel frequently contrasts Jesus and Moses, putting Moses in a negative light. And in chapter 8 of John, Jesus says to a group of Jews, "You are from your father, the devil."

So building on the Platonist philosophy of the time and on Christian ambivalence about the Jewish tradition, the Gnostics concluded that it was the inferior deity Ialdabaōth who created this world, not the pure and perfect Invisible Spirit.

But what about the rest of the creation story in Genesis? How and why did Ialdabaōth create Adam and Eve? If Ialdabaōth is the god of this world, what does this mean for human beings? And what can Wisdom do to correct the mistake that led to all this in the first place? In the next lecture we'll turn to human history and salvation in the Secret Book According to John.

Gnosticism on Creation, Sin, and Salvation
Lecture 4

The Gnostics believed that Genesis tells us how humanity came into being, how we lost our original knowledge of God, and how God is acting to help us. But Genesis has a major problem. Like most ancient people, the Gnostics believed that Moses wrote the first five books of the Bible—the Torah or Pentateuch—including Genesis. But they believed that Moses made a crucial mistake: He thought that Ialdabaōth is the true God. Thus, the Secret Book retells the stories of Genesis, but it "corrects" Moses. In this lecture, we will focus on three moments in this retelling: the creation of human beings, events in the Garden of Eden, and the flood survived by Noah and his family.

The Creation of Human Beings

- As you recall, after Ialdabaōth created this universe, he arrogantly claimed that he was the only god. His mother, Wisdom, repented for her act of independent thought that gave birth to Ialdabaōth, and the Invisible Spirit and the other aeons had mercy on her and restored her to harmony with the Entirety. Wisdom was temporarily united with the aeon Afterthought. Wisdom—or Afterthought— then works with Forethought (the Barbēlō) to regain the divine power that Ialdabaōth took from Wisdom.

- Their first approach is to inspire Ialdabaōth to create humanity. Forethought projects the light-filled image of a divine human being to the lower realms. Ialdabaōth and his fellow rulers decide to create a human being modeled after this image.
  - This act accords with God's words in Genesis: "Let us make humanity in our image." Notice that in this passage, humanity is made in a divine image and that multiple divine beings share in the creation.

- This is similar to the belief of other Jews and Christians of the time that God must have had helpers, probably angels, in making Adam and Eve.

- Ialdabaōth and the rulers create humanity twice. First, they make a purely spiritual human being, whose body is made of the stuff that constitutes the soul. Second, they make a material body into which the soul-body is placed.
  - This two-stage creation of humanity comes from the fact that the creation of human beings is narrated twice in Genesis (1:1–2:3 and 2:4–25). Modern scholars believe that the editor or compiler of Genesis combined two originally separate stories of creation into one book.

  - But most ancient Jews and Christians believed that God must have created people twice—the first time in a spiritual form, in God's image, and the second time in a material form, in a physical substance—dirt. Perhaps when God blows spirit into the material human being, he is uniting the spiritual human being with the material one.

- The Secret Book shares this idea—but with a twist. After Ialdabaōth and the rulers create the spiritual human being, it does not move. Wisdom and the Barbēlō send some divine beings disguised as lower rulers to Ialdabaōth, and these beings persuade Ialdabaōth that if he blows his spirit into the human being, he will live. Ialdabaōth does this, and indeed, the human being stands up.
  - But this has been a trick! Ialdabaōth has blown his share of the divine power from the Entirety into the human being. When the human being stands up, Ialdabaōth and the rulers realize that the human being is more intelligent and stronger than they are.

  - Ialdabaōth and the rulers then make a material body from dirt and put the spiritual human being into it. The idea is to obscure and obstruct the human being's thinking and to prevent him from realizing his superiority over them.

- o In response, the Barbēlō sends Wisdom in the form of Afterthought to hide within the human being and to guide his thinking to the Entirety.

- Here begins the great drama of salvation in the Gnostic myth. Wisdom and the Barbēlō seek to regain the divine power that Ialdabaōth has stolen and that's now present in humanity. In contrast, Ialdabaōth and his rulers try to prevent human beings from realizing that this power is within them and stop them from worshipping the higher God. This great struggle continues to this day.

The Garden of Eden

- The first moment in this struggle takes place in the Garden of Eden and within the family of Adam. As we have seen, Ialdabaōth had placed Adam in a material body, which tended to make him forget his true nature. But Wisdom, in the form of Afterthought, was hidden within Adam.

- According to the Secret Book, the rulers realize that Afterthought is within Adam, and they try to take possession of her by creating a female body in her image. When the rulers take a part of Adam and use it to make Eve, Afterthought leaves Adam and goes into Eve. But miraculously, this enables Wisdom to reveal herself more fully to Adam. Adam then awakens from his forgetfulness and recognizes that his true self is a fragment of the divine.

- The rulers next attempt to prevent Adam and Eve from eating from the tree of *gnōsis*—acquaintance with good and evil—but once again, Afterthought helps them by appearing as an eagle and encouraging them to eat from the tree. They do so, and their thinking is raised. Ialdabaōth becomes enraged that Adam and Eve recognize that he is not God and expels them from the garden.

- Ialdabaōth also sees that Afterthought—that is, Wisdom—is shining forth in Eve, and he decides to rape her. The Barbēlō sends divine beings who take Wisdom out of Eve, which means that Ialdabaōth rapes Eve but fails to harm Wisdom. Cain and Abel are born from the rape of Eve by Ialdabaōth, which helps to explain their rivalry and enmity.

- Ialdabaōth's rape of Eve is the origin of sexual intercourse, which clearly, the Secret Book sees as problematic. The desire for sex comes from the rulers, and sex itself results in the birth of material bodies in which the divine power that Ialdabaōth took is dispersed. Still, sex is not entirely bad because Adam and Eve have sex and beget Seth. Seth is begotten in the image of the archetypal divine Seth who resides in the Entirety; thus, he becomes the symbolic father of all people who have the divine power within them.

- This part of the story ends with the rulers giving Adam and Eve water of forgetfulness, with the result that human beings fall into oblivion and forget their true origins.

Noah and the Flood

- In Genesis chapter 6, strange beings called the "sons of God" take human women as wives, and the women give birth to giants. Following this, God sees that human beings are committing evil deeds. He regrets his creation and decides to destroy humanity through a flood. God saves only Noah and his family by commanding Noah to build an ark.

- Most ancient Jews and Christians believed that the "sons of God" were fallen evil angels, who had corrupted human women. Although the flood sent by God was catastrophic, ancient readers believed that it was a just punishment by God for a sinful humanity.

- In the Secret Book, Ialdabaōth also wants to destroy humans because they do not properly worship and serve him. The Barbēlō, however, instructs Noah to preach to about the truth. Noah fails to persuade most people, but many listen to him, in particular, a group called the "immovable race." Forethought saves Noah and the immovable race from Ialdabaōth's flood in a luminous cloud. Thus, the human beings who survive Ialdabaōth's flood are those who listened to the preaching of Noah and are faithful to true divinity.

- Ialdabaōth then sends his own angels to earth to mate with human women. At first, the women resist the evil angels, but then the rulers concoct a "counterfeit spirit" that leads human beings astray. Under the influence of the counterfeit spirit, human women have sex with the evil angels, and humanity loses its knowledge of the true God.

Salvation
- The Secret Book speaks about the saved people as part of a "posterity" that is descended from or linked with Seth. It also refers to the saved people as the "immovable race." This language makes it sound as if only some human beings have the divine power within them and will be saved.

- But in the Secret Book, the Savior talks about two forces that are active in the lives of human beings: the spirit of life that comes from above, from the Invisible Spirit and the Barbēlō, and the counterfeit spirit that comes from below, from Ialdabaōth and the rulers. These two spirits descend upon human beings and compete for influence over human souls.

- The Savior divides people into three groups to further explain salvation.
    - The first group consists of people upon whom the spirit of life descends and who become perfect and worthy of salvation. These souls receive eternal life. This first group must be the Gnostics and those who listen to Gnostic teaching and become Gnostics.

    - Second are the souls upon whom the counterfeit spirit descends and who are led into works of wickedness. These people are not Gnostics and reject the Gnostic message. When these people die, their souls are placed in new bodies, and they go through multiple lives until they become perfect and attain salvation.

    - The third group consists of people who "have gained acquaintance and then turned away." These souls will be tortured with eternal punishment, along with the rulers, at the end of time. In other words, apostates are the only human beings who will suffer eternal damnation.

In the Secret Book, Jesus does not save people by dying for our sins but by bringing us the message of the Barbēlō in human form.

- How will people be saved? The Secret Book frequently refers to people as lost in "oblivion" or "forgetfulness." We have forgotten who we really are—fragments of the divine from the Entirety. Thus, people need to be brought out of oblivion and returned to knowledge of God. It is Forethought or the Barbēlō who accomplishes this.

  ○ In the Secret Book, Forethought tells us that she has descended to humanity twice before but had to return to the Entirety, lest humanity be destroyed. Finally, she says that she has come to humanity a third and final time. She became incarnate in a human body and announced her message of salvation and awakening to human beings.

  ○ Because the Secret Book identifies Jesus as the Christ and Savior, it seems reasonable to conclude that Forethought's final visit to humanity in a body refers to her incarnation in Jesus. Through Jesus, the Barbēlō is calling human beings to wake up from our sleep, to recognize our true nature, to resist Ialdabaōth and the rulers, and to follow her. We can find salvation by joining the Gnostics.

Gnosticism on Creation, Sin, and Salvation
Lecture 4—Transcript

At the heart of any form of Christianity is the sense that human beings and the world we live in are not as they should be. The created world is full of beauty and wonder, and human beings are capable of great love and achievement. And yet the world is also full of suffering and pain, and human beings are capable of great disappointment and violence.

Even as we look at our own selves, we know that often we don't feel and act as we should. And sometimes we don't really know who we really are. Who's my true self? I like to think I am basically good, but then I think and say and do things that I know are wrong. As the Apostle Paul writes in his Letter to the Romans, "I do not do the good I want, but the evil I do not want is what I do. ... Who will rescue me from this body of death?"

All Christians agree that it's Jesus who rescues human beings from this wretched state. And it's Jesus who will somehow restore this world to perfection, love, and justice. But Christians have never fully agreed on how Jesus rescues people and how he will restore this world. And they have provided different explanations for why the world is the way it is—that is, how this world came into being and how it went wrong. They all believe that there is a problem called *sin*, but they don't all see this problem the same way.

The Gnostic myth provided one powerful answer to the questions of what's wrong with the world and human beings and how God is making things right through Jesus. We have already seen part of that answer in the Gnostic Secret Book According to John. The material universe in which we live is imperfect because the god who made it, Ialdabaōth, is himself imperfect. He is the mistaken and misshapen product of the divine aeon Wisdom's attempt to think without the consent of her consort.

Because Ialdabaōth made this universe as a copy of the spiritual world, our universe does share in the beauty of God; its form and order derive ultimately from the source of all being, the unknowable Invisible Spirit.

And yet because Ialdabaōth is a flawed version of divinity and because the material stuff that makes up our universe is inferior and corrupt, this world is flawed, inferior, and corrupt.

Yet we know somehow that there must be something better than this—something eternal and spiritual. And Gnostic myth says, yes, there is. It's the Entirety, the fullness of God's thoughts, where the Invisible Spirit, the Barbēlō, the Self-Originate, and the other aeons dwell in harmony and eternal peace.

But how do we know this? Is the Entirety our true home? If so, how can we return there? And what does Jesus have to do with all of this? The Secret Book explains all this as well, in a story that retells the biblical book of Genesis. The Gnostics believed that Genesis tells us how humanity came into being, how we lost our original knowledge of God, and how God is acting to help us. But Genesis has a major problem. Like most ancient people, the Gnostics believed that Moses wrote the first five books of the Bible—the Torah or Pentateuch—including Genesis. But unlike most ancient people, they believed that Moses missed a crucial fact. Moses mistakenly thought that Ialdabaōth, the arrogant and ignorant product of Wisdom, is really the true God.

So as the Secret Book retells the stories of Adam and Eve, the Garden of Eve, and the flood, it subtly and not so subtly changes what Genesis says, and it corrects, so to speak, Moses. At one point the Savior explicitly says to John, "It is not as Moses wrote."

The story that the Secret Book tells is complicated, so let's focus on three moments: the creation of human beings, Adam and Eve and their family, and the flood that Noah and his family survive. We can then sum up how God will bring human beings to salvation. And we should remember that this is what the myth wants to tell people—how we came to exist in the dark and evil world that Ialdabaōth has created and how God is going to save us from it.

Now to understand how God has acted to help and save human beings in these events, we must return briefly to the spiritual world of the Entirety. You may recall that, after Ialdabaōth created his fellow rulers and this universe, he arrogantly and ignorantly claimed that he was the only God. "There is no other god apart from me," he said. This upset his mother Wisdom, who began to move about in her distress. Wisdom repented for her reckless act of independent thought that gave birth to Ialdabaōth, and the Invisible Spirit and the other aeons had mercy on her and restored her to harmony with the Entirety. Wisdom was temporarily united with the aeon Afterthought—in Greek, *Epinoia.* Wisdom—or Afterthought—works with Forethought, that is, the Barbēlō, to rectify what Wisdom had done. Namely, they work to regain the divine power that Ialdabaōth took from Wisdom and by which he created this world.

The first way they do this is by inspiring Ialdabaōth to create humanity. Forethought projects the light-filled image of a divine human being to the lower realms. Ialdabaōth and his fellow rulers decide to create a human being modeled after this image, so that they might share in the light that they see. This accords with Genesis having God say, "Let us make humanity in our image." Notice that this passage says both that humanity is made in a divine image and that multiple divine beings shared in this creation—ancient people did not really have the modern idea of a royal "we." And so the Secret Book has Ialdabaōth make humanity with the assistance of many other rulers. This is very similar to the belief of other Jews and Christians of the time that, because God speaks in the plural—"Let us make humanity"—God must have had helpers in making Adam and Eve, most likely angels. Here, evil rulers assist Ialdabaōth.

Ialdabaōth and the rulers create humanity twice. First, they make a purely spiritual human being, whose body is made up of the stuff that constitutes the soul. Second, they make a material body into which the soul-body is placed.

This two-stage creation of humanity comes from a peculiar feature of Genesis. There, the creation of human beings is narrated twice. First, in Genesis chapter 1 and the first few verses of chapter 2, God creates human beings in his image on the sixth day of creation, as the last thing he makes, and God tells human beings to go forth and multiply. God then rests on the seventh day. But then in chapter 2 of Genesis the creation story seems to start all over again, and humanity is the first thing that God makes. God makes Adam by using dirt from the ground. He then blows his spirit into this human made of dirt to make him live. How are we to understand this double creation?

Modern scholars believe that the editor or compiler of Genesis combined two originally separate stories of creation into the single book. That's why creation seems to happen twice. But people in antiquity did not have access to this theory. Instead, they thought Moses wrote everything at once, and so the story has to make sense as it is. Most ancient Jews and Christians came up with the same solution as the Gnostics. God must have created people twice—the first time in a spiritual form, in God's image, and the second time in a material form, in a physical substance, dirt. Perhaps when God blows spirit into the material human being he is uniting the spiritual human being with the material one.

The Secret Book shares this idea—but with a twist. After Ialdabaōth and the rulers create the spiritual human being, this human being doesn't move. After all, Ialdabaōth and his fellow rulers aren't really God, so they're not very good at making things. Wisdom and the Barbēlō send some divine beings disguised as lower rulers to Ialdabaōth, and these divine beings persuade Ialdabaōth that, if he blows his spirit into the human being, the human being will live. And so Ialdabaōth does this, and indeed the human being stands up.

But this has been a trick! Ialdabaōth has blown his share of the divine power from the Entirety into the human being! When the human being stands up, thanks to this divine power, Ialdabaōth and the rulers realize that the human being is stronger and more intelligent than they are. That's when they make a material body from dirt and put the spiritual human being into it. The rulers do this in order to obscure and obstruct the human being's thinking and to prevent him from realizing his superiority over them.

In response, the Barbēlō sends Wisdom in the form of Afterthought to hide within the human being and to guide his thinking to the Entirety. Here begins the great drama of salvation in the Gnostic myth. Wisdom and the Barbēlō seek to regain the divine power that Ialdabaōth has stolen and that's now present in humanity. In contrast, Ialdabaōth and his rulers try to prevent human beings from realizing that this power is within them and stop them from worshiping the higher God, the Invisible Spirit. This is the great struggle that continues to this day.

The first great moment in this struggle took place in the Garden of Eden and within the family of Adam. As we have seen, Ialdabaōth had placed Adam in a material body, which tended to make him forget his true nature. But Wisdom, in the form of Afterthought, was hidden within the newly created human being, Adam—even though Wisdom was a female being. This was so that Wisdom could teach Adam about his true origin and lead him to his true destiny.

According to the *Secret* Book, the rulers realize that Afterthought is within Adam, and they try to take possession of her by creating a female body in her image. And indeed, when the rulers take a part of Adam and use it make the female Eve, Afterthought leaves Adam and goes into Eve. But miraculously, this enables Wisdom to reveal herself more fully to Adam. Wisdom, in the form of Afterthought, appears within Eve and addresses Adam. Adam awakens from his forgetfulness and recognizes that his true self is a fragment of the divine from above.

The rulers next attempt to prevent Adam and Eve from eating from the tree of *gnōsis*, or acquaintance with good and evil, but once again Afterthought helps them by appearing as an eagle—yes, an eagle, not a serpent—and encouraging them to eat from the tree. They do so, and as the Secret Book puts it, Afterthought is shown forth to them, raising their thinking. Ialdabaōth becomes enraged that Adam and Eve recognize that he is not really God, and so he expels them from the Garden.

But that's not all. Ialdabaōth sees that luminous Afterthought—that is, Wisdom—is shining forth in Eve, and he decides to rape her. The Barbēlō sends divine beings who rescue Wisdom and take her out from Eve, and so Ialdabaōth does rape Eve, but fails to harm Wisdom. Cain and Abel are born from the rape of Eve by Ialdabaōth, which helps to explain their rivalry and enmity, which led Cain to murder Abel. Although we may be shocked by the appearance of rape in a sacred story, in fact it was a fairly common plot element in ancient religious myths and stories. Think of the rape of Tamar in 2 Samuel in the Old Testament, or the rape of Lucretia in Roman legends.

Ialdabaōth's rape of Eve is the origin of sexual intercourse, which clearly the Secret Book sees as problematic. The desire for sex comes from the rulers, and sex results in the birth of material bodies, in which the divine power that Ialdabaōth took is dispersed. Still, sex is not entirely bad, for Adam and Eve have sex and beget Seth. Seth is begotten in the image of the archetypal divine Seth who resides in the Entirety, and thus Seth becomes the symbolic father of all people who have the divine power within them. In many of their texts the Gnostics call themselves "the seed of Seth" or "the descendants of Seth." Seth, unlike Cain and Abel, represents the hope that humanity can once again recognize the inferiority of Ialdabaōth and his rulers and see their true destiny in the Entirety. For this reason scholars sometimes call the Gnostics "Sethians."

Just before the rape of Eve, however, Wisdom returned to the Entirety. To make up for this, the Secret Book tells us that Forethought, or the Barbēlō, sent to humanity her spirit in a female image. This is probably an enigmatic reference to a Gnostic character named Nōrea, who appears in other Gnostic texts as Seth's sister and as a heroine of the Gnostics. We'll learn more about Nōrea in our sixth lecture.

This part of the story ends with the rulers giving Adam and Eve water of forgetfulness, so that human beings fall into oblivion and forget their true origins.

You can see how the Gnostic author of the Secret Book revises the story of Adam and Eve and the Garden of Eden from the view that the God of Genesis is the evil Ialdabaōth. The actions that Ialdabaōth takes—creating a material body for Adam, making Eve out of a part of Adam, expelling Adam and Eve from the Garden—are designed to prevent human beings from knowing about their true origin in the spiritual Entirety and realizing that he is a false god. The author explains also why Cain and Abel did not get along: They were really the offspring of Ialdabaōth.

In the Secret Book, little details in the biblical text become important to the Gnostic story of salvation. For example, Genesis 5:3 says that Adam begat Seth "according to his form and according to his image." The Bible does not say this about Cain and Abel. So, according to the Secret Book, Adam did not beget Cain and Abel; only Seth is according to Adam's form and image. Only Seth, therefore, is the father of the posterity that shares in the divine power that Ialdabaōth took and blew into Adam and Eve.

Let's look at how another episode from Genesis appears in the Secret Book. In Genesis Chapter 6, strange beings called "the sons of God" are attracted to human women because of their beauty. The sons of God take human women as wives, and the women give birth to giants. Following this, God sees that human beings are committing all sorts of evil deeds. He regrets his creation of humanity and decides to destroy people through a flood. God saves only Noah and his family by commanding Noah to build an ark. Along with two of every kind of animal, Noah, his wife, his sons, and their wives survive the flood, and humanity is able to make a fresh start.

This is a puzzling sequence of events, which ancient Jews and Christians struggled to understand. Most decided that the beings called "sons of God" were fallen evil angels, who corrupted human women and taught them all sorts of sins. That's why humanity went downhill and God decided to destroy people with the flood. Although it was catastrophic, ancient readers believed that the flood was a just punishment by God for a sinful humanity.

How does this story appear in the Secret Book According to John? Of course, we know that for this Gnostic author, the God of Genesis is actually Ialdabaōth, so surely the flood he causes is a bad thing, not a just punishment. And indeed, in the Secret Book, Ialdabaoth wants to destroy all humanity because, thanks to the works of Wisdom and the Barbēlō, they don't properly worship and serve him. The Barbēlō, however, instructs Noah to preach to human beings about the truth. Noah fails to persuade most people, but many do listen to him—a group that the text calls "the immovable race." Forethought saves Noah and the immovable race from Ialdabaōth's flood—not in an ark, however, but in a luminous cloud. Maybe the author of the Secret Book thought that a bunch of people in an ark wasn't very realistic. In any event, Ialdabaōth's plan to eliminate human beings with a flood fails—and the human beings who survive are those who listened to the preaching of Noah and are faithful to true divinity.

So Ialdabaōth makes a new plan. He sends his own angels to earth to mate with human women. At first these enlightened women resist the evil angels, but then the rulers concoct what the text calls a "counterfeit spirit." The counterfeit spirit looks like the spirit that comes from Wisdom and the Barbēlō, but it actually leads human beings astray into materialism and immorality. Under the influence of the counterfeit spirit, human women have sex with the evil angels, and humanity loses its knowledge of the true God.

It's interesting that the Secret Book reverses the order of the story as it appears in the Bible. In Genesis the "sons of God" mate with human women, human beings become worse, and then God causes the flood. Here, Ialdabaōth causes the flood because human beings are getting better, then the evil angels mate with human women, and then human beings become worse. This is a great example of how switching the character of God from good to bad leads to a real reversal in the logic of the biblical story.

Not only do the rulers mate with human beings in the Secret Book, but the rulers also manufacture the planets and stars, which exert control over human affairs. Destiny or fate works through the heavenly bodies. Fate does not force human beings to do bad things, but it does exert control over our lives, and it leads us to forget our true nature. Most ancient people, including faithful Jews and Christians, believed in some form of astrology—that is, that the planets and stars do have some power over our lives. They looked to God for protection from or even complete salvation from the influence of the stars.

The Secret Book says that, thanks to astrological fate and the counterfeit spirit, the hearts of human beings "became closed and hardened with the hardness of the counterfeit spirit, down to the present time." So this is how things are left when the Secret Book concludes its retelling of the Genesis story. The divine power that Ialdabaōth took from his mother Wisdom is now dispersed within human beings. Wisdom and the Barbēlō have sent a spirit from above to elevate our thinking, so that we will recognize that Ialdabaōth is a false god, that the true God is the Invisible Spirit, and that we belong to the spiritual realm. But Ialdabaōth and his rulers have clouded our thinking and left us oblivious to the true nature of our selves. We are in bondage to the destiny of the stars, and the counterfeit spirit leads us astray.

So how do people get saved from this situation? How will the divine power return to the Entirety? Will all human souls be saved? The Secret Book According to John discusses these questions at some length. Let's consider first who will be saved. We have seen that the Secret Book speaks about the saved people as part of a "posterity" that is descended from or linked with Seth. It also refers to the saved people as "the immovable race." This language makes it sound as if only some human beings have the divine power within them and will be saved. You have to be born as part of the posterity of Seth or the immovable race. You can't really change your lineage or race, can you? So it seems as if some people are simply saved by their very nature, their race, while everyone else is doomed. That's precisely how opponents of the Gnostics characterized Gnostic views of salvation: Only Gnostics, the descendants of Seth, can be saved, and they are born that way—already saved. Some modern scholars have said this about the Gnostics as well.

But the Secret Book seems to have a different view. The apostle John asks the Savior, "Lord, will all souls then be saved and go into the uncontaminated light?" In response, the Savior first says that this is a difficult question, one that really can only be revealed to members of the immovable race. But then the Savior goes on to talk about two forces that are active in the lives of human beings: the spirit of life that comes from above, from the Invisible Spirit and the Barbēlō, and the counterfeit spirit that comes from below, from Ialdabaōth and the rulers. These two spirits descend upon human beings and compete for influence over human souls. In addition, there is a divine power without which human beings cannot stand, just as the original human being that the rulers made could not stand until he received power from above. All human beings receive this power, the Savior says, because without it they could not stand. The question is which spirit—the spirit of life or the counterfeit spirit—increases and grows strong in people?

The Savior divides people into three groups. The first group consists of people upon whom the spirit of life descends and who become perfect and worthy of salvation. These souls receive eternal life. This first group must be the Gnostics and those who listen to their teaching and become Gnostics.

Second are the souls upon whom the counterfeit spirit descends and are led into works of wickedness. They forget their true origin in the spiritual realm. These are clearly people who are not Gnostics and who reject their message. These souls do not receive eternal life—but they are not eternally damned either. Rather, when these people die, their souls are handed over to the rulers, who place them in new bodies. That is, these people are reincarnated, and they go through multiple lives until they become perfect and attain salvation. Yes, the Gnostics are Christians who believe in reincarnation!

Finally, the third group consists of people who "have gained acquaintance and then turned away." These souls will indeed be tortured with eternal punishment, along with the rulers, at the end of time. In other words, apostates—people who join the Gnostics and then leave the group—are the only human beings that will suffer eternal damnation, according to the Secret Book. Everyone else can look forward to attaining salvation, perhaps after multiple lifetimes.

So the answer to who will be saved is, in the long run, just about everyone, all people except apostates from the Gnostic school of thought. If you think about it, this makes sense because if the point is to recover the divine power that Ialdabaōth took and dispersed in humanity, then as many people as possible need to be saved. Plus, it certainly encourages people to stay within the Gnostic group.

But then how are people saved? We have seen that the Secret Book frequently refers to people as lost in "oblivion" or "forgetfulness." We have forgotten who we really are—fragments of the divine from the Entirety—and we are deluded into thinking that the god who created this world is the true God. We have lost the knowledge that Ialdabaōth is just an evil ruler and that the real God is the Invisible Spirit, whom we can know through the Barbēlō.

So what people need is to be awakened, brought out of their oblivion and forgetfulness, and returned to *gnōsis*, knowledge of God. It's Forethought, or the Barbēlō, who accomplishes this. The Secret Book concludes with a poem of deliverance, in which Forethought herself speaks of how she saves humanity. She says that she has descended to humanity twice before, but had to return to the Entirety, lest humanity be destroyed. But finally she says she has come to humanity a third and final time. Here is what she says about her third coming to human beings:

> I brightened my face with light from the consummation of their realm, and I entered the midst of their prison, which is the prison of the body. I said, "Let whoever hears arise from deep sleep. ... I am the Forethought of pure light!"

In other words, Forethought became incarnate in a human body and announced her message of salvation and awakening to human beings. She goes on to call upon people to follow their root, the source of their being, which is she, and to be on their guard against the rulers of this world. She says that she will seal the saved person "in luminous water with five seals." We'll learn in a future lecture that "the water of the five seals" refers to a ritual of baptism.

Because the Secret Book identifies Jesus as the Christ and Savior, it seems reasonable to conclude that Forethought's final visit to humanity in a body refers to her incarnation in Jesus. Through Jesus, the Barbēlō is calling human beings to wake up from our sleep, to recognize our true nature, to resist Ialdabaōth and the rulers, and to follow her. We can find salvation by joining the Gnostics and undergoing the baptism that will seal us and protect us from death. This is the message of hope that the Secret Book According to John offers.

Notice that the Christian message of the Secret Book does not focus on the crucifixion of Jesus. Jesus does not save people by dying for our sins. Rather, he saves us by bringing to us the message of the Barbēlō in human form. The Barbēlō entered into our imprisonment in the body by coming in the form of Jesus. In this way she was able to wake us from our sleep and help us to see that this is not our true home. We really belong to the Entirety, to the spiritual realm of the Invisible Spirit.

Modern people sometimes think of the Gnostics as having a negative message. This world is an evil prison, made by a god who is not really God. Our bodies oppress us, and we need to escape from them. And yes, that's part of the Gnostic message. The Gnostics take seriously that this is a world of pain, suffering, and death, and they offer a straightforward explanation for this. Ialdabaōth made this universe, and he did not do a good job. We do indeed belong to a higher realm.

But ultimately, like all Christians, the Gnostics offer a message of hope and salvation. They reject the idea that Adam and Eve ate from the tree in the Garden of Eden and left us in a state of sin. Instead, eating from the tree was a good thing, one of the first moments in the history of Wisdom and the Barbēlō working for our salvation.

Surprisingly enough, one recent person who understands this is the pop singer Tori Amos. On her 2005 album *The Beekeeper*, Amos includes a song inspired by the Secret Book According to John, entitled "Original Sinsuality." This song suggests that eating from the tree of knowledge of good and evil did not lead to original sin. Rather, Amos suggests that it was Wisdom who urged Adam and Eve to eat. Even today, Wisdom is urging human beings to choose knowledge: "You must eat this." Yes, the song says, this is a world of darkness, but, as Amos sings, "You are not alone, You are not alone in your darkness."

We have spent so much time with the Secret Book According to John because it matches Irenaeus of Lyons's account of the Gnostic myth. So we know that the Secret Book came from the Gnostics. But Irenaeus also tells us about another book that the Gnostics created—the Gospel of Judas. In our next lecture we will examine that fascinating and surprising text.

Judas as a Gnostic Tragic Hero
Lecture 5

The name Judas has come to stand for treachery and betrayal. It may seem surprising, then, to learn that the Gnostics had a text called the Gospel of Judas, claiming that Jesus revealed the truth about God, the creation of this world and humanity, and the future to Judas alone. Further, when Judas hands Jesus over for crucifixion, he sets in motion events that will lead to the dissolution of the present world order and its replacement by a new regime. If the Secret Book According to John presented a new Gnostic version of the Genesis story of creation, then the Gospel of Judas presents a new Gnostic version of the gospels' stories about Jesus.

Discovery of the Gospel of Judas

- The Gospel of Judas was not found at Nag Hammadi. It's contained in another ancient Coptic codex now known as Codex Tchacos. Unfortunately, Codex Tchacos has suffered a great deal of damage, much of which occurred after it was discovered.

- Codex Tchacos was one of four codices found by some peasants in the late 1970s in an ancient burial cave about 35 or 40 miles from the Egyptian town of Al-Minyā. Given that Al-Minyā is well north of Nag Hammadi, it's unlikely that these manuscripts were ever part of the same collection as the Nag Hammadi codices.

- After it was discovered, the codex found its way into the hands of a series of antiquities dealers, who did not treat it well. Eventually, it ended up in the possession of the Maecenas Foundation for Ancient Art in Switzerland. Under the auspices of the foundation, a small team of scholars was able to reconstruct the fragmentary codex and translate its text. In the spring of 2006, the results of this labor were released to the world.

- But the story does not end there. It turns out that one of the dealers kept some fragments, which became available only a few years later. It's likely that still more fragments exist that have not yet been given to scholars.

Gnostic Myth in the Gospel of Judas

- In the first scene of the Gospel of Judas, Jesus comes upon the disciples "offering thanksgiving over the bread," and he laughs at them. The disciples ask Jesus, "Teacher, why are you laughing at our prayer of thanksgiving? What did we do? This is what's right." And Jesus replies, "I'm not laughing at you—you don't do this by your own will. Rather, by this your god receives praise." This is the first indication that the Gospel of Judas is Gnostic: It rejects the god that other Christians worship, that is, the god of the Old Testament.

- Jesus's pronouncement that the disciples' god is not his God angers the disciples, and Jesus challenges them: "Let whoever is strong among you people represent the perfect human being and stand before my face." In other words, Jesus wants to know whether any of the disciples belongs to the saved people and whether any of them can display their *gnōsis* before him.
  - ○ None of the disciples dares to answer Jesus, except for Judas Iscariot. Judas stands before Jesus and says, "I know who you are and where you have come from. You have come from the immortal aeon of the Barbēlō. But as for the one who sent you, I am not worthy to say his name."

  - ○ This scene is almost certainly modeled after the scene in the New Testament gospels in which Jesus asks the disciples, "Who do you say that I am?" They give various answers, but only Simon Peter answers properly: "You are the Christ, the Son of the living God." This scene establishes Peter as the leader of the disciples; only he declares Jesus's true identity.

  - ○ But in the Gospel of Judas, it's Judas who answers, and he says that Jesus comes from the Barbēlō aeon. Judas, however, says that he cannot name the one who sent Jesus. Surely, this unnamable God is the Invisible Spirit, the ultimate unknowable God from the Secret Book According to John.

- Later in the Gospel, when Jesus reveals to Judas the true nature of God and the cosmos, other elements of the Gnostic myth appear, including the Self-Originate and his four angelic attendants and the divine human being, Adamas. There are also numerous references to a "great undominated race" associated with Seth. There are two important ways, however, in which the Gospel of Judas differs from the Secret Book According to John.
    - First, there's much less interest in female characters, whether divine or human.

    - Second, in the Secret Book, it does not seem to have been God's will that Ialdabaōth come into existence. In the Gospel of Judas, however, Ialdabaōth and his assistant Saklas come into existence at the initiative of a divine figure, who seems to be Ēlēlēth, one of the Self-Originate's four attendants. It was the Invisible Spirit's plan to bring these lower rulers into existence to rule over the chaos of the material world.

- Despite these differences, the Secret Book According to John and the Gospel of Judas teach the same basic Gnostic myth. They agree that the god of the Old Testament is a lower, pseudo-divine being. The true God is the Invisible Spirit, and his primary emanations are the Barbēlō and the Self-Originate.

The Role of Judas

- As we said, Judas is the only character in the Gospel of Judas who has *gnōsis* of God and Jesus. The other disciples mistakenly worship Saklas (identified here as the god of the Old Testament) and think that Jesus comes from Saklas. This would seem to indicate that Judas is a privileged character, a member of the great race that the Gospel says will be saved.

- But Judas's role in the Gospel is not so positive. For example, Jesus says to Judas at one point, "I will tell you the mysteries of the kingdom, not so that you will go there, but so that you will be much grieved." That is, Jesus implies that Judas is not one of the saved people. Such passages would seem to indicate that Judas is a negative character.

- Most scholars tend to see Judas not as evil but as ambiguous. He's a kind of tragic hero: He plays an essential role in salvation, but one for which he suffers. His ultimate fate may not be to dwell in heaven, but he will receive an exalted position that gives him great power and authority.

The Gnostic Gospel of Judas narrates a series of conversations between Jesus and his disciples and between Jesus and Judas, the only one of the disciples who has true *gnōsis*.

- Interestingly, this view of Judas is not so different from what we see in the New Testament gospels. There, Judas's betrayal of Jesus is required for the salvation of humanity; it's part of God's plan and was predicted in the Old Testament, and Judas dies for his guilt. In the Gnostic gospel, Judas must also hand Jesus over, and he suffers for doing so, but he receives a much more prominent position in the universe.

- Perhaps the most controversial moment for understanding Judas in the Gospel of Judas is when Jesus addresses him as "you thirteenth *daimōn*."
  - In antiquity, the Greek word *daimōn* sometimes functioned as a general term for all divine beings, including gods. More often, however, it referred specifically to divine beings in an intermediate position between full-fledged gods, such as Apollo, and extraordinary human beings, such as Herakles.

- Even more specifically, ancient philosophers often used *daimōns* to refer to divine beings that lived and operated within our universe, while gods dwelled in a different domain. The gods delegated to *daimōns* the work of running this world under their supervision.

- It seems likely that the Gospel of Judas uses the term *daimōn* in this morally neutral sense, rather than to mean "demon." Thus, Jesus is telling Judas that he will receive a "promotion" from human being to divine ruler. This will come to Judas precisely because he alone knows the full truth about God and Jesus and because he was willing to perform the act that led to Jesus's saving crucifixion.

Cosmic Reorganization

- The ultimate message of the Gospel of Judas is a Gnostic vision of future cosmic reorganization—something that Judas helps to set in motion.
  - The divine Jesus tells Judas that Judas will sacrifice the human being in whom Jesus dwells, not the divine Savior himself. This act will set in motion a series of events that will lead to the dissolution of the current world order and its reestablishment under Judas, the *daimōn* in the highest heaven of our world, the thirteenth heaven.

  - The current rulers, led by Ialdabaōth and Saklas, will be overthrown; even the stars that are associated with them will be destroyed. Judas will take their place as ruler of the material cosmos, while the saved people will enter the spiritual kingdom.

- One interesting point in this vision is the role of the stars. As we saw in the Secret Book According to John, the Gnostics believed that one way Ialdabaōth and the other evil rulers try to impede our *gnōsis* of God is by controlling our decisions through fate, which can operate through the stars. According to the Gnostics, however, the Barbēlō has acted through Jesus to free human beings from fate and the stars by means of *gnōsis*.

○ The Gospel of Judas also speaks of the stars guiding and leading people, but it does not use the term *fate*, and it associates specific stars with individual human beings and groups of people. For example, Judas has his own star, which can guide him rightly or lead him astray.

○ This understanding of stars seems to be closer to ancient Jewish literature, in which the stars are beings, similar to angels or demons. They guide and influence events but as part of a wider scheme directed by God, and their influence is not as coercive as fate.

- It's also interesting to note that as the Gospel of Judas elevates Judas to the position of future world ruler, it depicts the other disciples as ignorant of religious truth.
  ○ In a strange vision, the disciples see themselves as priests making sacrifices at an altar. They offer up animals and even human beings to God and engage in a host of other sins—all in the name of Jesus. When the disciples tell Jesus their vision, he commands them sternly, "Stop sacrificing animals!" In other words, stop leading other Christians to their spiritual deaths.

  ○ Here, the Gospel strongly criticizes Christian leaders who claim to be the successors to the apostles, who act as priests, and who celebrate the Eucharist in Jesus's name as a new Christian sacrifice to God. That is, it depicts contemporary bishops and priests as false priests who are worshipping the false god of the Bible and leading their followers to damnation.

Suggested Reading

Jenott, *The "Gospel of Judas."*

Kasser, Meyer, and Wurst, eds., *The Gospel of Judas from Codex Tchacos.*

Krosney, *The Lost Gospel.*

Meyer, ed., *The Nag Hammadi Scriptures*, "The Gospel of Judas."

1. How did the author of the Gospel of Judas hope to make the Gnostic message persuasive to other Christians?

2. What do you think of the overall character of Judas in this work?

Judas as a Gnostic Tragic Hero
Lecture 5—Transcript

Judas. The name itself has come to stand for treachery and betrayal, for the friend who is really an enemy. According to the gospels of New Testament, it was Satan who inspired Judas to betray Jesus, and Judas suffered a miserable death, either as a suicide, as in the Gospel of Matthew, or in sudden spontaneous combustion, as in the Acts of the Apostles.

Imagine, then, the surprise of many people when, in the spring of 2006, a small group of scholars announced the publication of an ancient Gospel of Judas. The very idea seemed to be an insult to Christianity—a stick in its eye. And yet it really exists—a Gospel of Judas that's not only Christian, but also claims that other Christians are deluded and it alone has the truth about Jesus and salvation.

Many people throughout the world may have found this shocking, but scholars of Gnosticism did not. You might recall that in his writings from around 180, Irenaeus of Lyons claimed that the Gnostics had produced a book called the Gospel of Judas. After describing the teachings of the Gnostics, Irenaeus writes the following:

> And furthermore—they say—Judas the betrayer was thoroughly acquainted with these things; and he alone was acquainted with the truth as no others were, and (so) he accomplished the mystery of the betrayal. By him all things, both earthly and heavenly, were thrown into dissolution.

> And they bring forth a fabricated work to this effect, which they entitle the Gospel of Judas.

And that's exactly what we find in the newly discovered Gospel of Judas. Jesus reveals the truth about God, the creation of this world and humanity, and the future to Judas alone. The other disciples of Jesus are clueless. And when Judas hands Jesus over to his enemies for crucifixion, he sets in motion events that will lead to the dissolution of the present world order and its replacement by a new regime. If the Secret Book According to John presented a new Gnostic version of the Genesis story of creation, then the Gospel of Judas presents a new Gnostic version of the gospels' stories about Jesus.

Unlike the gospels in the New Testament, however, the Gospel of Judas does not tell us much about Jesus's life and ministry—there are no stories of Jesus being born; there are no travels around Galilee; no miracles. The author just says that Jesus "performed signs and great wonders for the salvation of humanity." Instead, the gospel narrates a series of conversations between Jesus and his disciples and between Jesus and Judas. These conversations take place in the days before Jesus's death. During these conversations Jesus deprecates all the disciples, including Judas, but he never criticizes Judas as harshly as he does the other disciples. None of the other disciples know anything true about Jesus, and Jesus compares them to evil priests who are leading their followers to their deaths.

Eventually Jesus delivers a speech of revelation to Judas, much like the Savior's revelation to John in the Secret Book According to John. After this revelation, the divine nature of Jesus departs toward heaven on a cloud, leaving only the human Jesus for Judas to betray. Next the human Jesus is with his disciples in the upper room of some house, presumably sharing the Last Supper. Outside Judas meets with Jewish leaders, accepts their money, and hands Jesus over to them. Then the gospel ends. The author assumes that the reader knows what happened next.

What's going on here? Why does Jesus criticize the disciples so strongly? What's the revelation that he makes to Judas? And what's Judas's role in salvation? These are the questions at the heart of understanding this Gnostic gospel.

But first let me tell you how the Gospel of Judas was discovered and why it did not become available to people until 2006. The Gospel of Judas was not found at Nag Hammadi. It's contained in another ancient Coptic codex now known as Codex Tchacos. Unfortunately, Codex Tchacos has suffered a great deal of damage, much of it after it was discovered.

It seems that it was one of four codices that some peasants found in the late 1970s in an ancient burial cave about 35 or 40 miles from the Egyptian town of Al-Minyā. Al-Minyā is well north of Nag Hammadi, and so it's unlikely that these manuscripts were ever part of the same collection as the Nag Hammadi codices. The other three books found in the cave near Al-Minyā contain a Greek mathematical text, a copy of the biblical book Exodus in Greek, and a copy of the letters of St. Paul in Coptic. I'm afraid that there are no exciting stories about the discovery of these codices. Instead, it's after the discovery that the tale turns tragic.

The codex that contains the Gospel of Judas ended up in the hands of an antiquities dealer. Thanks to the notoriety of the Nag Hammadi codices, this dealer knew he had something special, and so he tried to get people to pay millions of dollars for the codex. Of course, the people and institutions that would want the codex and who would know how to preserve and read it were scholars and universities; they did not have the kind of money that the dealer wanted. But his attempts to get buyers did lead a few scholars to realize that another important Coptic codex had been found. One scholar was allowed to read enough of the codex to see that "Judas" was an important character in it, but he thought this was the apostle Judas Thomas, not Judas Iscariot.

Meanwhile, more than one antiquities dealer entered the picture, and they did not treat the codex well. It spent some 16 years in a safe deposit box in a bank on Long Island in the United States. There it suffered the damage that comes from humidity and changes in temperature. Another dealer tried to separate the pages of the papyrus by freezing the manuscript and then thawing it, which did terrible harm. There's even evidence that pages in the codex were deliberately rearranged to make it more appealing to buyers.

Eventually—and fortunately—the codex ended up in the possession of the Maecenas Foundation for Ancient Art in Switzerland, thanks to the generosity of Frieda Nussberger-Tchacos. She named the codex after her father, Dimaratos Tchacos, and thus it's named the Tchacos Codex.

Under the auspices of the Maecenas Foundation, a small team of scholars from Switzerland, Germany, France, and the United States were able to undertake the painstaking work of reconstructing the fragmentary codex and editing and translating its texts. In the spring of 2006 they released the results of their labor to the world. Eventually the codex will be placed in the Coptic Museum in Cairo, joining the Nag Hammadi codices.

But the story does not end there. It turns out that one of the dealers kept some fragments, which became available only a few years later. It's likely that still more fragments exist somewhere but have not yet been given to scholars. As of the date of these lectures, just about all of the Gospel of Judas has been reconstructed—but there are still missing pieces. We can only hope that these pieces might surface in the years ahead.

When scholars could read the Gospel of Judas, they recognized it as coming from the Gnostics because it matched Irenaeus's description of Gnostics' Gospel of Judas. The first scene of the gospel lets us know that we're dealing with a view of God that's similar to that of the Secret Book According to John and that we are not dealing with the Christianity of a bishop like Irenaeus. Jesus comes upon the disciples "offering thanksgiving over the bread," and he laughs at them. The disciples ask Jesus, "Teacher, why are you laughing at our prayer of thanksgiving? What did we do? This is what's right." And Jesus replies, "I'm not laughing at you—you don't do this by your own will. Rather, by this your god receives praise."

Now, the word used for "thanksgiving" here is "eucharist." So when the disciples are portrayed as saying "thanksgiving over the bread," it looks like they are celebrating the Eucharist or Lord's Supper—even though that would be anachronistic because Jesus has not yet instituted the Lord's Supper. In any case, Jesus mocks this ritual as offering praise to what he calls "your god."

This is the first indication that the Gospel of Judas is Gnostic: it rejects the god that other Christians worship, that is, the God of the Old Testament. Let's remember that the Secret Book According to John calls the God of the Old Testament Ialdabaōth and Saklas, and depicts him as a malicious and false lower divinity.

In the Gospel of Judas, Jesus's pronouncement that the disciples' god is not his God angers the disciples, and Jesus challenges them: "Let whoever is strong among you people represent the perfect human being and stand before my face." In other words, Jesus wants to know whether any of the disciples belong to the saved people, those who are perfect, and whether any of them can display their *gnōsis* before him. None of the disciples dare to answer Jesus—except for Judas Iscariot. Judas stands before Jesus, albeit with his eyes averted, and says, "I know who you are and where you have come from. You have come from the immortal aeon of the Barbēlō. But as for the one who sent you, I am not worthy to say his name."

This scene is almost certainly modeled after the scene in three of the New Testament gospels where Jesus asks the disciples, "Who do you say that I am?" They give various answers, but only Simon Peter answers properly: "You are the Christ, the Son of the living God." This scene establishes Peter as the leader of the disciples—only he declares Jesus's true identity.

Here, however, it's Judas who answers, and he says that Jesus comes from the Barbēlō aeon. Judas says that he cannot name the one who sent Jesus. Surely this unnamable God is the Invisible Virgin Spirit, the ultimate unknowable and unnamable God whom we met in the Secret Book According to John.

So we see now the basic elements of the myth found in the Secret Book—the Invisible Spirit, and its first emanation, the Barbēlō. But it's Judas who has this knowledge, not John or any of the other disciples. They ignorantly and foolishly worship the creator of this world as the true God.

Later in the Gospel, when Jesus reveals to Judas the true nature of God and the cosmos, other elements of the Gnostic myth appear—including the Self-Originate, along with his four angelic attendants, and the divine human being, Adamas. There are also numerous references to a "great undominated race," associated with Seth. The members of this race possess the gift of the spirit, which will assure them of salvation.

There are two important ways, however, in which the Gospel of Judas differs from the Secret Book According to John. First, there's much less interest in female characters, whether divine or human. The Barbēlō aeon appears only once, in Judas's confession of Jesus's true identity, and Wisdom, or Sophia, does not appear at all. Eve is identified as the person through whom all human beings seek God, but otherwise Adam seems to be the major player.

Why is the Gospel of Judas more male-focused than the Secret Book? It's hard to say, but the author may have thought that less emphasis on female characters would appeal to non-Gnostic Christians.

In any case, the absence of Wisdom leads to the second major difference with the Secret Book. In the Secret Book, Ialdabaōth, the ignorant creator of the universe in which we live, came into existence because of Wisdom's error. It does not seem to have been God's will that Ialdabaōth exist, although Wisdom and the Barbēlō quickly work to bring good out of a bad situation.

In the Gospel of Judas, however, Ialdabaōth and his assistant Saklas—these are two different beings in this work—come into existence at the initiative of a divine figure, who seems to be Ēlēlēth, one of the Self-Originate's four attendants. You'll remember that in the Secret Book, Saklas was another name for Ialdabaōth. Here, Ialdabaōth is a higher ruler than Saklas. Saklas is identified as the God of Genesis, and he's the God that Jews and other Christians mistakenly worship. In the Gospel of Judas, it was the Invisible Spirit's plan to bring these lower rulers into existence to rule over the chaos of the material world. This, too, may be an attempt to appeal to other Christians. Rather than portraying the Invisible Spirit of the immortal aeons as fallible or as inadvertently creating the lower ruler, this Gospel says that God had all this in mind from the beginning, and everything is according to plan.

Despite these differences, the Secret Book According to John and the Gospel of Judas teach the same basic Gnostic myth. They agree that the God of the Old Testament, the god who created this world, is a lower pseudo-divine being. People who worship him as the ultimate God are still asleep or drunk. The true God is the Invisible Spirit, and his primary emanations are the Barbēlō and the Self-Originate. And so, even though they were found in different locations and are associated with different codices, there's no reason to doubt that both the Gospel of Judas and the Secret Book According to John come from the same group of Gnostic Christians.

Still, as we meet additional Gnostic writings in the next few lectures, we'll find that each author can introduce variations into the basic myth. This suggests that the Gnostics did not treat their myth as a set of unchanging doctrines or as absolute truth. Instead, they approached the myth in a way more like how we think of scientific knowledge. At any given moment scientists believe that they are offering the best and most probable explanation for what we can observe about the universe. But additional observations and experiments always lead them to make revisions to their basic understanding. And every now and then, someone like Copernicus or Albert Einstein comes along and changes the basic understanding in a revolutionary way.

The Gnostics, of course, did not base their myth on scientific observation and experimentation, but on close study of sacred texts and on experiences of revelation. But like a new scientific theory, the Gnostic myth must have been born in some moment of revolutionary new insight, brought about by the experience of Jesus. That new insight included the Invisible Spirit, the Barbēlō, and the true identity of the God of Genesis. The Gnostics, however, did not treat the myth that came from that extraordinary revelation as unchangeable. Instead, further reading in the Scriptures and works of philosophy or new experiences of revelation could lead them to revise details in the myth.

For the Gnostics, true *gnōsis*, true saving knowledge, was ultimately not about knowing the precise details of the myth—rather, it was about having a personal acquaintance with God, really knowing God in the most direct way possible. Which aeon did what and how many rulers Ialdabaōth has were not what's important; what mattered was to know the true God who sent Jesus—the Invisible Spirit—through the Barbēlō. The myth is a means to the ultimate end of *gnōsis*.

Now, as Irenaeus said, Judas is the only character in the Gospel of Judas who knows all this. The other disciples are ignorant: they mistakenly worship Saklas and think that Jesus comes from Saklas. This would seem to indicate that Judas is a privileged character, and if he has the true *gnōsis*—the true knowledge—of God and Jesus, then surely he must be a member of the great race that the Gospel says will be saved. This and some other ambiguous passages in the gospel led the first editors to promote it as showing us a good Judas—a Judas who's a hero.

But it turns out, especially as new fragments came to light, that Judas's role in the Gospel is not so positive. For example, Jesus says to Judas at one point, "I will tell you the mysteries of the kingdom, not so that you will go there, but so that you will be much grieved." That is, Jesus implies that Judas is not a member of the immortal race, not one of the saved people. When passages like this one became clear, some scholars then began to go in the exact opposite direction, and they argued that Judas is a thoroughly negative character, in fact a tool of Ialdabaōth. According to this view, the Gospel of Judas is not really a gospel, which means "good news." Instead, it's a parody of gospel: it looks like a gospel that brings good news, but it's really bad news. No one in the story is saved.

The problem with this view is that such a text would be unprecedented in early Christian literature. When a character receives a revelation from a savior figure, that's always a good thing; the human being who receives the revelation may be flawed or may not understand everything, but he or she is never evil or one of the damned. And so most scholars, including me, tend to see Judas not as evil, but as an ambiguous figure. He's a kind of tragic hero: He plays an essential role in salvation, but one for which he suffers. His ultimate fate may not be to dwell in heaven, but it is an exalted position that gives him great power and authority.

On the one hand, this view of Judas is not so different from what we see in the New Testament gospels. In the New Testament as well, Judas's betrayal of Jesus is required for the salvation of humanity; it's part of God's plan and was predicted in the Old Testament. And yet the New Testament portrays Judas as an evil betrayer, and he dies for his guilt. So, too, in this Gnostic Gospel, Judas must hand Jesus over—but he suffers for doing so.

On the other hand, as we are about to see, the Gospel of Judas gives Judas a much more prominent position in the universe than the New Testament gospels do.

Perhaps the most controversial and crucial moment for understanding Judas of the Gospel of Judas is when Jesus unexpectedly and rather mysteriously addresses him as "you thirteenth *daimōn*." What does it mean to call Judas the "thirteenth *daimōn*"? In antiquity, the Greek word *daimōn* sometimes functioned as a general term for all divine beings, including gods. More often, however, it referred specifically to divine beings in a kind of intermediate position between full-fledged gods like Apollo and extraordinary divine human beings like Herakles. The term was morally neutral: *daimōns* could be good or bad, helpful to humans, or harmful. In general terms, gods were beings that you would worship, pray to, and offer sacrifices to; *daimōns* you would deal with or negotiate with through rituals like magical spells.

Even more specifically, ancient philosophers often called *daimōns* those divine beings that lived and operated within our universe, within the planetary spheres. Gods, however, dwelled beyond the farthest planetary sphere, in their own domain. The gods delegated to *daimōns* the work of running this world, but under their overall supervision. When the Greek word *daimōn* is used in this way, modern scholars translate it into English as "god" (lower-case G), or as "spirit," or just leave it as *daimōn*.

In our period, however, Jews and Christians began to use the word *daimōn* in a completely negative sense. For them, angels were the only good intermediate-level beings, and a *daimōn* was an evil being, a fallen angel, and thus should be understood in English as a "demon."

So what's going on in the Gospel of Judas? Unfortunately, the text does not use the term *daimōn* other than in Jesus's address to Judas. But I think it's significant that the gospel uses the term "angel" to refer both to undeniably good divine beings like the Self-Originate and to undeniably bad divine beings like Saklas and his fellow rulers. So I think what's most likely happening here is that *daimōn* also functions in a somewhat neutral sense.

That is, Judas is going to get "promoted" from being a mere human being to being a divine ruler—in fact, the highest ruler in this universe. The text refers several times to Judas being persecuted—by the twelve disciples, and by other races of human beings. This certainly refers to the hatred that Judas receives for handing over Jesus. But Jesus also tells Judas that he will eventually rule over all those who persecute him—precisely because he alone knows the full truth about God and Jesus and because he was willing to perform the act that led to Jesus's saving crucifixion.

The gospel also says more than once that Judas will not enter into the divine realm of heaven. This, of course, sounds very negative, but I think it confirms that Judas will become the highest *daimōn* or divine being in this universe, serving as a kind of administrator for the Invisible Spirit, the Barbēlō, and the other divine beings—just as *daimōns* in the Greco-Roman world did. So I think that the title of this gospel is completely appropriate. This is good news about Judas: He did something for which many people, including most Christians, hate him, but he will ultimately rule this universe as God's representative.

So the ultimate message of the Gospel of Judas is a Gnostic vision of future cosmic reorganization—something that Judas helps to set in motion. The divine Jesus tells Judas that Judas will sacrifice the human being in whom Jesus dwells, not the divine Savior himself. This betrayal of a friend remains an evil act, but Jesus says that it will set in motion a series of events that will lead to the dissolution of the current world order and its reestablishment under Judas, the *daimōn* in the highest heaven of our world, the thirteenth heaven. The current rulers led by Ialdabaōth and Saklas will be overthrown—even the stars that are associated with them will be destroyed. Judas will take their place as ruler of the material cosmos in which we live. The saved people, however, will enter the spiritual kingdom above this world. The gospel calls these people "the strong and holy race."

This vision has a lot of interesting religious implications, but let's spend the rest of our time looking at just two—the role of the stars, and the criticism of the disciples other than Judas and of Christians who follow them.

First, the stars. We saw in the Secret Book According to John that the Gnostics believed that one way Ialdabaōth and the other evil rulers try to impede our *gnōsis* of God is by controlling our decisions through fate, and that fate can operate specifically through the stars. In some ways this is basic ancient astrology, which often taught that the stars exert influence on events or even control them. According to the Gnostics, however, the Barbēlō has acted through Jesus to free human beings from fate and the stars by means of *gnōsis*.

The Gospel of Judas, too, speaks of the stars guiding and leading people—in fact, it talks a lot more about stars than the Secret Book does. But there does seem to be a difference. The Gospel of Judas does not use the term *fate*, and it associates specific stars with individual human beings and groups of people. So, for example, Judas has his own star, which can guide him rightly and also lead him astray. So, too, the other disciples have stars, and certain races of human beings have stars.

The way the Gospel of Judas envisions stars appears to be more like ancient Jewish literature, in which the stars are beings like angels or demons. They guide and influence events, but as part of a wider scheme directed by God, and their influence is not as coercive as fate. Think of the star over Bethlehem that leads the wise men to baby Jesus in the Gospel of Matthew: That star plays an important role in divine and human affairs, but the wise men did not have to follow the star—they could have chosen to go home.

So, too, in the Gospel of Judas, stars can guide people rightly and wrongly, but people are free to resist. And the stars are closely linked to the people they guide, and so Jesus tells Judas that at the end of time, "your star will rule over the thirteenth aeon"—the highest aeon in this universe. That is, Judas's star will become more important and powerful than the twelve aeons or twelve stars of the Zodiac—which, it seems, are also the twelve stars of the twelve disciples.

And that brings us to our final point. As it elevates Judas to the position of future world ruler, the thirteenth *daimōn*, the Gospel of Judas depicts the other twelve disciples—the original eleven plus Judas's replacement—as ignorant of religious truth. In a strange vision, the disciples see themselves as twelve priests making sacrifices at an altar. There, they offer up animals and even human beings to God, just as they engage in a host of other sins and yet treat each other with respect. They do all this in the name of Jesus. When the disciples tell Jesus their vision, he commands them sternly, "Stop sacrificing animals!" That is, stop leading other Christians to their spiritual deaths.

Here the Gospel strongly criticizes Christian leaders who claim to be the successors to the apostles, who act as priests, and who celebrate the Eucharist in Jesus's name as a new Christian sacrifice to God. That is, it depicts contemporary bishops and priests as false priests who are worshiping the false God of the Bible and leading their followers to damnation. Of course, Irenaeus was one of these bishops that the Gospel of Judas condemned.

This harsh condemnation of other Christian leaders goes along with the differences in the Gnostic myth that we found in this gospel. On the one hand, the author has toned down the roles of female characters, and he has emphasized that the rulers of this world resulted from a divine plan. Perhaps he hoped that these changes would appeal to other Christians, who may have been put off by female divinities and the idea that the God of the Old Testament is a kind of mistake. On the other hand, the author depicts other Christian priests and bishops as sinful and ignorant, and he condemns the Eucharist as a false sacrifice. So he's basically saying to other Christians: The Gnostic message of Christianity is the correct one. What your bishops and priests are teaching you leads to death. Come over to our views before it's too late! If you don't do so, you will perish forever!

Irenaeus, of course, strongly disagreed. According to him, it's the Christians who follow the Gospel of Judas who will be damned to hell. The Gospel of Judas, Irenaeus said, is not a genuine revelation from Jesus, but a false gospel, fabricated by the Gnostics.

We've now looked at two ancient religious texts that came from the Gnostics: the Secret Book According to John and the Gospel of Judas. We know these works are Gnostic thanks to Irenaeus's description of the Gnostic school of thought. But are there other surviving ancient books that came from the Gnostics, ones other than those mentioned by Irenaeus? Yes there are, and in the next three lectures we will look at some of them, starting with The Revelation of Adam and The Reality of the Rulers.

Gnostic Bible Stories
Lecture 6

A s we've seen in the Secret Book According to John and the Gospel of Judas, the Gnostics retold stories from the Bible, almost always stories from the first chapters of Genesis. In this lecture, we'll discuss two other Gnostic texts that also rewrite the early chapters of Genesis: the Revelation of Adam and the Reality of the Rulers. These fascinating texts helped Gnostic readers see how the stories in Genesis related to them and their salvation. And they help to explain certain features of the biblical text that Gnostics and other ancient people saw as problematic or unclear.

Background on the Texts
- The Revelation of Adam and the Reality of the Rulers were originally written in Greek and probably date to the 2nd or early 3rd century.

- The Revelation of Adam presents itself as Adam's final revelation to his son Seth. Adam explains how he and Eve were created and what happened to them in the Garden of Eden. Then he looks forward to future events in Genesis, such as the flood and Sodom and Gomorrah.

- The Reality of the Rulers claims to be sent from a Gnostic teacher to a student who had asked about the reality of the spiritual beings that appear in the New Testament letter to the Ephesians. The author of Ephesians writes, "Our contest is not against flesh and blood, but against the authorities of the world and the spiritual hosts of wickedness." The Gnostic author seeks to explain the origin and nature of the spiritual rulers of this world.

Retelling Biblical Stories
- Jews and Christians retell biblical stories for a number of reasons. One motivation, for example, is to resolve contradictions between different accounts of events in the Bible. People also may want

The Christmas nativity scene is just one example of how Christians retell stories from their Bible, combining elements from the Gospels of Matthew and Luke into one coherent narrative.

to fill in gaps in certain stories or add elements that the Bible doesn't mention. In addition, people may retell biblical stories to make theological points or to connect themselves more closely to the stories.

- Ancient Jews and Christians retold biblical stories for the same reasons. For example, some of the most fascinating texts to survive from ancient Judaism are a group of books called the *targums*. These are revised versions of the books of the Bible in Aramaic. Such books were necessary because nearly all of the Jewish Bible is written in Hebrew, but during the first few centuries A.D., most ordinary Jews in Palestine spoke Aramaic.

- The targums don't simply translate biblical stories but also revise them. In so doing, they highlight the concerns of ancient Jews. Consider, for example, the book known as the Targum Pseudo-Jonathan. Its final form dates perhaps to the 8th century A.D., but it contains traditions and materials that go back to the time of the Gnostics in the 2nd and 3rd centuries.

- This targum retells Genesis, and it's clear that one thing that concerned the author is the nature and character of God in Genesis. For example, in the biblical story of the Garden of Eden, God asks Adam, "Where are you?" This question makes God seem human and ignorant. But in the targum, it's not God himself who walks around in the garden but the Word of God (Aramaic: *Memra*), a kind of lower manifestation of the ultimate God.

- The Targum Pseudo-Jonathan also makes the biblical story of Genesis more relevant to contemporary Jews. At the time the targum was composed, the rabbis were encouraging Jews to base their lives on closely following the Law as found in the Bible. But in the Bible, the Law does not appear until the time of Moses. In the targum, however, God gives the Law to Adam and Eve in the garden, placing contemporary religious beliefs and practices into the story of the first human beings.

Gnostic Retelling of the Creation

- Both the Revelation of Adam and the Reality of the Rulers spend time discussing the creation of human beings; their primary concern is the passage of the divine spirit or power into and out of Adam and Eve.

- As we saw in the Secret Book According to John, divine power came to human beings through Ialdabaōth and became dispersed into humanity. This divine power enables human beings to know the true God, and the story of salvation is the story of how God works to return this power to the spiritual realm of the Entirety.

- In the Revelation of Adam, Ialdabaōth and his fellow rulers create humanity in two stages, just as in the Secret Book. But here, the author makes clear that the original spiritual human being was an androgyne, made up of both Adam and Eve. In fact, many Jews and Christians in the ancient world thought that the original human was androgynous because of the wording of the creation story in the Bible: "And God made the human being; according to God's image he made it; male and female he made them" (Gen. 1:27).

○ Recall that in chapter 2 of Genesis, creation seems to restart. Here, God makes Adam and places him in a garden, but he can find no suitable partner for Adam from among the other animals; thus, God constructs a woman from Adam's rib.

○ As we've mentioned, modern biblical scholars believe that Genesis represents the combination of two originally separate creation accounts into one somewhat confusing story. But ancient Jews and Christians believed that a single divinely inspired author, Moses, wrote all of Genesis; thus, they had to make sense of the two accounts as a single coherent narrative.

○ One widespread solution was to say that Genesis 1 narrates the creation of an ideal androgynous human being, and Genesis 2 tells of the division of this human being into male and female beings, with good and bad effects.

○ This is the situation in the Revelation of Adam. When Adam and Eve were first created, they were a single being, and the divine power or glory dwelled in them and made them superior to the rulers who made them. But when the rulers split Adam and Eve into two beings, the divine power left them and went to dwell in a special people, namely, the seed of Seth.

• The Reality of the Rulers is also intrigued by the division of Adam and Eve, and here, too, the result is a loss of divine power. In this text, the original human being seems to be just Adam, but he has within himself the divine power or spiritual helper, which is portrayed as female. The evil cosmic rulers try to get this divine power by creating Eve, and in fact, the divine power leaves Adam and dwells in the newly created Eve.

○ On the positive side, this means that the spiritual helper can now speak directly to Adam and inspire him. On the negative side, the rulers still want to possess the power or helper and try to rape Eve.

- ○ But the power departs from Eve and goes into the snake in the Garden of Eden. The rulers succeed in raping Eve, but the spiritual helper speaks to Adam and Eve through the snake and encourages them to eat from the tree of knowing good and evil. In this way, Adam and Eve become aware that they lack the divine power.

- Although these two Gnostic texts do not agree on precisely what went wrong, they both conclude that the separation of humanity into male and female brought with it tragic consequences.

Gnostic Retelling of the Flood

- Both the Revelation of Adam and the Reality of the Rulers also retell the story of Noah and the flood. The flood story is a classic problem in considering the nature and character of the biblical God. Would God really change his mind and destroy nearly all of humanity?
  - ○ Our Gnostic texts clearly believe that no true God would do such a thing. Instead, it was the evil Ialdabaōth who did this to stop human beings from realizing that he's not the real God.

  - ○ In both texts, Noah is not even a good character. Ialdabaōth saves him from the flood because he worships Ialdabaōth.

  - ○ If Ialdabaōth uses the flood to wipe out human beings who will not worship him, and Noah is actually an adherent of Ialdabaōth, then who will be saved? How do the Gnostics put themselves in the biblical story?

- In the Revelation of Adam, the saved people are represented by a group called the seed of Seth, or Those People. The seed of Seth survives Ialdabaōth's attacks on them because the spiritual aeons from the Entirety rescue them and keep them safe. Clearly, the seed of Seth represents the Gnostics.

- In the text, Adam tells Seth that in the future, a human being will come and perform signs and wonders to bring knowledge of God to human beings and to awaken the seed of Seth. The rulers will punish the body of that human being, but to no avail.

- Adam also predicts that at the end of time, the saved people will receive eternal life, but the human beings who have not recognized the true God will perish, along with the rulers of this world.

- In the Reality of the Rulers it's not Seth who is the ancestor of the Gnostics but a new Gnostic character, Nōrea, the sister of Seth.
  - When Eve gives birth to Nōrea after Seth, she says, "[God] has begotten on me a virgin as an assistance for many generations of humankind." Nōrea becomes the female spiritual helper for all of humanity. When she helps human beings to improve spiritually, the rulers decide to destroy humanity with the flood.

  - And just as the rulers wanted to rape Eve when the divine power and spiritual helper dwelled in her, they try to do the same to Nōrea. But she defies the rulers and cries out to God for assistance.

  - God sends to rescue her Ēlēlēth, one of the four Luminaries who attend the Self-Originate. Ēlēlēth reveals to Nōrea that she is the mother of the saved human beings, whom he calls Nōrea's "offspring." The evil rulers of this world cannot approach the offspring of Nōrea because in them dwells the spirit of truth. They possess *gnōsis* and exist immortal among dying humankind.

  - As Adam prophesied in the Revelation of Adam, Ēlēlēth tells Nōrea that sometime in the future, a human being will reveal the existence of the spirit of truth, teach the offspring of Nōrea about the Eternity, and free them from the blindness and death of the rulers. Then, this world and its rulers will perish, and the children of light will receive salvation.

Suggested Reading

Brakke, "The Seed of Seth at the Flood."

Layton, *The Gnostic Scriptures*, "The Revelation of Adam" and "The Reality of the Rulers."

Luittikhuizen, *Gnostic Revisions of Genesis Stories and Early Jesus Traditions*.

Meyer, ed., *The Nag Hammadi Scriptures*, "The Revelation of Adam" and "The Nature of the Rulers."

Questions to Consider

1. People often say that the Gnostics rejected or rebelled against the Bible. Does this seem like a good way of understanding their attitude?

2. It's clear that the writings we call Gnostic differ on many mythic details. Why might various Gnostic authors tell the same stories in different ways or introduce new characters, such as Nōrea?

Gnostic Bible Stories
Lecture 6—Transcript

At Christmas time, in many Christian homes you'll see a crèche, a modeled scene of the birth of Jesus. There was always one in my house when I was growing up. It had Mary, Joseph, and the baby Jesus in a manger, of course. They were surrounded by the three wise men with their gifts of gold, frankincense, and myrrh, and by shepherds with some sheep. There were some more barnyard animals, like a donkey and a cow. And above it all hovered an angel attached to the top of the stable. Unfortunately, the angel was missing part of its left wing because our dog had chewed on it one year.

Now my family and I knew that this is what Jesus's birth looked like because we had read about it in the Bible. This nativity scene reproduced the story of the nativity in the New Testament. And it indeed did so—but not exactly. The Gospels of Matthew and Luke each tell about Jesus's birth, but in Matthew, only the magi visit the baby Jesus—and they do so some weeks or months after the baby is born. In Luke, there are no wise men, only shepherds, and they visit Jesus very soon after he is born. So to have both magi and shepherds together, at the stable, shortly after Jesus is born is not quite what's in the Bible—the crèche is based on the Bible, but it changes the Bible in this and other ways.

The Christmas nativity scene is just one example of how Christians retell stories from their Bible and usually change them in doing so. Both Jews and Christians have been doing this as long as there has been a Bible. In fact, already in the Bible we see stories being retold and changed. The Old Testament books of Chronicles are basically the stories of the kings of Israel you find in the books of Samuel and Kings—just told differently.

The Gnostics also retold stories from the Bible, almost always stories from the first chapters of Genesis. We have already seen that the Secret Book According to John not only includes philosophical discussion of the nature of God, but also retells the Genesis stories of Adam and Eve and the flood. The Secret Book does this because its author believed that when Moses wrote these stories in Genesis he mistakenly thought that the god who created the world is the true God, when in fact he is the evil Ialdabaōth or Saklas. So the Gnostic author tells the "correct" version of the story.

Likewise, the Gospel of Judas creates new scenes of Jesus talking with his disciples that are not in the New Testament gospels, but it ends with something from the New Testament gospels—Judas betraying Jesus after the Last Supper. So the Gospel of Judas both adds to and revises the story of Jesus in the New Testament.

Other Gnostic authors do the same thing. In this lecture I'm going to discuss two Gnostic texts that rewrite the early chapters of Genesis: the Revelation of Adam and The Hypostasis of the Archons, or in plain English, the Reality (or Nature) of the Rulers. These fascinating texts help Gnostic readers to see how the stories in Genesis are really about them and their salvation. And they help to explain certain features of the biblical text that Gnostics and other ancient people saw as problematic or unclear.

We don't know who really wrote the Revelation of Adam and the Reality of the Rulers. We do know, however, that they were originally written in Greek and probably date to the 2nd or early 3rd century. The Revelation of Adam presents itself as Adam's final revelation to his son Seth. Adam explains how he and Eve were created and what happened to them in the Garden of Eden. Then he looks forward to future events in Genesis, like the flood and Sodom and Gomorrah. These events may be in the past for us and the original readers of the text, but for Adam and Seth they are in the future.

The Reality of the Rulers, in contrast, claims to be sent from a Gnostic teacher to a student who had asked about the reality of the spiritual beings that appear in the New Testament Letter to the Ephesians. The author of Ephesians writes, "our contest is not against flesh and blood, but against the authorities of the world and the spiritual hosts of wickedness." The Gnostic author wants to explain the origin and nature of the spiritual rulers of this world that Ephesians mentions. But as we'll see, about halfway through, there is a new narrator, a female character named Nōrea.

How do we know that the Revelation of Adam and The Reality of the Rulers came from the Gnostics? We don't know it for certain, but nearly all scholars agree that these are Gnostic texts because the stories that they tell so clearly match what we have seen in The Secret Book According to John and the Gospel of Judas, texts that we know came from the Gnostics thanks to the report of Irenaeus. Like the Secret Book and the Gospel of Judas, the Revelation of Adam and The Reality of the Rulers feature such Gnostic characters as Ialdabaōth, the four Luminaries, and Wisdom—and they present new versions of biblical stories.

Before we look at these Gnostic texts in detail, we should ask why Jews and Christians retell biblical stories at all. Isn't just reading the Bible sufficient? Let's return to my example of the Christmas nativity scene. As I pointed out, nearly all such crèches have both magi and shepherds visiting the baby Jesus just after his birth, even though this is not what's really in the biblical text. Part of the reason for doing this is simply the constraints of having a single modeled scene to set up on your fireplace mantle. You want to get all the characters in the scene, even if they really don't belong all together.

But more than this, Christians have often wanted to combine the two stories of Jesus's birth in Matthew and Luke into one story. These two accounts really are different in several respects, but when they retell the story, Christians put the two accounts together and they gloss over their differences. This is one motivation for people to retell Bible stories—they resolve contradictions between different accounts within the Bible to create a single biblical narrative.

They also fill in gaps in the story or add stuff that the Bible story does not tell us about. Let's think about what the Bible says about the wise men or magi who visit the baby Jesus. Matthew tells us that these magi come from the East, led by a star. After visiting King Herod and telling him about their journey, they visit the baby Jesus in his house—he's not in a stable—they worship him and give him gifts of gold, frankincense, and myrrh. A dream tells them not to go back to Herod, so they head straight home. That's all the Bible story says about them.

Now in almost any nativity scene, you will see three magi, and almost always one of them is dark-skinned, even black. But none of this is in the Bible. It's traditional to think that there are three wise men because they bring three gifts: gold, frankincense, and myrrh. But there's no reason to think that the number of gifts equals the number of magi. Perhaps a group of ten brought these gifts. In any event, when Christians retell the story, they fill in this gap. They use clues in the text to say something the text does not say.

And why is one of the magi usually depicted as dark-skinned or black? The Bible says only that the magi came from "the East." So Christians eventually decided which Eastern lands they came from, usually settling on Persia, Arabia, and India. So often the dark-skinned wise man is supposed to have come from India. This is how Western Christians have tended to imagine the magi, and by doing so they are making a theological point: The wise men represent that not only Jews worship the messiah Jesus, but so do people from all over the world. So the multi-racial character of the wise men signifies an important point about the universality of the Christian message. Christians make this point by putting it right into the biblical story—even though they have to augment or revise the biblical text to do so.

Interestingly, however, Christians in China have traditionally believed that all three magi did not come from just anywhere in the East—they came from China. Chinese Christians make the magi Chinese so that people from their land are included in the life of Jesus from the start. This makes the biblical story more relevant to Chinese Christians—and it brings Chinese people right into the biblical story! We were there, they are saying, even though, of course, they probably weren't. So here we have seen four reasons that people change a biblical story as they retell it—to solve problems in the text, to fill in gaps or explain what it does not say, to make a theological point, and to connect themselves more closely to the story.

Ancient Jews and Christians did the same thing. For example, some of the most fascinating texts to survive from ancient Judaism are a group of books that are called the *targums*. The targums are revised versions of the books of the Bible in Aramaic. Such books were necessary because nearly all of the Jewish Bible is written in Hebrew, but during the first few centuries

A.D., most ordinary Jews in Palestine did not read or speak Hebrew. Their language was Aramaic. So the targums retell the Bible in Aramaic so that Jews could understand them.

But the targums don't simply translate the biblical stories; they revise them as they retell them. And in so doing they show us what ancient Jews worried about as they read the biblical stories. Consider the book known as the Targum Pseudo-Jonathan. Its final form dates perhaps to the 8th century A.D., but it contains traditions and materials that go back much earlier, to the time of the Gnostics in the 2nd and 3rd centuries.

This targum retells Genesis, and it's clear that one thing that worried the author very much is the nature and character of the God in Genesis. For example, in the targum, when God creates the sun and moon, the moon says slanderous things against the sun. That's not in the Bible, so why is it in the targum? Because in the Bible God makes the sun greater than the moon, and Genesis calls the moon "lesser" than the sun. Why did God make the sun greater than the moon? The author of the targum does not want this to be an arbitrary or unfair act on God's part, so when he retells the story, he makes clear that God made the moon lesser than the sun because the moon had committed a sin.

Likewise, in the Bible, God acts in ways that are not very god-like. He walks around in the Garden of Eden, and he asks Adam, "Where are you?" These actions make God seem human and ignorant. So in the targum it's not God himself who walks around in the Garden, but the Word of God—in Aramaic, God's *Memra*—a kind of lower manifestation of the ultimate God. The Gnostics were not the only ancient people to imagine that God has emanations! And in the targum God does not ask Adam, "Where are you?" but "Where are the commandments that I commanded you?"—clearly a rhetorical question that accuses Adam of sinning.

Not only does the Targum Pseudo-Jonathan change the biblical story to make clear that God is just and not at all weak or ignorant, but it makes the story more relevant to contemporary Jews. At the time the targum was composed, the rabbis were encouraging Jews to base their lives on closely following the Law as found in the Bible. Now in the Bible the Law does not show up until the time of Moses, but in the targum, God already gives the Law to Adam and Eve in the Garden. So there has always been the Law. In this way, the author of the targum puts the religious beliefs and practices of the Jews of his day right into the Genesis story of the first human beings.

Now as we turn to the Gnostic retellings of Genesis in the Revelation of Adam and The Reality of the Rulers, we realize that they are not unique. Other ancient Jews and Christians retold biblical stories to clear up problems in the biblical text, like the nature and character of God, and to make the story more relevant to them and their religious lives. How did the Gnostics do this? Let's look at three key moments or themes: the creation of humanity, Noah and the flood, and who's going to be saved.

First, both of these texts spend some time discussing the creation of human beings, and their primary concern is the passage of the divine spirit or power into and out of Adam and Eve. We saw in the Secret Book According to John that divine power came to human beings through Ialdabaōth and then became dispersed into humanity. It's this divine power that enables human beings to know the true God, and the story of salvation is the story of how God works to return this power to the spiritual realm of the Entirety.

In The Revelation of Adam, Ialdabaōth and his fellow rulers create humanity in two stages, just as in the Secret Book. But here the author makes clear that the original spiritual human being was an androgyne, made up of both Adam and Eve. Many Jews and Christians in the ancient world thought this. That's because in the first creation story it says:

And God said, "Let us make a human being according to our image and likeness, and let them rule the fish of the sea, and the birds of the heaven, and the cattle, and all the earth, and all the reptiles that creep on the earth." And God made the human being; according to God's image he made it; male and female he made them.

Note the fluctuation between the singular and plural pronouns in the ancient Greek text that ancient people read. It's kind of ambiguous whether God made multiple human beings who are either male or female, or whether he made a single humanity or human being, who is both male and female.

Then, remember that in chapter 2, creation seems to start all over again. Here, God makes the male Adam and places him in a garden, but God can find no suitable partner for Adam from among the other animals. And so God performs surgery on Adam:

> And God cast a trance on Adam, and he slept. And he took one of his ribs and filled up the flesh equal to it. And God constructed the rib that he took from Adam into a woman, and he led her to Adam. And Adam said, "This now is bone from my bone and flesh from my flesh. She will be called woman because she was taken from her man."

From here the story goes downhill, as the serpent tricks Eve into eating fruit from the forbidden tree, Adam eats as well, and God sentences humanity to death.

You'll recall how modern biblical scholars explain this double creation: the editor or editors of Genesis combined two originally separate creation accounts into one somewhat confusing story. But ancient Jews and Christians did not have access to that hypothesis; rather, they believed that a single divinely inspired author, Moses, wrote the entire thing, and so they had to make sense of the two creation accounts as really a single coherent narrative.

One very widespread solution, doubtless inspired in part by Plato's *Symposium*, was to say that Genesis 1 narrates the creation of a single ideal androgynous human being and that Genesis 2 tells of the division of this human being into two male and female beings, with good and bad effects. That's what we have in the Revelation of Adam. It says that when Adam and Eve were first created, they were a single being, and the divine power or glory dwelled in them and made them superior to the rulers who had made them.

But when the rulers split Adam and Eve into two beings, the divine power left them, and it went to dwell in a special people, namely the seed of Seth, the descendants of their son Seth. We'll come back later to the importance of the seed of Seth in the Revelation of Adam, but let's just notice that the division of Adam and Eve in Genesis 2 is a tragic event, one that means a loss of divine power for them and many other people.

The Reality of the Rulers is also intrigued by the division of Adam and Eve, and here, too, the result is a loss of the divine power. In this text, the original human being seems to be just the male Adam; but thanks to the work of God, Adam has within himself the divine power or spiritual helper, which is portrayed as female. The evil cosmic rulers try to get this divine power by creating the female Eve, and in fact the divine power does leave Adam and dwell in the newly created Eve.

On the positive side, this means that the spiritual helper can now speak directly to Adam and inspire him. On the negative side, the rulers still want to possess the power or helper, and so they try to rape Eve. But the power departs from Eve and goes into the snake in the Garden of Eden. The rulers— not just Ialdabaōth, as in the Secret Book—succeed in raping Eve, but the spiritual helper speaks to Adam and Eve through the snake and encourages them to eat from the tree of knowing good and evil. In this way, Adam and Eve become aware that they lack the divine power.

So, although these two Gnostic texts do not agree on precisely what went wrong, they both conclude that the separation of humanity into male and female brought with it some tragic consequences. One can see how the Gnostics might conclude this since even in the Bible, the creation of Eve leads to sin, the fall, and death. Still, it's remarkable how, for the Gnostics, the problem is not really the creation of a woman, but the separation of the male and female. You'll recall how in the Secret Book, the evil Ialdabaōth comes into being when Wisdom tries to produce a thought without the consent of her male consort. So the problem of separating male and female shows up throughout Gnostic myth.

I suspect that it was not androgyny itself that Gnostics valued—that is, they did not devalue masculinity or femininity in favor of androgyny. Rather, they valued the original unity that androgyny represented. Once upon a time, humanity enjoyed unity with itself and with God, and the loss of that unity meant the loss of *gnōsis* of God.

Both the Revelation of Adam and the Reality of the Rulers also retell the story of Noah and the flood. The flood story is a classic problem in considering the nature and character of the biblical God—the problem that so concerned the author of the Targum of Pseudo-Jonathan. Would God really change his mind and destroy nearly all of humanity? Our Gnostic texts answer this question clearly: No true God would do such a thing. Instead, it was the evil Ialdabaōth who did this, in order to stop human beings from realizing that he's not the real God and worshiping the Invisible Spirit instead. In the Revelation of Adam Ialdabaōth makes another attempt to wipe out good human beings at Sodom and Gomorrah.

In both of our texts, even Noah is not a great character: Ialdabaōth saves him from the flood because he worships Ialdabaōth, which of course is not a good thing. So if Ialdabaōth uses the flood to wipe out human beings who will not worship him, and Noah is actually an adherent of Ialdabaōth, then who gets to be saved? How do the Gnostics put themselves in the biblical story?

In the Revelation of Adam, the saved people are represented by a group called the seed of Seth or, very mysteriously, Those People. The seed of Seth survive Ialdabaōth's attacks on them in the flood and Sodom and Gomorrah because the spiritual aeons from the Entirety rescue them and keep them safe. Clearly the seed of Seth represent the Gnostics. Just as Chinese Christians have imagined that the magi were their spiritual ancestors in the biblical story of Jesus's birth, so, too, the Gnostics placed themselves in Genesis in the guise of the seed of Seth, or Those People.

Noah's posterity, then, represents people who are not Gnostics. The Revelation of Adam divides Noah's descendants into two groups. Noah's son Shem and his descendants make a covenant with the ruler of this world, to serve him and follow his commandments. They clearly stand for the Jews. Noah's sons Ham and Japheth and their descendants form twelve kingdoms separate from the descendants of Shem. They probably represent the Gentiles, non-Jews. Then 400,000 of the descendants of Ham and Japheth leave their families and join the seed of Seth—converts to the Gnostic sect. So the Revelation of Adam carefully makes biblical characters in Genesis represent religious people in the Roman Empire: Jews, Gentiles, and Gnostics.

Adam then tells his son Seth that in the future, a human being will come and perform signs and wonders in order to bring knowledge of God to human beings and to awaken the seed of Seth. The rulers will punish the body of that human being, but to no avail. Here Adam seems to be predicting the incarnation of a savior in Jesus. But even more, Adam predicts that at the end of time the saved people, Those People, will receive eternal life, but the human beings who have not recognized the true God will perish, along with the rulers of this world.

The Revelation of Adam emphasizes that the saved people are the seed of Seth, to whom Adam reveals the secrets of *gnōsis*. In the Reality of the Rulers, however, it's not Seth who is the ancestor of the Gnostics, but a new Gnostic character, Nōrea, the sister of Seth. You may recall that the Secret Book According to John says briefly and enigmatically that Forethought or the Barbēlō sent to humanity her spirit in a female image. In the Reality of the Rulers, that female image takes clear shape in the person of Nōrea.

When Eve gives birth to Nōrea after Seth, she says, God "has begotten on me a virgin as an assistance for many generations of humankind." Nōrea becomes the new female spiritual helper for all of humanity. When she helps human beings to improve spiritually, the rulers decide to destroy humanity with the flood. And just as the rulers wanted to attack and rape Eve when the divine power and spiritual helper dwelled in her, they try to do the same to Nōrea. But she defies the rulers: "You are accursed," she tells them. "I am not your descendant; I have come from the world above." She then cries out to God for assistance.

God sends to rescue her Ēlēlēth, one of the four Luminaries who attend the Self-Originate in the Entirety. Ēlēlēth reveals to Nōrea that Nōrea is the mother of the saved human beings, whom he calls Nōrea's "offspring" and also "That Race." The evil rulers of this world cannot approach the offspring of Nōrea, for in them dwells the spirit of truth. They possess *gnōsis* or acquaintance with the truth, and so they exist immortal among dying humankind.

As Adam prophesied in the Revelation of Adam, Ēlēlēth tells Nōrea that sometime in the future a human being with a body will reveal the existence of the spirit of truth, teach the offspring of Nōrea about everything, and free them from the blindness and death of the rulers. Then this world and its rulers will perish, and the children of light will receive salvation. They will return to *gnōsis* of God and thus to their full potential as people with shares of the divine spirit. With this revelation from Ēlēlēth, the Reality of the Rulers comes to an end.

Both the Revelation of Adam and the Reality of the Rulers find ways to include the Gnostics in the stories of Genesis, and both do so by making the Gnostics the descendants or offspring of an ancient person. In the Revelation of Adam, they are the descendants of the biblical Seth, but in the Reality of the Rulers they are the offspring of a new character, Seth's sister, Nōrea. The character of Nōrea goes along with the prominence of Eve in the Reality of the Rulers, which emphasizes the female gender of the spiritual power or divine helper in humanity.

The Reality of the Rulers does an especially good job of sounding very much like Genesis itself. It combines word-for-word repetition of the biblical text with new material that is written to sound just like it. For example, consider how it describes the births of Seth and Nōrea:

> And Adam knew his female counterpart Eve, and she became pregnant, and bore Seth to Adam. And she said, "I have borne another man through God, in place of Abel."

> Again Eve became pregnant, and she bore Nōrea. And she said, "He has begotten on me a virgin as an assistance for many generations of human kind."

The first part of this passage, about the birth of Seth, virtually reproduces the biblical text. The second part, about the birth of Nōrea, is totally new, but it's written in the biblical style and sounds totally plausible as coming from Genesis. It looks like the author may be trying not just to supplement or retell Genesis, but to replace it with a new scripture that sounds just like the original.

When the Gnostics made themselves descendants of a biblical character, they were following an important theme in Genesis. Genesis frequently includes lengthy genealogies; there are lots of lists of fathers and sons—"Seth begat Enosh, and Enosh begat Kenan," and so on. It's the descendants of Abraham who eventually become God's chosen people. In Genesis, family lineage is an important marker of religious identity. Characters worship the god of their fathers.

So the Gnostics were remaining true to the overall theology of Genesis when they identified themselves as descendants of a child of Adam and Eve, whether Seth or Nōrea. It's unlikely that they thought of this literally: that is, they probably did not think that they were the literal genetic ancestors of Seth or Nōrea. By this time Christians had learned to think of this religious ancestry in symbolic terms. For example, in his Letter to the Galatians, Paul told Christians that they become children of Abraham through the ritual of baptism.

Is it possible that the Gnostics became members of the seed of Seth or offspring of Nōrea by means of a ritual as well? Indeed it is. According to the Revelation of Adam, the seed of Seth "receive his name upon the water." In our next lecture we will learn more about the Gnostic ritual of baptism and other ways in which the Gnostics worshiped God.

Gnosticism's Ritual Pathway to God
Lecture 7

I n their texts, the Gnostics referred to themselves as the seed of Seth, Adam and Eve's third son, or the offspring of Nōrea, Seth's sister. But it's probably not the case that one had to be born into Gnosticism. Instead, it seems that people became offspring of Nōrea or descendants of Seth through a ritual of baptism. No Gnostic text gives us a clear description of this ritual, but in this lecture, we will look at five new Gnostic writings from Nag Hammadi that offer evidence for baptism and other forms of Gnostic worship: First Thought in Three Forms, the Holy Book of the Great Invisible Spirit (Egyptian Gospel), the Three Tablets of Seth, Zōstrianos, and the Foreigner.

Gnostic Baptism

- We've seen brief references to water and salvation and even to baptism in some of the Gnostic texts we've already discussed, such as the Secret Book According to John and the Revelation of Adam. Another Gnostic text, First Thought in Three Forms, is a lengthy poetic retelling of the Gnostic myth. It concludes with First Thought (the Barbēlō) explaining how she washes and saves a person.

- The Barbēlō describes the act of being washed in the water of baptism, as well as more mysterious actions: enthroning, glorifying, and snatching up, all carried out by divine beings. At the end, the baptized person experiences "the luminous place," probably a reference to the Entirety.

- This description of baptism concludes with a fragmentary mention of the five seals that belong to First Thought. The "five seals" seem to have been a distinctive feature of Gnostic baptism, but we don't know what they were. Perhaps they refer to the five actions in the baptismal ritual: enrobing, washing, enthroning, glorifying, and snatching up.

- The Gnostics celebrated baptism as part of a larger worship service, as we know from the Holy Book of the Great Invisible Spirit, a kind of Gnostic liturgy that culminates in baptism. The Holy Book tells the Gnostic myth, with stops at multiple points so that divine beings can be praised with hymns. It also promises that those who undergo baptism will receive *gnōsis* and will not taste death.

- Baptism was not the only time when the Gnostics sang hymns. A book called the Three Steles of Seth consists of seven hymns and concludes with directions on how they are to be used. The hymns are arranged so that they lead the worshipers upward toward contemplation of God, at which point they are to be silent; then, the hymns lead the worshipers downward again.

Zōstrianos and the Experience of *Gnōsis*

- The book Zōstrianos tells the story of an ancient person with that name who desires to contemplate God and other spiritual realities. He turns away from material things and engages in a program of bodily discipline, philosophical study, and teaching. Through his hard work, Zōstrianos learns to see the ordinary world of material things as petty and insignificant, and he formulates deep questions about higher reality. But because he does not reach his goal of contemplating God directly, he finds himself anguished and suicidal.

- The "angel of *gnōsis*" appears to Zōstrianos and invites him to ascend through the lower realms of this cosmos up to the Entirety. The hero abandons his physical body and is carried upward on a luminous cloud. He meets several divine revealers, undergoes repeated baptisms, and gains increasingly esoteric knowledge of our universe and the Entirety. His journey takes him higher, not only in a cosmic sense but also intellectually, as he contemplates increasingly abstract levels of reality.

- Eventually, he ascends into the Barbēlō aeon, the highest level of divinity that human beings can know. At this apex of his journey, Zōstrianos seeks to understand the Invisible Spirit, but this act is

Excerpts from Gnostic Texts

Description of Baptism, First Thought in Three Forms*
And I delivered him to the Baptists and they baptized him—Micheus,
Michar, Mn[e]sinous—and they immersed him in the spring of the
[Water] of Life. And I delivered him to those who enthrone—Bariēl,
Nouthan, Sabēnai—and they enthroned him from the throne of glory.
And I delivered him to those who glorify—Ariōm, Ēlien, Phariēl—and
they glorified him with the glory of the Fatherhood. And those who
snatch away snatched away—Kamaliēl, [missing name], and Samblō,
the servants of [the] Great holy Luminaries—and they took him into the
light-[place] of his Fatherhood.

Thanksgiving Hymn, Holy Book of the Great Invisible Spirit**
I have been formed within the orbit of the riches of the light.
For the light is within my bosom, bestowing form upon the various
      engendered beings by unreproachable light.
I shall truly declare your praise,
For I have comprehended you:
It is yours, O Jesus! Behold, O eternally omega, O eternally epsilon,
      O Jesus!

Hymn in Praise of the Barbēlō, Three Steles of Seth**
We praise you—we who, in our capacity as those who are perfect and
      particular, have become wholly saved,
We who are perfect because of you,
We who became perfect along with you.
O you who are perfect!
O you who are perfect!
O you who are perfect through all these [spiritual beings]!
O you who are everywhere similar!
O thrice-male!
You have stood at rest: you stood at rest in the beginning.

You have become divided everywhere: you have remained One.
And you have saved whomever you desired: and you desire that all
worthy people become saved.
You are perfect! You are perfect! You are perfect!

*Adapted from James M. Robinson's *The Nag Hammadi Library* (New York: HarperOne, 1990).

**Excerpts from Bentley Layton's *The Gnostic Scriptures: A New Translation with Annotations and Introductions* (New Haven: Yale University Press, 1995).

described as "reckless." Zōstrianos then descends, returns to his physical body, and preaches a message of moral reformation and *gnōsis* with God to others.

- The idea of traveling through heavenly realms to gain knowledge of the cosmos and God came from a long tradition of Jewish apocalypses, such as 2 Enoch. In that book, the hero is extremely righteous in following Jewish Law and displays special fidelity to the God of Israel. For these reasons, he is led on a tour through the heavens and learns important secrets of the universe. Eventually, he experiences a vision of God; he then returns to earth and exhorts other Jews to follow the Law and be faithful to God.
  - We see several similarities between Zōstrianos's heavenly journey and that of Enoch. In both stories, the main figures journey upward through the heavens, guided by one or more angels, and learn divine information about the universe. Both experience some sort of contact with God, then descend to preach and teach others.

  - However, there are also important differences between the two stories that show the distinctiveness of the Gnostic religious vision. First, Enoch receives his heavenly journey as a reward for following Jewish Law and being faithful to the

God of Israel. Zōstrianos, in contrast, undertakes a program of asceticism and study; he follows the path of philosophy until it can take him no further and God must step in.

○ Second, the information that Enoch learns on his journey mostly concerns the creation and structure of this universe and God's future judgment. Zōstrianos also sees how God created the world and how he will judge people, but he sees other things, as well. He is shown the aeons of the Entirety, and he sees the eternal forms after which things in this world were copied. In other words, Zōstrianos sees the important philosophical concepts of the Gnostic myth.

○ Finally, Enoch's journey culminates in a vision of God's face, but when Zōstrianos asks to understand the ultimate God, his request is deemed "reckless." The ultimate God of the Gnostics cannot be understood, nor does it have a face that can be seen.

• In the story of Zōstrianos, the Gnostics have combined a Jewish apocalyptic tradition of gaining *gnōsis* of God through a heavenly journey with a philosophical tradition of knowing God through study and contemplation. This philosophical path can be traced to Plato.
  ○ Plato's most famous description of how a human being can experience mystical knowledge of God is found in the *Symposium*. In this book, a group of educated men entertain themselves after dinner by giving speeches in praise of Eros, the god of erotic love.

  ○ In the climactic speech, we learn that erotic desire is meant to lead us to love God. Here, the man of philosophy undertakes a journey of increasing abstraction, starting with love of the beauty of a particular human body and moving to the beauty of the body in general, the beauty of the soul, and so on, up to beauty itself. If a man trains himself in this way, Plato says, he might be fortunate enough to be granted "all of a sudden" a vision of beauty itself, which is God.

○ What we see in Zōstrianos is the adaption of Plato's method of knowing God to the idea of a revelatory heavenly journey. Zōstrianos, as Plato advises, takes up the study of philosophy, and during his heavenly journey, he contemplates increasingly abstract levels of reality, including the eternal ideas that Plato said are the models for everything in this universe.

○ The only "mistake" that Zōstrianos makes is that he recklessly tries to gain understanding of the ultimate God. But according to Plato, such a vision cannot be forced; it will happen "all of a sudden." Plato also says that the person who is granted this vision becomes "immortal." *Gnōsis* of God grants a person salvation from this material world and eternal life. Zōstrianos may not achieve *gnōsis* of the Invisible Spirit, but he gets what's possible in this life: divine knowledge of the cosmos and the Entirety, culminating in *gnōsis* of the Barbēlō. This brings him salvation and eternal life.

The Foreigner and the Experience of *Gnōsis*

- The book entitled the Foreigner is similar to Zōstrianos. Its hero, named simply "the Foreigner," is a mythical human being from long ago—possibly Seth. The Foreigner also experiences a heavenly journey, guided by an angel named Iouēl. Like Zōstrianos, the Foreigner ascends as high as the Barbēlō aeon, the level of reality just below the Invisible Spirit. Iouēl tells the Foreigner that he will receive a revelation of the unknowable God after a period of 100 years.

- The Foreigner spends the time preparing himself for this experience. When the century is over, he is taken outside his body to a holy place. There, divine beings instruct him in how to contemplate God by turning his attention toward himself and contemplating sequentially the structures of his mind.
  ○ This process of mental withdrawal is like Plato's ascent through levels of abstraction of love, but it's totally intellectual and self-oriented. We must know our true selves, that is, our intellects, in order to know God.

- ○ We can do this because it was the Invisible Spirit's own act of self-knowledge—of thinking about itself—that generated the Barbēlō and the other aeons of the Entirety. The structure of our minds is a fragment or miniature version of the structure of the Entirety, which is God's mind.

- As the Foreigner performs this self-contemplation, he gains knowledge of aspects of the Barbēlō aeon that are also in his own intellect: blessedness, vitality, and reality. He gains *gnōsis* of himself and discovers the Barbēlō as "that which existed within me."

- The Foreigner then receives a vision of the Invisible Spirit. He wants to understand this vision, but the divine beings explain that the Invisible Spirit is not knowable. Ultimately, what the Foreigner learns is a paradox: He understands the Invisible Spirit precisely by not understanding it. In the end, the Foreigner ascends to acquaintance with God by journeying through his own intellect, and he receives *gnōsis* of the Invisible Spirit as a gift.

- Here, we reach what must have been the ultimate appeal of Gnostic teachings. The Gnostics acknowledged that this world is flawed and full of misery and saw that our bodies and the physical world can obstruct our contemplation and understanding of higher spiritual realities. But there is a spiritual realm of truth and perfection beyond this universe, and our dissatisfaction with this world is a sign that we belong to that higher realm. If we contemplate rightly, we can experience—however briefly—*gnōsis* of the true God. Such an experience confirms the reality of what the Gnostics teach.

Suggested Reading

Layton, *The Gnostic Scriptures*, "First Thought in Three Forms," "The Holy Book of the Great Invisible Spirit," "Zōstrianos," "The Foreigner," and "Three Tablets of Seth."

McGinn, *The Foundations of Mysticism*, chapters 1–2 and 4.

Meyer, ed., *The Nag Hammadi Scriptures*, "Three Forms of First Thought," "The Holy Book of the Great Invisible Spirit," "Zostrianos," "Allogenes the Stranger," and "The Three Steles of Seth."

Turner, "Ritual in Gnosticism."

Questions to Consider

1. Some scholars argue that the Gnostics did not actually perform baptisms with real water because the Gnostics did not think much of the body and because the language they use for baptism is so mythological. Rather, baptism is a metaphor for *gnōsis*. What do you think?

2. Can you imagine engaging in the mystical contemplation that the Foreigner describes? How might you try to do it?

Gnosticism's Ritual Pathway to God
Lecture 7—Transcript

In their mythic texts the Gnostics referred to themselves as the seed or descendants of Seth, Adam and Eve's third son, or as the offspring of Nōrea, Seth's sister. They also called themselves "the immovable race," "the undominated race," and more mysteriously, "Those People." Does this mean you had to be born a Gnostic? That being a Gnostic was genetically determined, like the blond hair that might run through a family?

Most likely not. Instead, it seems that people became offspring of Nōrea or descendants of Seth through a ritual of baptism. No Gnostic text gives us a clear description of this ritual, but in this lecture I will explain what we know and don't know about Gnostic baptism. I will talk about five new Gnostic writings, all of which come from Nag Hammadi—First Thought in Three Forms, the Holy Book of the Great Invisible Spirit—also known as the Egyptian Gospel—the Three Tablets of Seth, Zōstrianos, and the Foreigner. It's impossible to date any of these works precisely, but they probably originated sometime between 150 and 275 A.D.

In these works we'll find evidence not only for baptism, but for other forms of Gnostic worship as well, such as the singing of hymns. And the Gnostics did believe that it might be possible in this lifetime to experience direct *gnōsis* or acquaintance with the Barbēlō, or Forethought, the aeon closest to the ultimate God, the Invisible Virgin Spirit. They seem to have practiced a ritual of mystical ascent that enabled this amazing spiritual experience.

There are brief references to water and salvation and even to baptism in some of the Gnostic texts that I have already discussed. At the end of the Secret Book According to John, Forethought says that she will seal the saved person "in luminous water with five seals." The Revelation of Adam says that the seed of Seth "received his name upon the water." It also identifies three deities who "preside over holy baptism and living water"—Micheus, Michar, and Mnēsinous. These three divine beings accuse non-Gnostic people of "defiling the water of life." So according to the Revelation of Adam, there is a "holy baptism," but there are other forms of baptism that are not holy, that in fact defile true baptism.

Given the beliefs of the Gnostics, you can bet that they did not baptize people "in the name of the Father, Son, and Holy Spirit"! But what did they do? Some other Gnostic texts give us hints. For example, First Thought in Three Forms is a lengthy poetic retelling of the Gnostic myth. It concludes with First Thought, that is, the Barbēlō, explaining how she washes and saves a person. Her description is very mythological and features a lot of divine characters. For example, the divine beings who actually wash the baptized person are Micheus, Michar, and Mnēsinous, the ones who appear as the baptismal divinities in the Revelation of Adam. These three characters are only the first of many new divinities we're going to meet in this lecture.

The text is fragmentary, and symbolic, but here's what First Thought or the Barbēlō says:

And I stripped him of it, and I put upon him a shining Light, that is, the knowledge of the Thought of the Fatherhood.

And I delivered him to those who give robes—Yammon, Elasso, and Amenai—and they [covered] him with a robe from the robes of the Light.

This must refer to the candidate taking off his or her clothes and then being given a special robe to wear. As in other ancient Christian texts, this mundane activity becomes a symbol for removing one's old state of being and putting on a new state of salvation. Notice that this is given great religious significance: the candidate does not receive the robe from just anyone, but from the enrobing deities Yammon, Elasso, and Amenai. This, by the way, is all we know about these divine beings or any of the others that follow.

Let's see what happens next. More actions and more new deity names! The Barbēlō continues:

And I delivered him to the baptists, and they baptized him— Micheus, Michar, and Mnēsinous—and they immersed him in the spring of the water of life.

And I delivered him to those who enthrone—Bariēl, Nouthan, and Sabēnai—and they enthroned him from the throne of glory.

And I delivered him to those who glorify—Ēriōm, Ēlien, and Phariēl—and they glorified him with the glory of the Fatherhood.

And those who snatch away, snatched away—Kamaliēl [there's a missing name] and Samblō—the servants of the great holy Luminaries, and they took him into the light place of his Fatherhood.

This starts with an action that we can easily understand—being washed in the water of baptism—but then come actions that are more mysterious—enthroning, glorifying, and snatching up. Did the Gnostics act these out in some way? For example, did they have an impressive chair for the enthroning? We just don't know. We do know that the Gnostics believed that divine beings carried out these ritual actions, and that somehow the baptized person experienced "the luminous place"—probably a reference to the Entirety, where all the aeons dwell.

Now all this may sound rather grandiose—divine beings enthroning and glorifying people and snatching them away to heaven—but Christians tended to talk about their baptismal rituals in this way. The New Testament Letter to the Ephesians likewise speaks of baptized Christians being raised up and seated with Christ in the heavenly places. These rituals looked like they happen on earth, with simply human actors, but the meaning of these actions was cosmic and divine.

Did anything else happen at Gnostic baptism? There are a few brief references to anointing—that is, to having oil applied to the body, usually the head. This was a feature of baptism in many Christian congregations, but the evidence for anointing at Gnostic baptism is inconclusive.

Far more important are frequent references to "five seals." In fact, the description of baptism in First Thought in Three Forms concludes with a fragmentary mention of the five seals that belong to First Thought. The five seals seem to have been a distinctive feature of Gnostic baptism. But we don't know what they were. Perhaps they refer to the five actions we have seen in the baptismal ritual—enrobing, washing, enthroning, glorifying, and snatching away—each of which has a set of deities. Maybe the candidate was dunked in water or had water poured over him or her five times. Maybe the person was anointed with oil five times or in five places, so that maybe five openings of the body were sealed with oil—possibly the two ears, the two eyes, and the mouth. We just don't know.

We do know that the Gnostics celebrated baptism as part of a larger service of worship of God. The Holy Book of the Great Invisible Spirit is a kind of Gnostic liturgy that culminates in baptism. It tells the Gnostic myth from the Invisible Spirit and its emanations, through the creation of the world and the flood, down to Seth's incarnation in Jesus, and the establishment of baptism. The narration of the myth stops at multiple points, so that divine beings can be praised with hymns.

You can compare the Holy Book to an Easter Vigil service today in Christianity. At the Easter Vigil, excerpts from the Bible, from the creation through the fall and to the incarnation of Christ, are interspersed with psalms and hymns. It all leads to a celebration of baptism for new Christians.

This is how the Holy Book of the Great Invisible Spirit works, but it leads to Gnostic baptism and a hymn of thanksgiving. It promises that those who undergo baptism will receive *gnōsis*, acquaintance or knowledge, and they will not taste death. The thanksgiving hymn reads in part:

> I have been formed within the orbit of the riches of the light.
> For the light is within my bosom, bestowing form upon the various
> engendered beings by unreproachable light.
> I shall truly declare your praise,
> For I have comprehended you:
> It is yours, O Jesus! Behold, O eternally omega, O eternally
> epsilon, O Jesus!

Baptism was not the only time when the Gnostics sang hymns. A book called the Three Steles (or Tablets) of Seth consists of seven hymns and concludes with directions as to how they are to be used. The hymns are arranged so that they lead the worshipers upwards toward contemplation of God, at which point they are to be silent, and then the hymns lead the worshipers downwards again.

Here's an excerpt from a hymn in praise of the Barbēlō:

> We praise you—we who, in our capacity as those who are perfect
>   and particular, have become wholly saved,
> We who are perfect because of you,
> We who became perfect along with you.
> O you who are perfect!
> O you who perfect!
> O you who are perfect through all these (spiritual beings)!
> O you who are everywhere similar!
> O thrice-male!
> You have stood at rest: you stood at rest in the beginning.
> You have become divided everywhere: you have remained One.
> And you have saved whomever you desired: and you desire that all
>   worthy people become saved.
> You are perfect! You are perfect! You are perfect!

In these hymns the Gnostics praise the Barbēlō for her divine qualities, declare their own perfection and salvation, and give thanks to the Barbēlō for saving and perfecting them. The language can sound formal, but the hymns express a religious attitude of devotion to God, confidence in one's own salvation, and thanksgiving for what God has done. In other words, Gnostic hymns show that the Gnostics felt a genuine closeness to God and had experiences of God's presence. The Barbēlō was not just a remote aeon, perfect in every way, but the perfecter and savior of the Gnostics. As for the strange term "thrice-male," we'll talk about that in the next lecture.

Not only this, but the Gnostics believed that the human intellect could have brief experiences of *gnōsis*, that is, direct knowledge of the Barbēlō within this mortal life. Two Gnostic works, Zōstrianos and the Foreigner, portray a human being receiving this *gnōsis*. The people in these texts experience knowledge of God in two ways: One is through a journey upward through the cosmic heavens; the other is through interior contemplation of one's own intellect. Let's consider each of these.

The Gnostic book Zōstrianos tells the story of an ancient person with that name who desires to contemplate God and other spiritual realities. By means of his own intellect he turns away from material things and engages in a program of bodily discipline, philosophical study, and teaching. Through his hard work, Zōstrianos learns to see the ordinary world of material things as petty and insignificant, and he formulates deep questions about higher reality. But he does not reach his goal of contemplating God directly, and so he finds himself anguished and depressed—even suicidal.

At this point an angel called "the angel of *gnōsis*" appears to Zōstrianos and invites him to ascend through the lower realms of this cosmos and up to the Entirety. The hero abandons his physical body and boards a luminous cloud. The cloud carries him on an upward journey in which he meets several divine revealers, he undergoes repeated baptisms, and he gains increasingly esoteric knowledge of our universe and the Entirety. His journey takes him higher and higher not only in a cosmic sense, but also intellectually. Zōstrianos contemplates increasingly abstract levels of reality.

Eventually he ascends into the Barbēlō aeon, the highest level of divinity that human beings can know. At this apex of his journey Zōstrianos seeks to understand the Invisible Virgin Spirit itself, but this act is described as "reckless." Zōstrianos's "reckless" desire to gain *gnōsis* of the Invisible Spirit is something like Wisdom's failed attempt to think on her own in the Gnostic myth. In any event, Zōstrianos then descends and returns to his physical body. He then preaches a message of moral reformation and *gnōsis* with God to other people.

The Gnostics got this idea of traveling through the heavenly realms in order to gain knowledge of the cosmos and God from a long tradition of Jewish apocalypses in which this happens. An excellent example is a book entitled 2 Enoch, which tells about the heavenly journey of Enoch. Unfortunately, the date of this text is uncertain, but it comes from some time in the first few centuries A.D. Enoch appears briefly in Genesis as one of Seth's descendants.

According to Genesis 5, Enoch lived 165 years, but he did not really die. The Bible says, "Enoch was well pleasing to God, and he was not found, because God transferred him." So Enoch is a good character to imagine ascending up into the heavens, because God transferred him there.

In 2 Enoch the hero is extremely righteous in following the Jewish Law, and he displays special fidelity to the God of Israel. For these reasons, he is led on a tour up through the heavens, and he learns important secrets of the universe. Angels guide him, teach him, and answer his questions, and eventually he experiences a vision of God himself. "In a moment of eternity," Enoch says, "I saw the Lord's face, but the Lord's face is ineffable, marvelous, very awful, and very, very terrible." Enoch then returns to earth and exhorts other Jews to follow the Law and to be faithful to God.

When you compare Zōstrianos's heavenly journey to that of Enoch, there are several similarities. Both are serious religious men from long ago. Both journey upward through the heavens, guided by one or more angels, and they learn divine information about the universe that other human beings don't have. Both experience some sort of contact with God, and then they descend to preach and teach other people. And of course, in both cases, we have a text that describes the journey and shares with us the secrets that the hero learned.

So ancient people who knew stories like Enoch's would have found the Gnostic book Zōstrianos pretty familiar. But they would have noticed some important differences that show how distinct the Gnostic religious vision was. First, Enoch receives his heavenly journey as a reward for following the Jewish Law and being faithful to the God of Israel. Zōstrianos, in contrast, undertakes a program of asceticism and philosophical study. Philosophy is the path that Zōstrianos follows, until it can take him no further. That's when God has to step in.

Second, the information that Enoch learns on his journey mostly concerns the creation and structure of this universe and God's future judgment. For example, he is granted a vision of God creating the world; he sees where the angels store snow; and he is shown how God will judge and punish the wicked at the end of time. Zōstrianos also sees things like this, including how God created the world and will judge people. But he sees other things as well—most importantly, he is shown the aeons of the Entirety, and he sees the eternal forms after which things in this world were copied. In other words, Zōstrianos sees, so to speak, the important philosophical concepts of the Gnostic myth—that there is an Entirety made up of eternal aeons and that this world is an imperfect copy of the spiritual world. We see here not just Jewish apocalypticism, but also Platonist philosophy.

Third and finally, Enoch's heavenly journey culminates in a vision of God's face. The Lord's face may be ineffable, impossible to describe in words, but God does have a face, and Enoch sees it. Zōstrianos, in contrast, asks to understand the ultimate God of all, the Invisible Spirit, but his request is "reckless." The ultimate God of the Gnostics cannot be understood—much less does it have a face that someone could see.

So the Gnostics take a Jewish tradition of heavenly journeys and give it their own spin. It's no surprise that their hero Zōstrianos does not follow the Jewish Law or worship the God of Israel, because the Gnostics believe that the God of Israel is actually Ialdabaōth. But more than this, the Gnostics show a lot more interest in abstract philosophy. The hero prepares for his journey by studying philosophy; he sees abstract things like the aeons, and the Gnostic God is the unknowable God of Platonism.

What the Gnostics have done is combined a Jewish apocalyptic tradition of gaining *gnōsis* of God through a heavenly journey with a philosophical tradition of knowing God through study and contemplation. This philosophical path is the second way of knowing God in Gnostic texts. And it goes back, as you might expect, to Plato.

Plato's most famous description of how a human being can experience mystical knowledge of God is found in his book the *Symposium*. In this book a group of highly educated men entertain themselves after dinner by giving speeches in praise of Eros, the god of erotic love. The men present different visions of Eros, but they all agree that erotic desire, or love for what is beautiful, is a basic component of the human soul.

In the climactic speech we learn that our erotic desire is meant to lead us to love God, who is beauty itself. How this works is that a man starts by desiring the beautiful body of an adolescent male—this is all very male-oriented. In Plato's Greece, the young male body was seen as the epitome of physical beauty, and it was assumed that all adult males would find a beautiful adolescent male attractive, even as they would also carry on sexual relationships with women.

What a philosophical man should do, however, is learn to love not just the beauty of that particular teenage boy's body, but the beauty of the human body in general. From there he should love the beautiful soul, and then the principles that govern the soul, and so on up to loving simply beauty itself. You can see how this is a journey of increasing abstraction: You start by loving a specific material beautiful thing; then you love things that are more spiritual and abstract, like the soul; and eventually fields of knowledge, like mathematics, which are themselves beautiful. This is where philosophical study of the kind Zōstrianos pursues plays an important role.

If a man trains himself in this way, Plato says, he might be fortunate enough to be granted, "all of a sudden," a vision of beauty itself, which is God. Here is how Plato describes this beauty itself, or God:

> First, it is eternally existent: It neither comes into being nor perishes; neither grows nor diminishes. Next, it is not partly beautiful and partly ugly; nor is it one at one time and the other at another time; nor is it beautiful in one respect and ugly in another; nor is it beautiful in one situation and ugly in another so that it seems beautiful to one person and ugly to another. Nor again will the Beautiful appear to him as a face or hands or any other body part, not as a particular discourse or a particular science, not existing somewhere in another something, such as an animal, earth, heaven, or anything else. Rather, (it will appear) independently, eternally existing in a single form: all the other beautiful things participate in it in such a way that, although the others come into being and perish, it becomes neither greater or lesser, nor is it affected in any way.

This sounds a lot like the Gnostics' Invisible Spirit, doesn't it?

Indeed, what you see in a Gnostic book like Zōstrianos is the adaption of Plato's method of knowing God to the idea of a revelatory heavenly journey. Zōstrianos, as Plato advises, takes up the study of philosophy, and during his heavenly journey he contemplates increasingly abstract levels of reality, including the eternal ideas that Plato said are the models for everything in this universe.

The only mistake, so to speak, that Zōstrianos makes is that he "recklessly" tries to gain understanding of the ultimate God, the Invisible Spirit. But according to Plato, a person cannot force such a vision: It will happen "all of a sudden," like a gift. And also—very important—Plato says that the person who is granted this vision of God becomes immortal. *Gnōsis* of God grants a person salvation from this material world and eternal life. Zōstrianos may not achieve *gnōsis* of the Invisible Spirit, but he does get what's possible in this life—namely, divine knowledge of the cosmos and of the Entirety, culminating in *gnōsis* of the Barbēlō. This brings him salvation from the material world and eternal life.

Well, that's all well and good for Zōstrianos, you might think. He was clearly a devout heroic man from the past, who went on a journey into the heavens. If you were an ordinary Gnostic living in Rome in the 2nd or 3rd century, what hope did you have of gaining *gnōsis* of God if leaving your body, getting on a luminous cloud, and journeying through the heavens is what's required? This is where this second mode of knowing God comes into play. You can know God also, the Gnostics claim, by contemplating higher and more abstract levels of reality, just as Plato taught. But of course, the Gnostics did not follow Plato in suggesting that we do this through erotic love, by first desiring the body of a beautiful young man. The Gnostics, we have seen, did not have such a positive view of sexual desire. Instead, if you want to start with something lower and then ascend to God through study and contemplation, start with your own mind. After all, your own intellect is a miniature version of God's intellect, the Entirety.

We learn all this from our final new Gnostic book, which is entitled the Foreigner. This book is a lot like Zōstrianos. Its hero, named simply "the Foreigner" or "One Who is Other," is a mythical human being from long ago. It's possible that he's Seth. Genesis calls Seth "another seed"—that is, a kind of seed different from that of Cain and Abel. An ancient enemy of the Gnostics tells us that some Gnostics did call Seth "the foreigner." Well, whoever he is, the Foreigner experiences a heavenly journey much like that of Zōstrianos, guided by an angel named Iouēl. Like Zōstrianos, the Foreigner ascends as high as the Barbēlō aeon, the level of reality just below the Invisible Spirit. Iouēl tells the Foreigner that he will receive a revelation of the Unknowable God, but after a period of 100 years.

Rather than being discouraged by this news, the Foreigner spends the next 100 years preparing himself for his experience. When the century is over, he is taken outside his body to a holy place. There, divine beings instruct him in how to contemplate God. It's these instructions that a Gnostic could have tried to follow.

The Foreigner learns that he must turn his attention toward himself and contemplate sequentially the structures of his own mind. This is a process of interior contemplation through increasingly abstract stages of mental "withdrawal." This is like Plato's ascent through levels of abstraction through love, but it's totally intellectual and self-oriented. We must know our true self, that is, our intellect, in order to know God. We can do this because it was the Invisible Spirit's own act of self-knowledge, of thinking about itself, that generated the Barbēlō and the other aeons of the Entirety. The structure of our mind is a fragment or copy or miniature version of the structure of the Entirety, which is God's mind.

As the Foreigner performs this self-contemplation, he gains knowledge of aspects of the Barbēlō aeon that are also in his own intellect: blessedness, vitality, and reality. He gains *gnōsis* of himself—"as I really am," he says. And in that way he discovers the Barbēlō as "that which existed within me." The Foreigner then receives a vision of the Invisible Spirit—in the sudden, gratuitous way that Plato had said in the *Symposium*. The Foreigner wants to understand his vision, but instead the divine beings explain at length that the Invisible Spirit is not knowable. Ultimately, what the Foreigner learns is a paradox: He understands the Invisible Spirit precisely by not understanding it. As an eternal being tells him, "Do not attempt to comprehend it, for this is impossible. Rather, if, through a luminous thought, you should happen to understand it, be uncomprehending of it."

Ultimately, the Foreigner ascends to acquaintance with God by journeying through his own intellect, and he receives *gnōsis* of the Invisible Spirit as a gift. Here we reach what must have been the ultimate appeal of Gnostic teachings. The Gnostics acknowledged that this world is flawed and full of misery. They saw how our bodies and the physical world can obstruct our contemplation and understanding of higher spiritual realities. They suggested that the flawed nature of this world can be traced back to its creator, Ialdabaōth, who is a flawed version of divinity. He tried to make this world as a copy of the spiritual realm, but he did a poor job. Now he arrogantly thinks that he is the ultimate God and he wants human beings to serve and worship him.

But, the Gnostics say, we know that there is a spiritual realm of truth and perfection beyond this universe. And there is a higher God who is unchanging and eternal and perfect. Our dissatisfaction with this world is a sign that we, too, belong to that higher realm; in fact, within us, is a fragment of the spiritual power that Ialdabaōth took from his mother, Wisdom. If we wake up to our true selves, get baptized with the five seals, and worship the Barbēlō rather than Ialdabaōth, we shall return to the spiritual realm after this life.

But even now, if we contemplate rightly, we can experience, however briefly, *gnōsis* or acquaintance of the true God. Such an experience confirms the reality of what the Gnostics teach.

Perhaps now we can appreciate the appeal of the complexity of Gnostic myth and the different stories the Gnostics tell about Adam and Eve and the flood. The Gnostics needed to understand the aeons of the Entirety in all their complexity because the Entirety is God's intellect. Our intellect is a miniature version of God's, and it's by knowing and contemplating our own intellect that we can gain knowledge of God in this life. That's why they wanted to know the Entirety in as great detail as possible.

The Gnostics needed to retell Genesis because they needed to explain how it was that the spiritual power persists in human beings and why it is that most people have failed to understand the true nature of Ialdabaōth. These matters could not be simple because Genesis got some things right and some things wrong. But by revising Genesis and seeing how they, the Gnostics, fit into the story, the Gnostics gained assurance that the Barbēlō and Wisdom have been acting to save them and protect them.

And perhaps the complexity of Gnostic myth and literature was itself appealing. If the path to knowing God is through our intellect, then maybe the intellectual difficulty of mastering the Gnostic myth and following its stories seemed like an essential part of that path.

I think that this promise of achieving *gnōsis* of a God beyond this world and beyond our conceptions of God constituted the great appeal of Gnostic teaching in the ancient world. But modern scholars have suggested something else that may have been appealing—the Gnostic interest in assertive female character like Eve and Nōrea, and female divinities like the Barbēlō and Wisdom. In the next lecture I will consider women, gender, and sexuality in Gnostic myth.

The Feminine in Gnostic Myth
Lecture 8

When scholars first began to read texts from Nag Hammadi in the 1960s and 1970s, they were astonished to find how frequently these books depict God and other divine beings as female. This strong female element suggested that the Gnostics had a more inclusive, less patriarchal notion of the divine than did orthodox Jews and Christians. Since the 1970s, however, scholars have become less enthusiastic about the roles of women and the feminine in Gnostic myth. In this lecture, we'll look at three examples of the feminine in Gnostic texts: the feminine divine in the Secret Book According to John, the feminine revealer in The Thunder: Perfect Intellect, and the feminine heroine in the Reality of the Rulers.

The Feminine Divine

- The Secret Book According to John describes the Barbēlō as follows: "She became the universal womb, for she precedes everything, the mother-father, the first human, the holy spirit, the triple male, the triple power, the androgynous one with three names, the aeon among the invisible beings, the first to come forth."

- This description twice balances male and female elements: The Barbēlō is the "mother-father" and "androgynous." At one point, the author makes the Barbēlō seem female: She is "the universal womb," yet he also calls her "the triple male" or "thrice male." (*Thrice* seems to be Gnostic jargon for "supremely" or "very.") Thus, the Barbēlō is supremely male, yet she is also a womb—and androgynous. How can this all be true?

- In modern thought, *androgynous* might be taken to refer to equal shares of two equal principles. In other words, to be androgynous is to be equally male and female, and these qualities are equal in value. But this may not have been how ancient people thought of androgyny.

○ As mentioned in an earlier lecture, humanity is created twice in the first two chapters of Genesis. In chapter 1, the text reads: "And God made the human being; according to God's image he made it; male and female he made them" (Gen. 1:27). It's difficult to know whether God made multiple human beings who are either male or female or whether he made a single human being who is both male and female.

○ In chapter 2, God constructs a female mate for Adam from Adam's rib—removing the female as a part of the male. This does not seem to refer to the separation of two equal halves. Instead, the female appears to be less than the male. In fact, many ancient people did not think of male and female as two opposite and equal genders, but they considered the female to be a derivative aspect of the male. To be female was to be "not enough" male.

○ In this understanding, androgyny is not the union of two equal genders but the proper incorporation of the female into the more fundamental and superior male.

• This seems to be precisely what we see in the Barbēlō. The Secret Book depicts her primarily as a female character because her other name, Forethought, is a feminine name in Greek, and at some point, she conceives the Self-Originate from the gaze of the Invisible Spirit. But as a perfect divine being, the Barbēlō is essentially masculine. She is, in fact, "thrice-male" because she includes within her masculinity the features of femininity. The Gnostic view of God incorporates feminine elements, but it does not dislodge the superiority of the masculine.

• The aeon Wisdom (Sophia in Greek) is an even more clearly female character than the Barbēlō because she has an unnamed male aeon as her consort and she is the mother of Ialdabaōth. She is also a good example of the ambiguity of the divine feminine in Gnostic myth.

- On the one hand, it's Wisdom who enlightens human beings about their true origins in the Entirety and teaches them about the way to *gnōsis*.

- On the other hand, it's her error that leads to the generation of Ialdabaōth and the loss of the divine power to him in the first place. And remember, her error is daring to think on her own, without the consent of her male partner.

- The author of the Secret Book strongly emphasizes harmony. By pondering on her own, Wisdom disturbs the harmony that should exist between male and female aeons.

The Feminine Revealer

- One of the most remarkable Gnostic texts from Nag Hammadi is The Thunder: Perfect Intellect, probably written before 300 A.D. It consists entirely of a revelation monologue spoken by a female divine revealer. In some passages, this speaker exhorts her audience to listen to her message and to realize their true selves. In other passages, she talks about herself in paradoxes. For example:

  > I am the first and the last.
  > I am the honored one and the despised one.
  > I am the whore and the holy one.
  > I am the wife and the virgin. …
  > I am the bride and the bridegroom
  > And it is my husband who begot me.

- What did these paradoxes mean for the ancient Gnostics? One persuasive hypothesis is that these statements form a riddle that reveals the identity of the speaker. What woman is both revered and despised, is seen as both holy and a harlot, and has a husband who gave birth to her? The female revealer in The Thunder would seem to be Eve but Eve as the embodiment of the female divine, whether Wisdom or Forethought, the Barbēlō.

- As the revelation monologue of a female divinity, The Thunder resembles at least two other ancient texts, one Jewish and one "pagan."

  o In the Old Testament book of Proverbs, God's Wisdom is personified as a female figure. The Hebrew word for wisdom, *hochmah*, is feminine, just as Sophia is in Greek. Proverbs depicts Wisdom as God's helper in creating the world, and she addresses human beings directly,

Isis was an Egyptian goddess, but temples devoted to her spread throughout the ancient Mediterranean world.

inviting them to follow her. It's virtually certain that the Gnostic author of Thunder modeled his divine female revealer on the Wisdom of Proverbs. By doing so, he indicates that the true Wisdom of God can be found in Gnostic myth.

  o The author may have been equally inspired by a famous text called the Isis Aretalogy (Discourse on Virtues). This text is famous because it shows a goddess—not a god—making grand claims about her powers. In the text, Isis lists her many virtues and reminds human beings of all that she has done for them: "I divided the earth from the heaven. / I showed the path of the stars. / I ordered the course of the sun and the moon."

The Feminine Heroine

- The Gnostics are famous not only for having female divinities but also for giving the human female Eve a larger role in the Genesis story and for including the new biblical character Nōrea, sister of Seth, who is prominent in the Reality of the Rulers. In contrast to all other Gnostic writings, this text characterizes the Gnostics as the descendants, not of Seth but of Nōrea, who leads humanity to improve and defies male human beings, including Noah and the evil rulers.

- That Reality of the Rulers is distinctive for how it places gender and sexual violence at the center of its story. From the start, the divine power that enters this world is coded as feminine, and the evil rulers of this world experience an erotic attraction to it. They create Adam and Eve precisely so that they can possess the divine power from above. When the divine spirit enters Eve, the rulers want to rape her.

- But the divine spirit laughs at the rulers, leaves Eve, and becomes a tree, probably the tree of life in the Garden of Eden. The divine spirit leaves behind a fleshly Eve, a shadow of herself, and it is this fleshly Eve whom the rulers rape. The female spiritual principle mocks the rulers and escapes, but they succeed in raping the human Eve.

- When Nōrea becomes the female source of divine knowledge, she, too, comes into conflict with the rulers. First, when the rulers decide to destroy humanity with a flood, Nōrea tries to escape the flood with Noah on the ark. When Noah refuses to let her onboard, Nōrea causes the ark to be destroyed by fire, and Noah must build another.

- At this point, the rulers decide to attack Nōrea. The chief ruler says to her, "Your mother Eve came to us." But Nōrea replies: "It is you who are the rulers of darkness; you are accursed. And you did not know my mother; instead it was your female counterpart that you knew. For I am not your descendant; rather, it is from the world above that I am come." The chief ruler is undeterred, and Nōrea cries out to God for help. The Luminary Ēlēlēth arrives to rescue her, and he reveals to her that she is the mother of all the saved people.

- It's difficult to call the depiction of women and gender in this Gnostic tale wholly positive or wholly negative. On the one hand, the female divine spiritual principle always manages to outwit the evil rulers, and Nōrea is an assertive woman who defies both Noah and the rulers. On the other hand, women and the feminine are the repeated objects of sexual violence.

- In general, Gnostic myth depicts a negative view of sexual desire. To be sure, some instances of sexual intercourse have good consequences. For example, Adam and Eve produce Seth, and in the Entirety, the conception of the Self-Originate by the Invisible Spirit and the Barbēlō closely resembles sexual intercourse. But sexual desire itself is never seen as good.

  - In the Reality of the Rulers, sexual desire motivates the evil rulers to attack Eve and Nōrea. In the Secret Book According to John, Ialdabaōth rapes Eve, and the rulers later seduce human women, leading to human sinfulness.

  - After Ialdabaōth rapes Eve, the author of the Secret Book writes: "To this day sexual intercourse has persisted because of the first ruler." In other words, sex as we know it comes from Ialdabaōth, and sexual desire is a major means by which the counterfeit spirit leads human beings astray.

  - If the Gnostics were not positive about sex, neither were most early Christians. In 1 Corinthians, Paul told his followers that he wished all Christians could be celibate, and he encouraged single Christians not to get married. This does not mean that the Gnostics or other early Christians thought that marriage was wrong. It was acceptable for Christians to get married, but reproduction was the only good reason to have sex. Christians universally agreed that sex for pleasure—out of desire—was wrong.

Suggested Reading

King, *Images of the Feminine in Gnosticism.*

———, "Reading Sex and Gender in the *Secret Revelation of John.*"

Layton, *The Gnostic Scriptures*, "The Secret Book According to John," "The Thunder—Perfect Intellect," and "The Reality of the Rulers."

———, "The Riddle of the Thunder."

McGuire, "Women, Gender, and Gnosis in Gnostic Texts and Traditions."

Meyer, ed., *The Nag Hammadi Scriptures*, "The Secret Book of John," "Thunder," and "The Nature of the Rulers."

Pagels, *The Gnostic Gospels*, chapter 3.

Questions to Consider

1. Would you characterize the Gnostic perspective on women and sexuality as predominantly positive, negative, or ambiguous?

2. Why do you think rape figures prominently in several Gnostic writings?

The Feminine in Gnostic Myth
Lecture 8—Transcript

As the Holy Book of the Great Invisible Spirit tells the Gnostic myth, it begins with the ultimate God, the ineffable parent of everything—that is, the Invisible Spirit. But we can't really know that God. Instead, we can know the aeons or powers that emanate from that God. Unlike what you see in some other Gnostic texts, the first three aeons that emanate from the Invisible Spirit are called the Father, the Mother, and the Son.

When scholars first began to read the texts from Nag Hammadi in the 1960s and 1970s, they were astonished to find how frequently these books depict God and other divine beings as female. Not only in the Holy Book but also in the Secret Book According to John, a trilogy of Father, Mother, and Son lies at the heart of the divine realm. The Barbēlō aeon is also called Forethought—in Greek, *Pronoia*, a feminine noun—and so she is referred to with feminine pronouns. Other than the Barbēlō, the most active divine aeon is Wisdom—*Sophia* in Greek, also feminine, and she is clearly portrayed as a female character, the mother of Ialdabaōth.

And when Wisdom and Forethought speak through human beings, they do so through female characters, namely Eve and Nōrea, the mother and sister of Seth, respectively.

This strong female element in Gnostic mythology suggested to scholars that the Gnostics had a more inclusive, less patriarchal notion of the divine than did orthodox Jews and Christians. While non-Gnostics thought of God as a Father who might have a Son, the Gnostics could speak of a divine Mother.

In her groundbreaking 1979 book *The Gnostic Gospels*, the great scholar of early Christianity Elaine Pagels argued that Gnostic myth challenged the emerging patriarchal theology of the Christian Church. She suggested that, because Gnostics worshiped a God who was both Father and Mother and because their myth featured prominent female characters, Gnostic communities would have been more open to female leadership than other Christian groups. A more inclusive idea of God, one that embraced the feminine rather than rejecting it, would have supported a more inclusive religious community, one that gave women a greater voice than did the emerging Catholic Church. Pagels found support her for her argument in the writings of the Gnostics' enemies, who accused the Gnostics of allowing women to lead men and of mixing women and men too easily.

Pagels and other feminists hoped that Gnostic literature might provide resources for modern Christian women looking for more liberating religious texts than those in the official Bible of the Church.

Since the 1970s, however, these same scholars, including Pagels, have become less enthusiastic about the roles of women and the feminine in Gnostic myth. For one thing, historians of religion are no longer confident that the prominence of female characters in a religion necessarily leads to greater roles for women in religious communities. Consider the Roman Catholic Church in the Middle Ages: The Virgin Mary became a very important figure in Catholic devotion. Christians prayed to Mary and honored images of her in their churches. Mary was nearly as visible and prominent as Christ. And yet this did not lead to women leading churches or having a bigger role in the Church. One could argue that devotion to the Virgin had the opposite effect: Real human women looked imperfect and ordinary in comparison to a woman who was perfect and sacred.

But even deeper, how positive is the feminine in Gnostic myth? To be sure, Gnostic myth has more of the feminine than traditional Christian theology, but is it necessarily better, or more affirming? Let's look at three examples of the feminine in Gnostic texts: the feminine divine in the Secret Book According to John, the feminine revealer in a text that we have not yet discussed, called Thunder: Perfect Intellect, and the feminine heroine in the Reality of the Rulers.

As we have seen, one of the core convictions of the Gnostics is that the ultimate God, the Invisible Virgin Spirit, is beyond any concepts that we might have, including concepts of divinity. The Secret Book According to John goes on at some length about how we cannot even think about the Invisible Spirit, much less talk about it. So surely the Invisible Spirit transcends any concept of gender.

And yet the Invisible Spirit is also called a "virgin spirit." Now certainly a virgin can be either male or female, but the point is that a virgin pretty much has to be either a male or a female. If we understand as "virgin" someone who has not had sex, then you pretty much have to have a sex in order to have or not have sex. So even when they are talking about the immeasurable, indescribable, incorporeal Invisible Spirit, the Gnostics cannot escape thinking that a living being must have gendered qualities.

Things become more complex with the emanation of the first aeon from the Invisible Spirit—Forethought, or the Barbēlō. Here is how the Secret Book describes the Barbēlō:

> She became the universal womb, for she precedes everything, the mother-father, the first human, the holy spirit, the triple male, the triple power, the androgynous one with three names, the aeon among the invisible beings, the first to come forth.

This description twice balances male and female elements: the Barbēlō is the "mother-father" and also "androgynous." Once, the author makes the Barbēlō seem female—she is the "universal womb." And yet he also calls her triple male, or "thrice male." *Triple* or *thrice* seems to be Gnostic jargon for "supremely" or "very." Thus the Barbēlō is supremely male, very male. And yet she is also a womb—and androgynous. How can this all be true?

We must ask first what it means—or rather, what it meant in antiquity—to be androgynous, both male and female. We might think it means to include equal shares of two equal principles. To be androgynous is to be equally male and female, and these qualities are equal in value. Well, that may not have been how some ancient people thought of androgyny.

Let's return to something we've considered before—the creation of humanity in the first two chapters of Genesis. Let's remember that the creation of humanity is narrated twice, in chapter 1 and then a second time in chapter 2. Again, chapter 1 says this:

And God said, "Let us make a human being according to our image and likeness, and let them rule the fish of the sea, and the birds of the heaven, and the cattle, and all the earth, and all the reptiles that creep on the earth." And God made the human being; according to God's image he made it; male and female he made them.

Note again the fluctuation between the singular and plural pronouns in the Greek text that ancient people read. It's kind of ambiguous whether God made multiple human beings who are either male or female, or whether he made a single humanity or human being, who is both male and female.

Then, remember that in chapter 2, creation seems to start all over again. Here, God makes the male Adam and places him in a garden, but God can find no suitable partner for Adam from among the other animals. And so God performs surgery on Adam:

And God cast a trance on Adam, and he slept. And he took one of his ribs and filled up the flesh equal to it. And God constructed the rib that he took from Adam into a woman, and he led her to Adam. And Adam said, "This now is bone from my bones and flesh from my flesh. She will be called woman because she was taken from her man."

From here the story goes downhill, as the serpent tricks Eve into eating fruit from the forbidden tree; Adam eats as well, and God sentences humanity to death.

You'll recall that ancient people often understood these two stories as one. In the first chapter, God creates an androgynous human being, who is both male and female, and then in chapter 2, God separates the human being into male and female.

But now notice how God does this: He removes the female from the male, as a part of the male—the rib. This does not look like the separation of two equal halves. Instead, the female appears to be less than the male, derivative of the male; the woman "was taken from her man." And in fact, many ancient people did not think of male and female as two opposite and equal genders, but instead they considered the female or the feminine as a lesser, derivative aspect of the male or the masculine. To be female is not to be something separate and different from the male. Rather, the female is a lesser version of the male; to be female is not to be enough male. It was sometimes believed that children who are born female simply did not develop long enough in the womb: they literally did not cook long enough in the heat of the uterus. In this view, there aren't really two genders—just one, which is male when it's perfect and female when it's imperfect.

Now when ancient people understood the Genesis story in this way, then the removal of the female Eve from the male Adam does leave him missing something, namely the feminine: Adam now cannot be a womb and cannot bear children. But still, the masculine is the basic and superior form. From this point of view, androgyny is not the union of two equal genders. Instead, it's the proper incorporation of the female into the more fundamental and superior male.

That is precisely what I think we see in the Barbēlō. The Secret Book depicts her primarily as a female character because her other name, Forethought, is a feminine name in Greek, and she at some point conceives the Self-Originate from the light gaze of the Invisible Spirit. But, as a perfect divine being, the Barbēlō is essentially masculine. She is in fact thrice-male, supremely male, precisely because she includes within her masculinity the features of femininity.

And so when the Gnostics sang a hymn to the Barbēlō, now found in the Three Tablets of Seth, they addressed her with masculine pronouns and praised her as "the masculine, virgin, first aeon Barbēlō."

So yes, the Gnostic view of God incorporates feminine elements, but it does not dislodge the superiority of the masculine. We see this as well in the case of the aeon Wisdom—*Sophia* in Greek. She is an even more clearly female character than the Barbēlō, for she has an unnamed male aeon as her consort, and she is plainly called the mother of Ialdabaōth.

Wisdom is a great example of how ambiguous the divine feminine is in Gnostic myth. On the one hand, she and Forethought work tirelessly to help humanity. It's Wisdom who enlightens human beings about their true origin in the Entirety and teaches them about the way to *gnōsis*. On the other hand, it's her error that leads to the generation of Ialdabaōth and the loss of the divine power to him in the first place. And what was her error? She dares to think on her own, without the consent of her male partner. This is how the Secret Book puts it:

> She wanted to bring forth something like herself, without the consent of the Spirit, who had not given approval, and without her consort and without his consideration. The male did not give approval. She did not find her consort, and she considered this without the Spirit's consent and without the knowledge of her consort.

Notice how strongly the author emphasizes harmony. There should be harmony between male and female aeons. By pondering on her own, Wisdom disturbs that harmony and produces a flawed divine being. And notice too how this harmony is expressed: The male consort must give his consent to Wisdom's thought. Wisdom may be a female divinity, but things go wrong when she acts without a male divinity's consent.

Wisdom, of course, repents of her mistake, and she works with Forethought to rectify what she has done by teaching humanity and working to recover the divine power that is dispersed within us. And so Wisdom and Forethought, both female beings, do a lot of talking, for they must reveal to humanity the truth about God and the spiritual realm. Forethought in particular gives long speeches in works like the Secret Book According to John and First Thought in Three Forms.

But one of the most remarkable Gnostic texts from Nag Hammadi is The Thunder: Perfect Intellect (or Perfect Mind). Like so many of the Nag Hammadi works, we can't be sure of when the Greek original was written, but it must be from before 300 A.D. It consists entirely of a revelation monologue spoken by a female divine revealer.

The speaker talks in two different ways. In some passages, she exhorts the listeners to listen to her message and to realize their own true selves. Here's an excerpt:

You who listen, listen to me!
You who are waiting for me, take me to yourselves
And do not chase me away from your sight. ...
Keep watch! Do not be ignorant of me!

In other passages, she talks about herself in paradoxes. For example:

I am the first and the last.
I am the honored one and the despised one.
I am the whore and the holy one.
I am the wife and the virgin. ...
I am the bride and the bridegroom
And it is my husband who begot me.

These amazing paradoxes have for some readers expressed the problem of being a woman in a patriarchal society. Women are simultaneously seen as whores and as virgins; they are revered and despised. In 2005, Jordan Scott, the daughter of the famous movie director Ridley Scott, made a commercial for Prada showing a beautiful woman at various places in a city while a female narrator reads from The Thunder. For Scott, this lengthy poem expresses the paradoxical dilemma of femininity.

But what did these paradoxes mean for the ancient Gnostics? One very persuasive hypothesis is that these statements make a riddle, which reveals the identity of the speaker. What woman is both revered and despised? What woman is seen as both holy and a harlot? What woman has a husband who gave birth to her?

The answer would seem to be Eve, who, for example, was created from the side of her husband, Adam. We have seen that in some versions of the Gnostic myth, Wisdom, in the person of Afterthought, speaks to Adam and all humanity through Eve. Eve captures, then, a larger Gnostic paradox: The divine principle to which we should listen is also present within us as the divine power that Ialdabaōth took from his mother, Wisdom.

This female revealer in Thunder is Eve, but Eve as the embodiment of the female divine, whether Wisdom or Forethought, the Barbēlō.

As the revelation monologue of a female divinity, The Thunder: Perfect Intellect resembles at least two other ancient texts, one Jewish and one "pagan." In the Old Testament book of Proverbs, God's Wisdom is personified as a female figure. The Hebrew word for wisdom, *hochmah*, is feminine, just as *Sophia* is in Greek. Proverbs depicts Wisdom as God's helper in creating the world, and she addresses human beings directly, inviting them to follow her:

> And now, my children, listen to me:
> Happy are those who keep my ways.
> Hear instruction, and be wise, and do not neglect it.
> Happy is the one who listens to me,
> Watching daily at my gates,
> Waiting beside my doors.
> For whoever finds me finds life
> And obtains favor from the Lord;
> But those who miss me injure themselves;
> All who hate me love death.

It's virtually certain that the Gnostic author of Thunder modeled his divine female revealer, his Wisdom, on the Wisdom of Proverbs. And by doing so he was saying to Jews and Christians, "If you are looking for the true Wisdom of God, you'll find her in Gnostic myth."

The author may have been equally inspired by a famous text called the Isis Aretalogy, or discourse on virtues. Isis was an Egyptian goddess, but temples devoted to her spread throughout the ancient Mediterranean world. The Isis Aretalogy is so famous because it shows a goddess, not a god, making very grand claims about her powers. The version of the Isis Aretalogy that we have comes from Greece in the 2nd century, but the text is certainly much older. As the title suggests, Isis talks about her many virtues, and she especially reminds human beings of all that she has done for them. Isis says:

> I gave and ordained laws for human beings, which no one can
> change.
> I am eldest daughter of Kronos.
> I am wife and sister of King Osiris.
> I am she who finds fruit for men. ...
> I divided the earth from the heaven.
> I showed the path of the stars.
> I ordered the course of the sun and the moon.
> I devised business in the sea.
> I brought together woman and man. ...
> I revealed mysteries unto human beings.

Whether or not the author of the Thunder knew this text—and he probably did—we see again how the voice of Gnostic Wisdom would have competed with other female divine voices from the ancient world.

But why is this Gnostic book called The Thunder? We may have the answer from a Christian bishop named Epiphanius, who lived in the 4th century. He reports that the Gnostics have a book called the Gospel of Eve, in which the speaker seems to be drunk because she, as he puts it, "randomly utters statements that are not compatible." This sounds a lot like our text, The Thunder. But Epiphanius goes on to say that in this lost Gospel of Eve the voice that speaks comes as "a voice of thunder." Perhaps we are to imagine the voice of our text as being like thunder: magnificent, awe-inspiring, and scary, all at the same.

But the Gnostics are famous not only for female divinities, but also for giving the human female Eve a bigger role in the Genesis story—and for including the new biblical character, Nōrea, sister of Seth, who is so prominent in the Reality of the Rulers. In contrast to all other Gnostic writings, the Reality of the Rulers characterizes the Gnostics as not the descendants of Seth, but the descendants of his spunky sister, Nōrea, who leads humanity to improve and defies male human beings like Noah as well as the evil rulers.

That text, the Reality of the Rulers, is distinctive for how it places gender and sexual violence at the center of its story. From the start, the divine power that enters this world is coded as feminine, and the evil rulers of this world experience an erotic attraction to it. They create Adam and later Eve precisely so that they can possess the divine power from above.

When the divine spirit enters Eve, the rulers become attracted to her and want to rape her. Here is what happens:

> When they saw Adam's female counterpart speaking with him, they became agitated with great agitation; and they became enamored of her. They said to one another, "Come, let us sow our seed in her," and they pursued her. And she laughed at them for their witlessness and their blindness; and in their clutches, she became a tree, and left before them her shadowy reflection resembling herself; and they defiled it foully, and they defiled the stamp of her voice so that by the form they had modeled, together with their own image, they made themselves liable to condemnation.

When the rulers try to rape Eve, the divine spirit laughs at them, and she leaves Eve and becomes a tree. Most likely this is the tree of life that Genesis says was in the Garden of Eden. This detail also is reminiscent of the Greek myth of Daphne, a nymph who escapes from the erotic interest of Apollo by transforming herself into a tree. The divine spirit leaves behind simply a fleshly Eve, a shadow, a modeled form, and it's this fleshly Eve whom the rulers rape. The female spiritual principle mocks the rulers and escapes, but they succeed in raping the human Eve.

When Nōrea becomes the female source of divine knowledge, she too comes into conflict with the rulers. First, when the rulers decide to destroy humanity with a flood because human beings aren't worshiping them, Nōrea tries to escape the flood with Noah on the ark. Noah refuses to let her on board—in this text Noah is not a good character—and so Nōrea blows upon the ark and causes it to be destroyed by a fire. So Noah has to build another ark.

At this point the rulers decide to attack Nōrea as they did Eve. The chief ruler says to Nōrea, "Your mother Eve came to us." But Nōrea will have none of this. She says to the rulers:

> It is you who are the rulers of darkness; you are accursed. And you did not know my mother; instead it was your female counterpart that you knew. For I am not your descendant; rather, it is from the world above that I am come.

The chief ruler is undeterred, and so Nōrea cries out to God for help. The Luminary Ēlēlēth arrives to rescue her, and he reveals to her that she is the mother of all the saved people.

Again, it's hard to call the depiction of women and gender in this Gnostic tale as wholly positive or wholly negative. On the one hand, the female divine spiritual principle always manages to outwit the evil rulers, and Nōrea is an assertive woman who defies both Noah and the rulers. She proudly and defiantly declares her divine origin when the rulers try to attack her.

On the other hand, women and the feminine are the repeated objects of sexual violence, and the rulers do in fact rape the human being Eve. Nōrea herself dismisses this rape as inconsequential: "You did not know my mother," she tells the rulers. "Rather, it was your female counterpart that you knew." Well, OK, as Nōrea says, the fleshly Eve whom the rulers raped did not have the divine spirit. Still, I think we can agree that her rape is a horrible thing nonetheless.

In general, Gnostic myth depicts a negative view of sexual desire. To be sure, some instances of sexual intercourse turn out okay. For example, Adam and Eve do produce Seth, and in the Entirety, the conception of the Self-Originate by the Invisible Spirit and the Barbēlō closely resembles sexual intercourse. But sexual desire itself is never seen as a good. In the Reality of the Rulers sexual desire is what motivates the evil rulers to attack Eve and Nōrea. In the Secret Book According to John, Ialdabaōth rapes Eve, and rulers later seduce human women, leading to all sorts of human sinfulness.

After Ialdabaōth rapes Eve, the author of the Secret Book writes: "To this day, sexual intercourse has persisted because of the first ruler." So sex as we know it comes from Ialdabaōth.

It's interesting that the different manuscripts of the Secret Book disagree about what comes next. According to one manuscript, Ialdabaōth planted sexual desire in Eve, so that humans would have sex and produce new bodies in which the spiritual power can be trapped. But in two other manuscripts, Ialdabaōth puts sexual desire in Adam, not Eve. Scholars are not sure which is the more original. My guess is that the original text had sexual desire put in Adam because the Secret Book and other Gnostic texts tend to depict women as the objects of male lust, rather than as the source of lust. Perhaps a later editor—a later editor who was male—changed it to Eve because ancient men did tend to think that women were less able to control their sexual desire than men were.

In any case, all the manuscripts agree that Ialdabaōth created sexual desire and that it's a major means by which the counterfeit spirit leads human beings astray. The Gnostics were not sex-positive.

But then again, neither were most early Christians. From the beginning, Christians showed little appreciation for the goodness of sexual love. In his First Letter to the Corinthians, chapter 7, Paul told his followers that he wished all Christians could be celibate as he was, and he encouraged single Christians not to get married. He conceded that some Christians would not be able to control their need to have sex, and he said in that case, they should marry. "Better to marry," he said, "than to be aflame with passion."

Most Christians followed Paul in preferring virginity to marriage, and so the Gnostics were not unique in this respect. This does not mean that the Gnostics or other early Christians thought that marriage was wrong or that husbands and wives should abstain from sex. It was OK for Christians to get married and to produce children. But reproduction was the only good reason to have sex. Christians universally agreed that sex simply for pleasure, out of desire, was wrong.

The Gnostics seem to have thought the same way. Sexual desire came from Ialdabaōth, and the rulers use sex to deceive human beings and to produce new material bodies. But Gnostic myth includes good families—not only Adam and Eve and their children, Seth and Nōrea—but also the divine family we met at the beginning of this lecture, the divine Father, Mother, and Son.

The Gnostics may have had female divinities and assertive female characters, but their overall attitudes seem to have been fairly typical for the ancient world. Being male was superior to being female.

You can find no better expression of this idea than in the Christian Gospel According to Thomas. At the end of that gospel, the apostle Peter says to Jesus that Mary Magdalene should leave their group because, as he says, "females are not worthy of life." Jesus replies, "Look, I will guide her to make her male so that she, too, may become a living male spirit like you. For every female who makes herself male will enter the kingdom of heaven."

This astonishing statement sounds really misogynist, but we're going to have to examine it more closely to figure out what it's trying to say.

In my next two lectures, I'll discuss the Gospel of Thomas, perhaps the most famous writing from Nag Hammadi. It's frequently called a "Gnostic Gospel." But did it really come from the Gnostics? If not, then how should we understand it? And what does it mean for Mary to make herself male?

The Gospel of Thomas's Cryptic Sayings
Lecture 9

The Gospel According to Thomas, which contains more than 100 sayings of Jesus, is probably the most widely known "Gnostic" gospel. For many people, this gospel is what "Gnosticism" is all about. But as we'll see, Thomas lacks most of the distinctive teachings and practices that we have seen in Gnostic literature. Thus, scholars are increasingly reluctant to call it Gnostic. Instead, we need to appreciate the Gospel of Thomas for its own sake and try to understand its unique teachings about how Jesus can lead people to *gnōsis* with God.

Background on the Gospel of Thomas

- Scholars always knew that a text called the Gospel According to Thomas existed because several early Christian authors mention it. One father of the church, Hippolytus (fl. 3rd c.), even gives a short quotation from Thomas that was later found to match a saying of Jesus found in the Nag Hammadi text of the gospel.

- Once scholars had the gospel in Coptic, they realized that they also had fragments of it in Greek, found in excavations at Oxythynchus around 1900. Scholars date these Greek fragments to the 200s, which means that the original gospel must have been written sometime before 200.

- The Gospel of Thomas begins as follows: "These are the secret sayings that the living Jesus spoke and Didymus Judas Thomas recorded." But no historians believe that it was actually written by the disciple Thomas. Most early Christian gospels, including those in the New Testament, were originally composed anonymously. Only later were such titles as "According to Matthew" or "According to Luke" assigned to these books.

- Almost all biblical scholars agree that the earliest gospel written was Mark, which probably comes from around the year 70. They agree also that the authors of Matthew and Luke used Mark in writing their gospels. There is no consensus about whether the author of John had read any of the other gospels. Did the author of the Gospel of Thomas know and use Matthew, Mark, Luke, or John?

- ○ Historians disagree on this point. Some believe that the author of Thomas did not have access to the other gospels, and thus, it probably dates to the 1st century. Most scholars, however, think that the author of Thomas did use the gospels in the New Testament, which means it probably comes from the early 2nd century.

- ○ The answer to this question primarily matters to scholars who are interested in studying what Jesus himself taught. If the Gospel of Thomas is not dependent on the New Testament gospels, then it provides an independent witness to teachings that Jesus may have said and his followers passed down orally.

Message of the Gospel

- • Unlike the New Testament gospels, the Gospel of Thomas is not a story about Jesus. Instead, it's a *wisdom book*, a collection of wise sayings. In the gospel, Jesus speaks in a similar vein as Wisdom in the book of Proverbs: He speaks about himself, and he calls people to follow him in devotion to God. In fact, we probably say that in Thomas, Jesus is Wisdom—or, at least, the voice of Wisdom. In this respect, Jesus is something like the aeon Wisdom in Gnostic texts. He's the voice of the divine calling us to understand our true selves, and he's the divine potential within us that makes up our true selves.

- • With the opening sayings of Thomas, we learn that what the gospel teaches is a matter of life and death, a matter of salvation. The source of salvation is present in the sayings of Jesus, the meaning of which we must seek. Ultimately, what we seek is not far away but within us.

- • Because Jesus is God's Wisdom, he is eternal and alive. The gospel is not interested in a Jesus who lived years ago in Palestine. It repeatedly calls Jesus "the living Jesus"—the Jesus who lives now and is present to people.

- As Wisdom, Jesus is the source of all that is, and he is present in all creation: "I am the light that is over all things. I am all: from me all came forth, and to me all attained. Split a piece of wood; I'm there. Lift up the stone, and you'll find me there." (77).

- Jesus is the divine presence in all that is, but he is especially present in the words that he says. He tells the disciples that they will understand who he is from the things he says to them. Even more, the light that is Jesus is also within human beings. We ourselves are from the spiritual realm: "There is a light within a person of light, and it shines on the whole world. If it does not shine, it is dark" (24).

- When we hear the message of Jesus, we realize that the kingdom of heaven is within us, that knowing Jesus is knowing our true selves. If we do not recognize the light within us, we remain in darkness. But if we do recognize it, we essentially become Jesus, who is the light.

Differences between Thomas and Gnosticism

- In some respects, the teaching of the Gospel of Thomas resembles that of the Gnostics. We belong to the spiritual realm of light, and the spiritual realm is present within us as light. Jesus saves us by waking us up to this fact, by revealing to us our true natures, by bringing us the *gnōsis*—the saving knowledge—that we need.

- But the Gnostics did not emphasize knowledge of the self as knowledge of God as strongly as Thomas does. They were concerned with how distant we are from God and the fact that we did not identify ourselves closely with God. For the Gnostics, to experience *gnōsis* of God, we don't simply recognize our true selves. Instead, we must ascend through levels of abstraction to contemplate the Barbēlō aeon.
    - o In Gnostic myth, it was the Barbēlō who spoke through the human Jesus, and it was Wisdom who guided Adam and Eve, Seth, and Nōrea toward God.

- In contrast, the Gospel of Thomas does not have a divine aeon named the Barbēlō, nor does it separate Wisdom from Jesus. Indeed, the gospel does not have the complicated divine realm that we saw in Gnostic myth at all.

- The Gospel of Thomas shares with the Gnostics the idea that we have within ourselves divine potential that we must recognize. And like the Gnostics, it teaches that Jesus came to reveal this truth about ourselves. There are also hints in Thomas that this world is controlled by inferior divine beings. But otherwise, Thomas lacks the distinctive characters of the Gnostic myth.

- For these reasons, most scholars of early Christianity are reluctant to use the term *Gnostic* for the Gospel of Thomas. This gospel teaches salvation by *gnōsis*, but it does not share the mythology and rituals of the Gnostic school of thought. Instead, Thomas represents another path to salvation through *gnōsis* within the great diversity of early Christianity.

Apocalyptic Eschatology

- One important way in which Gnostic myth is closer to emerging orthodox Christianity than the Gospel of Thomas is in its view of history and the future. The New Testament, the early church fathers, and Gnostic myth all agree that history is moving toward the end of the world as we know it and the establishment of a new kingdom of God. But Thomas explicitly rejects this teaching: There is no future kingdom of God; salvation is available right now!

- According to the New Testament, Jesus proclaimed, "The time is fulfilled, and the kingdom of God has come near; repent, and believe in the gospel" (Mark 1:15). When the disciples ask Jesus when the kingdom will come, he gives a paradoxical answer. On the one hand, there will be signs, such as war, famine, and acts of sacrilege. On the other hand, we need to be prepared because we can never know precisely when the kingdom will come.

- Scholars call this teaching about a future kingdom of God *apocalyptic eschatology*. The term refers to a religious view that emphasizes revealed knowledge about the end of the world. Apocalyptic eschatology can be found in the Old Testament and the Jewish tradition, among the early Christians, and in the teaching of the Gnostics.

- But the Gospel According to Thomas explicitly rejects apocalyptic eschatology. The kingdom of God is not some future event to which history is moving. The kingdom is already

© Steven Wynn/iStock/Thinkstock.

In the New Testament, Jesus says that his healing of the sick was a sign that Satan's rule of this world was coming to an end.

present, hidden within each of us. When we awaken to this fact, we will experience the kingdom and gain full salvation.

- In the opening of the gospel, Jesus rejects the idea that the kingdom is a place or an external reality: "The kingdom is inside of you, and it is outside of you." It seems not to be a place at all but an experience, something that happens when "you come to know yourselves."

- As they do in the New Testament gospels, the disciples in Thomas ask Jesus when the kingdom will come. Jesus answers by rejecting the idea that it is coming in the future: "His disciples said to him, 'When will the rest for the dead take place, and when will the new

Excerpts from the Gospel of Thomas*

Saying 1
He said, "Whoever finds the interpretation of these sayings will not taste death."

Saying 2
Jesus said, "Let one who seeks not stop seeking until one finds. When one finds, one will be disturbed. When one is disturbed, one will be amazed, and will reign over all."

Saying 3
Jesus said, "If your leaders say to you, 'Behold, the kingdom is in the sky,' then the birds in the sky will get there before you. If they say to you, 'It is in the sea,' then the fish will get there before you. Rather, the kingdom is inside you and outside you. When you know yourselves, then you are children of the living Father. But if you do not know yourselves, then you live in poverty, and embody poverty."

Saying 96
Jesus said, "The kingdom of the Father is like a woman who took a little yeast, hid it in dough, and made large loaves of bread. Whoever has ears ought to listen."

Saying 98
Jesus said, "The kingdom of the Father is like someone who wanted to put a powerful person to death. He drew his sword at home and thrust it into a wall to find out whether his hand would go through. Then he killed the powerful person."

Saying 107
Jesus said, "The kingdom is like a shepherd who had a hundred sheep. One of them, the largest, went astray. He left the ninety-nine and looked for the one until he found it. After he had toiled, he said to the sheep, 'I love you more than the ninety-nine.'"

Saying 108

Jesus said, "Whoever drinks from my mouth will become like me; I myself shall become that person, and the hidden things will be revealed to him."

Saying 113

His disciples said to him, "When will the kingdom come?" Jesus said, "It will not come by looking for it. Nor will it do to say, 'Behold, over here!' or 'Behold, over there!' Rather, the kingdom of the Father is spread out on the earth, but people do not see it."

*Excerpts adapted from Marvin W. Meyer's *The Gnostic Gospels of Jesus: The Definitive Collection of Mystical Gospels and Secret Books about Jesus of Nazareth* (New York: HarperOne, 2005) and Robert J. Miller's *The Complete Gospels* (Salem, OR: Polebridge Press, 2010).

world come?' He said to them, 'What you are looking forward to has come, but you don't know it.'"

- Some of the parables Jesus tells in this gospel express the danger of not recognizing the kingdom: "Jesus said, 'The kingdom of the Father is like a woman who was carrying a jar full of meal. While she was walking along a distant road, the handle of the jar broke, and the meal spilled out behind her along the road. She didn't know; she didn't understand how to toil. When she reached her house, she put down the jar and discovered that it was empty.'"

  ○ This woman's ignorance of the fact that the meal is spilling out of her jar represents the ignorance of those who go through life unaware of the presence of God within them. Just as this woman comes to the end of her journey and has nothing, people without *gnōsis* come to the ends of their lives without having discovered the truth about themselves and the divine.

  ○ Notice that the woman is said not to have understood how to toil. The gospel makes clear that Jesus has revealed the truth to us, but we must expend effort to grasp and understand his revelation.

○ The toil that *gnōsis* requires is the hard work of trying to understand the often perplexing sayings of the Gospel According to Thomas. If we do, we will discover our true selves and experience the kingdom of God—not in some future time but now!

Suggested Reading

Davies, *The Gospel of Thomas and Christian Wisdom.*

Layton, *The Gnostic Scriptures*, "The Gospel According to Thomas."

Meyer, ed., *The Nag Hammadi Scriptures*, "The Gospel of Thomas with the Greek Gospel of Thomas."

———, *The Gnostic Discoveries*, chapter 3.

Pagels, *Beyond Belief.*

Questions to Consider

1. Why do you think the author of Thomas turned against the idea of a future kingdom of God?

2. How is Thomas similar to and different from the Gnostic writings?

The Gospel of Thomas's Cryptic Sayings
Lecture 9—Transcript

If there's one symbol that everyone associates with Christianity, it's the cross. Crosses appear on top of and inside churches, and many Christians wear a cross around their neck or, these days, even have one tattooed on their body. And we all know why this is: Jesus was crucified, and Christians believe that by dying on the cross Jesus saved human beings from sin. If you read any of the four gospels in the New Testament—Matthew, Mark, Luke, or John—they all focus on Jesus's death on the cross as the most important fact about him.

We have seen that the Gnostics didn't really think of Jesus as saving them by dying on the cross. Instead, Jesus is the incarnation of Forethought, sent to reveal to us our true origin in the spiritual Entirety. And yet even the Gnostics frequently mention the crucifixion of Christ. The Gospel of Judas ends with Judas turning Jesus over to the authorities, so that the human being whom the Savior inhabits can be killed.

Imagine, then, Christianity without the cross. A Christianity in which Jesus's death and resurrection really don't play a major role. And imagine a Christian gospel that's all about Jesus and yet never even mentions how or why Jesus died.

That's what we have in the Gospel According to Thomas, which is certainly the most famous text from the Nag Hammadi codices. When scholars first read Thomas in the 1950s, they were astonished to find that it does not tell any story about Jesus at all. There's no biographical narrative about Jesus— no description of his birth, no baptism by John the Baptist, no stories of Jesus walking on water or healing people or feeding 5,000—and above all, no account of Jesus's last days, his death, and resurrection. Instead, the Gospel of Thomas consists entirely of over 100 sayings of Jesus, nearly all of them introduced by little more than the phrase, "Jesus said."

And although some of the sayings in Thomas appear also in the New Testament gospels, others are completely new—and many are very strange. For example, Number 80: "Jesus said, 'Whoever has come to know the world has discovered the body, and whoever has discovered the body, of that one the world is not worthy.'"

What does this mean? Did Jesus actually say these things?

The Gospel According to Thomas rapidly became widely known as the most important "Gnostic" gospel. For many people, this gospel really is what "Gnosticism" is all about. But we're going to see that Thomas lacks most of the distinctive teachings and practices that we have seen in Gnostic literature. So scholars are increasingly reluctant to call it "Gnostic." Instead, we need to appreciate the Gospel of Thomas for its own sake and try to understand its unique teachings about how Jesus can lead people to *gnōsis* with God.

Let's start with what historians do and do not know about this gospel. As in the case of the Gospel of Judas, scholars always knew that there had been a Gospel According to Thomas because several early Christian authors mention it—always warning Christians not to read it. One father of the Church, Hippolytus, who lived in the 3rd century, even gives a short quotation from Thomas. When the Gospel According to Thomas showed up in the Nag Hammadi codices, it contained a saying of Jesus that matched Hippolytus's quotation—not exactly, but close enough to confirm that what we have is a Coptic translation of the Gospel of Thomas that Hippolytus read in Greek in the 200s.

Not only that, but scholars realized that they had fragments of the Gospel of Thomas in Greek. Around 1900 archaeologists excavated an ancient trash dump in the Egyptian city of Oxyrhynchus. The dump was full of discarded pieces of papyrus, and among these were three small fragments that contain sayings of Jesus in Greek. These sayings did not match any of the gospels about Jesus known at the time, whether in the New Testament or not. But they did match sayings in the Coptic Gospel According to Thomas discovered about 50 years later at Nag Hammadi. Again, the texts were not precisely the same, but they provided additional confirmation that Thomas was originally written in Greek. Scholars date these Greek fragments to the 200s. So the gospel must have been written in Greek before the year 200.

How much earlier than 200? That's not so clear. The gospel begins like this: "These are the secret sayings that the living Jesus spoke and Didymus Judas Thomas recorded."

So the gospel claims that the author was Thomas, the disciple of Jesus. But no historians believe this. Most early Christian gospels, including those in the New Testament, were originally composed anonymously. Only later were titles like "According to Matthew" or "According to Luke" assigned to these books. We do not believe that any of Jesus's original disciples wrote a gospel that we have.

For one thing, all of the New Testament gospels indicate that they were written after the Romans destroyed the Jewish Temple in Jerusalem during a war in the year 70, some 40 years after the crucifixion of Jesus. Second, all of these gospels, and Thomas as well, were written in educated, if not very sophisticated, Greek. The disciples of Jesus, however, were native speakers of Aramaic and did not have education in Greek. So, anonymous Greek-speaking Christians composed all the gospels, including Thomas, sometime around or after the year 70.

Almost all biblical scholars agree that the earliest gospel written was Mark, which probably comes from around the year 70 or shortly thereafter. They agree also that the authors of Matthew and Luke used Mark in writing their gospels. There is no consensus as to whether the author of John had read any of the other gospels.

Did the author of the Gospel of Thomas know and use Matthew, Mark, Luke, or John? Historians disagree sharply on this point. Some believe that the author of Thomas did not have access to the other gospels, and thus it most likely dates to the 1st century, before the year 100, perhaps even earlier than the year 70. Probably a majority of scholars, however, think that the author did use the gospels in the New Testament, and therefore it probably comes from the early 2nd century, after the year 100. All of this depends on close analysis on how the sayings found in Thomas are similar to and different from related sayings in the New Testament. Even the order in which the sayings appear may indicate whether the author was using gospels like Matthew and Luke or was working on his own without them.

What difference does the answer to this question make? It primarily matters when scholars are interested in studying what Jesus himself taught. If the Gospel of Thomas is not dependent on the New Testament gospels, then it provides an independent witness to teachings that Jesus may have said and that his followers passed down orally. If the author used the other gospels, then it does not provide this kind of evidence for Jesus.

But that's really not our question here. We are not trying to find out what Jesus said and did, but what early Christians believed about Jesus. In that case, the exact date of Thomas and whether it used the other gospels are not important issues for us.

For what it's worth, my personal view is that the version of the Gospel of Thomas that we have from Nag Hammadi does show contact with the other gospels, and so I expect that it probably dates to the first half of the 2nd century. And yet I think also that some of the sayings in Thomas are probably earlier or more primitive than sayings in the other gospels. Most likely the gospel was revised more than once in its history. But what we want to understand is Thomas's unique views on salvation, Jesus, and *gnōsis* of God. And for that purpose which sayings may be early and which may be later does not really matter.

Unlike the New Testament gospels, Thomas is not a story about Jesus. Instead, it's a *wisdom book*, a collection of wise sayings. It resembles the book of Proverbs in the Old Testament. You'll recall that in my last lecture I discussed how in Proverbs God's Wisdom, personified as a woman, speaks to people about herself and calls people to follow her in devotion to God and in righteous living. In the Gospel of Thomas Jesus speaks like Wisdom in Proverbs: He speaks about himself, and he calls people to follow him in devotion to God. In fact, I would say that in Thomas, Jesus is Wisdom— or, at least, the voice of Wisdom. In this respect Jesus is something like the aeon Wisdom in Gnostic texts. He's the voice of the divine calling us to understand our true selves, and he's the divine potential within us that makes up our true selves.

Let's look at how the gospel opens. The first few sayings read like this:

> These are the secret sayings that the living Jesus spoke and Didymus Judas Thomas recorded.
>
> He said, "Whoever finds the interpretation of these sayings will not taste death."
>
> Jesus said, "Let one who seeks not stop seeking until one finds. When one finds, one will be disturbed. When one is disturbed, one will be amazed, and will reign over all."
>
> Jesus said, "If your leaders say to you, 'Behold, the kingdom is in the sky,' then the birds in the sky will get there before you. If they say to you, 'It is in the sea,' then the fish will get there before you. Rather, the kingdom is inside you and outside you. When you know yourselves, then you are children of the living Father. But if you do not know yourselves, then you live in poverty, and embody poverty."

In these first sayings, we learn that what the Gospel teaches is a matter of life and death, a matter of salvation. The source of salvation is present in the sayings of Jesus, the meaning of which you must seek and find. And ultimately, what you seek is not far away, but within you.

These teachings echo what Moses says to the Israelites in Deuteronomy, Chapter 30:

> This commandment that I command you today is not excessive, nor is it far from you. It is not in the sky, saying, 'Who will go up to the sky to get it for us? And when we hear it, we shall do it.' Neither is it beyond the sea, saying, 'Who will cross to the other side of the sea for us and get it for us? And when we hear it, we shall do it.' The word is very near to you, in your mouth and in your heart and in your hands, to do it. See, I have given before you today life and death, good and evil. ... And choose life, so that you and your offspring may live.

Like the Gnostics, the author of Thomas subtly rewrote the biblical book to make the sayings of Jesus replace the words of Moses. It's now the sayings of Jesus, the voice of Wisdom, that offer life and that are in your heart.

Because Jesus is God's Wisdom, he is eternal and alive. The gospel is not interested in a Jesus who lived years ago in Palestine. It constantly calls Jesus "the living Jesus"—the Jesus who lives now and is present to people. Jesus has come from the realm of spiritual unity to reveal the truth. He proclaims: "I am from the one who is whole. I disclose my mysteries to those who are worthy of my mysteries." (61–62)

As Wisdom Jesus is the source of all that is, and he is present in all creation: "I am the light that is over all things. I am all: From me all came forth, and to me all attained. Split a piece of wood; I'm there. Lift up the stone, and you'll find me there."

You find Jesus as well in his sayings: He tells the disciples that they will understand who he is from the things that he says to them. Jesus is the divine presence in all that is, but he is especially present in the words that he says. And even more, the light that is Jesus is also within human beings. We ourselves are also from the spiritual realm: "There is a light within a person of light. And it shines on the whole world. If it does not shine, it is dark."

When we hear the message of Jesus, we realize that the kingdom of heaven is within us, that knowing Jesus is knowing our true selves. That is, *gnōsis* of God means *gnōsis* of ourselves. If we do not recognize the light within us, we remain in darkness. But if we do recognize it, we essentially become Jesus, who is the light. "Jesus said, 'Whoever drinks from my mouth'—that is, becomes enlightened by the sayings of Jesus—'will become like me; I myself shall become that person, and the hidden things will be revealed to him.'"

On the one hand, the teaching of the Gospel of Thomas resembles that of the Gnostics. We really belong to the spiritual realm of light, and the spiritual realm is actually present within us as light. Jesus saves us by waking us up to this fact, by revealing to us our true natures, by bringing us the *gnōsis*—the saving knowledge—that we need.

On the other hand, the Gnostics did not emphasize so strongly knowledge of the self as knowledge of God. They were concerned with how distant we are from God and did not identify our selves with God so closely. For the Gnostics, to experience *gnōsis* of God, you don't just recognize your true self. Instead, you need to ascend through levels of abstraction to contemplate the Barbēlō aeon.

In Gnostic myth, it was Forethought, the Barbēlō, who spoke through the human Jesus, and it was Wisdom who guided Adam and Eve, Seth, and Nōrea toward God. The Gospel of Thomas does not have a divine aeon named the Barbēlō, nor does it separate Wisdom from Jesus. Thomas does not have the complicated divine realm that we saw in Gnostic myth; it speaks only of the Father from whom Jesus comes and makes brief references to God's Holy Spirit and Jesus's true Mother, who are probably the same thing. In general, though, the divine is much simpler in Thomas: There is the Father and Jesus, and the Father really doesn't show up that much. It's all about Jesus.

So the Gospel of Thomas shares with the Gnostics the idea that we human beings have within ourselves divine potential that we must recognize. And like the Gnostics, it teaches that Jesus came to reveal to us this truth about ourselves. And there are also hints that the author believes that this world is under the control of inferior, lower divine beings. But otherwise, Thomas lacks the distinctive characters of the Gnostic myth. There is no Invisible Virgin Spirit, no Barbēlō, no Self-Originate and his Four Luminaries, no Ialdabaōth. It does not call saved people the seed of Seth or the offspring of Nōrea. And when it talks about baptism—which it does—it does not mention the deities Micheus, Michar, and Mnēsinous or the five seals. For these reasons most scholars of early Christianity are reluctant to use the word *Gnostic* for the Gospel of Thomas. This gospel does teach salvation by *gnōsis*, but it does not share the mythology and rituals of the Gnostic school of thought. Instead, Thomas represents another path to salvation through *gnōsis* within the great diversity of early Christianity.

In fact, there's one very important way in which Gnostic myth is closer to emerging orthodox Christianity than is the Gospel of Thomas—and that's how the Gnostics view history and the future. In short, if you read the New Testament, the early Fathers of the Church like Irenaeus, and Gnostic myth, they all agree that history is moving towards a major climax—the end of the world as we know it and the establishment of a new kingdom of God. The Gospel of Thomas explicitly rejects this teaching: There is no future kingdom of God; salvation is available right now!

Let's consider this important difference further. When you read the gospels in the New Testament, they report that Jesus proclaimed, "The time is fulfilled, and the kingdom of God has come near; repent, and believe in the gospel." Jesus warned his listeners that the world as we know it is controlled by Satan—as anyone could see in the sick people and people possessed by demons whom Jesus healed. Jesus said that his healing of the sick and his casting out of demons showed that Satan's rule of this world was coming to an end, and that God's new kingdom was coming. The kingdom of God—or as Matthew calls it, the kingdom of heaven—is not here yet, but it's on the way.

In the Gospels of Matthew, Mark, and Luke, the disciples ask Jesus about when the kingdom will come. What signs of its arrival will they see? Jesus gives a paradoxical answer. On the one hand, there will be signs, such as war and famine and acts of sacrilege. On the other hand, you can never know precisely when the kingdom will come. It will come like a thief in the night—so you need to be prepared.

People need to be prepared because when the kingdom comes, there will be a resurrection of the dead and a judgment. Both people who are alive when this kingdom arrives and those who are dead will be judged and either granted eternal life or condemned to eternal punishment.

Now, this emphasis on the future kingdom of God is toned down in the Gospel of John. In this gospel, Jesus can speak of people receiving eternal life when they believe, and he can say that the important moment of judgment is when people respond immediately to his message. But he still preaches that history is moving toward a future kingdom that God has planned.

Scholars call this teaching about a future kingdom of God *apocalyptic eschatology*, which comes from the Greek terms that mean "revelation" and "final things." Apocalyptic eschatology is a religious view that emphasizes revealed knowledge about the end of the world as we know it.

Apocalyptic eschatology can be found in the Old Testament and Jewish tradition, which is of course the origin of Christianity. The Old Testament book of Daniel is a great example of apocalyptic eschatology: It tells the Jews who are oppressed by foreign rulers that God is in charge of history and will rescue them from their oppression. An anointed one, a messiah, will bring in a new kingdom of God—not a heavenly kingdom, but this world transformed and made righteous. If you understand world events rightly, you can see that history is moving according to God's plan.

Among the early Christians this was the teaching of Paul in the New Testament, as well. We saw in an earlier lecturer how Paul warned his followers that the day of the Lord would come unexpectedly and that Jesus would return to judge all people and grant salvation to the chosen ones, including Gentiles who have faith in Christ. Christians needed to prepare themselves for this future moment of judgment and salvation.

And this was the teaching of the Gnostics as well. Especially in the Secret Book According to John, the Revelation of Adam, and the Reality of the Rulers, revealers like Christ and Adam look forward to a future moment in which Ialdabaōth and his fellow rulers will be destroyed. In his revelation, Adam tells Seth that at the end of time, people will acclaim the Gnostics: "Blessed are the souls of Those People, for they have become acquainted with God in acquaintance with truth. They will live for ever and ever!" On the other hand, the damned will lament: "We have done everything in the folly of the powers. … Now we know that our souls are going to die with death." Most likely the damned will be utterly destroyed, along with this cosmos and its evil rulers.

The Gnostics looked forward to a future in which this universe, controlled by the rulers, will come to an end. Human beings will then receive full salvation, because they will return to the Entirety from which they came.

This is not the teaching of the Gospel According to Thomas. It explicitly rejects apocalyptic eschatology. The kingdom of God is not some future event to which history is moving; the kingdom is already present, hidden within each of us. When we awaken to this fact, then we experience the kingdom and gain full salvation. By the time this gospel was written, Jesus had not come back, and a new kingdom had not arrived. Some Christians evidently concluded that the kingdom of God is not some future event that was still to come. Jesus must have already brought the salvation for which they had been waiting.

We have already seen that in the opening of the gospel, Jesus rejects the idea that the kingdom is a place or an external reality. It's not in heaven or in the sea. "The kingdom is inside you," he says, "and it is outside you." It seems not to be a place at all. Rather, it's an experience, something that happens to you when, as he puts it, "you come to know yourselves."

As they do in the New Testament gospels, the disciples in Thomas ask Jesus when the kingdom will come. Jesus answers by rejecting the idea that it is coming in the future at all. For example: "His disciples said to him, 'When will rest for the dead take place, and when will the new world come?' He said to them, 'What you are looking forward to has come, but you don't know it.'" Or again: "His disciples said to him, 'When will the kingdom come?' Jesus said, 'It will not come by looking for it. Nor will it do to say, "Behold, over here!" or "Behold, over there!" Rather, the kingdom of the Father is spread out on the earth, but people do not see it.'"

You can see that the problem is not that the kingdom still lies in the future and will come at any moment so that you have to be ready. Instead, the problem is that the kingdom is present and available, but you have not yet recognized it or become aware of it.

Some of the parables that Jesus tells in this gospel show how the kingdom of God is right here, but people might miss it or fail to see it. Consider this parable: "Jesus said, 'The kingdom of the Father is like a woman who took a little yeast, hid it in dough, and made large loaves of bread. Whoever has ears ought to listen.'"

There would be no bread if there were not leaven in it, but people might not understand or be aware of the presence of leaven in the bread. But surely people should; without the leaven there would be no bread, just as without the presence of the light or of God within us, there would be no us.

Here's a parable that expresses the danger of not recognizing the kingdom:

> Jesus said, "The kingdom of the Father is like a woman who was carrying a jar full of meal. While she was walking along a distant road, the handle of the jar broke, and the meal spilled behind her along the road. She didn't know; she didn't understand how to toil. When she reached her house, she put the jar down and discovered that it was empty."

This woman's ignorance of the fact that the meal is spilling out of her jar represents the ignorance of those who go through life unaware of the presence of God within them. Just as this woman comes to the end of her journey and has nothing, people without *gnōsis* come to the ends of their lives without having discovered the truth about themselves and the divine.

Notice, too, that the woman is said not to have understood how to toil. The Gospel of Thomas makes clear that discovering the truth of the kingdom requires effort. Yes, Jesus has revealed the truth to us, but we must endeavor to grasp and understand his revelation. Here's a parable that's similar to one Jesus tells in the New Testament, but the moral of the story is somewhat different from what one sees in the New Testament:

> Jesus said, "The kingdom is like a shepherd who had a hundred sheep. One of them, the largest, went astray. He left the ninety-nine and looked for the one until he found it. After he had toiled, he said to the sheep, 'I love you more than the ninety-nine.'"

In the New Testament the one sheep that goes astray seems to represent a sinful person, and Jesus is the shepherd who goes to rescue the sheep and bring it back. In Thomas, however, we are the shepherd, and the sheep represents salvation. We all should abandon the 99 other things in our lives that don't really matter. And like the shepherd, we should toil to seek salvation—the largest and most valuable sheep—and we should value it more than everything else. The kingdom of God is the discovery of the large sheep, the discovery of *gnōsis*. We should value *gnōsis*, salvation through Jesus, more than anything else.

And notice again that the kingdom is an individual experience; it's finding the lost sheep, experiencing *gnōsis*, something any of us can experience at any time—but only if we make the effort.

One of Thomas's strangest parables conveys the determination and energy that *gnōsis* requires:

> Jesus said, "The kingdom of the Father is like someone who wanted to put a powerful person to death. He drew his sword at home and thrust it into a wall to find out whether his hand would go through. Then he killed the powerful person."

Surely Jesus is not urging people to commit murder, but the gospel says that we do need the focus and intensity of this assassin to find salvation. We must work hard to grasp the revelation that Jesus brings. As the opening of the gospel says, we must endeavor to find the meaning of the sayings in the Gospel of Thomas. "Whoever finds the interpretation of these sayings will not taste death," Jesus says. "Let one who seeks not stop seeking until one finds."

The toil that *gnōsis* requires, then, is the hard work of trying to understand the often perplexing sayings of the Gospel According to Thomas. If we do, we will discover our true selves and experience the kingdom of God—not in some future time, but right now!

In the next lecture, I'll say more about what Thomas teaches about our true selves, and I'll explore the gospel's theology of baptism and of becoming an integrated and whole self.

The Gospel of Thomas on Reunifying the Self
Lecture 10

The shortest saying in the Gospel of Thomas is: "Jesus said, 'Be passersby.'" We belong to the realm of spirit and light, not this world of flesh and darkness. Thus, Jesus commands that we should live our lives in this world as "passersby." In our last lecture, we learned that the Gospel of Thomas shares with the Gnostics the belief that salvation comes through *gnōsis*, the special knowledge of God that Jesus brings; for Thomas, *gnōsis* is knowledge of our true selves. We need to regain knowledge of our true selves through the sayings of Jesus. In this lecture, we'll learn more about this true self and what it means to become "passersby."

The True Self

- Basic to everything that the Gospel of Thomas teaches about human beings is the idea that our bodies are not who we are. Our true selves are completely spiritual, immaterial, not flesh. The body and flesh are poor and useless in comparison to the wealth and wonder of the soul and spirit.

- The gospel teaches that our souls existed in a spiritual realm of light before they came to dwell in our bodies, and our destiny is to return to that realm. For example, Jesus says, "The end will be where the beginning is," and "Blessed are those who are solitary and chosen: you will find the kingdom. For you have come from it, and you will return there again."

- Most people are like the woman with the jar of meal that we met earlier: They go through life unaware of their true selves. But when we listen to the message of Jesus, we wake up from our stupor and come to realize who we really are. When that happens, we can experience the rest and repose of the spiritual realm—even in this world. According to Thomas, that is the kingdom of God.

- Much of this comes from the philosophy of Plato. For Plato, too, human beings essentially are souls. Our souls existed before we were born into this material word, and they will continue to exist after our bodies die. According to Plato's dialogue *Timaeus*, the gods made our souls with a seed of the divine within them. We were educated about the universe, then sent down to live in bodies. In our bodies, we tend to forget what we were taught when we existed only as souls, but through philosophy and education, we remember and can achieve happiness.

- The Gospel of Thomas shares this basic Platonist view of the origin and destiny of human beings, but it insists that it's Jesus, not philosophy, who brings insight to our souls, reveals to us our origins in the world of spirit and light, and offers us the way back to our origins.

Becoming Unified

- In Thomas, Jesus says, "Blessed are those who are solitary and chosen." In fact, many of the sayings in Thomas refer to individuals who have achieved *gnōsis* and salvation as "solitary" or a "single one."

- In the Gospel of Thomas, the terms *single one* and *solitary* refer to a person who has overcome the divisions and multiplicity of life in this world and has become unified. In response to a question from the disciples, Jesus explains that salvation comes from combining opposites:

- Jesus said to them, "When you make the two into one, and when you make the inside like the outside and the outside like the inside, and the upper like the lower, and when you make male and female into a single one, so that the male will not be male nor the female be female; when you make eyes in place of an eye, a hand in place of a hand, a foot in place of a foot, an image in place of an image, then you will enter the kingdom." (22)

- The idea here seems to be that before we are saved, we don't really know our true selves, and for this reason, we're divided. We have one self who lives in this world, has a family and a job, and thinks that those things constitute life. But that is a false self. There is another self who does not belong to this world but is spirit and light. When we achieve *gnōsis*, the two selves will become one.

- But overcoming this division is only part of the story. When we know ourselves, we also know Jesus, and we realize that we are light, as Jesus is. Thus, the difference between the self and Jesus also fades away.

- This idea—that the division between the believer and Jesus is also overcome—is symbolized by name of the supposed author of this gospel, Didymus Judas Thomas.
  - Both the names *Didymus* (Greek) and *Thomas* (Aramaic) could mean "double" or "twin" in their respective languages. Therefore, Didymus Judas Thomas was believed by some early Christians to be Jesus's twin brother in the sense that they looked very much alike.

  - The twinship of Thomas and Jesus becomes a metaphor for the relationship between every human soul and Jesus. As we have seen, in the Gospel of Thomas, *gnōsis* of self is *gnōsis* of God. Our true selves are divine, just as Jesus is divine. Within us is the light that Jesus is. Thus, when we know ourselves as divine light, then we will know Jesus and recognize our essential unity. Jesus and the individual soul are one—twins, like Thomas and Jesus.

Baptism in the Gospel of Thomas
- One of the divisions that salvation overcomes is that between male and female. Jesus says that Christians will enter the kingdom when they "make the male and the female be one and the same, so that the male might not be male nor the female be female." We have seen already in Gnostic myth that the division between male and female was a powerful religious symbol.

- Some early Christians clearly believed that baptism restored human beings to the image of God, which they had lost when they sinned. In Galatians, this renewal overcomes divisions among human beings: "There is no longer Jew or Greek, there is no longer slave or free, there is no longer male and female; for all of you are one in Christ Jesus" (3:28). Saying 22 in the Gospel of Thomas also tells us that salvation comes when people overcome divisions.

In the ritual of baptism, the old self is stripped away when one's clothing is removed, and a new self emerges from the baptismal waters.

- In the New Testament gospels, Jesus often compares his followers to children. The Gospel of Thomas goes even farther: Jesus's followers are not simply children but nursing infants. Such newborns are pre-sexual; they have not yet divided into male and female. Thus, nursing infants provide a good metaphor for what the gospel is saying: The new human being is beyond male and female, like an infant.

- With this understanding of baptism, salvation, and unity, we can now better understand the last saying of Thomas: "Simon Peter said to them, 'Make Mary leave us, for females are not worthy of life.' Jesus said, 'Look, I will guide her to make her male, so that she too might become a living male spirit, like you. For every female that makes herself male will enter the kingdom of heaven'" (114).

○ Peter and Mary here are symbolic of male and female elements, and the female element must be made male to achieve the kingdom of heaven. Again, we see that the ancient author does not understand overcoming male-female division as the union of two equal things but as the return of the female element to the more basic male element.

○ To be saved, both Peter and Mary must recover a state in which female is not separated from male. Neither alone will be sufficient. The two must become one, and the saved person must be a "solitary"—fully integrated and beyond divisions of any kind. That is the experience of the kingdom of heaven.

Gnostic Ethics

• This is a compelling vision of human salvation, but what does it mean in practical terms? How should a person who follows the Gospel of Thomas live in this world?

○ Because Gnostic literature is mostly mythology and apocalyptic visions, it's difficult to pinpoint the ethics or lifestyle of the Gnostics. We saw that they had a negative view of sexual desire, but they did not have a negative view of marriage and family. And we see some aspects of their worship life, such as meditation, hymn singing, and baptism, but otherwise, Gnostic literature does not give much practical direction about the religious life.

○ In contrast, the Gospel of Thomas tells its readers specifically: "Be passersby." Thomas urges people to live in this world as if they are just passing through.

• Sayings in Thomas reject the traditional features of conventional religion in the ancient world. For example, Jesus says, "If you fast, you'll bring sin upon yourselves, and if you pray, you'll be condemned, and if you give to charity, you'll harm your spirits" (14). Fasting, giving alms, and praying were the basic activities of a devout life among ancient Jews and most Christians, but in Thomas, Jesus rejects these acts of piety as harmful. What's important is cultivation of the soul, the divine light within us, not external activities.

- In some of the New Testament gospels, commitment to Jesus is placed before one's family in importance. For example, in Luke 14, Jesus says that people must hate their parents, siblings, spouses, and children if they are to be his disciples. We find similar teachings in Thomas. For example, Jesus says: "Whoever does not hate father and mother cannot be my disciple, and whoever does not hate brothers and sisters and carry the cross as I do will not be worthy of me" (55).

- Several sayings also suggest that true followers of Jesus will embrace poverty, homelessness, and begging. For example, in saying 14, after telling his disciples not to fast or give alms, Jesus instructs them to depend on others for their food and support. Not surprisingly, Thomas also strongly condemns making money and engaging in business.

- Did any Christians actually live the lifestyle of wandering and begging that the Gospel of Thomas recommends? Evidence shows that such wandering Christians existed throughout the early centuries of Christianity, especially in Syria and Mesopotamia. But it was the ideas of the Gospel of Thomas that had a much greater influence in the history of ancient religions: that *gnōsis* of one's self is *gnōsis* of God and that salvation is the integration of a divided self.

Suggested Reading

Davies, *The Gospel of Thomas and Christian Wisdom*.

Layton, *The Gnostic Scriptures*, "The Gospel According to Thomas."

Meyer, ed., *The Nag Hammadi Scriptures*, "The Gospel of Thomas with the Greek Gospel of Thomas."

———, *The Gnostic Discoveries*, chapter 3.

Pagels, *Beyond Belief*.

1. Compare the idea of gender in Thomas to what we saw in the Gnostic writings.

2. How do you think people who believed in the message of Thomas actually might have lived their lives?

The Gospel of Thomas on Reunifying the Self
Lecture 10—Transcript

Jesus said, "Be passersby."

That's the shortest saying in the Gospel According to Thomas. It sums up how this gospel thinks about life in this world. We don't belong here, really. We belong to the realm of spirit and light, not this world of flesh and darkness. The *gnōsis* that Thomas offers is the knowledge of ourselves—that we have the divine within us, and that we don't belong here. And so, Jesus commands that we should live our lives in this world as "passersby"—people who are just temporarily passing through.

In our last lecture we learned that the Gospel of Thomas shares with the Gnostics the belief that salvation comes through *gnōsis*, through the special knowledge of God that Jesus brings. Like the Gnostics, Thomas teaches that this world is not our true home; rather, we belong to the eternal realm of light. We need to regain knowledge of our true self through the sayings of Jesus. Let's learn more about this true self and what it means to become "passersby."

Basic to everything that the Gospel of Thomas teaches about human beings is the idea that our bodies are not who we are. Our true selves are completely spiritual, immaterial, not of flesh. The body and flesh are poor and useless in comparison to the great wealth and wonder of the soul and spirit. Jesus says, "I marvel at how this great wealth has come to dwell in this poverty."

The gospel teaches that our souls existed in a spiritual realm of light before they came to dwell in our bodies. Jesus tells the disciples that if they are asked where they are from, they should say, "We have come from the light, where the light came into being by itself and stood at rest." The spiritual realm of light is a condition of rest or repose, while this world is a place of agitation or movement.

Our destiny is to return to that realm of light from which we came. The gospel puts this in different ways. For example, Jesus can say, "The end will be where the beginning is." Or, "Blessed are those who are solitary and chosen: you will find the kingdom. For you have come from it, and you will return there again." We will come back to the idea of being solitary and chosen, but notice that our ultimate end is to return to where we came from.

Nonetheless, we can experience some repose and rest now. For when we realize this truth about ourselves, we immediately experience a new spiritual condition of serenity. This change is compared to a drunk sobering up:

> Jesus said, "I stood at rest in the midst of the world and in flesh I appeared to them. I found them all drunk, and I did not find any of them thirsty. My soul ached for the human race, because they are blind in their hearts and they do not see. For they came into the world empty, and they also seek to depart from the world empty. But meanwhile, they are drunk. When they shake off their wine, then they will change their ways."

Most people are like the woman with the jar of meal that we met in the last lecture: They go through life unaware of their true selves. They think that their physical lives as parents, children, people with jobs, and so on are what's important. They're like drunks, who aren't really aware of their surroundings. When we listen to the message of Jesus, we can wake up from our drunken stupor and come to realize who we really are. When that happens, we can experience the rest and repose of the spiritual realm even in this world. That's the kingdom of God, according to Thomas.

Now much of this is simply the philosophy of Plato. For Plato too, human beings have souls; or better, human beings essentially are souls. Our souls existed before we were born into this material word, and they are immortal, so they will continue to exist after our bodies die. According to Plato's dialogue *Timaeus*, which influenced the Gnostics so much, the gods made our souls with a seed of the divine within them. We were educated about the universe and then sent down to live in bodies. Because we have bodies, we tend to forget the things we were taught when we existed only as souls, but through philosophy and education we remember, and achieve happiness.

The Gospel of Thomas shares this basic Platonist view of the origin and destiny of human beings. But it insists, in a way that no pagan Platonist would, that it's Jesus, not philosophy, who brings insight to our souls and reveals to us our true origins in the world of spirit and light. And it's Jesus, not philosophy, who offers us the way back to where we came from.

Now, we have heard Jesus say in the gospel, "Blessed are those who are solitary and chosen." Many of the sayings in Thomas refer to people who have achieved *gnōsis* and salvation as "solitary" or a "single one." In fact, some sayings in Thomas are just like those in the New Testament, except for the addition of calling saved people "single ones" or "solitaries." For example:

Jesus said, "Perhaps people think that I have come to bring peace to the world. They do not know that I have come to bring conflict to the earth: fire, sword, war. For five people will be in a house: it will be three against two and two against three, father against son and son against father, and they will stand at rest as solitaries."

Although this saying may sound somewhat strange, in fact, nearly all of this appears in pretty much the same way in the Gospels of Matthew and Luke: When people accepted Jesus's message, this would often divide them from even their closest friends and family members—for example, parent against child. But the last line in Thomas is truly new: "And they will stand at rest as solitaries."

It's interesting to note that the Greek word that Thomas uses for "solitary" is *monachos*, which later in Christian history will become the word used for monks, men and women who live alone as "solitaries." But when Thomas was written in the early 2nd century, there were not yet any Christian monks. So what does this gospel mean by this term?

The terms "single one" and "solitary" refer to a person who has overcome the divisions and multiplicity of life in the world and has become unified— what we might call integrated. Here's an important saying, number 22, that we will want consider closely:

Jesus saw some babies nursing. He said to his disciples, "These nursing babies are like those who enter the kingdom." They said to him, "So do we have to enter the kingdom as babies?" Jesus said to them, "When you make the two into one, and when you make the inside like the outside and the outside like the inside, and the upper like the lower, and when you make male and female into a single one, so that the male will not be male nor the female be female; when you make eyes in place of an eye, a hand in place of a hand, a foot in place of a foot, an image in place of an image, then you will enter the kingdom."

This saying talks about Christians as transformed people. People will experience salvation when we combine opposites, like inside and outside, above and below, and male and female, and when we replace our old image with a new one. We need to make the two one.

The idea seems to be that, before we are saved, we don't really know ourselves, our true selves. We live in ignorance of who we really are. And so we are divided: There's the me who lives in this world, has a family and a job, and thinks this is what his life is all about. This is the me I know. But it's a false me. There is in fact another me, the true me, the me who does not belong to this world, who is spirit and light. This is the me I don't know. So there are two of me.

When, however, I achieve knowledge of myself, when I understand who I really am and where I am from, then these two mes become one. I know the real me. So there is no longer a false me. I am a single one.

But overcoming this division within myself is only part of the story. When I know myself, I also know Jesus, and I realize that I am light as Jesus is. So the difference between me and Jesus also fades away. "Whoever drinks from my mouth will become like me," Jesus says. "I myself shall become that person, and the hidden things will be revealed to him." The two have become one.

This idea—that the division between the believer and Jesus—is also overcome is symbolized by the apostle Thomas himself. According to the opening, this gospel is attributed to "Didymus Judas Thomas." This is an important name because it suggests that Thomas, the author of this gospel, is not only an apostle, but also Jesus's double or twin. How can this be?

First, the Thomas here is also said to be Judas. Obviously this is not meant to be Judas Iscariot, but another disciple of Jesus whom we usually call in English "Jude." In the New Testament there's a letter of Jude, and there, the author calls himself "brother of James." James was a very prominent disciple and apostle and was known to be the brother of Jesus. In other words, "Judas Thomas" is the brother of James, who's the brother of Jesus. Hence, our Judas Thomas is also a brother of Jesus.

Not only this, but he is called Didymus Judas Thomas. *Didymus* was a Greek proper name for a man, just as *Thomas* was an Aramaic proper name for a man. And both names in their respective languages could also mean "double" or "twin." Therefore, Didymus Judas Thomas was believed by some early Christians to be Jesus's twin brother. Not his twin in the sense that they were born at the same time, but in the sense that they looked alike.

This idea shows up in other early Christian texts about Thomas, like The Book of Thomas the Contender Writing to the Perfect and The Acts of Thomas. In The Acts of Thomas, the physical similarity between Jesus and Thomas is sometimes used for comic effect: People think they are talking to the apostle Thomas, but they are really speaking to his double, the Lord Jesus.

The twinship of Thomas and Jesus becomes a metaphor for the relationship between every human soul and Jesus. As we have seen, in the Gospel of Thomas, *gnōsis* of self is *gnōsis* of God. My true self is divine, just as Jesus is divine. Within me, at the core of myself, is the light that Jesus is. When I know myself as divine light, then I know Jesus as well, and I recognize our essential unity. Jesus and I are one: We are doubles, twins, like Thomas and Jesus. The two—the individual soul and Jesus—have become one.

You'll remember that in saying 22, one of the divisions that salvation overcomes is that between male and female: Jesus says that Christians will enter the kingdom when they "make male and female into a single one, so that the male will not be male, nor the female be female." We have seen already in Gnostic myth how powerful a religious symbol the division between male and female was. We saw that many early Jews and Christians interpreted Genesis to be saying that the original human being, made in the image of God, was both male and female, an androgyne. Here, too, we see Christianity's indebtedness to Plato. For it was Plato who in the *Symposium* suggested that human beings were originally joined pairs, with most people having been in a male-female coupling. The separation of the male and female left people with a longing—a desire for their lost other half.

In Jewish and Christian interpretations of Genesis, the separation of humanity into male and female, Adam and Eve, was also something of a loss, for it led to the fall and to sin and death.

It's clear that some early Christians believed that baptism restored human beings to the image of God, which they lost when they sinned. The old self was stripped away when one's clothing was removed, and a new self emerged when the person was washed in baptism. Here's how the New Testament Letter to the Colossians puts it:

You have stripped off the old self with its practices and you have clothed yourself with the new self, which is being renewed according to the image of its Creator. In that renewal there is no longer Greek and Jew, circumcised and uncircumcised, barbarian, Scythian, slave and free; but Christ is all and in all!

Notice how renewal in the image of God in baptism overcomes divisions among human beings, like Jew versus Greek and slave versus free. How about male versus female? Well, that, too, according to St. Paul. When he quotes this formula in his Letter to the Galatians, he says:

As many of you as were baptized into Christ have clothed yourselves with Christ. There is no longer Jew or Greek, there is no longer slave or free, there is no longer male and female; for all of you are one in Christ Jesus.

Elements of these passages from Colossians and Galatians appear in our saying 22 from the Gospel of Thomas, which we can now see is alluding to baptism. Here too salvation comes when people overcome divisions, including that between male and female, and they become one. This is being made into a new image; or better, it's being restored to our original image—the image of God.

You might notice, too, that in Thomas the baptized Christians are compared to children—which makes sense because they are reborn, they are beginning new lives, and they are new remade selves. In the New Testament gospels Jesus also compares his followers to children. He says that his disciples should be humble, just like little children. But in the Gospel of Thomas, Jesus says that his followers are not simply children—they are nursing infants. So these are children that are, so to speak, pre-sexual; they have not yet divided, really, into male and female. So nursing infants, newborns, provide a good metaphor for what the gospel is saying: The new human being is beyond male and female, beyond sexuality, like infants.

This idea shows up in another saying:

The disciples said, "When will you be appear to us, and when will we see you?" Jesus said, "When you strip without being ashamed, and you take your clothes and put them under your feet like little children and trample them, then you will see the son of the Living One and you won't be afraid."

This saying almost certainly is also a reference to baptism. Like the passage in Colossians, it talks about taking off clothes, which was an important step in the baptismal ritual. In Colossians and in Gnostic literature, removing one's clothes and becoming naked symbolizes removal of one's old self and its bad ideas and practices. Here in Thomas the baptized people actually tread on their clothes, all the better to show their rejection of their old selves and ways of thinking. But they are also naked without being ashamed, just like small children who don't think of themselves as sexual beings, as male or female. This saying too suggests how for Thomas, salvation represents overcoming divisions—above all, the separation between male and female.

We can now perhaps understand better the last saying of Thomas, which we looked at briefly in an earlier lecture:

> Simon Peter said to them, "Make Mary leave us, for females are not worthy of life." Jesus said, "Look, I will guide her to make her male, so that she too may become a living male spirit, like you. For every female who makes herself male will enter the kingdom of heaven."

As with nearly all the sayings in Thomas, there's probably not a single correct meaning for this passage. Let's remember that discovering the interpretation of these sayings is meant to be hard work.

Still, I think in the context of what we have seen about baptism, salvation, and the union or overcoming of male and female, we should understand Peter and Mary in this saying as symbolic of male and female elements. The female element must be made male in order for the kingdom of heaven to be achieved. Again, we see that an ancient author does not understand overcoming male-female division or recovering androgyny as the union of two equal things, male and female, but the return of the female element to the more basic male element.

To be saved, both Peter and Mary must recover a state in which female is not separated from male. Neither alone will be sufficient. The two must become one, and the saved person must be a "solitary" or "single one"— fully integrated and beyond divisions of any kind. That's the experience of the kingdom of heaven.

This is a compelling vision of human salvation, but what does it mean in practical terms? How should a person who follows the Gospel of Thomas live in this world? Gnostic literature is mostly mythology and apocalyptic visions, so it's hard to tell what the ethics or lifestyle of the Gnostics were. We saw that they had a negative view of sexual desire, but they did not have a negative view of marriage and family in general. And we could see some aspects of their worship life, such as meditation, hymn-singing, and baptism. But otherwise, their literature does not give a lot of practical directions about the religious life.

In contrast, the Gospel of Thomas does give its readers specific advice about how to conduct their lives. "Be passersby," Jesus says. Thomas urges people to live in this world as if they are just passing through. We don't really belong to this world, after all, and so we should not treat it as our home. Or, as Jesus also states: "If you do not abstain from the world, you will not find the kingdom. If you do not keep the Sabbath a Sabbath, you will not see the Father." (27) Somehow you should abstain from the entire world, and you should treat every day like the Sabbath—a day free from the concerns of everyday life and devoted completely to God.

Sayings in Thomas reject the traditional features of conventional religion in the ancient world. At one point the disciples ask Jesus, "Do you want us to fast? How shall we pray? Shall we give to charity? What food may we eat?" Jesus replies, "Do not lie, or do what you dislike." In another saying, he states outright: "If you fast, you'll bring sin upon yourselves, and if you pray, you'll be condemned, and if you give to charity, you'll harm your spirits."

Fasting, giving alms, praying—these were the basic activities of a devout life among ancient Jews and most Christians. In the New Testament gospels, especially Matthew, Jesus gives his followers specific directions on how they should do these things. For example, he teaches them how to pray with the so-called Lord's Prayer, and he tells people not to look sad when they fast. In Thomas, however, Jesus rejects these traditional acts of piety as harmful to the person. What's important is cultivation of your soul—the divine light within you—not these external activities.

As in other gospels, the Jesus of Thomas urges his followers to reject family life. We tend to forget how radical some of Jesus's teachings in the New Testament really are. Today people often equate Christianity with so-called "family values," with marriage and having children. But in Matthew chapter 19, Jesus praises men who have made themselves eunuchs for the sake of the kingdom of heaven. And in Luke chapter 14, he says that people must hate their parents, siblings, spouses, and children if they are to be his disciples. The gospel demands total commitment and must be placed before your family.

We find similar teachings in Thomas. Jesus says: "Whoever does not hate father and mother cannot be my disciple, and whoever does not hate brothers and sisters and carry the cross as I do will not be worthy of me." Here is the only reference to the cross in the Gospel of Thomas. Most scholars, including me, think that a scribe added it to make this saying more like those in the New Testament gospels. But it does capture what the gospel teaches: Followers of Jesus should abandon their families and live like the "single ones" and "solitaries" that they are.

Several sayings suggest that true followers of Jesus will embrace poverty, homelessness, and begging. For example, after telling his disciples not to fast or give to charity, he instructs them to depend on others for their own food and support: "When you go into any region and walk about in the countryside, when people take you in, eat what they serve you and heal the sick among them. After all, what goes into your mouth won't defile you; what comes out of your mouth will."

As this gospel presents it, those who receive its message will wander about, teaching and healing others, and receiving from people food and shelter. They truly will be "passersby."

Not surprisingly, then, Thomas strongly condemns making money and engaging in business. Jesus forbids lending money at interest, and he tells rich people that they should renounce their possessions. Two parables make clear the danger to salvation that wealth and business pose. The first one also appears in the Gospel of Luke in pretty much the same form:

Jesus said, "There was a rich man who had a great deal of money. He said, 'I shall invest my money so that I may sow, reap, plant, and fill my storehouses with produce, that I may lack nothing.' These were the things he was thinking in his heart, but that very night he died. Whoever has ears to hear should listen."

Wealth is a distraction, something that prevents us from focusing on what's really important—our salvation. A second parable is also one that appears in the New Testament gospels, but Thomas adds a unique moral to the story:

Jesus said, "A man was receiving out-of-town visitors. When dinner was ready, the host sent a slave to invite the guests. The slave went to the first one and said, 'My lord invites you.' The guest said, 'Some merchants owe me money and they are coming to me tonight. I must go to give instructions to them. Please excuse me from the dinner.'

"The slave went to another guest and said, 'My lord invites you.' The guest said, 'I have bought a house, and I have been called away for the day. I have no time.'

"The slave went to another guest and said, 'My lord invites you.' The guest said, 'My friend is to be married and I must arrange the dinner, so I shall not be able to come. Please excuse me from dinner.'

"The slave went to yet another guest and said, 'My lord invites you.' The guest said, 'I have bought a farm and I am going to collect the rent, so I shall not be able to come. Please excuse me.'

"The slave returned and said to lord, 'Those whom you have invited to dinner have asked to be excused.' The lord said to the slave, 'Go out on the streets and bring back whomever you find to eat my dinner.' Business people and merchants will not enter the realm of my Father."

People who have recognized their true selves will give up their business activities because they are things that pull them into the world that they should renounce. Imagine all the things that demand our attention today—all our electronic gadgets, media, as well as our jobs. Today people might agree to attend the dinner, but they would spend it looking at their smartphones. The Gospel of Thomas calls these things distractions, things that connect us to this world and draw us away from knowledge of our true selves, which is the kingdom of God.

A parable that appears only in Thomas makes the general point:

> Mary said to Jesus, "Whom are your disciples like?" He said, "They are like children living in a field that is not theirs. When the owners of the land come, they will say, 'Give our field back to us.' The children will take off their clothes in the presence of the owners and thus give the field back and return it to them."

This saying draws together many of the themes that we have explored. Those who follow Jesus are like children—people who have not yet become divided by sexuality and the concerns of this world. They strip off their old selves and reject the world in which they live because it is not their true home.

Did any Christians actually live the lifestyle of wandering and begging that the Gospel of Thomas recommended? Yes, they did. We have evidence that such wandering Christians existed throughout the early centuries of Christianity, especially in areas like Syria and Mesopotamia. By the late 4th century, such Christians were being condemned as heretics and nuisances. They were despised by more respectable Christians, who looked down on them as some modern people might be annoyed by street people.

But it was the ideas of the Gospel of Thomas that had a much greater influence in the history of ancient religions. That *gnōsis* of one's self is *gnōsis* of God, that salvation is making the two one and integrating a divided self, that we have a kind of divine twin with whom we must unite—these ideas will live on to influence two of antiquity's greatest religious thinkers: Valentinus and Mani. In our next lecture we'll meet Valentinus.

Valentinus, Great Preacher of *Gnōsis*
Lecture 11

When Irenaeus wrote his *Against the Heresies* in 180, his greatest fear was that Christians would listen to teachers he called Valentinians, followers of Valentinus. Valentinian Christians, Irenaeus said, are "wolves in sheep's clothing," ready to pounce on unsuspecting Christians and lead them into satanic error. Why was Valentinus such a threat? Why did other Christian leaders attack him so frequently and so viciously? In short, because Valentinus was a brilliant and eloquent Christian theologian who turned the Gnostic myth into a powerful Christian message and started a Christian movement that lasted for centuries. Valentinus invited people to find in Jesus true *gnōsis* of the Father and of themselves and to experience God directly, immediately, and above all, joyfully.

Life of Valentinus

- Valentinus was probably born around the year 100 and may have spent his early years in Alexandria in Egypt. By around the year 140, he was a popular and effective teacher in Rome. We don't know when Valentinus died, but he was certainly dead before Irenaeus wrote his massive work against Gnostics and Valentinians in 180.

- In his lifetime, Valentinus was never declared a heretic. Despite the fact that many Christian teachers considered his views wrong, he had a substantial following. In addition, at the time, there was no single Christian church that could officially declare someone a heretic. Only later did church authorities agree that Valentinus should be condemned.

- Unfortunately, as a result of this condemnation, nearly all of Valentinus's writings have been lost. We have about a half dozen fragments from his works that his critics quote and a short poem quoted by an ancient author. In addition, many scholars believe that a sermon found at Nag Hammadi called the Gospel of Truth is by Valentinus.

"Summer Harvest"

○ Valentinus's short poem "Summer Harvest" highlights his willingness to express himself in innovative ways:

> In spirit I see that all things are hanging
> In spirit I know that all things are being carried
> Flesh hanging from soul
> Soul cleaving to air
> Air hanging from upper atmosphere
>
> Crops coming forth from the deep
> A baby coming forth from the womb.

- Note that the speaker here does not communicate someone else's views, nor does he claim to interpret the Bible or some other religious text. Instead, the speaker says, "I see" and "I know," underscoring his personal experience of truth and insight.

- "Summer Harvest" has two parts. In the first five lines, the poet conveys the interdependence of all that is. Everything that exists hangs from, or is carried by, or clings to something more spiritual than itself. These first lines communicate a peaceful cosmos of unity and stability.

- But the last two lines suggest motion, generation, and birth. Stability and interdependence are interrupted by creation and fertility. The poem then vividly expresses the life and vitality that lie behind the universe and, indeed, all of existence. It leaves the reader suspended between two truths: All of reality is stable and interconnected, yet at the base of reality is tremendous life-giving force.

- The last two lines are also typical of Valentinus in that they create a religious feeling by drawing on specific terms and images that the reader may or may not recognize. For example, the poem refers to the source of life as "the deep" and "the womb," and we know from other ancient sources that Valentinus referred to the ultimate high God as "The Deep."

- In "Summer Harvest," we see the characteristics that made Valentinus such an attractive preacher. He expresses a vision of deep personal insight, and he does so in a way that brings together several religious traditions: Gnostic myth, the Gospel of Thomas, the New Testament, and Greek philosophy. He leaves readers with feelings of wonder at divine stability and creativity and suggests that others, too, can have the same kind of personal insight that he has experienced.

The Valentinian Myth

- One of the sources for Valentinus's thought was the Gnostic myth, but Valentinus modified the myth significantly to make it more explicitly Christian and to remove some of its more anti-Jewish features.

- Like the Gnostics, Valentinus considered God to be a complex structure of emanations, but Valentinus used biblical names for his aeons: Truth, Life, Word, and Church. The Gnostics called the divine realm the Entirety, but Valentinus called it the Fullness.

- Like the Gnostics, Valentinus believed that one aeon, Wisdom, did something wrong. But in the myth of Valentinus, Wisdom does not produce a flawed divinity and cast him out of the Entirety. Instead, Wisdom herself leaves the Fullness and enters our world. Valentinus then calls this aeon the Mother.
  - The Mother generates multiple divine beings. The first is Christ, who takes from the Mother her share of divine spirit, then returns to the Fullness. Next, without divine spirit, the Mother emits a second being, whom Valentinus calls the Craftsman and the Almighty. This is the creator of this world and the God of Genesis.

  - Valentinus agreed with the Gnostics that the God of Genesis is a lower divine being, but his creator god is not malicious and does not persecute human beings. He is simply lower and less spiritual than the ultimate God.

○ In this way, Valentinus's myth is less hostile toward Jewish tradition than the Gnostic myth, and it's more similar to how other Christians thought about God.

● Finally, in Gnostic myth, Wisdom and Forethought work together to enlighten human beings, to recover the divine power from the rulers, and to restore what had been lost to the Entirety. Valentinus, however, does not emphasize the recovery of stolen divine power. Instead, he highlights the divine essence within humanity as our connection to God, that which enables us to know our selves and God and to realize our superiority to mortal existence.

○ The divine being who helps us is primarily God's Word, or Logos, who is also God's Son and God's Name. It is this Word who reveals to us God and to our selves and who became incarnate in Jesus.

Valentinus's message of salvation is centered on Christ—the Word, Son, and Name of the Father, who is present within us and was embodied in Jesus.

○ According to Valentinus, when the creator god and his angels made human beings, they were awestruck in the presence of humanity because the Word of God planted a seed of higher essence in humanity. The Name of God, present to and within human beings, fulfills what's lacking in us because we were created by lower beings. The Word is the divine potential that lies within all of us.

- ○ This same Word of God is how God the Father reveals himself to human beings. God visits the hearts of human beings and purifies them of evil spirits. In this way, through the Son of God, a person can gain a pure heart and see God, just as Jesus promises in Matthew 5:8: "Blessed are the pure in heart, for they shall see God."

- ● For Valentinus, the salvation that the Word of God brings unlocks the divine potential within us and enables us to triumph over the corruption and decay of the material world. The Gospel of Thomas urged Christians "to abstain from the world" because it's not their true home. Valentinus goes further: He tells his disciples to "abolish the world." Christians who have gained *gnōsis* through Christ activate the immortality they have always had. Through them, death dies, and they prevail over everything that is created and suffers corruption.

The Gospel of Truth

- ● The most complete statement of Valentinus's spirituality is the sermon entitled the Gospel of Truth. Although we don't know for certain that Valentinus wrote this gospel, many scholars attribute it to him. The sermon is an invitation to every Christian to experience the repose and joy of knowing God the Father through his Son, Jesus.

- ● The sermon defines sin—what separates us from God—as ignorance. Salvation—our return to God—is discovering the Father through the power of the Savior, the Word. This is the heart of the Christian message for Valentinus, and in the sermon, he explains how ignorance came to be, how Christians gain knowledge through Jesus, and what the experience of joy is for these Christians.

- ● According to Valentinus, the material world in which we live is the result of ignorance. Ultimately, everything that exists is in God the Father, and all truly real beings are emanations from him. For all beings, joy and blessedness are to know the Father and to be known by him. But to have that kind of relationship, we must be separate from the one we want to know, and separation introduces the possibility of ignorance.

- For Valentinus, ignorance of the Father became a kind of fog that condensed into matter; matter was then formed into a universe of things by a personified female character, Error. Ultimately, then, the material world in which we live is not real: It is ignorance, and it becomes irrelevant as soon as our ignorance is dispelled by *gnōsis*. It is Jesus who makes possible the *gnōsis* that removes ignorance and brings joy.

- Valentinus tells us that Jesus came to humanity to enlighten us and guide us to truth. Error, the personification of the forces of ignorance, persecuted Jesus and caused him to be crucified.
  - Valentinus evokes the crucifixion from the New Testament, but instead of a cross, Jesus is nailed to "a tree," and on this tree, he becomes "fruit of the Father's acquaintance." This is an allusion to the traditional story of the fall of humanity in Genesis. But for Valentinus, to eat from the fruit of knowledge—which is Jesus—is not ruin but joy, the discovery of the Father of whom people were ignorant.

  - People can eat the fruit that is the crucified Jesus in the Christian ritual of the Eucharist, and they can discover the Father within themselves. The Father is within us, just as we are within the Father, because all beings that are truly real are emanations of the Father.

- In another passage, Valentinus uses a book as a metaphor. All knowledge is "the living book of the living, which is written in the Father's heart and intellect." No one can read this book, and no one even dares to pick it up, except Jesus.
  - Here again, Valentinus reverses an image from the Bible, this time, from chapter 2 of Colossians. There, Jesus's crucifixion

is described as nailing to the cross the edict of God's condemnation of us for our sins.

○ But in Valentinus, through the crucifixion, Jesus makes available the book of knowledge of the Father, which had been closed. The Entirety that comes from the Father is in that book, and now it can be known. Readers of the book learn about themselves and, thus, return to the Father.

Suggested Reading

Dawson, *Allegorical Readers and Cultural Revision in Ancient Alexandria*, chapter 3.

Layton, *The Gnostic Scriptures*, "The Writings of Valentinus."

Meyer, ed., *The Nag Hammadi Scriptures*, "The Gospel of Truth."

———, *The Gnostic Discoveries*, chapter 5.

Thomassen, *The Spiritual Seed*, chapters 30–32.

Questions to Consider

1. Why would some people find Valentinus's message so appealing?

2. Why did some Christian leaders find his message so dangerous?

Valentinus, Great Preacher of *Gnōsis*
Lecture 11—Transcript

In the early 300s, several Christian leaders were engaged in a vicious debate over the nature of God. Are God the Father and God the Son equally divine? If God is one, how can God also be three—Father, Son, and Spirit?

A priest named Arius found himself accused of being a heretic because of his answers to these questions. Arius wrote an impassioned letter to his bishop, defending himself against charges of heresy. Arius explained his theological views and said that they were traditional Christian teachings and not at all heretical. At one point Arius proclaimed, "I do not teach that the Son of God is an emanation of the Father, as Valentinus taught."

One of the most effective ways for Arius to defend himself was to say that he did not teach the same thing as the great heretic Valentinus. Valentinus lived in the middle of the 2nd century, nearly 200 years before Arius. But Christians still considered Valentinus one of the most dangerous heretics, still a threat to Christian orthodoxy.

You may remember that when Irenaeus of Lyons wrote his *Detection and Overthrow of Gnōsis, Falsely So-Called* in 180, his greatest fear was that Christians would listen to teachers he called Valentinians, followers of Valentinus. Valentinian Christians, Irenaeus said, are "wolves in sheep's clothing," ready to pounce on unsuspecting Christians and lead them into satanic error.

Why was Valentinus such a threat? Why did other Christian leaders attack him so frequently and so viciously? In short, because Valentinus was a brilliant and eloquent Christian theologian who turned the Gnostic myth into a powerful Christian message, and who started a Christian movement that lasted for centuries. Valentinus invited people to find in Jesus true *gnōsis* of the Father and of themselves, and to experience God directly and immediately and, above all, joyfully.

We don't know much about Valentinus's life. He was probably born around the year 100. Much later sources say that he spent his early years in Alexandria in Egypt, and this makes sense. Alexandria was one of the Roman Empire's most cosmopolitan and intellectually exciting cities. We have already met Philo, the Jewish philosopher who lived and taught in Alexandria around the time of Jesus and Paul. You may remember that many scholars think that the Gnostic school of thought probably originated in Alexandria as well. In Alexandria, Valentinus could have studied with philosophers of all kinds, and he would have interacted with diverse Christian teachers.

We do know that by around the year 140 he was teaching in Rome. He was a popular and effective teacher. Many of his students went on to become important Christian theologians on their own. In the next few lectures, I'll discuss the Valentinian school of Christian thought that arose from Valentinus's teaching and preaching. Valentinus was so compelling a preacher that one Christian community in Rome almost elected him their bishop.

We don't know when Valentinus died, but he was certainly dead before Irenaeus wrote his massive work against Gnostics and Valentinians in 180. In his lifetime Valentinus was never declared a heretic. For one thing, he was pretty popular, and although many other Christian teachers considered his views wrong, he found a substantial following among other Christians. But even more, when Valentinus lived, there was no single Christian church that could declare someone an official heretic. Only later did church authorities all agree that Valentinus was a heretic who must be condemned.

Unfortunately, due to his later condemnation, nearly all of Valentinus's writings have been lost. We have about a half-dozen fragments from his works that critics quote, and one ancient author quotes an entire short poem that Valentinus wrote. In addition, many scholars, including me, believe that a sermon found at Nag Hammadi called the Gospel of Truth is by Valentinus. We believe this for two reasons. First, the style and vocabulary of the sermon match the fragmentary quotations of Valentinus. Second, Irenaeus tells us that Valentinians placed high value in a book called the Gospel of Truth. It makes sense that Valentinus would be the author of a book that his students admired so much. For these reasons, I will include the Gospel of Truth in my presentation of Valentinus's thought, but please be aware that many other scholars would not.

Let's see what made Valentinus such a compelling Christian teacher by looking at his short poem entitled "Summer Harvest." It reads in full:

In spirit I see that all things are hanging
In spirit I know that all things are being carried
Flesh hanging from soul
Soul cleaving to air
Air hanging from upper atmosphere

Crops coming forth from the deep
A baby coming forth from the womb.

The first thing to say is that it's remarkable enough for a Christian theologian in the 100s to have simply written a poem. This is very rare, and it's a sign of Valentinus's willingness to express himself in innovative ways.

Note, too, that the poem expresses a personal vision. The speaker does not communicate someone else's view of things, nor does he claim to be interpreting the Bible or some other authoritative religious text. "I see" and "I know," he says. In other words, I have *gnōsis* and have seen and experienced truth and insight.

Gnostic authors did not write in their own names. Instead, they attributed their works to ancient figures like Adam or Zōstrianos, or to more recent Christian leaders like the apostle John. Valentinus, however, speaks in his own voice, from his own mystical knowledge of God. According to one of his Christian enemies, Valentinus claimed to have had a visionary experience of God's Logos or Word in the person of a newborn baby. This poem ends with the image of a baby being born. In the Gospel of Truth, Valentinus proclaims, "I have been in the place of repose." That is, I have experienced true *gnōsis* of God and the serenity that it brings.

You may recall, too, that the Gospel of Thomas said that transformed Christians were like newborn babies. And Thomas called salvation "repose." Valentinus surely had read the Gospel of Thomas, and he was profoundly influenced by that gospel's teaching that *gnōsis* of God is *gnōsis* of one's self. Imagery from Thomas, like repose and newborn babies and sleeping and awakening, appear throughout Valentinus's works.

This poem has two movements, so to speak. In the first five lines, the poet conveys the interdependence of all that there is. Everything that exists hangs from, or is carried by, or clings to something more spiritual than itself. The vocabulary here—flesh, soul, air, the upper atmosphere—is philosophical, reminiscent of how Greek philosophers would talk about the cosmos and its elements. These first lines communicate a peaceful cosmos of unity and stability, with also hierarchy—lower things depend on higher things.

But then the last two lines suggest motion and generation and birth. Stability and interdependence are interrupted by creation and fertility. The poem then vividly expresses the life and vitality that lie behind the universe and, indeed, all of existence. It leaves the reader suspended between two truths: all of reality is stable and interconnected, and yet at the base of reality is tremendous life-giving force.

These last two lines are also typical of Valentinus in that they create a religious feeling by drawing on specific terms and images that the reader may or may not recognize. For example, the poem refers to the source of life as "the deep" and "the womb." The reader may just find these terms evocative, or you may think [they] simply refer to the human womb. But we know from other ancient sources that Valentinus referred to the ultimate high God, the god that the Gnostics called The Invisible Spirit—Valentinus called this god "The Deep." That is, when the poem uses the term "the deep," it's also referring to the unknowable source of all that is, the highest God. And you may recall that the Gnostics called the Barbēlō aeon "the womb of the Entirety"; could Valentinus be alluding to that as well?

And, of course, the image of a baby being born can simply convey the life-giving power of God. But for Christians, the image may also remind them of the birth of Christ.

Valentinus draws on imagery and terms from Gnostic myth, his own mythological views, and traditional Christianity to create a compelling vision of God as the source of all life.

In "Summer Harvest" we see the characteristics that made Valentinus such an attractive teacher and preacher: He expresses a vision of deep personal insight, and he does so in a way that draws on and brings together several different religious traditions: Gnostic myth, the Gospel of Thomas, the New Testament, Greek philosophy. He leaves the reader with powerful and even paradoxical feelings of wonder at divine stability and creativity. He suggests that you, too, can have the same kind of personal insight that he has.

Irenaeus and bishops like him did not appreciate this message of visionary insight, nor did they celebrate this combination of diverse religious and philosophical traditions. Instead, Irenaeus attacked Valentinus by saying that he had adapted his ideas from the Gnostics, whom Irenaeus said are clearly heretics. Irenaeus's claim is meant to disparage Valentinus. Nonetheless, it does appear to be true: One of the sources for Valentinus's thought was the Gnostic myth. But Valentinus modified the myth significantly, to make it more explicitly Christian and to remove some of its more anti-Jewish features.

We cannot have as detailed a knowledge of Valentinus's myth as we had of the Gnostic myth because so little of what Valentinus wrote survives. Irenaeus does give a summary of Valentinus's myth, but it's very brief, and he seems to assume that readers can fill in the gaps from his summaries of other myths. And some scholars argue that Valentinus did not really have a complicated myth like that of the Gnostics. Still, we can see some of the important ways that Valentinus used and revised the Gnostic myth.

Like the Gnostics, Valentinus considered God to be a complex structure of emanations that come from the ineffable ultimate God. Also, just as the Gnostic Entirety had first a set of ten aeons, and then a set of twelve, so too Valentinus's God has a set of ten powers and then another set of twelve powers.

But Valentinus used less exotic vocabulary for his aeons. The Gnostic aeons had strange or technical names like Barbēlō, Divine Self-Originate, and Ēlēlēth. In contrast, the names of the aeons in Valentinus's system are almost all biblical—names like Truth, Life, Word, and Church. The Gnostics called the divine realm the Entirety, but Valentinus called it the Fullness. He probably took that term from the Gospel of John, which reads in chapter one, "From his fullness we have all received grace, grace upon grace."

So Valentinus retained the idea of a complex God consisting of aeons, but he made this God sound less philosophical or intellectual and more biblical and Christian. He drew more of his ideas and vocabulary from the New Testament. Like the Gnostics, Valentinus believed that one aeon did something wrong. In Gnostic myth, the aeon Wisdom tries to think on her own, and the result is the flawed divinity, Ialdabaōth. Wisdom casts Ialdabaōth out of the Entirety. He is the malicious and ignorant ruler who created this universe.

In the myth of Valentinus, it seems also to be Wisdom who goes astray in some fashion. But she does not then produce a flawed divinity like Ialdabaōth and throw him out of the Entirety. Instead, it's Wisdom herself who leaves the Fullness and enters our world. Valentinus then calls this aeon the Mother. The Mother generates multiple divine beings. The first is Christ, who takes from the Mother her share of divine spirit. Christ then returns to the Fullness.

Next, without divine spirit, the Mother emits a second being, whom Valentinus calls the Craftsman and the Almighty. This is the creator of this world and the God of Genesis. Here we see perhaps the most important difference between Valentinus and the Gnostics. Valentinus agreed with the Gnostics that the God of Genesis, the god who created this universe, is a lower divine being. But Valentinus did not call him Ialdabaōth. Instead, he used the term *Craftsman* or *Demiurge*, the term that Plato used for the creator god in the *Timaeus*. And he used the name *Almighty*, which comes from the Bible, of course.

And above all, Valentinus's Creator God is not malicious, arrogant, or evil; he is simply lower and less spiritual than the ultimate God. The God of Genesis may result from one aeon going wrong, and he may be less divine than the ineffable Father of all, but he is not arrogant or evil, and he does not persecute human beings.

In this way, Valentinus's myth is less hostile toward Jewish tradition than was the Gnostic myth. And it's less different from how other Christians thought about God. This is probably one of the most important reasons that Valentinus's version of the Gnostic myth was more appealing to other Christians—and thus more frightening to leaders like Irenaeus.

A final example of how Valentinus revised Gnostic myth is the identity of the divine being who acts to save humanity. In Gnostic myth, Wisdom—the aeon who caused the lack of divine power—and Forethought work together to enlighten human beings, to preserve the divine power from the rulers, and to restore what had been lost to the Entirety.

In contrast, Valentinus does not emphasize the theme of recovery of stolen divine power. Instead, like the Gospel of Thomas, he highlights the divine essence within humanity as our connection to God, that which enables us to know our selves and God and to realize our superiority to mortal existence. The divine being who helps us is primarily God's Word or Logos, who is also God's Son and God's Name. It is this Word or Son or Name of God who reveals to us God and our selves. And it is this Word of God who became incarnate in Jesus.

And so Valentinus says that when the Creator God and his angels made human beings, they were awestruck in the presence of humanity, for the Word of God planted a seed of higher essence in humanity, which enables humanity to speak freely, with a voice unknown to these lower divinities. The Name of God, present to and within human beings, fulfills what's lacking in us because we were created by lower beings. The Word is the divine potential that lies within all of us.

This same Word or Son of God is how the God the Father reveals himself to human beings. God visits the hearts of human beings and purifies them of evil spirits. In this way, through the Son of God, a person can gain a pure heart and thereby see God, just as Jesus promises in the Gospel of Matthew when he says, "Blessed are the pure in heart, for they shall see God."

And of course, this same Word of God became human in Jesus. According to one report, Valentinus had such a strong sense of Jesus's divinity that he did not believe that Jesus ate and drank like a normal human being. Instead, Jesus did not experience any corruption in his body, so that his food did not become excrement within him.

For Valentinus, the salvation that the Word of God brings to us unlocks the divine potential within us and enables us to triumph over the corruption and decay of the material world. Here is an astonishing fragment from one of Valentinus's sermons to a group of Christians:

> From the beginning you are immortal, and you are children of eternal life. And you wanted death to be apportioned to yourselves so that you might spend it and deplete it, and so that death might die in you and through you. For when you abolish the world and are not yourselves destroyed, you rule over creation and over all decay.

You might remember that the Gospel of Thomas urged Christians "to abstain from the world" because it's not their true home. People really belong to the realm of spirit. Valentinus goes beyond this. He tells his disciples to "abolish the world"—to cancel it, deny it, simply ignore it. Christians who have gained *gnōsis* through Christ activate the immortality that they have always had. Through them death dies, and they prevail over everything that is created and suffers corruption.

This is a powerful message of salvation, and it's all centered on Christ— the Word, Son, and Name of the Father, who is present within us and was embodied in Jesus.

The most complete statement of Valentinus's spirituality is the sermon the Gospel of Truth. The sermon survives only in two fragmentary Coptic translations from Nag Hammadi. Even in Coptic, however, the eloquence of the original Greek shines through. Remember that the idea that Valentinus wrote the Gospel of Truth is a hypothesis—the manuscripts do not give it an author. But I think it make complete sense as a sermon of Valentinus. It's his remarkable invitation to every Christian to experience the repose and joy of knowing God the Father through his Son, Jesus.

Here's how the sermon begins:

> The gospel of truth is joy for people who have received grace from the Father of truth, so that they might know him through the power of the Word. The Word has come from the Fullness in the Father's thought and mind. The Word is called "savior": a term that refers to the work he is to do to redeem those who had no known the Father; and the term "gospel" refers to the revelation of hope, since it is the means of discovery for those who seek him.

You can hear in this passage the language of the New Testament—the Father, the Word, gospel, truth, fullness, savior, redeem, hope. The sermon is dense with allusions to the Bible, especially the New Testament, and we'll look at a couple of these images in a moment.

But notice, too, how Valentinus defines sin and salvation. Sin—what separates us from God—is ignorance. We have fallen ignorant of the Father, and we are now searching for him. Salvation—our return to God—is discovering the Father, learning to know him, and that happens through the power of the savior, the Word. This is the heart of the Christian message for Valentinus, and in the rest of the sermon, he explains how ignorance came to be, how Christians gain knowledge through Jesus, and what the experience of joy is for these Christians.

According to Valentinus, the material world in which we live is the result of ignorance. Ultimately, everything that exists is in God the Father. The Father is the source of all being; indeed, he is all being. All truly real beings are emanations of the Father, just as in Gnostic myth. For all beings, joy and blessedness are to know the Father and to be known by him. But to have that kind of relationship—to know someone and be known by them—you have to be separate from the one you want to know. And once there's separation, there's the possibility of ignorance. That is, in order for the emanations of the Father to know him and be known by him, they must also be separate from the Father. And that separation leads to ignorance—not knowing the Father.

As Valentinus tells it, ignorance of the Father became a kind of fog, and it condensed into matter. Valentinus introduces a personified female character named Error, who combines the roles that Wisdom and Ialdabaōth played in Gnostic myth. According to Valentinus, "Error found strength and labored at her matter in emptiness."

In other words, the material world in which we live is the product of ignorance. It's the condensation of ignorance, formed into a universe of things by Error. Ultimately, then, the material world in which we live—this world so full of pain and disappointment and injustice—this world of sin is not real. It's ignorance, and it becomes irrelevant to us as soon as our ignorance is dispelled by *gnōsis*. Remember how Valentinus told Christians in another sermon to abolish the world, cancel it.

It's Jesus Christ who makes possible the *gnōsis*—the acquaintance with the Father—that removes ignorance and brings joy. Valentinus describes how this happens:

> The hidden mystery Jesus Christ shed light upon those who were, because of forgetfulness, in darkness. He enlightened them and gave them a way, and the way is the truth, about which he instructed them. For this reason Error became angry with him and persecuted him. She was constrained by him and became inactive. He was nailed to a tree and became fruit of the Father's acquaintance. Yet it did not cause ruin because it was eaten. Rather, to those who ate of it, it gave the possibility that whomever he discovered within himself might be joyful in the discovery of him. And as for him, they discovered him within them—the inconceivable, uncontained, the Father, who is perfect, who created the Entirety.

This passage neatly sums up Valentinus's view of salvation. Jesus came to humanity to enlighten us and to guide us to truth. Error, the personification of the forces of ignorance, persecuted Jesus and caused him to be crucified.

And then Valentinus brings together the New Testament, Genesis, and Christian ritual. He evokes the crucifixion from the New Testament in the nailing of Jesus to the cross. But Valentinus calls the cross "a tree," and on this tree Jesus becomes "fruit of the Father's acquaintance." Now he alludes to Genesis, and the tree of the knowledge of good and evil in the Garden of Eden. This is the traditional story of where human beings eat from the fruit and fall into sin and ruin. But no, says Valentinus, to eat from the fruit of knowledge, which is Jesus, is not ruin, but joy, the discovery of the Father of whom people were ignorant.

But how can people eat the fruit that is the crucified Jesus? In the Christian ritual of the Eucharist. In the Gospel of Judas, the Gnostics vehemently rejected the Eucharist as a mistaken sacrifice to the false God of the Old Testament. But Valentinus embraces the Eucharist as an intimate encounter with Jesus, the Word who saves us from our ignorance of the Father.

And where do Christians actually discover the Father? Within themselves. The Father is within them, just as they are within the Father. For all beings that are truly real are emanations of the Father.

In the end, the Father, the Son, and the Christian are not really distinct beings at all. Ignorance separates people from God, but once people know the Son, they know the Father—and they know themselves as containing and being contained by the Father.

In this passage Valentinus has used the imagery of eating to explain the saving effect of the crucifixion. This imagery draws from the Garden of Eden story in Genesis and from Christian celebration of the Eucharist.

In another passage, he uses the publication of a book as his metaphor. All knowledge, the entirety of everything, Valentinus says, is like a book—what he calls "the living book of the living, which is written in the Father's heart and intellect." No one can read this book, and no one even dares pick it up—until Jesus:

> The merciful and faithful Jesus became patient and accepted the sufferings even unto taking up that book: inasmuch as he knew that his death would mean life for many. Before a will is opened, the extent of the late property owner's fortune remains a secret; just so, the Entirety was concealed. Since the Father of the Entirety is

invisible—and the Entirety derives from him, from whom every way emanated—Jesus appeared, wrapped himself in that document, was nailed to a piece of wood, and published the Father's edict upon the cross. ... And those who would learn, namely the living enrolled in the book of the living, learn about themselves, recovering themselves from the Father, and returning to him.

Once again, Valentinus takes an image from the Bible and reverses it—this time from the Letter to the Colossians. In chapter 2 of Colossians Jesus's crucifixion is described as nailing to the cross the edict of God's condemnation of us for our sins. Valentinus takes this idea—that the crucifixion is the public display of a written text—and makes it a metaphor for salvation.

In the crucifixion, Jesus publishes and makes available the book of the knowledge of the Father, which had been closed. The Entirety that comes from the Father is in that book, and now it can be known. But what do the readers of that book learn? They learn about themselves, and so they return to the Father. Yet again, the *gnōsis* of the Father that Jesus makes possible is also *gnōsis* of ourselves.

I think you can see why Irenaeus and other Christian bishops found Valentinus so frightening. Valentinus used all the same words, scriptures, and rituals that they used—the Garden of Eden, the crucifixion, the Eucharist, the Letter to the Colossians—but he proclaims that when we know ourselves, we know God—not a message that Irenaeus endorses at all.

Some of the most striking passages in the Gospel of Truth describe the close relationship that the believer can have with the Father thanks to Jesus. For example:

As for everyone who loves truth, because the truth is the mouth of the Father, his tongue is the Holy Spirit. He who is joined to the truth is joined to the Father's mouth by his tongue whenever he is to receive the Holy Spirit, since this is the manifestation of the Father and his uncovering to his aeons. He manifested what was hidden of him. He explained it.

This erotic, even sexual imagery vividly expresses the joy and intimacy of knowing the Father. Kissing, uncovering, and revealing one's self—these are actions in which two people know each other as deeply as possible. This is the kind of knowledge of God that Jesus brings, according to Valentinus.

This sermon, the Gospel of Truth, has been called the first great classic work of Christian mysticism. Mysticism is the experience of having direct, immediate contact with God. Throughout history, Christian mystics have struggled to put into words how it feels and what it means to know God directly, with nothing between them and God. They have often used the language of sexuality to express this experience.

Throughout history as well, some Christian leaders have found this talk threatening. It seems to erase the distinction between God, the ruler of the universe, and human beings, his creatures—and, in fact, that's precisely the point for Valentinus, as for the Gospel of Thomas before him.

Some ancient Christians were indeed disturbed by Valentinus's teaching, but others found it thrilling. In the next lecture we'll see how Valentinus himself described the reactions to his teaching, and we'll learn about the popular branch of Christianity that he inspired.

God and Creation in Valentinian Myth
Lecture 12

I n the 140s, when Valentinus was preaching his version of the gospel in Rome, there were many small groups of Christians worshipping together in separate house churches or studying the Scriptures with different teachers. Valentinus's proclamation of *gnōsis* caused a disturbance among such Christian communities. One prominent Christian teacher, Justin, denounced Valentinus's teachings as inspired by demons, but another Christian community nearly elected him its bishop. We don't know precisely how Valentinus taught his students, but we can guess that they read the Bible and other texts and that Valentinus explained what these texts revealed about God the Father, his Son, and salvation. In this lecture, we'll look at what Christians might have learned from Valentinus.

The Valentinian School
- We know the names of some of the most prominent students of Valentinus who became important Christian theologians, including Ptolemy, Heracleon, and Theodotus. Eventually, a network of Christian teachers inspired by Valentinus's theology spread across the Roman Empire. This network is known as the Valentinian school.

- Valentinianism related to other forms of Christianity in diverse ways. In its most basic form, it was just a type of Christian theology, a way of understanding the Christian message, with which any educated Christian could engage without necessarily joining a Valentinian group.
  - The Valentinians, however, also formed study groups that operated alongside other Christian communities. These Valentinian groups seem to have been the most prevalent form of Valentinianism in the 2nd century and, perhaps, the 3rd.

  - By the 300s, Valentinians had completely separate churches. At some point, it probably became too difficult for Valentinians to participate in other Christian churches that rejected their theology.

- Whatever social form they took, Valentinians invited non-Valentinian Christians to learn about their teachings. In fact, Valentinus had encouraged his followers to bring his message of *gnōsis* to others: "Unto those who are weary give repose. And awaken those who wish to arise. For it is you who are unsheathed intelligence" (Gospel of Truth).

Later Versions of the Valentinian Myth

- As we saw in the last lecture, Valentinus had revised the Gnostic myth to make it more explicitly Christian and less anti-Jewish. Later students of Valentinus continued to revise and augment the myth.

- We have two major complete narratives of the Valentinian myth. One is Irenaeus's summary of the myth that Ptolemy taught. The second is a long text from Nag Hammadi that scholars call the Tripartite Tractate. This anonymous work probably comes from the middle of the 3rd century, about 70 years after Irenaeus. Given that difference in time, it's no surprise that it differs from Ptolemy's myth in important ways.

- Like the Gnostics and Valentinus, the Valentinians believed that everything comes from a single ultimate divine being, which they called the Deep and the Father **(see Figure 2)**. This God is unknowable, ineffable, beyond our concepts of divinity and thinking. Yet the Father desires to be known, and he thinks, and his thinking generates a series of aeons.
  - In the Tripartite Tractate, the aeons of the Fullness are without number and are not individually named. At the center of the Fullness are the Father and the Son; then, multitudes of aeons form what the author calls the Church.

Figure 2. View of God in the Tripartite Tractate

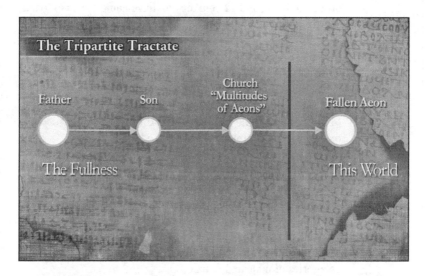

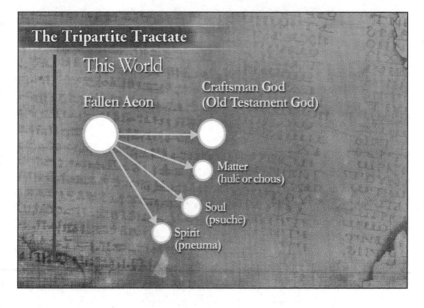

- In Ptolemy's myth, there are precisely 30 aeons, arranged into groups of 8, 10, and 12, and they all have names, such as Truth, Word, Motionless, and Hope. The final aeon is Wisdom.

- These aeons exist in male-female pairs, just as we saw in the Gnostic myth. Valentinian theology greatly values harmony and stability, and the pairing of male and female aeons provides these. This pairing also explains how God can move from unity to multiplicity. Male and female are different, yet they are also one humanity, complements of each other.

- According to Irenaeus, some Valentinians taught that even the ultimate Father has a female consort, named Silence. The feminine name Silence would express the ineffability of the ultimate principle, while the masculine names Father and Deep would express its generative power. Irenaeus tell us that other Valentinians, however, argued that the Father exists beyond the categories of male and female.

- Just as in Gnostic myth, the creation of this world happens after one aeon disrupts the harmony and stability of the Fullness by trying to know the Father on its own. This aeon presumptuously moves toward the Father, disturbing the serenity and order of the aeons. In Ptolemy's version of the myth, this aeon is, of course, Wisdom. In the Tripartite Tractate, the aeon is not named; it's called simply "the youngest aeon" or "a *logos*."

- In the Valentinian myth, this aeon becomes the primary source for the cosmos in which we live. The aeon's desire to know the Father directly is, of course, misguided because it disrupts the stability of the Fullness. Thus, the aeon is temporarily removed from the Fullness. It then emits three substances, the building blocks for the universe in which we live and for us. These three elements are matter or dirt (Greek: *hulē* or *chous*), soul (*psuchē*), and spirit (*pneuma*).
    - Matter is the physical stuff that we find in everything from rocks to plants to animals; in humans, it makes up our flesh. Matter has its origins in the fallen aeon's ignorance, grief, and fear.

- The fallen aeon repents of its passionate desire to know the Father and asks for forgiveness. This repentance produces soul. Soul is the somewhat physical, somewhat spiritual stuff that makes things live and breathe. It's an intermediate element between matter and spirit.

- When the Father and the other aeons accept the repentance of the fallen aeon, it is restored to its divine status. And because it is divine, its thinking produces spirit. This is the nearly immaterial element that enables humans and other spiritual beings to understand higher realities and possibly gain *gnōsis* of God. Spirit can be present in people but not in plants and animals.

The Three Elements

- In our world, matter, soul, and spirit exist in various beings and things in different proportions. They make individual beings, including angels and people, more or less spiritual (and closer to the Fullness) or more or less material (and closer to animals and other lower beings).

- At the end of time, the three elements will be separated and placed in their proper realms or conditions. The spiritual element will return to the Fullness. The material element will perish because it has no real basis in true existence; it comes from ignorance, fear, and other emotions that will pass away. The soul element will take a place lower than that of the Fullness—sometimes called the "midpoint"—but it will not pass away.

- For the Valentinians, just as the three elements of matter, soul, and spirit are the building blocks of the cosmos, so too, they are present in differing amounts and proportions in human beings. In fact, human beings can be divided into three categories based on which element predominates in them.

  - The highest element, spirit, predominates in spiritual people. These are the Valentinians themselves, who possess *gnōsis* of

God and of themselves. Obviously, these people will be saved and enter the Fullness.

○ The lowest element, matter, predominates in material people. These are non-Christians, including pagans, Jews, and anyone who does not believe in Jesus. Like the material element to which they are oriented, these people will perish at the end of the world.

○ The middle element, soul, predominates in animate people. These are non-Valentinian Christians—people who do not yet have the full *gnōsis* that Christ brought. These Christians have not reached perfection, but they have made the choice to worship Christ and to avoid idolatry and immorality. The sources disagree on the destiny that awaits animate people.

○ Animate people and the soul element have the freedom either to turn toward God, live righteous lives, and receive salvation or to turn away from God, live sinful lives, and perish with the material people. According to Irenaeus, the Valentinians said that righteous animate people would spend eternity with the lower craftsman god in the "midpoint." Other sources suggest that some Valentinians thought that the animate people would eventually share fully in salvation within the Fullness.

• What determines whether people are spiritual, animate, or material? Here, too, our sources disagree.
  ○ According to Irenaeus, the Valentinians taught that the three categories are three different kinds or species of human beings, descended or derived from the three sons of Adam and Eve. Cain is the father of the material people, Abel is the father of the animate people, and Seth is the father of the spiritual people. People are simply born into these categories.

  ○ As Irenaeus presents it, the spiritual people will be saved no matter what, and the material people will be destroyed no matter what. The only people who have any kind of free will are the animate people: They can either live righteous lives as Christians and gain limited salvation, or they can live sinful lives and be condemned. Again, according to Irenaeus, the Valentinians themselves had no reason to be concerned about behaving ethically; they did not need to live righteous lives because they will be saved by nature!

- ○ According to most modern scholars, however, the Valentinians probably thought that every person consists of all three elements. Each person chooses whether to live righteously or sinfully, whether to follow Christ, whether to accept Valentinian teachings, and so on. Over time, these choices determine which element predominates and, thus, whether a person is spiritual, animate, or material.

- Some scholars find an even deeper intellectual problem in this line of Valentinian thought. The Valentinians believed that when this universe comes to a conclusion, these three substances will be separated and have their appropriate ends—the spiritual element in the Fullness, the material element in destruction, and the soul element somewhere in between. In this sense, then, the destinies of these three elements are fixed.
  - ○ Human beings, too, are made up of these three elements and, thus, must experience in some way the same fixed destinies. By placing human beings in three categories that correspond to the elements, the Valentinians seem to be saying that individual people also have such fixed destinies.

  - ○ Yet the Valentinians clearly tried to persuade other Christians—the animate people—to become Valentinians. It seems that somehow human beings can orient themselves toward one of these three elements, or they can make one of these three elements dominate within them, enabling them to participate in that specific fate.

Dunderberg, *Beyond Gnosticism*.

Layton, *The Gnostic Scriptures*, "Ptolemy's Version of the Gnostic Myth (According to St. Irenaeus)."

Marjanen and Luomanen, eds., *A Companion to Second-Century "Heretics,"* "The School of Valentinus."

Meyer, ed., *The Nag Hammadi Scriptures*, "The Tripartite Tractate."

Thomassen, *The Spiritual Seed*, chapters 5–6.

Questions to Consider

1. What are the most important similarities and differences between the Valentinian myth and the original Gnostic myth?

2. How might the question of whether people are born into one of the three categories of people have affected Valentinian life and practice?

God and Creation in Valentinian Myth
Lecture 12—Transcript

In the last lecture, we met Valentinus, the great visionary teacher of Christian *gnōsis*. Valentinus had read the Gnostic myth, and he developed his own mythological teachings about God and the universe in response to it. But, in contrast to the Gnostics, Valentinus's vision was deeply personal, mystical, even radical—and sometimes very puzzling. For example, at one point during his sermon, the Gospel of Truth, Valentinus tells a parable about a set of jars. He says:

> This is like people who moved from one house to another. They had jars around that were not good and they broke, but the owner suffered no loss. Rather, the owner was glad because instead of these defective jars, there were full jars that were perfect. This is the judgment that has come from above and has judged every person: a drawn, two-edged sword, cutting on this side and that, since the Word that is in the heart of those who speak, the Word appeared. It is not merely a sound, but it was embodied. A great disturbance occurred among the jars, for some were empty and others were filled; some were ample and others were depleted; some were purified and others were broken.

Unfortunately, but somewhat typically, Valentinus does not explain what the parable means. He leaves it to the hearer to puzzle it out, to discover the insight the parable contains.

One clue is that the Word comes as not merely a sound, but it came in a body. That would seem to be a reference to the incarnation of the Word in the person of Jesus. As we saw last time, Valentinus preached that the Word of God came in Jesus to remove our ignorance and bring us *gnōsis* of the Father and of ourselves.

The message or proclamation of the Word causes a disturbance among the jars, and this disturbance affects the jars in different ways—from being well-filled, to being half-full, to having leaked dry or having broken. One plausible theory is that the jars represent different people and how people respond differently to the incarnation of Jesus. Some reject the message, while others embrace it and become full.

It's possible that Valentinus was applying this parable to his own situation as well. In the 140s, when he was preaching and teaching his version of the gospel in Rome, there were many small groups of Christians worshiping together in separate house churches or studying the Scriptures with different Christian teachers. Like the voice of the Word in the parable, Valentinus's proclamation of *gnōsis* caused a disturbance among the Christian communities of Rome. One prominent Christian teacher, Justin, later known as Justin Martyr, denounced Valentinus's teachings as inspired by demons. But another Christian community nearly elected Valentinus its bishop. Like the jars in the parable, Christian groups in Rome reacted to the striking message of Valentinus in diverse ways.

Some Christians found Valentinus to be such a compelling teacher that they became his students. We don't know precisely how Valentinus taught his students, but we can guess that they read the Bible, other sacred texts, and works of philosophy in his classes, and he would have explained what they revealed about God the Father, his Son, and salvation.

In one of his surviving fragments, Valentinus explains that many of the teachings found in non-Christian literature are also found in Christian scriptures and theological books. There is, Valentinus said, a "law that is written in the heart," and this law speaks even through the hearts of non-Christians.

After they concluded their education with Valentinus, some of his students went on to become Christian theologians and teachers in their own right. We know the names of some of the most prominent students of Valentinus who became important Christian theologians: among these are Ptolemy, Heracleon, and Theodotus. We know that Ptolemy did much of his teaching in Rome. Heracleon and Theodotus may have worked in Alexandria. Eventually, a network of Christian teachers inspired by Valentinus's theology spread across the Roman Empire. Ancient people called this network "the Valentinian School," or "the Valentinians," and modern historians still use these terms today.

Valentinian forms of Christianity lasted for centuries. In the late 300s, a Christian mob attacked a Valentinian chapel, so we know there were still communities of Valentinians 200 years after Valentinus.

Valentinianism related to other forms of Christianity in diverse ways. In its most basic form, Valentinianism was just a type of Christian theology. It was a way of understanding the Christian message with which any educated Christian could engage without necessarily joining a Valentinian group. There must have been bishops and priests in local communities whose preaching and teaching reflected Valentinian ideas without any awareness on their part or that of their followers that their ideas were peculiar or out of the mainstream. Today a Christian minister may preach sermons that are heavily influenced by the theologian Karl Barth or by liberation theology, but that does not make him or her part of a separate church. We know that in the 190s, a Valentinian named Florinus served as a priest under the non-Valentinian Bishop Victor.

The Valentinians, however, also formed study groups that operated alongside and as a supplement to other Christian communities. A Christian might worship weekly in a house church that wasn't Valentinian, but also participate in meetings of study and discussion led by a Valentinian teacher. These Valentinian groups that were alongside other Christian communities seem to have been the most prevalent form of Valentinianism in the 2nd century, and perhaps the 3rd as well. But we know too that by the 300s Valentinians had completely separate churches. At some point it probably became too difficult for Valentinians to participate in the churches that rejected their theology.

Whatever social form they took, Valentinians reached out to non-Valentinian Christians and invited them to learn about Valentinian teachings. Valentinus had encouraged his followers to bring his message of *gnōsis* to other people: "Unto those who are weary give repose," he said in the Gospel of Truth. "And awaken those who wish to arise. For it is you who are unsheathed intelligence." That's a cool image: The Valentinians are like the knives ancient people carried to get things done, and they are drawn out of their sheaths, ready to accomplish good things in the world. Certainly, opponents of the Valentinians might find this image somewhat scary.

And in fact we know that Valentinians did try to recruit new followers among other Christians. According to the complaints of Irenaeus, the Valentinians would approach people and offer to guide them to an advanced, more profound understanding of Christianity. I imagine that, after a Eucharist or prayer meeting, a Valentinian might approach a promising non-Valentinian and say something like, "Were you intrigued by the discussion of the resurrection of the dead we heard today in Paul's Letter to the Corinthians? There's a group of us who meet on Wednesday evenings with a really great teacher, and he helps us to understand things like the resurrection in greater depth. These meetings have really helped me grow in my relationship to the Father through Jesus." This approach must have appealed to Christians who were interested in a more intellectual and mystical understanding of the faith than they were getting in their congregations.

But this is the kind of thing that so infuriated Irenaeus. He feared that not just ordinary Christians, but even church leaders like bishops might not recognize that what they would learn from Valentinian teachers might sound like Christianity, but that it was really demonic heresy. That's why he wrote *Detection and Overthrow of Gnōsis, Falsely So-Called*—to help Christians detect and then refute the false *gnōsis* of the Valentinians.

So what would Christians learn from a Valentinian teacher? In part, they would learn yet another version of the Gnostic myth. Valentinus had already revised the Gnostic myth to make it more explicitly Christian and less anti-Jewish. He got rid of names like the Barbēlō and Ēlēlēth and focused on biblical figures like the Wisdom of God and the Word of God. He made the God of the Old Testament less negative—no longer the evil and ignorant Ialdabaōth—instead, he became the craftsman, a lower and less perfect god, but one not hostile to the human race. In these ways, Valentinus made the myth more appealing to other Christians.

His students continued to revise and augment the myth, and so the Valentinian myth is not completely the same as what Valentinus himself taught. Our evidence for the Valentinian myth and for other Valentinian teachings comes from the two sources that we are now used to. First, Irenaeus and other heresiologists describe Valentinian teachings and sometimes quote word-for-word from Valentinian documents. We have a long philosophical letter from the Valentinian theologian Ptolemy just because an enemy of the Valentinians chose to quote it entirely. Second, we have Valentinian writings from the Nag Hammadi codices. None of these writings explicitly call themselves Valentinian, but based on their content and vocabulary, we can tell that they came from Valentinians.

We have two major complete narratives of the Valentinian myth. One is Irenaeus's summary of the myth that Ptolemy taught. It's as complex and elaborate as any of the myths we have seen so far. Even though Irenaeus was an enemy of the Valentinians, there are sources against which scholars can check various details of what he says, and most of the time what he tells us appears to be corroborated. The other important source is a long text from Nag Hammadi that scholars call the Tripartite Tractate. This anonymous work probably comes from the middle of the 3rd century, about 70 years or so after Irenaeus. Given that difference in time, it's no surprise that it differs from Ptolemy's myth in some important ways. Valentinians must have continued to revise and augment the myth, and there's no reason to think that individual Valentinian theologians all had to agree about everything.

Some scholars argue that the Valentinian myth attributed to Ptolemy by Irenaeus and the myth in the Tripartite Tractate also represent two branches of the Valentinian movement: a Western one, based mainly in Rome and represented by Ptolemy, and an eastern one, based primarily in Alexandria and represented by the Tripartite Tractate. Some ancient heresiologists report the division of Valentinianism into these two schools. Other historians, however, are skeptical that Valentinians can be divided into these two groups.

There's no reason for us to solve this historical question here. Rather than going through the two versions of the myth point by point, I'm going to highlight the most distinctive features of Valentinian mythology. Along the way, I will point out some of the key differences between Ptolemy and the Tripartite Tractate.

Like the Gnostics and Valentinus, the Valentinians believed that everything comes from a single ultimate divine being, which they called the Deep and also the Father. This god, as you will expect, is unknowable, ineffable, beyond our concepts of divinity and thinking. Yet the Father desires to be known, and he does think, and his thinking generates a series of aeons. In the Tripartite Tractate the aeons of the Fullness are without number and are not individually named. At the center of the Fullness are the Father and the Son, and then the multitudes of aeons form what the author calls the Church.

In Ptolemy's myth, however, there are precisely 30 aeons, arranged into groups of 8, 10, and 12. And they all have names, which are religious terms or aspects of God, such as Truth, Word, Motionless, and Hope. The final aeon is Wisdom.

It's very important that in Ptolemy's myth, the 30 aeons exist in male-female pairs, just as we saw in the Gnostic myth. Valentinian theology greatly values harmony and stability, and so that's a key feature of God's Fullness as the Valentinians envision it. The pairing of male and female aeons provides stability and harmony, and it also explains how God can move from unity to multiplicity. How do you get from having a single God to the multiplicity of the cosmos and the divine realm? The male-female conception provides a kind of metaphor for that movement. Male and female are different, and yet they are also one humanity, complements of one another.

According to Irenaeus, some Valentinians taught that even the ultimate Father or the Deep has a female consort, namely Silence. The feminine name Silence would express the ineffability of the ultimate principle, while the masculine names Father and Deep would express its generative power. Irenaeus tell us that other Valentinians, however, argued that the Father exists beyond the categories male and female, which therefore appear only in the aeons that emanate from the Father. And yet Father remains an undeniably masculine concept. Here we see that, like the Gnostics and the Gospel of Thomas, the Valentinians may have used androgyny as a symbol of wholeness and unity, but androgyny remained asymmetrical—that is, the masculine is the base gender, so to speak, and the feminine, derivative of it. In any case, we'll see a bit later how this male-female principle plays an important role in the Valentinian idea of salvation.

Just as in Gnostic myth, the creation of this world happens after one aeon disrupts the harmony and stability of the Fullness. One aeon tries to know the Father on its own. This aeon presumptuously and passionately moves toward the Father, disturbing the serenity and order of the aeons. In Ptolemy's version of the myth, this aeon is, of course, the last aeon, Wisdom. In the Tripartite Tractate, the aeon is not named: It's just called "the youngest aeon" or "a *logos*" or "word."

You'll recall that in Gnostic myth, Wisdom's attempt to think a new thought resulted in the production of the flawed divinity Ialdabaōth. Ialdabaōth then formed the material world as a bad copy of the spiritual realm.

In the Valentinian myth, the passionate aeon, whether called Wisdom or not, becomes the primary source for the cosmos in which we live. The aeon's passionate desire to know the unknowable Father directly is, of course, misguided because it disrupts the stability of the Fullness. So the aeon is, at least temporarily, removed from the Fullness. There it emits three substances, the building blocks for the universe in which we live—and for us as well. These three elements are, first, matter or dirt (in Greek, *hulē* or *chous*); second, soul (in Greek, *psuchē*); and third, spirit (in Greek, *pneuma*). Let's take these in order.

First, the unruly passions of the fallen aeon produce matter. Matter is the physical stuff that you find in everything from rocks to plants to animals, and in us it makes up our flesh. Matter has its origins in the fallen aeon's ignorance, grief, fear, and terror. You may recall that Valentinus taught that matter originated in ignorance.

Second, the fallen aeon repents of its passionate desire to know the Father and asks for forgiveness. This repentance produces soul. Soul is the somewhat physical, somewhat spiritual stuff that makes things live and breathe. So there isn't any soul in rocks, but there is soul in plants and animals and, of course, in human beings as well. It's an intermediate element between matter and the third element, spirit.

So finally, third, the Father and the other aeons in the Fullness accept the repentance of the fallen aeon. The aeon retains or is restored to its status as a divine aeon of the Fullness. Because it is a divine aeon, its thinking produces spirit. Spirit is the nearly immaterial element that enables human beings and other spiritual beings to understand higher realities and possibly gain *gnōsis* of God. Spirit can be present in people, but not really in plants and animals.

Now, what I have sketched out simplifies an episode in the Valentinian myth that is very complicated in whichever version one reads. In Ptolemy's story, for example, the fallen aeon, Wisdom, actually splits into two beings: a higher Wisdom that truly belongs to the Fullness, and a lower Wisdom called Achamōth, which belongs primarily outside the Fullness. Similarly complex events occur in the Tripartite Tractate. But the most important point of this episode is the production of the three elements that make up the cosmos and human beings.

In the world we live in, these three elements are mixed up, existing in various beings and things in different proportions. They make individual beings, including angels and people, more or less spiritual or more or less material. The more spiritual and less material you are, the closer your nature is to that of the spiritual Fullness. The less spiritual and more material you are, the closer your nature is to that of animals and other lower beings.

At the end of time the three elements will be separated out and placed in their proper realms or conditions. The spiritual element will return to the Fullness, just as in Gnostic myth the divine power that Ialdabaōth took will return to the Entirety. The material element will perish because it has no real basis in true existence: It comes from ignorance and fear and other emotions that will pass away. The soul element will take a place lower than that of the Fullness itself, sometimes called "the midpoint," but it will not pass away like the material.

The idea that the world is made up of these three elements—matter, soul, and spirit—was common in ancient thought, but philosophers did not agree on how to define these materials, where they were to be found, and so forth. More important for the Valentinians, however, was that the Apostle Paul used these terms in his letters. In his First Letter to the Corinthians, he talks about different bodies as being made of matter, soul, or spirit. Notice that there can be bodies of spirit, so even spirit, the highest substance, is not really immaterial. According to Paul, our present bodies are "psychic" or "soul-ish," made up of *psuchē*, but the resurrected bodies of the saved people will be "spiritual," made up of *pneuma*.

Paul in the same letter uses these adjectives to talk about people as well. Specifically, he calls some people "psychic," made of or oriented to *psuchē*—in English, "soul-ish" or "animate." And he calls some other people "pneumatic," made of or oriented to *pneuma*—in English, "spiritual." In the second chapter of 1 Corinthians, he says, "The psychic or animate people do not receive the gifts of God's Spirit, for the gifts are foolishness to them and they can't understand them because they are discerned spiritually. But the spiritual people discern all things, and they are discerned by no one." So for Paul, psychic or animate people are less spiritually advanced than spiritual people.

Inspired by Paul, the Valentinians used these terms and the elements they describe to talk about people in particular and not just the cosmos in general. Just as the three elements of matter, soul, and spirit are the building blocks of the cosmos, so too they are present in differing amounts and proportions in human beings. In fact, human beings can be divided up into three categories, based on which element predominates in them.

The highest element, spirit, predominates in spiritual people. These are the Valentinians themselves. In fact, in their literature the Valentinians tend not to call themselves Valentinians; instead, they call themselves "the spiritual ones." They consider themselves to be the spiritual people who Paul said "discern all things and are discerned by no one." They possess *gnōsis* of God and of themselves. Obviously these people are going to be saved and enter the Fullness.

The lowest element, matter, predominates in material people. These are non-Christians—pagans, Jews, anyone who does not believe in Jesus. They clearly lack *gnōsis*. Like the material element to which they are oriented, they will perish at the end of the world. As Valentinus puts it in the Gospel of Truth, "Whoever lacks acquaintance until the end is a modeled form of forgetfulness, and will perish along with it."

The middle element, soul, predominates in animate people. These are non-Valentinian Christians—people who do not yet have the full *gnōsis* that Christ has brought. These Christians have not reached perfection, but they have made the choice to worship Christ and to avoid idolatry and immorality. These are the "soul-ish" people who Paul said are good but can't understand spiritual things—at least not yet.

If spiritual people will enter the Fullness and material people will dissolve into nothing, what kind of destiny awaits the animate people? This is a point on which our sources disagree. The basic idea seems to be that animate people and the soul element have the freedom either to turn toward God, live righteous lives, and receive salvation, or to turn away from God, live sinful lives, and perish with the material people. But what kind of salvation will the righteous animate people receive? According to Irenaeus, the Valentinians said that they would spend eternity with the lower craftsman god in the "midpoint," where the soul element belongs. But other sources suggest that some Valentinians thought that the animate people would eventually share fully in salvation within the Fullness.

What's interesting about this issue is that the Valentinians thought about how to include in final salvation their fellow Christians who did not become Valentinians. Gnostic writings suggested that the Gnostics saw their religious community as the only path to salvation. You may remember that the Secret Book According to John teaches that non-Gnostics will be reincarnated, even multiple times, until they achieve *gnōsis*. But still, it's the Gnostic concept of *gnōsis* that people must at some point embrace. The Valentinians, in contrast, taught that non-Valentinian Christianity was also a path to salvation, whether to full salvation or to some lesser form of it.

But what determines whether people are spiritual, animate, or material? Is this predetermined? Or do people choose which type of person they are? Here, too, our sources disagree, and this may be a function of an ambiguity within Valentinian theology.

According to Irenaeus, the Valentinians taught that the three categories really are three different kinds or species of human beings, and he said that these three kinds of people were descended from or derived from the three sons of

Adam and Eve. Cain is the father of the material people, who are made up only of the material element. Abel is the father of the animate people, who are made up of the material and soul elements. And Seth is the father of the spiritual people, who are made up of all three elements. People are simply born into these categories.

As Irenaeus presents it, the spiritual people will be saved no matter what, and the material people will be destroyed no matter what. The only people who have any kind of free will are the animate people: They can either live righteous lives as Christians and gain limited salvation, or they can live sinful lives and be condemned. By "righteous" lives, the Valentinians meant what other Christians meant—worshiping only Jesus and his God, telling the truth, leading a chaste sexual life, and so on.

According to Irenaeus, however, the Valentinians themselves had no reason to be concerned about behaving ethically. They did not need to live righteous lives because they will be saved by nature!

Most modern scholars are not so sure about what Irenaeus says. We believe that it's much more likely that every person consists of all three elements—spirit, soul, and matter. Each person chooses whether to live righteously or sinfully, whether or not to follow Christ, whether or not to accept Valentinian teachings, and so on. Over time, these choices determine which element predominates in the person and thus whether the person is a spiritual, animate, or material person.

Several Valentinian sources clearly talk about people becoming saved—that is, changing their religious situation—or as receiving grace from God in baptism and other rituals. But these discussions are always somewhat ambiguous. For example, here's how the Tripartite Tractate explains the three kinds of human beings:

> Now, humanity came to exist as three kinds with respect to essence—spiritual, animate, and material. ... The essences of the three kinds can each be known from its fruit. They were nevertheless not known at first, but only when the Savior came to them, shedding light upon the saints and revealing what each one was.

This passage seems to be saying two things. On the one hand, humanity eventually "came to exist" in the three kinds. So people weren't always in these three categories; something happened to divide them into these three groups. On the other hand, the passage suggests that when the Savior came, he revealed what each person already was. This suggests that people already had their distinct essences, and the coming of Jesus just made clear what they were.

The text goes on to say that the three kinds of people reacted to the Savior in three different ways. The spiritual people immediately rushed to the Savior and received *gnōsis* immediately. The material people did not accept the Savior and even hated the Lord. Animate people hesitated, but eventually embraced the Savior and received instruction for future hope.

Again, the text is somewhat ambiguous about what all this means. Do the three kinds of people react to the Savior the way they do because they already belong to the three kinds? Or do the people belong to the three kinds because of the different ways they reacted to the Savior? The text really is ambiguous on this point.

And some scholars would say that's because there's a more basic ambiguity or intellectual problem within Valentinian thought. The Valentinians believed that the universe in which we live is made up of these three elements—spirit, soul, and matter. These are real substances, the building blocks of everything that exists. And they believed that at some point this universe will come to a conclusion, and these three substances will be separated and have their appropriate ends—the spiritual element in the Fullness, the material element in destruction, and the soul element somewhere in between. In this sense, then, the destinies of these three elements are fixed.

And yet, this is difficult to project onto human beings. We, too, are made up of these three elements, and so we must experience in some way the fixed destinies that these substances have. And by placing human beings in three categories that correspond to these elements, the Valentinians seem to be saying that individual people also have such fixed destinies. And yet, the Valentinians clearly tried to persuade other Christians, the animate people, to become Valentinians, and they devoted themselves to educating and guiding these other Christians. It seems that somehow, human beings can orient themselves toward one of these three elements, or they can make one of these three elements dominant within them, so that they participate in that specific fate.

In the end, there are all sorts of problems that arise when the Valentinians talk about human beings in terms of cosmic substance.

We have only begun to understand Valentinian *gnōsis* by exploring their myth. The Valentinians also practiced several rituals, including baptism and the Eucharist. Through these rituals, we can learn more about how the Valentinians understood *gnōsis* and salvation, and that's the topic of our next lecture.

"Becoming Male" through Valentinian Ritual
Lecture 13

The Valentinians appear to have had a rich worship life, filled with such rituals as baptism and celebration of the Eucharist. This may be surprising given that they considered matter to be the lowest of the three elements that make up this cosmos. Unlike spirit and soul, matter originated in ignorance and fear and would perish at the end of time. How, then, could material things, such as water and bread, convey salvation? For the Valentinians, in this universe, it's impossible for truth to come to us without such material symbols. In this lecture, we will explore the Valentinian sacraments, drawing from two sources: the Excerpts from Theodotus and the Gospel According to Philip.

The Eucharist

- In his sermon the Gospel of Truth, Valentinus said that the Eucharist is a means by which Christians gain *gnōsis*. On the cross, Valentinus said, Christ became the fruit of the Father, and by eating that fruit, Christians come to know the Father within themselves.

- Several excerpts in the Gospel According to Philip consider the symbolism of the bread and wine in the Eucharist. For example, the bread represents the spiritual nourishment that human beings did not have until Christ came and brought them his "bread from heaven." The bread also reminds Christians of the crucifixion of Christ, when he spread out his body on the cross, just as the bread is broken and handed out to others. And just as ordinary bread is made holy in the Eucharist, so too, the body of the individual Christian becomes holy.

- In fact, as we see in the Gospel of Philip, the Eucharistic bread represents and even brings about the resurrection of Christians.
  - The author of the gospel criticizes two opposing views on the question of whether people in the resurrection will have "flesh." On the one hand, some Christians believe that when

the resurrection comes, people will have bodies made of the same flesh we have now. The Valentinian author rejects that idea because we must divest ourselves of this world, which is not our true home. On the other hand, other Christians say that there is no sense in which the flesh will arise from death. The author rejects this view, as well.

- o Instead, he argues that it's the flesh of Jesus that will rise up. The flesh of Jesus is the bread of the Eucharist, in which the Word of God comes to us. By partaking of the bread, Christians participate in the Word; they join with the Word and, thus, experience resurrection in the present, not at some future resurrection of the dead.

Valentinian Baptism

- Baptism, of course, initiates a person into Christianity and begins the relationship with Christ that leads to *gnōsis* and resurrection. For the most part, Valentinian Christian baptism seems to have resembled the baptisms of other Christian groups in the 2nd and 3rd centuries.
  - o First, there was a period of instruction and training (Greek: *catechesis*) for the interested candidates. If a candidate proved worthy, there was then a more intense period of preparation consisting of "fasts, supplications, prayers, laying on of hands, and kneelings." These acts of physical discipline focused the mind of the candidate and symbolized his or her withdrawal from the sinful practices of the world. They were also designed to remove evil spirits.

  - o When it was time to be baptized, the candidates undressed, which symbolized liberation from the body and the giving up of one's old life. The candidates also renounced the evil rulers of this world. They were then immersed in water, and the name of the Father, Son, and Holy Spirit was spoken over them. This was considered the single Name of God, and it was called being "sealed."

○ After the immersion, there was an anointing with oil, through which the candidates became Christians. The candidates then dressed themselves, and once again, hands were laid upon them with prayers. Then, the new Christians received the Eucharist for the first time.

• For the Valentinians, baptism accomplished at least three important objects: the removal of unclean spirits, the provision of freedom from the evil rulers of this world, and the sealing of the candidate with the Name of God.

○ Ultimately, the true Name of God is Christ. "The Son is the Name of the Father," Valentinus said in the Gospel of Truth. This means that one knows the Father through the Son. The Son reveals who the Father is, just as a name identifies who a person is.

○ Unlike ordinary human names, which are basically arbitrary, God's Name belongs uniquely to him and truly reveals who he is. In baptism, Christians are stamped or sealed with that Name.

The Male and Female in Baptism

• Valentinians also talked about baptism with the language of male and female. For example, consider this passage from the Excerpts from Theodotus:

• So long as the seed is still without form, they say, it is a child of the female. But when it is given form, it is changed into a male and becomes a son of the bridegroom. It is no longer weak and subject to the cosmic powers, whether visible or invisible; rather, having been made male, it becomes a male fruit.

• This should remind us of the Gospel According to Thomas, which discussed salvation in terms of integration. The separation between male and female was one of the divisions that salvation and baptism removed. But, again, this did not mean uniting two equals—male and female. Rather, it meant returning the female to the more basic male.

- In addition, recall that the pairing of male and female aeons in Valentinian myth provides harmony and stability in the Fullness. It stands to reason, then, that separating the male and female would be negative in Valentinian thought, and that's precisely the case. Valentinian thinkers identified the separation of Eve from Adam as the beginning of death. Christ, they said, came to heal this division:
  - If the female had not separated from the male, she and the male would not die. That being's separation became the source of death. Christ came to rectify the separation that had been present since the beginning and join the two; and to give life unto those who had died by separation and join them together. (Gospel According to Philip)

- Does this mean that each of us has a lost half of the other gender with whom we need to reunite? The answer is yes—but there's more. It's not the case that each of us must reunite with our partner of the opposite gender, because our identities as men and women belong to our bodies, which are not our true selves. Our true selves are our spiritual selves, the parts of us that originated from above—and our true spiritual selves are all female.

- Genesis 1:27 tells us: "In the image of God he created them; male and female he made them." For the Valentinians, this refers not to the creation of male and female human beings but to two created selves, angelic selves and human selves, which are male and female, respectively **(Figure 3)**. We humans are all female elements, and we exist in a kind of alienation from our higher masculine selves, the angels. We are like the divine male-female aeon pairs, but we are all female aeons and are separated from our male consorts.

- The separation of Eve from Adam represents that alienation on the level of human difference.

Figure 3. Male and Female Selves in Valentinian Thought

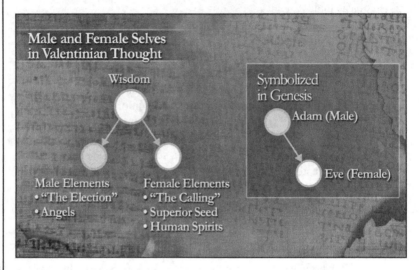

- The original Adam, created in Genesis 1, indicated the original union of the male angels with the female superior seed, and the separation of Eve from Adam in Genesis 2 demonstrated the separation of the female element from the male.

- The Genesis account makes clear that the female element is derivative of the male. The female selves that we have now are the lower, derivative aspects of our true masculine angelic selves.

- Salvation, then, is not simply the reunion of male and female or the coupling of our angelic and spiritual selves. It is, rather, the return of the derivative female element to the higher male element.

- The Valentinians understood this process of being made male and reuniting with one's true angelic self as beginning in baptism and being gradually accomplished through the rituals and practices of the church.

The Bridal Chamber and Marriage

- Several sources mention a ritual or a symbol of the reunion with one's true angelic self called the *bridal chamber*. Most modern historians believe that this term was probably a symbolic way of speaking about the union of our male and female selves that happens through baptism, Eucharist, and other rituals and is completed after our deaths.

- Salvation will not be complete until the end of this world, when our spiritual elements, our female selves, will unite definitively with our angelic bridegrooms and join the aeons of the Fullness as eternal male-female pairs. Ultimate salvation is to be the union of the angelic male selves and the human female selves within the Fullness—this is the ultimate bridal chamber **(Figure 4)**.

- If the division of Adam and Eve represents on a worldly level the division between the male angelic elements and the female spiritual elements, then ordinary marriage provides an image or representation of this final consummation. Marriage is a mystery—

Figure 4. Ultimate Bridal Chamber (Ultimate Salvation)

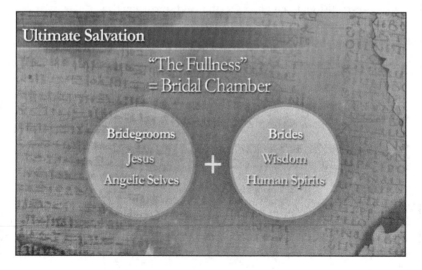

that is, something symbolic—which provides an image not simply of our final salvation but of the underlying male-female organizing principle of the cosmos.

Ransom

- One ritual practiced by the Valentinians alone was *apolutrōsis* (Greek), meaning "ransom" or "redemption," a ritual for someone who was dying.

- According to Irenaeus, in this ritual, the dying person was anointed with a mixture of oil and water. These two elements, oil and water, would have reminded the person of his or her baptism, when the Christian was immersed in water and anointed with oil. Thus, one meaning of this ritual was to complete the process of salvation that was begun in baptism.

- But the ritual mainly prepared the person for what would happen after death. Remember that according to the Valentinians, human beings are made up of spirit, soul, and matter, and each element must go to its proper place. The ritual of ransom made the person ready to abandon the material body and leave it here on earth. Freed from the material body, the soul and spirit would ascend.

- Next, the ritual gave the dying person secret words to say to the cosmic rulers and to the creator God. After saying these words, the person would leave the soul with the creator God, and only the spirit would ascend into the Fullness. There, the spiritual element, the lower female self, would unite with its angelic male self. Salvation would then be complete in the heavenly bridal chamber.

Suggested Reading

Foerster, *Gnosis*, "Valentinianism V."

Layton, *The Gnostic Scriptures*, "The Gospel According to Philip."

Lewis, "*Apolytrosis* as Ritual and Sacrament."

Meyer, ed., *The Nag Hammadi Scriptures*, "The Gospel of Philip."

Turner, "Ritual in Gnosticism."

Questions to Consider

1. Would a Valentinian worship service have looked different from a non-Valentinian Christian worship service?

2. Did the Valentinians have a positive or negative view of the female and femininity?

"Becoming Male" through Valentinian Ritual
Lecture 13—Transcript

"It is not the bath [of baptism] alone that liberates, but also the *gnōsis*: Who were we? What have we become? Where were we? Into what place have we been thrown? Where are we going?"

This may be one of the most famous quotations from a Valentinian theologian or from any teacher of Gnosticism. The speaker is Theodotus, a Valentinian theologian of the 2nd century. It seems to capture the essence of what makes Valentinian Christianity Gnostic. You need more than the ritual of baptism to be saved, you also need *gnōsis*: the knowledge that tells you where you have come from and where you are going. That *gnōsis* is what Valentinian teachers provided.

That may be true, but Valentinians certainly considered baptism necessary for salvation, and they also, like other Christians, celebrated the Eucharist as well. In fact, the Valentinians appear to have had a rich worship life, filled with ritual and ceremony. The water of baptism, the oil of anointing, the bread and wine of the Eucharist—these were the substances with which Valentinian Christians worshiped and through which they received blessings from God. The Valentinians, we will see, even developed the earliest known ritual for dying Christians.

This may be surprising because, as we saw in the previous lecture, the Valentinians considered matter the lowest of the three elements that make up this cosmos. Unlike spirit and soul, matter, they believed, originated in ignorance, fear, and other bad emotions, and it would perish at the end of time. How, then, could material things like water and bread convey salvation?

Basically, in this universe it's impossible for Truth to come to us without such material symbols. One Valentinian author wrote, "Truth did not come to the world nakedly; rather, it came in prototypes and images; the world will not accept it in any other form." We can't receive truth directly in its spiritual form as long as we live in the body, so we need material images through which Truth can come to us. True spiritual rebirth really exists, but in order for us to be reborn spiritually, we must experience rebirth through its material image: baptism.

In addition, the power of God makes the material elements spiritual and holy. In the Eucharist, for example, the power of the Name or Son of God makes the bread and wine holy. They remain the same visibly, but they are changed into a spiritual power. If we explore the spiritual power of the Valentinian sacraments, we will learn more about how they thought about salvation.

The two main sources for Valentinian rituals are fragmentary—not because the manuscripts have been damaged, but because they are ancient collections of excerpts. In the late 2nd century, Clement of Alexandria, a Christian critic of the Valentinians, created an anthology of excerpts from Valentinian theologians, now called the Excerpts from Theodotus. Not all the excerpts come from Theodotus, but he is the only Valentinian theologian cited by name in the text. This book is a kind of research notebook, in which Clement collected quotations from multiple Valentinian theological works. Maybe Clement was planning to write a refutation of Valentinian thought, because every now and then, Clement adds his own critical remarks about what he has quoted. Whatever the reason, Clement included several statements about the sacraments, especially baptism.

The second important source is the Gospel According to Philip. It was found at Nag Hammadi, and so it's a Coptic translation of an originally Greek text. Despite its title, the Gospel According to Philip is not a book about the life and teachings of Jesus, nor does it really have much to do with the apostle Philip. Philip is the only male apostle mentioned in the book, but otherwise he plays no important role. I suspect that the author did not create the title, but it was added later.

The Gospel of Philip is like the Excerpts from Theodotus: It's an anthology of excerpts from mostly Valentinian theologians. But unlike the Excerpts, a Valentinian probably created this anthology because it does not contain any critical remarks. It does, however, feature many passages about baptism, the Eucharist, anointing, and something called the bridal chamber. For this reason, the Gospel According to Philip is one of our most important sources for Valentinian rituals.

You may recall that Valentinus himself, in his sermon the Gospel of Truth, said that the Eucharist is a means by which Christians gain *gnōsis*. On the cross, Valentinus said, Christ became the fruit of the Father, and by eating that fruit, Christians come to know the Father within themselves.

Several excerpts in the Gospel According to Philip consider the symbolism of the bread and wine in the Eucharist. For example, the bread represents the spiritual nourishment that human beings did not have until Christ came and brought them his "bread from heaven." The bread also reminds the Christian of the crucifixion of Christ, when he spread out his body on the cross, just as the bread is broken and handed out to others. And just as ordinary bread is made holy in the Eucharist, so too the body of the individual Christian becomes holy.

In fact, the Eucharistic bread represents and even brings about the resurrection of Christians. In the next lecture I'll say more about the Valentinian view of the resurrection. But one passage in the Gospel of Philip discusses whether people in the resurrection will have "flesh." The author criticizes as incorrect two opposite views. On the one hand, there are Christians who believe that when the resurrection comes, people will have bodies made up of the very same flesh we have now. The Valentinian author rejects that idea because we must divest ourselves of this world, which is not our true home. As Saint Paul said in 1 Corinthians, "Flesh and blood will not inherit the kingdom of God."

On the other hand, there are Christians who say that there is no sense in which the flesh will rise from death. The author rejects this view as well. Instead, he argues that it's the flesh of Jesus that will rise up. The flesh of Jesus is the bread of the Eucharist, in which the Word of God comes to us. By partaking of the bread, Christians participate in the Word, and they join with the Word and so experience resurrection—that is, freedom from this mortal world. The Valentinians believed that Christians do not need to wait for a future resurrection of the dead to experience resurrection; they experience resurrection now, in their communion with Christ in the Eucharist.

Baptism, of course, initiates a person into Christianity and begins the relationship with Christ that leads to *gnōsis* and resurrection. As in the case with the Gnostics, no Valentinian source gives us a clear description of what happened at baptism, but there are enough references to specific actions that we have a pretty good idea. For the most part Valentinian Christian baptism looked like the baptisms of other Christian groups in the 2nd and 3rd centuries.

First, there was a period of instruction and training for the interested candidates. The Greek term for this was *catechesis*. We don't know how long this period of instruction lasted, but some ancient sources tell us that Valentinians required a longer period of catechesis than other Christians did.

If a candidate proved to be worthy of initiation, then there was a more intense period of preparation consisting of "fasts, supplications, prayers, laying on of hands, and kneelings." These acts of physical discipline focused the mind of the candidate and symbolized his or her withdrawal from the sinful practices of the world. They were also designed to remove evil spirits from the person. Like other ancient Christians, the Valentinians believed that non-Christians had demons or unclean spirits within them. It was important that these unclean spirits be removed before baptism. If they were not, then the evil spirits would be sealed up with the person in baptism and become incurable— which would leave the person even worse off than they were before!

When it was time to be baptized, the candidates undressed, which symbolized liberation from the body and giving up one's old life. The candidates also renounced the evil rulers of this world. The candidates were then immersed in water, and the name of the Father, Son, and Holy Spirit was spoken over them. This was considered the single Name of God, and it was also called being "sealed." After the immersion, there was an anointing with oil, which may have been scented oil. The name "Christ" means "anointed one," and through anointing the candidates became Christians. The candidates then dressed themselves, and once again hands were laid upon them with prayers. Then the new Christians received the Eucharist for the first time.

As I said, this is very similar to what we find in other Christian texts from this period. A Valentinian baptism may not have looked much different from any other Christian baptism. Plus, many Valentinians probably were baptized in non-Valentinian congregations. As we saw in the previous lecture, some Valentinian groups were more like study circles or reading groups that supplemented rather than replaced going to a non-Valentinian church. So many of the references to baptism in Valentinian texts may not be to a special Valentinian ritual, but simply to baptism in any Christian church. In that case, what the Valentinian texts give us is how Valentinians understood baptism—what it's true meaning was according to them.

We have already seen one important thing that baptism accomplished according to the Valentinians—removal of unclean spirits and freedom from the evil rulers of this world. Unlike the Gnostics, the Valentinians did not think that the god who created this world was evil and hostile to human beings; instead, they saw him as a more neutral divinity, who is simply lower than the ultimate God, the Father.

But the Valentinians did believe that hostile powers are active in this universe, and that they try to enslave and corrupt human beings. One way the demonic powers enslave us is through fate. When astrologers tell non-Christians what's going to happen to them, they are right because non-Christians are under the power of the rulers and fate. But Christians are not. Before baptism candidates renounce the evil rulers of this world, and when they are sealed by the Name of God in the water, they are freed from the rulers and from the power of fate.

Being sealed with the name of God was another thing that the Valentinians believed happened in baptism. The Name of God was an important symbol in Valentinian theology. Ultimately, the true Name of God is Christ. The Son is the Name of the Father, Valentinus said in the Gospel of Truth. This means that one knows the Father through the Son. The Son reveals who the Father is, just as a name identifies who a person is. But ordinary human names are, however, basically arbitrary. My parents could have chosen any names other than the one they gave me; you don't really learn anything important from that name. Not so with the Name of God—God's Name belongs uniquely to him and truly reveals who he really is.

In baptism, Christians are stamped or sealed with that name. Just as an animal might be branded with the name of its owner, so that it can be returned to the owner if it's lost, so too the Christian bears an inscription that indicates to spiritual beings to whom he or she belongs. The Valentinians also compared this to a coin that bears the stamp of the Emperor, indicating whose coin it is.

But not every Christian received the Name in baptism. Here's a passage from the Gospel According to Philip:

> Anyone who goes down into the water and comes up without receiving anything and says, "I am a Christian," has borrowed the name. But one who receives the Holy Spirit has the name as a gift. A gift does not have to be paid back, but what is borrowed must be paid. This is how it is with us, when one of us experiences a mystery.

The term "mystery" is one that early Christians often used to refer to the rituals that would later become known as "sacraments." Another saying in Philip associates the term mystery with five things: "The Lord did all things by means of a mystery: baptism, chrism [which means "anointing"], Eucharist, ransom, and bridal chamber."

It's not clear whether this refers to five different rituals or simply five kinds of actions that have a deeper meaning—a mystery. In any case, the saying about baptism suggests that the Valentinians believed that some baptisms were incomplete: The person did not actually receive the Holy Spirit and so did not receive the Name of God as a gift, but only as a loan that will be taken back. Maybe this is how Valentinians explained people who left Christianity—they weren't really Christians in the first place. Or maybe this passage is saying that non-Valentinian baptism is incomplete. We saw earlier that the Valentinian theologian Theodotus said that baptism is not enough—you also need *gnōsis*. To truly have the Name of God and thus to be a Christian you need to complete your baptism with the *gnōsis* that Valentinianism offers.

Valentinians also talked about baptism with the language of male and female. For example, consider this passage from the Excerpts from Theodotus:

> So long as the seed is still without form, they say, it is a child of the female. But when it is given form, it is changed into a male and becomes a son of the bridegroom. It is no longer weak and subject to the cosmic powers, whether visible or invisible; rather, having been made male, it becomes a male fruit.

We have already seen the idea that baptism liberates a person from slavery to the cosmic powers, but now we see that the person also moves from being "a child of the female" to being "a male fruit."

This should remind us of the Gospel According to Thomas. That gospel talked about salvation in terms of integration—overcoming division and becoming one. The separation between male and female was one of the divisions that salvation and baptism removed. But, as we have noticed several times, this did not mean uniting two equals—male and female. Rather, this meant returning the female to the more basic male. Jesus said, "Every female that makes itself male will enter the kingdom of heaven." It looks like we have the same idea here among the Valentinians: Baptism and salvation mean overcoming the male-female division by making the female more male.

But there's much more to this in Valentinian thought. First, let's remember that in Valentinian myth the aeons in the Fullness exist in male-female pairs, perhaps even the unknown Father himself. The pairing of aeons in male-female couples provides harmony and stability in the Fullness.

It stands to reason, then, that separating the male and female would be something negative in Valentinian thought, and that's precisely the case. Valentinian thinkers identified the separation of Eve from Adam as the beginning of death. Christ, they said, came to heal this division. Here are two passages from the Gospel According to Philip:

> In the days when Eve was [in] Adam, death did not exist. When she was separated from him, death came into existence. If he [reenters] and takes it unto himself, death will not exist.

Or:

> If the female had not separated from the male, she and the male
> would not die. That being's separation became the source of death.
> Christ came to rectify the separation that had been present since the
> beginning and join the two; and to give life unto those who had died
> by separation and join them together.

Now what does this mean? Does each of us have a lost other half of the other
gender with whom we need to reunite?

The answer is yes, but it's not quite what you might think. It's not the case
that each of us is male or female and must reunite with our partner of the
opposite gender, for our identities as men and women belong to our bodies,
which are not our true selves. Our true selves are our spiritual selves, the
parts of us that originated from above—and our true spiritual selves are all
female. To understand this, we must understand what Genesis is teaching at
a higher level. This is what we find in the Excerpts from Theodotus:

> The Valentinians say that the passage, "In the image of God he
> created them; male and female he made them" (Gen. 1:27), refers to
> the noblest emission of Wisdom, of which the male elements are the
> election and the female the calling. And they call the male elements
> angelic and the female themselves, the superior seed.

> Likewise, in the case of Adam, the male element remained in him,
> but the entire female seed was removed from him and became Eve,
> from whom (derive) the female beings, just as the males (derive)
> from him.

> Therefore, the male elements were united with the Word, but the
> female elements, when they have been made male, unite with the
> angels and enter into the fullness. This is why it is said that the
> woman is changed into a man and the church that is here into angels.

This is a pretty dense statement, so let's unpack each step in what it's saying. When we understand the creation of humanity as male and female in Genesis 1:27 at a higher level, we learn that it refers not to the creation of male and female human beings, but to two created selves: angelic selves and human selves, which are male and female respectively. We human beings are all female elements, and right now we exist in a kind of alienation from our higher, masculine selves, the angels. We are like the divine male-female aeon pairs, but we are all the female aeons and we are separated from our male consorts. We all have a kind of divine alter ego—or, better, we all have a true divine self, our male angels from whom we are now separated.

The separation of Eve from Adam represents that alienation on the level of human difference. The original Adam, created in Genesis 1, indicated the original union of the male angels with the female superior seed, and the separation of Eve from Adam in Genesis 2 demonstrated the separation of the female element from the male, leaving Adam simply male. The Genesis account makes clear that the female element is derivative of the male, as Eve was of Adam. The female selves that we have now are the lower, derivative aspects of our true masculine angelic selves.

Salvation, then, is not simply the reunion of male and female or the coupling of our angelic and spiritual selves. It is, rather, the return of the derivative female element to the higher male element. It's Eve being reincorporated into Adam. And so it's the female being made male.

Here's another example of Valentinians talking about their salvation:

> For as long as we were children of the female only, as though of a shameful coupling, we were incomplete, infantile, unwise, weak, and formless, brought forth like abortions (1 Cor. 15:8); we were children of the woman. But because we have been given form by the Savior, we have become children of the male and of the bridal chamber.

Before people are saved, they are "children of the female"—that is, they have their origin only in their lower female selves. They need to become "children of the male"—reunited with their male angelic selves. The important thing to remember here is that we are all the females who must become male.

So when Jesus said that Mary must make herself male in the Gospel of Thomas, the Valentinians would not have understood this as referring only to Mary, nor as referring only to women; instead, all of us are Mary, who must become male.

The Valentinians understood this process of being made male and reuniting with one's true angelic self as beginning in baptism and being gradually accomplished through the rituals and practices of the Church. Several sources mention a ritual or a symbol of this reunion called the bridal chamber, as we have just seen. When we are saved, we "become children of the male and of the bridal chamber." What did the Valentinians mean by bridal chamber?

Some scholars believe that the Valentinians had a special ritual called the *bridal chamber*. This ritual would have acted out or symbolized or even made effective the union of our lower female selves with our angelic male selves. Enemies of the Valentinians, like Irenaeus, were also convinced that the Valentinians practiced a secret ritual called the bridal chamber, and you can imagine what Irenaeus thought they did during this ritual. He charged that the Valentinians performed ritualized sex.

Most historians, however, believe that there was no separate ritual called the bridal chamber. Now that we have sources from the Valentinians themselves, we can search them for evidence of any ritual activities associated with bridal chamber, and we can't find any. Instead, bridal chamber is probably a symbolic way of speaking about the union of our male and female selves that happens through baptism, Eucharist, and other rituals—and is completed after our deaths. Bridal chamber refers to the highest and most profound meaning of these rituals.

In any event, salvation will not be complete until the end of this world, when our spiritual elements, our female selves, will unite definitively with our angelic bridegrooms and join the aeons of the Fullness as eternal male-female pairs.

> Then the spiritual elements lay aside the souls, and at the same time as the Mother [Wisdom] receives the bridegroom [Jesus], they too receive the bridegrooms, their angels; they enter into the bridal

chamber within the boundary [that is, within the Fullness] and they come to the vision of the Father, becoming intellectual aeons, [entering] into the intellectual and eternal marriage of the pair.

Ultimate salvation is to be the union of the angelic male selves and the human female selves within the Fullness—this is the ultimate bridal chamber.

If the division of Adam and Eve represents on a worldly level the division between the male angelic elements and the female spiritual elements, then it's ordinary marriage that provides an image or representation of this final consummation. Marriage is a mystery, that is, something symbolic, which provides an image not simply of our final salvation, but of the underlying female-male organizing principle of the cosmos. Thanks to sin and sexual desire, that image may exist in the midst of pollution, but it does provide such an image.

The Valentinians were noteworthy among early Christians for the high esteem in which they held marriage. They were not unique on this point, however. Already in the New Testament, the Letter to the Ephesians compares marriage to the relationship between Christ and the Church. Christ is the bridegroom, and the Church is the bride. The author calls this "a great mystery."

It's very likely that this passage in chapter 5 of Ephesians served as one source for the Valentinian idea of the bridal chamber. Notice that it calls marriage a mystery, precisely the term that Valentinians later used for the true power and meaning of Christian rituals. But even more, the Valentinians considered the male angels to be the entourage or bodyguard of the spiritual Jesus. And the Church, of course, is made up of human beings. So when the author of Ephesians says that marriage symbolizes the union of Christ and the Church, the Valentinians understood this to be referring to Jesus and his male angelic companions on the one hand—that's Christ—and their female human selves on the other hand—that's the Church.

Baptism, Eucharist, and marriage were rituals that the Valentinians shared with other Christians. But there was one ritual the Valentinians had that they alone practiced: a ritual for the dying person called "ransom" or "redemption"—in Greek, *apolutrōsis*.

Irenaeus gives us a description of this ritual and says that a group of Valentinians who followed a teacher named Mark practiced it. Of course, it's Irenaeus who tells us that the followers of Mark and other Valentinians had ritual sex in the bridal chamber. But in the case of the ransom ritual, we do have evidence from other texts that corroborates what Irenaeus says.

According to Irenaeus, the dying person was anointed with a mixture of oil and water. These two elements, oil and water, would have reminded the person of his or her baptism, when the Christian was immersed in water and anointed with oil. So one meaning of this ritual was to complete the process of salvation that was begun in baptism.

But the ritual mainly prepared the person for what would happen after death. Remember that, according to the Valentinians, human beings are made up of spirit, soul, and matter, and each element must go to its proper place. The ritual of ransom made the person ready to abandon the material body and leave it here on earth. Freed from the material body, the soul and spirit would ascend.

Next the ritual gave the dying person secret words to say to cosmic rulers and to the Creator God. First, the person would need to say certain things to the evil rulers, so that they will allow the soul and spirit to ascend higher. These words began, "I am a son from the Father, the pre-existing Father and a son in him who is pre-existent."

Once past the rulers, the soul and spirit would ascend to the Creator God and say more words beginning with, "I am a vessel more precious than the female who formed you." At this point the person would leave the soul with the Creator God, and only the spirit would ascend into the Fullness.

There in the Fullness, the spiritual element—the lower female self—would unite with its angelic male self. Salvation would then be complete in the heavenly bridal chamber.

We may have evidence for all this from an amazing inscription that survives on a memorial stone that was found in an ancient tomb in Rome. It's dated to the 2nd century, and it commemorates the death of a Christian woman named

Flavia Sophe. According to the inscription, Flavia was "eager to see the divine faces of the aeons," and in death she entered the bridal chamber of the Father. Flavia had prepared for this by being "anointed in the bath of Christ with imperishable ointment." Flavia was certainly a Valentinian Christian who had been baptized, but perhaps she had also experienced the Valentinian ritual of ransom.

The Valentinians are the first Christians in history known to have developed a Christian ritual for the dying. The ransom ritual for dying Christians was a unique feature of Valentinian Christianity.

But the Valentinians were like other Christians in many ways. They taught many of the same doctrines—like the resurrection of the dead and the divinity of Christ—and they read the same Bible. But they understood these things in their own way. In the next lecture, we'll explore how Valentinians and other Christians debated the Bible, the resurrection of the dead, and the nature of Christian authority.

Valentinian Views on Christian Theology
Lecture 14

T he Valentinians frustrated Christian leaders, such as Irenaeus, because it was so difficult to tell that they were, in fact, "false" Christians. The Valentinians professed the same doctrines as other Christians, but they had different interpretations for these doctrines. Irenaeus presents this problem as misinterpretation on the part of the Valentinians, while all genuine Christians agreed on the truth. But in fact, during the early centuries of their religion, Christians were still trying to work out many of their teachings. In antiquity, the Valentinians participated in lively debates about various aspects of Christian theology. To understand and appreciate what the Valentinians taught, we must put them in the context of the diverse Christian beliefs of their day.

Christian Views of Resurrection

- Christianity began when followers of Jesus believed that he had risen from the dead after his crucifixion. They concluded that Jesus's resurrection was the "first fruits" of a more general resurrection. But how would people rise from the dead? Would they have bodies, and if so, what kind? Christians generally agreed that their own resurrection would be similar to that of Jesus, but that did not solve the problem because how Jesus rose from the dead was also unclear.

- The apostle Paul gives us a view of the resurrection that is spiritual and transformative. In 1 Corinthians, Paul first refutes Christians who believed that there would be no resurrection of the dead, at least not one that involves the body. Paul reminds the Corinthians that he and other believers saw Jesus after his death; thus, they know that Jesus was raised. And he says that the resurrection is the basic hope of Christians: Without it, the Christian faith is futile.

- Then, Paul turns to the problem of what kind of bodies people will have when they rise.

o He first points out that there are different kinds of bodies, made up of different kinds of materials. The flesh of fish is different from the flesh of human beings, and the bodies of heavenly beings, such as the sun, are not the same as the bodies of earthly beings.

o He further says that the bodies we have in the resurrection will not be the same as our current bodies. The current body is related to the resurrected body as a seed is related to a plant. The seed is not the same as the plant, but when you sow the seed in the ground, it is transformed into the plant. After our current body of soul is sown into the ground at death, it will be transformed into a body of spirit at the resurrection. There is continuity but also a major transformation.

o Paul is certain that the resurrected body will not have flesh similar to what we have now: "Flesh and blood will not inherit the kingdom of God" (1 Cor. 15:50).

- It's important to note that Paul never mentions that Jesus's tomb was empty, which would surely indicate that the flesh of Jesus was somehow raised. Most historians conclude that Paul did not know of any claim that Jesus's tomb was empty. Instead, Paul based his idea of what Jesus's resurrected body was like on the appearances of Jesus to himself and others. In Paul's mind, Jesus had a spiritual body, not one of flesh; we, too, will have spiritual bodies in the resurrection.

- If Paul's view of the resurrection was spiritual and transformative, the gospels tend to have a view that is more fleshly and stable. In the gospels, the tomb is empty: It's obvious that Jesus's fleshly body was brought back to life. And his body is less transformed than what Paul envisioned. Jesus walks, talks, and eats after his death.

Valentinian View of Resurrection
- This question of the resurrected body was complicated for the Valentinians because they believed that human beings were made

of three elements: matter, soul, and spirit. Because they knew that matter would eventually perish, Valentinians could not follow the idea of a resurrection of the flesh. They believed that the only element of a person that would enter the Fullness is spirit. What did it mean, then, for this spiritual element to be resurrected?

- A Valentinian teacher tries to answer this question in a letter addressed to a student named Rheginus; this letter is known as the Treatise on Resurrection.

The idea of the empty tomb would become one of the most important claims of Christianity; it was proof that Jesus had risen from the dead.

  ○ The teacher first explains that Jesus came to reveal the truth to human beings and to manifest the superior element in us, that is, our spirit or intellect. Jesus demonstrated that we should turn away from the corruptible realm of the flesh and, instead, seek the eternal realm of the spirit. By doing this, the Savior "swallowed up" death, made visible to us what is invisible, and gave us the way to immortality.

  ○ According to this view, the point is not that Jesus had any kind of body after his death. Instead, it's the movement from the material world of corruption to the spiritual world of truth that constituted the resurrection of Jesus. The same is true of our resurrection.

- o The Valentinian teacher tells us that this world is not our true home and our bodies are not our true selves. The real part of us is our spiritual selves, which are present in the material world only temporarily. Further, our spiritual selves are like rays from the sun, which is Jesus. Resurrection is the process of the rays being "retracted" back to their origin. This resurrection of the spirit eliminates any resurrections of the soul or flesh.

- Obviously, the return of the rays to the sun, or the return of our spirits to the Fullness, is an ongoing process, happening right now. Christians need not wait for some future resurrection of the dead at the end of time. They can have resurrection now—if they receive *gnōsis*, recognize their true spiritual nature, and contemplate higher reality.

Christian Views of the Old Testament
- Another major question that early Christians faced was what to do with the Jewish Bible.
  - o When Paul and other early believers agreed that Gentile Christians did not need to convert to Judaism and follow the Law, they thought that they were building on what the Bible taught about Gentiles, the Messiah, and the coming day of the Lord.

  - o But during the 2nd century, there were more Gentile Christians and fewer Jewish Christians. These Gentile believers often did not have much prior exposure to the Jewish Bible, and some began to question the relevance of the Bible and its God to their Christian faith.

- As we saw in an earlier lecture, the Christian teacher Marcion argued that the Jewish Bible had no relevance for Gentile Christians. The god of the Old Testament was a relentlessly demanding god of righteousness, who severely punished human beings for failing to fulfill his Law. Jesus came as the Son of a more forgiving and loving God. He paid the price for our sins to the Old Testament god, and he brought a message of forgiveness and grace. Therefore, Marcion said, Christians no longer needed the Jewish Bible as Scripture.

- The Gnostics did not discard the Bible. They believed that the Bible, especially Genesis, gave them information about the origins of the cosmos and humanity and about the history of salvation. But they also believed that the Bible required corrections for errors made by Moses.

- Other Christians, such as Irenaeus, continued to believe that the God of the Old Testament was the Father of Jesus Christ and that the Jewish Bible was the inspired Word of God. The same God who sent Jesus gave the Jews this book—and now it also belonged to the Christians. These Christians read the Bible as a story that leads to the coming of Jesus and interpreted passages about the Law symbolically, not literally.

Valentinian View of the Old Testament

- The Valentinian view of the Old Testament comes to us in a letter from the theologian Ptolemy to a non-Valentinian Christian woman named Flora. Ptolemy opens the letter by explaining that Christians disagree about the status of the Old Testament. He identifies two positions that he considers wrong.
  - The first is that the Old Testament comes from the perfect God and Father. This is the position of Irenaeus and other Christians who used allegorical interpretation in their reading of the Bible. According to Ptolemy, this position is incorrect because the Old Testament itself is imperfect and required fulfillment in Jesus. Therefore, it could not come from the perfect ultimate God.

  - The other false position is that the Old Testament comes from the devil. This is almost certainly a reference to the Gnostics. Ptolemy says that this position is wrong because Christian texts teach that the god who created this world is just and hates evil.

○ Ptolemy stakes out a middle position: The Jewish Law does not come from the ultimate perfect God, nor does it come from an evil god.

• Using what Jesus says in the gospels, Ptolemy argues that the Old Testament has no single author. Rather, only some of the material comes from God. Other rules and commandments come from Moses, and still others are traditions of the Jewish elders. It's only the material that comes from God that applies to Christians, and this material itself can be divided into three categories.

○ First, there is legislation that is pure but imperfect. It's good and comes from God, but Jesus needed to come to fulfill it. A good example of this is the Ten Commandments. They come from God and are entirely good, but Jesus came to bring them to perfection.

○ Second, there is legislation that contains injustice and that Jesus abolished. The best examples of this are the Commandments that require retribution—an act that is violent and unjust.

○ Finally, there is legislation that's symbolic, consisting mainly of ritual laws. Ptolemy argues that these laws should be understood allegorically, as symbolic references to moral principles; they are not meant to be followed literally.

• Then, Ptolemy asks: What is the nature of the god who would establish such laws? This god cannot be evil because the laws he established have good principles in them. But this god also cannot be the ultimate perfect God because the laws he established required fulfillment by Christ and because Christ abolished some of them. Thus, Ptolemy concludes, this god must be somewhere between good and evil; this god is simply just.

Suggested Reading

Dunderberg, *Beyond Gnosticism*, chapter 5.

Layton, *The Gnostic Scriptures*, "Ptolemy's Epistle to Flora" and "Treatise on Resurrection (Epistle to Rheginus)."

Meyer, ed., *The Nag Hammadi Scriptures*, "The Treatise on Resurrection."

Pagels, *The Gnostic Gospels*, chapter 1.

Thomassen, *The Spiritual Seed*, chapter 11.

Questions to Consider

1. Why might ancient people have found one or another of the early Christian views of resurrection persuasive or unconvincing?

2. What ideas about the Jewish Scriptures did all early Christians share? On what points did they differ?

Valentinian Views on Christian Theology
Lecture 14—Transcript

The Valentinians frustrated Christian leaders like Bishop Irenaeus of Lyons because it was so hard to tell that they were in fact false Christians—false according to Irenaeus, of course. The Valentinians, Irenaeus complained, use the same words we do, but they mean different things. That is, Valentinians professed the same doctrines as other Christians—things like the divinity of Christ, the resurrection of the dead, the importance of the Eucharist—but they interpreted these doctrines differently from how Irenaeus and his allies did.

Irenaeus presents this problem as the Valentinians just having a wrong interpretation, while all true Christians agree on the true one. But in fact, during the early centuries of their religion Christians were still trying to figure out what many of their teachings really mean—and they are still doing so today. In antiquity the Valentinians were participating in lively debates about various aspects of Christian theology. To understand and appreciate what the Valentinians taught, we have to put them in the context of the diverse Christian beliefs of their day.

Let's consider first the resurrection of the dead. Christianity began when followers of Jesus believed that Jesus had risen from the dead after his crucifixion. They concluded that Jesus's resurrection was "the first fruits" of a more general resurrection. But what did this mean? How would people rise from the dead? Would they have bodies? If so, what kind? And when will this happen? Christians generally agreed that their own resurrection would be similar to that of Jesus, but that did not really solve the problem because how Jesus rose from the dead was also not clear.

We should start with the New Testament, and we'll find that it contains different ways of understanding the resurrection of Jesus and that of Christians. We can put these on a spectrum ranging from highly spiritual and transformative on the one side to very fleshly and stable on the other side.

For a view of the resurrection that is spiritual and transformative, we can turn to Paul, the 15th chapter of his First Letter to the Corinthians. In this letter, Paul first has to refute Christians who believed that there would be no resurrection of the dead, at least not one that involves the body. In response, Paul reminds the Corinthians that he and other believers saw Jesus after his death, so they know Jesus was raised. And he says that the resurrection is the basic hope of Christians; without it, the Christian faith is futile.

But then Paul turns to the problem of what kind of body people will have when they rise. He first points out that there are in fact different kinds of bodies, made up of different kinds of materials. The flesh of fish is different from the flesh of human beings, and the bodies of heavenly beings like the sun and the moon are not the same as the bodies of earthly beings like us.

He goes on to say that the same is true of the resurrection. The bodies we have in the resurrection will not be the same as our current bodies. He calls our current bodies *psuchic* in Greek—made up of *psuchē* or soul. Our resurrected bodies will be *pneumatic*—made up of *pneuma* or spirit. The current body is related to the resurrected body as a seed is related to a full plant. The seed is not the same as the plant, but when you sow the seed in the ground, it's transformed into the plant. So, too, after our current body of soul is sown into the ground at death, it will be transformed into a body of spirit at the resurrection. There is continuity, but a major transformation: "We will all be changed," Paul says.

One thing Paul is sure of: The resurrected body will not have flesh like what we have now. "Flesh and blood," he says, "cannot inherit the kingdom of God."

It's important to note that during this entire discussion Paul never mentions that Jesus's tomb was empty. This would be a very relevant point to his argument because surely the empty tomb would indicate that the flesh of Jesus was somehow raised. But Paul never mentions this. Most historians conclude that Paul did not know of any claim that Jesus's tomb was empty. The idea of the empty tomb would, of course, become one of the most important claims at the heart of Christianity. It was proof that Jesus had really risen from the dead. Paul did not deny that the tomb was empty—he just doesn't seem to have known about it. Instead, Paul based his idea of what Jesus's resurrected body was like on the appearances of Jesus to him and others. And so to his mind, Jesus had a spiritual body, not one of flesh, and so we, too, will have spiritual bodies in the resurrection.

If Paul's view of the resurrection was spiritual and transformative, the gospels tend to have a view that is more fleshly and stable. In the gospels the tomb is empty: it's obvious that Jesus's fleshly body was brought back to life. The stone that covered the tomb was rolled away, suggesting that Jesus had to walk out through an open entrance. In the Gospel of Luke, the resurrected Jesus walks with two disciples, and for a while they think that he's an ordinary man. And he later asks the disciples to touch him and see that he has flesh and bones and is not a ghost. In the Gospel of John, Jesus eats fish with his followers. So here, the resurrected body is made of flesh, and it's less transformed than what Paul envisioned. Jesus walks and talks and eats and can be touched. And yet there is some transformation because Jesus can appear and vanish in Luke, and in John he shows up in a closed room.

So you can see that Christians have available to them in the New Testament different ways of understanding the resurrection. Throughout history, some Christians have emphasized, like Paul, how different the resurrected body will be, how spiritual and transformed, and other times they have stressed, like the gospels, that the very flesh we have now will be raised, just even better. All these views were circulating during the time of the Valentinians.

You can figure that this question would be complicated for the Valentinians because they believed that human beings were made up of three elements: matter (which is our flesh), soul, and spirit. They knew that matter would eventually perish, so Valentinians could not follow the idea of a resurrection of the flesh, as a literal reading of the gospels would suggest. They believed that the only element of the person that would enter the Fullness is spirit. So what did it mean for this spiritual element to be resurrected?

A Valentinian teacher tries to answer this question in a text called Treatise on Resurrection, which was found at Nag Hammadi. This text is about the resurrection, but it's not really a treatise. Instead, it's a letter, addressed to a student or disciple named Rheginus. Rheginus has asked the teacher (whose name we don't know) about resurrection, and this letter is the teacher's response.

Like other Christians, this Valentinian theologian starts with the resurrection of Jesus. What was it like? The teacher explains that Jesus came to reveal the truth to human beings and to manifest to us the superior element in us, that is, our spirit or intellect. Jesus demonstrated to us that we should turn away from the corruptible realm of the flesh and instead seek the eternal realm of the spirit. By doing this, the Savior swallowed up death, made visible to us what's invisible, and gave us the way to immortality.

According to this view, the point really is not that Jesus had any kind of body after his death. Instead, it's the movement from the material world of corruption to the spiritual world of truth that constituted the resurrection of Jesus. He raised himself up from the body to the spirit.

The same is true for us. Here's what the author says:

> Because we are visibly present in this world, we wear the garment of the world. From the Savior we radiate like beams of light, and we are sustained by him until our sunset, our death in this life. We are drawn upward by him, like rays by the sun, and nothing holds us down. This is the resurrection of the spirit, which swallows the resurrection of the soul and the resurrection of the flesh.

This is an amazing image. This world is not our true home, not our true selves. Instead, the real part of us is our spiritual selves, which are present in this material world only temporarily. Our bodies are like garments that we are wearing and that we can remove. And our spiritual selves are like rays from the sun, who is Jesus. Resurrection is the process of the rays withdrawing from the world and being retracted, so to speak, back into their origin, the sun. This resurrection of the spirit "swallows"—that is, it does away with any resurrections of the soul or the flesh. The author goes on to say, as Valentinus did, that ultimately this material world is not real; it's an apparition. Resurrection into the realm of spirit is what's real.

Obviously, the return of the rays to the sun, or the return of our spirits to the Fullness, is an ongoing process, happening right now. And in fact, Christians need not wait for some future resurrection of the dead at the end of time. They can have resurrection now if they receive *gnōsis*, recognize their true spiritual nature, and contemplate higher reality. "Leave the state of dispersion and bondage," the teacher tells Rheginus, "and then you already have resurrection."

We saw in the last lecture that some Valentinians had a ritual that prepared the dying person for the ascent of the spiritual element into the Fullness and union with its male angelic self. The Valentinians, then, did not think that the resurrection that Christ brought revived a dead soul and body; instead, resurrection was available now as you turn away from this material world to the eternal realm.

Another major question that we have seen early Christians face is what to do with the Jewish Bible, what some Christians began to call the Old Testament. When Paul and other early Jesus believers agreed that Gentile Christians did not need to convert to Judaism and follow the Law, they believed that they were building on what the Bible taught about Gentiles, the Messiah, and the coming day of the Lord. But during the 2nd century, more and more Christians were Gentiles, and the number of Jewish Christians became very small. These Gentile believers often did not have much prior exposure to the Jewish Bible. And because they did not need to follow its laws about diet and Temple sacrifice, some began to question the relevance of the Bible and its God to their Christian faith.

Early in the course we met Marcion, a Christian teacher who argued that the Jewish Bible had no relevance for Gentile Christians. The God of the Old Testament was not the Father of Jesus Christ. Instead, he was a relentlessly demanding god of righteousness, who severely punished human beings for failing to fulfill his Law. Jesus came as the Son of a more forgiving and loving God. He paid the price for our sins to the Old Testament God, and he brought a message of forgiveness and grace. Therefore, Marcion said, Christians no longer need the Jewish Bible as Scripture. All they need to read is a gospel about Jesus and the letters of Paul, who preached salvation by faith in Christ, not by works of the Law.

The Gnostics, we have seen, did not discard the Bible as Marcion did. On the matter of the God of the Old Testament, they were more radical than Marcion: They called this god the evil and ignorant Ialdabaōth, not an overly righteous God. But as for the Bible itself, they still read it—and rewrote it. The Gnostics believed that the Bible, especially Genesis, gave them information about the origins of the cosmos and humanity and about the history of salvation, as long as they corrected it for the errors that Moses made.

Other Christians, of course, continued to believe, as Paul did, that the God of the Old Testament was the Father of Jesus Christ. Irenaeus is a good example of these Christians. Irenaeus and people like him believed that the Jewish Bible was the inspired Word of God. The same God who sent Jesus gave the Jews this book—and now it belonged to the Christians as well. But if Christians did not have to do many of the things that the Bible commanded, how should they read it and make it useful to them?

These Christians read the Bible as a story that leads to the coming of Jesus: there was the creation and fall in Genesis, then God's covenants with the people of Israel, and his promises to them of a future messiah. All of this, they argued, was leading to Jesus.

As for all the laws about a kosher diet and making sacrifices in the Temple and so on, such Christians understood these rules to be symbolic, not literal. A Christian text from the early 100s called the Epistle of Barnabas explains why the laws about diet that Moses commanded are still relevant to Christians, even though they do not have to follow them literally. For example, in Leviticus, Moses commands that the Israelites not eat swine. Moses, the author of Barnabas explains, "spoke spiritually." The command not to eat swine does not mean you should not eat swine. Rather, it means that you should not associate with people who are like swine—that is, who only care about God when they need something but otherwise ignore God. And when Moses commanded not to eat the eagle or hawk, he was spiritually saying that you should avoid people who do not grow or earn their own food, but rob food from others.

Christians interpreted other kinds of Old Testament passages symbolically as well, especially so that they would refer to Christ or the Church. Abraham's near-sacrifice of his son Isaac in Genesis they considered symbolic of God the Father sending his son to die for humanity. Or, when the Israelites celebrate Passover with a roasted lamb, this, too, was a symbol for Christ, the Lamb of God. The cross-shaped spit upon which people roasted lamb pointed to the cross on which Jesus died.

We call this kind of symbolic reading of the Bible *allegorical interpretation.* Allegory comes from a Greek phrase that means "say something different." In allegorical interpretation, the biblical text is understood to be saying something different from what it literally says. Allegorical interpretation allowed Christians to maintain a connection with the Jewish Bible and make it relevant to them and their Christian faith. For Christians who believed that the Old Testament came from the same God who sent Jesus, it was an essential tool for applying the Bible to their lives.

What did the Valentinians teach about the Old Testament? On this point we have a remarkable letter from the Valentinian theologian Ptolemy to a woman named Flora. Ptolemy was one of Valentinus's most famous students, and he was active in Rome in the middle of the 2nd century. You may recall that we looked at Ptolemy's version of the Valentinian myth in some detail. We have Ptolemy's letter to Flora in the original Greek because a later Christian author quoted it completely. We know that Flora, the woman to whom Ptolemy wrote the letter, was a Christian, but she was not a Valentinian. Ptolemy uses his letter to explain what Valentinians think about the Old Testament and to invite Flora to learn more about Valentinian thought.

Ptolemy opens the letter by explaining that Christians do disagree about the status of the Law or the Old Testament. He identifies two positions that he considers wrong. One is that the Old Testament comes from the perfect God and Father. This is the position of Irenaeus and other Christians who used allegorical interpretation to interpret the Bible. But Ptolemy says that this position is incorrect because the Old Testament itself is imperfect and required fulfillment in Jesus. Therefore, it could not come from the perfect ultimate God.

The other false position, according to Ptolemy, is that the Old Testament comes from the devil. This is almost certainly a reference to the Gnostics because they considered Ialdabaōth, the God of the Old Testament, to be evil. Ptolemy says this position is wrong as well because the Gospel of John and other Christian texts teach that the god who created this world is just and hates evil. Therefore, the Gnostics are wrong, too.

So Ptolemy sets himself up to stake out a middle position: The Jewish Law does not come from the ultimate perfect God, nor does it come from an evil god. Now it sounds like Ptolemy may have a position like that of Marcion— the Old Testament comes from a righteous God who is not the Father of Jesus. And in fact, his view is close to that of Marcion, as we'll see. But unlike Marcion, Ptolemy and the Valentinians still retain the Old Testament as scripture for Christians.

Ptolemy bases his case on the teachings of Jesus in the gospels. Using what Jesus says, Ptolemy argues that the Old Testament has no single author. Rather, only some of the material comes from God. Other rules and commandments come from Moses, and still others are traditions of the Jewish elders. So the Old Testament cannot be read as a single unified text; rather, some of its teachings come from Moses, some from the elders of the nation, and some from God. It's only the material that comes from God that applies to Christians.

This part of Ptolemy's teaching is amazingly modern. When he distinguished among different kinds of materials in the Old Testament, Ptolemy teaches something like what modern biblical scholars say. They, too, argue that the Bible has no single source. Rather, even individual books are made up of different traditions that later editors have put together. Ptolemy's view is a simpler version of that way of looking at the Bible.

Now, once Ptolemy has established that only some of the rules and commandments in the Old Testament come from God, he divides even the material that God wrote into three kinds. First, there's legislation that's pure, but imperfect. It's good and comes from God, but Jesus needed to come to fulfill it. A good example of this is the Ten Commandments. They come from God and are entirely good, but Jesus came to bring them to perfection. For instance, the Ten Commandments say, "Do not commit murder"—which is perfectly good—but Jesus brought this to perfection by commanding his followers not even to hate other people.

Second, there's legislation that contains injustice and that Jesus abolished. The best examples of this are the commandments that require retribution—such as the commandment in Leviticus to pluck out someone's eye in retaliation for plucking out someone else's eye, or the commandment to execute a murderer. Certainly, the crimes of murder and plucking out an eye are worthy of punishment, but the act of retribution is equally violent and unjust. Therefore, Christ abolished this kind of law.

Finally, there's legislation that's symbolic. This consists mainly of ritual laws, like circumcision, Temple sacrifices, dietary laws, and so on. Just as we saw in the Epistle of Barnabas, Ptolemy argues that these laws should be understood allegorically, as symbolic references to moral principles, and they are not meant to be followed literally.

To summarize, Ptolemy recognizes that only some of the rules and commandments in the Old Testament come from God. And out of these, some are pure but required fulfillment by Christ, some contain unjust elements and have been abolished by Christ, and some are purely symbolic. All of this sounds very much like what other Christians believed, especially the interpretation of many laws as symbolic.

But then Ptolemy introduces the distinctively Valentinian approach to the Old Testament. What is the nature of the god who would establish such a law, he asks? He says that this god cannot be evil because the laws he established have good principles in them. That position opposes the Gnostics. But this god also cannot be the ultimate perfect and good God because the laws he established required fulfillment by Christ, and Christ even abolished some of them. That opposes Christians like Irenaeus. So, Ptolemy concludes, this god must be an intermediate god, somewhere between good and evil—this god is simply just.

But this position sounds a lot like that of Marcion, who said that the God of the Old Testament is merely righteous and is not the Father of Jesus Christ. According to Marcion, the just God of the Old Testament is completely separate from the Father of Jesus Christ, and we need to be saved from his unforgiving punishments. Ptolemy does not believe this, and so he goes on to say that the God of the Old Testament may not be the ultimate perfect God, but he came into being in the image of the higher God. Unlike Marcion, Ptolemy and the Valentinians argue that the God of the Old Testament is lower than the ultimate God, but somehow related to him, not foreign to him.

Now, let's remember that Flora, the recipient of the letter, was not a Valentinian Christian. So she may have been puzzled by Ptolemy's claim that the God of the Old Testament is not the ultimate God, but somehow comes from the ultimate God. Ptolemy hoped that Flora would not only be puzzled, but also be intrigued. He wanted her to become his student and learn more about Valentinian teachings. At the end of the letter, he tells Flora that he can teach her about how the ultimate God engendered this lower god and other beings—if she proves worthy of learning these higher truths.

Here we see one way that a Valentinian teacher recruited new followers from among non-Valentinian Christians. He raised an important question of dispute among Christians—in this case, the status of the Old Testament and its God. He then refuted the opposing positions and argued for the Valentinian one. He then invited the potential student to learn more from him about these important doctrines, and he made this advanced Valentinian teaching sound like a special privilege. "In the future these teachings will be of the greatest help to you," Ptolemy told Flora—"at least if, like good, rich soil that has received fertile seeds, you bear fruit." Did Flora bear fruit and prove to be worthy of Valentinian teaching? Was she enticed by Ptolemy's letter and pursue further study with him? Unfortunately, we don't know.

From Ptolemy's letter and from other stuff that we've seen, it's clear that there were a variety of Christian teachers and theologians competing for followers and students during the 2nd century. These Christian teachers were, of course, competing not only with each other, but also with non-Christian teachers and philosophers, who also offered interested people instruction in matters like God and ethics. Teachers offered to lead students in reading sacred and philosophical texts and in becoming more virtuous and happy people.

These diverse teachers all thought that they were offering the truth. Ptolemy believed that the Valentinian view of the Old Testament God was the correct one, and that the views of the Gnostics and Marcion were false. But there was also money and prestige at stake. If Flora chose to study with Ptolemy, she undoubtedly would have given him financial support in return for his wisdom and guidance. If, as we suspect, Flora was a remarkably well-educated and financially prosperous woman, then if she joined the Valentinian school, her presence would help attract more followers.

So how did Christian teachers like Ptolemy present themselves as authoritative? Why should someone like Flora have considered Ptolemy worthy of her discipleship? We have seen that Valentinus claimed that his wisdom came from his mystical experiences of God. Valentinus had experienced *gnōsis*, and thus he was a trustworthy guide to others who sought *gnōsis* for themselves.

Valentinus's students such as Ptolemy emphasized that they had studied with Valentinus. And they claimed that the tradition that they received from Valentinus came from the apostles. That is, the Valentinians were among the first Christians to claim what came to be known as "apostolic succession." Apostolic succession is the idea that the apostles learned the truth of Christianity from Jesus. In turn, the apostles taught a select group of special students to pass on their teachings. In turn, those students taught their own followers. And so on—from Jesus, through the apostles, to the teachers of today.

In the case of the Valentinians, they claimed that their teacher, Valentinus, had studied with a man named Theudas, and that in turn Theudas had been a disciple of Paul. The chain of teachers reaching back to Paul authenticated the Valentinian doctrine as having roots in the time of the apostles, and coming ultimately from Jesus himself.

And so in his letter to Flora, Ptolemy referred to his teaching as "the apostolic tradition, which even we have received by succession." And the author of the Treatise on Resurrection told his student Rheginus that he received his doctrine on the resurrection "through the generosity of the Lord," and he was now passing this on to his students.

I and other scholars believe that the Valentinians had a special ritual of anointing, called *chrism*, that symbolized this handing down of tradition. Here's a passage from the Gospel According to Philip:

> The chrism is superior to baptism, for it is from the word "chrism" that we have been called "Christians," certainly not because of the word "baptism." And it is because of the chrism that "the Christ" has his name. For the Father anointed the Son, and the Son anointed the apostles, and the apostles anointed us. He who has been anointed possesses everything. He possesses the resurrection, the light, the cross, the Holy Spirit. The Father gave him this in the bridal chamber.

This passage summarizes the remarkable claims of the Valentinians. From the Father to the Son, from the Son to the apostles, and from the apostles to the Valentinians—the anointing that the Valentinians offered contained everything, including resurrection. The Valentinians offered a higher salvation of *gnōsis*. Christians could receive everything the Father has to give right now, in the bridal chamber.

Did Flora accept this invitation from Ptolemy? As I said, we don't know. We do know, however, that the Valentinians did have success in recruiting women. We have seen, too, that the imagery of male and female played an important role in Valentinian thought.

In the next lecture I want to examine one particular early Christian woman who famously appears in Valentinian literature and other early Christian texts—Mary Magdalene, possibly the favorite apostle of Jesus.

Mary Magdalene as an Apostle of *Gnōsis*
Lecture 15

M ary Magdalene, one of the few original disciples of Jesus who was a woman, appears in many Valentinian and other "heretical" texts. For example, the Gospel According to Philip tells us: "There were three who always walked with the Lord: Mary his mother and his sister and the Magdalene, the one who was called his companion." In another passage, the apostles wonder why Jesus loves Mary more than he does them. There is also an ancient Christian text called the Gospel According to Mary, in which Jesus gives Mary Magdalene a special revelation. In this lecture, we'll see why Mary was so prominent in these alternative gospels and why she and the apostle Peter are often portrayed as antagonists.

Witnesses to the Resurrection

- To early Christians, the Greek word *apostolos* ("apostle") simply referred to an envoy or a representative. Christian apostles were those sent by Jesus to proclaim his message. The earliest Christian author, Paul, uses the term to refer to Christians who had seen Jesus after his resurrection and whom the risen Jesus had commissioned to spread the gospel. According to Paul (1 Cor. 15:3–9), there were far more than twelve of these people.
  - It's important to note that Paul seems to consider the order in which Jesus appeared to people after his death to be significant.

  - That Jesus appeared to Paul last—perhaps about three years after the crucifixion—indicated that he was "the least of the apostles." Presumably Peter, the first person to see Jesus, was greatest among the apostles.

- When we turn to the New Testament Gospels, the picture becomes more complicated. All the gospels tell us that Mary Magdalene, sometimes accompanied by other women, found the empty tomb and brought the news to the male disciples. In Matthew and John, Mary—not Peter—is the first disciple to see the risen Jesus. As noted, Paul shows that at least some early Christians considered the order in which Jesus appeared to the apostles to be important; thus, we can see the makings here of a rivalry between Mary and Peter.

The Valentinian View of Mary

- A passage in the Gospel According to Philip reads as follows:
    - As for the Wisdom who is called "the barren one," she is the mother [of the] angels. And the companion of the [...] Mary Magdalene. [...loved] her more than [all] the disciples [and used to]

In the Christian tradition, Mary Magdalene is often called "the apostle to the apostles" because she brought the good news of Jesus's resurrection to the male apostles.

kiss her [often] on her [...]. The rest of [the disciples...]. They said to him, "Why do you love her more than all of us?" The savior answered and said to them, "Why do I not love you like her? When a blind man and one who sees are both together in darkness, they are no different from one another. When the light comes, then the one who sees will see the light, and the one who is blind will remain in darkness."

- As you recall, the Valentinians believed that we all have higher, more divine selves. These are our angelic selves, which Wisdom emitted, along with our human selves. Our higher angelic selves are designated male, and our lower human selves are designated female. Thus, the Valentinians talked about salvation as a reunion of male and female selves.

281

- This passage in the Gospel According to Philip refers to Wisdom producing the angels, our higher male selves, who form a kind of retinue for Jesus in the Valentinian myth. Thus, this passage seems to present Jesus and Mary as having a special relationship, but not one that symbolizes male and female divine principles. Rather, it symbolizes the relationship between our angelic male selves and human female selves. We are all Mary Magdalene—all of us are called to have a special relationship with our higher angelic self, represented by Jesus.

- The Gospel According to Philip accepts the idea that the real people Jesus and Mary had a stronger and closer relationship than Jesus did with Peter and the male disciples. Like the Gospel of Thomas, it depicts the male disciples as questioning this relationship. The Gospel of Philip makes the bond between Jesus and Mary a symbol for true salvation.
  - Consider this passage from Philip: "Three women always used to walk with the Lord—Mary his mother, his sister, and the Magdalene, who is called his companion. For 'Mary' is the name of his sister and his mother, and it is the name of his partner."

  - The name *Mary* becomes a symbol for the female in relationship to God. But this is not a female divine being. Rather, we are all female in our relationship to the Lord and to our higher angelic selves.

  - When Peter and the male disciples question the relationship between Jesus and Mary, they reveal that they do not yet understand the higher meaning of this relationship. They are still in darkness, in need of the light that the Valentinian myth can provide.

The Gospel According to Mary
- Conflict between Mary Magdalene and Peter and the other male disciples becomes a primary theme in the Gospel According to Mary—the only early Christian gospel attributed to a woman. We

have two short Greek fragments of this text and a longer fragment that is a Coptic translation.

- Although the Gospel of Mary has some ideas similar to Gnostic myth, it does not contain any of the distinctive teachings of the Gnostics. It shows, in fact, more signs of contact with the Gospel According to Thomas and with Valentinian ideas.

- At the beginning of the surviving text, Jesus is teaching the disciples after his death and resurrection. When Jesus finishes his discourse, he tells the disciples to go forth and preach the gospel; then, he goes away.
  - Rather than going out to preach, the disciples become distressed and weep. They fear that people will kill them as they did Jesus. Mary stands up and tells them that God's grace will protect them; thus, they should be resolute.

  - Peter then asks Mary to reveal any teachings that Jesus gave her that he and the other apostles do not know. Mary tells how the Savior appeared to her in a vision and told her that the human soul must ascend past hostile powers to reach its heavenly home.

  - When Mary finishes her revelation, Andrew and Peter charge that she is lying. Andrew says that the ideas she claims that Jesus taught her are strange, and Peter argues that Jesus would not reveal such things to a woman in private.

  - But the apostle Levi comes to Mary's defense. He accuses Peter of being prone to anger and says that Jesus did, in fact, love Mary more than he loved the men because he knew her so well. Levi tells his colleagues that they need to go preach the good news. In the Coptic translation, the gospel ends with all the apostles going forth to preach; in the Greek fragment, only Levi does so.

- Clearly, there are two issues that cause conflict between Mary and the male disciples: the content of the teaching that she reveals, which Andrew calls "strange," and the fact that Mary, a woman, is teaching it.

- As mentioned, in the Gospel According to Mary, the resurrected Jesus gives teachings to the disciples that are not recorded in the New Testament gospels, and what he teaches sounds similar to what we have seen in Valentinianism.
  - First, Jesus says that matter and the material world are ultimately not real. At some point, matter will dissolve and cease to exist.

  - Second, Jesus explains that what we call "sin" is actually what we produce when we fall into ignorance and turn away from the Good.

  - Third, Jesus condemns passion—meaning unhealthy emotions, such as anger or resentment—as arising from matter and ignorance. These emotions lead to immoral acts. Instead, Jesus urges his disciples to be content and inwardly peaceful.

  - Finally, the Savior tells the apostles to go and preach the good news, and he warns them not to add any rules or laws beyond the things that he has commanded.

- The secret teaching that Jesus reveals to Mary is even more similar to what we have seen among Valentinians. The Savior tells Mary that the human soul will need to ascend past certain hostile powers, such as Darkness, Desire, and Ignorance. These powers try to prevent the soul from ascending to its true home, but when the soul tells them about its true nature, it can pass them by. This seems similar to the Valentinian ritual for the dying that we studied earlier.

- The Gospel According to Mary seems to teach a theology very similar to that of the Valentinians, but one that may not actually come from the Valentinians. Instead, we see that some Valentinian ideas, such as the origin of sin in ignorance, were shared by other Christians. And some of these ideas, especially the soul's ascent past hostile powers, were controversial among Christians. Indeed, Andrew labels the idea of the soul's ascent as "strange." He must represent critics of this idea among early Christians.

- The Gospel According to Mary also reveals a division among early Christians over the role of women in the church and the nature of religious authority in general.
  - Peter objects to Mary's revelation for two reasons: She is a woman, and she received these teachings in private, without the other disciples knowing. Doubtless, Peter represents Christians who did not believe that women should teach in the church and who questioned revelations from Christ that were not generally known.

  - In defending Mary, the male disciple Levi makes three points: (1) Peter is prone to anger—one of the passions that the Savior said Christians must renounce; (2) Mary was Jesus's most beloved disciple and, thus, the most reliable source of revelation; and (3) the apostles should follow Jesus's original teachings and not impose rules that differ from what the Savior said.

- According to the Gospel of Mary, certain other Christians have developed rules and regulations that don't follow the original message of Jesus. They have turned away from that message and the new understanding of God it brings. Most likely, the rules that this gospel condemns are those that prohibited female leadership, that restricted Christian truth to official books, and that discounted the revelations that worthy people receive from Jesus.

- Somewhat like the Gnostic Gospel of Judas, the Gospel According to Mary condemns emerging power structures in the Church that restricted authority to male priests. Mary Magdalene, the first person to see the empty tomb, became a rallying point for this protest, just as Peter, the first person to see the risen Jesus (according to Paul), became a symbol for the emerging church structure of bishops and priests. In the long run, of course, Peter won this contest with Mary Magdalene.

Suggested Reading

King, *The Gospel of Mary of Magdala*.

Meyer, ed., *The Nag Hammadi Scriptures*, "The Gospel of Mary with the Greek Gospel of Mary."

Tuckett, *The Gospel of Mary*.

Questions to Consider

1. How did differing accounts of the resurrection support different views of leadership in early Christianity?

2. Why was Mary Magdalene a more appealing role model than Peter for some ancient Christians?

Mary Magdalene as an Apostle of *Gnōsis*
Lecture 15—Transcript

In 2003, Dan Brown published his novel *The Da Vinci Code* and created a worldwide sensation. The book has sold over 80 million copies and has been translated into over 40 languages. The movie based on the novel made over $700 million. All of this for a book that purports to explain the true meaning of Leonardo da Vinci's painting *The Last Supper*.

At the heart of *The Da Vinci Code* lies Mary Magdalene, one of the few original disciples of Jesus who was a woman and has a name. Mary Magdalene appears a lot in Valentinian and other so-call "heretical" texts. That's our topic for this lecture. Why did these Christians find Mary so fascinating? Why was she so important to them?

Now, later Christians often thought of Mary as a reformed prostitute, a remarkable example of repentance. Actually, we'll see that the early texts about Mary show no signs of this idea. But in *The Da Vinci Code*, Mary Magdalene becomes even more meaningful: She represents a feminine aspect of the divine, which organized Christianity has worked for centuries to suppress. Mary's unique and intimate relationship with Jesus expresses a unity of male and female divinity that Christianity's God the Father conceals. The novel finds clues to these truths not only in da Vinci's painting, but also in the Gospel According to Philip, the very same Valentinian work that we have studied. In the Gospel of Philip we find this remarkable passage: "There were three who always walked with the Lord: Mary his mother and his sister and the Magdalene, the one who was called his companion. His sister and his mother and his companion were each a Mary."

In another passage, the apostles wonder why Jesus loves Mary more than he does them. And you'll recall that Mary appears not only in Philip, but also in the Gospel According to Thomas, where Peter suggests Mary should leave because women are not worthy of life. In response, Jesus promises to make Mary male. And even more, there's an ancient Christian text called the Gospel According to Mary. In this work we find Mary and Peter once again opposed, and Jesus gives Mary a special revelation.

Why is Mary Magdalene so prominent in these alternative gospels? And why are she and Peter often portrayed as antagonists? And what does the Gospel According to Philip mean when it calls Mary Jesus's "companion" and "partner"? Was Mary an apostle? And what's the Gospel According to Mary all about? To answer these questions, we must return to the very birth of Christianity—to the resurrection of Jesus.

First we need to think about what an "apostle" originally was. While most Christians today would say that there were twelve apostles, all male, in fact the earliest Christians did not use the term in this limited way. The Greek word *apostolos* simply meant a person who had been sent, an envoy or delegate or representative. Christian apostles were persons sent by Jesus to proclaim his message. The earliest Christian author, Paul, uses the term to refer to Christians who had seen Jesus after his resurrection from the dead and whom the risen Jesus had commissioned to spread the Gospel. There were far more than twelve of these people. Here's Paul writing to his congregation in Corinth:

> For I handed on to you as of first importance what I in turn had received: that Christ died for our sins in accordance with the Scriptures, and that he was buried, and that he was raised on third day in accordance with the Scriptures … and that he appeared to Cephas, then to the twelve. Then he appeared to more than 500 brothers and sisters at one time, most of whom are still alive, though some have died. Then he appeared to James, then to all the apostles. … Last of all, as to one untimely born, he appeared also to me. For I am the least of the apostles, unfit to be called an apostle because I persecuted the church of God.

Notice a couple things here. First, Paul recognizes that there was a special group of twelve, but "the apostles" includes more people than that, most obviously Paul himself. Elsewhere Paul refers to another Christian missionary, Apollos, as an apostle, and in his Second Letter to the Corinthians he complains about a group of very talented missionaries whom he sarcastically calls the "super-apostles." Were there women among the apostles? Apparently so, because in his Letter to the Romans Paul refers to Andronicus, a man, and Junia, a woman, as "outstanding among the apostles."

But notice that Paul referred only to Jesus appearing to people after his resurrection. He nowhere mentions the discovery of the empty tomb, and he never refers to Mary Magdalene, who, as we shall see, the Gospels identify as one of the first persons to see that Jesus's tomb was empty.

Finally, Paul seems to consider the order in which Jesus appeared to people to be significant. That Jesus appeared to Paul last of all—we think about three years after the crucifixion—indicated that he was "the least of the apostles." Presumably Peter, the first person to see Jesus, was greatest among the apostles. Typically, however, Paul challenges this idea by going on to say, "I worked harder than any of them!" And in his Letter to the Galatians, he recounts a major disagreement with Peter and refers to him and other key leaders sarcastically as "so-called pillars of the church." But all this only underscores that the order of Jesus's appearances—who saw him first— created a kind of pecking order among the apostles, and here Peter seems to come out on top.

But things get more complicated, and Mary Magdalene enters the picture when we turn to the Gospels, all of which were written in the decades after Paul died in the early 60s. The Gospel of Mark does not describe the risen Jesus appearing to anybody. Rather, three women—Mary Magdalene, Mary the mother of James, and Salome—discover that the tomb is empty. A young man dressed in white instructs them to tell "the disciples and Peter" to go to Galilee, where they will see Jesus. Then the Gospel ends.

Mark doesn't tell us much about who Mary Magdalene was. She and the two other women first appear at the crucifixion of Jesus, watching from afar. The title "Magdalene" indicates that Mary came from the village of Magdala in the Galilee. Mark says that Mary and other women used to follow Jesus and supported him financially. So perhaps Mary came from a somewhat higher economic or social level than did Jesus and the male disciples. Above all, Mary is one of three women who observe the crucifixion and then discover the empty tomb.

In Matthew, two women—Mary Magdalene and "the other Mary"—find the tomb and meet the angel. But then Jesus himself appears to the women and repeats the message that the disciples should go to Galilee. In Galilee, Jesus appears to the eleven disciples as a group, and then the story ends. Here, Jesus appears first to Mary Magdalene and her companion. Peter, however, does not get his own appearance.

In the Gospel of Luke, matters get even more complicated. Here, a whole group of women, including Mary Magdalene, finds the empty tomb. They go and tell the male apostles, who don't believe them. Peter then goes to see the tomb for himself and goes home amazed. Then Jesus appears to two unnamed disciples who are walking to Emmaus. When they report this to the others back in Jerusalem, they learn that Jesus has also appeared to Peter, but Luke does not narrate this appearance to Peter. Then Jesus himself appears to the entire group and later ascends into heaven. In Luke Peter does get his own appearance, although it's not narrated, but even better, he gets to see the empty tomb as well.

Luke also adds an interesting biographical detail about Mary Magdalene not present in the other gospels. Mary, Luke tells us, had been possessed by seven demons, but she had been cured of this affliction. Luke does not say that it was Jesus who cast the demons out of Mary, but that seems to be implied.

Finally, there's the Gospel of John. It adds another character to the events, a disciple called simply "the one whom Jesus loved" and whom modern scholars call the Beloved Disciple. In John, Mary Magdalene alone discovers the empty tomb. She goes and tells Peter and the Beloved Disciple. And here's what happens:

> Then Peter and the other disciple set out and went toward the tomb. The two were running together, but the other disciple outran Peter and reached the tomb first. He bent down to look in and saw the linen wrappings, but he did not go in. …
>
> Then Simon Peter came, following him, and went into the tomb. He saw the linen wrappings lying there, and the cloth that had been on Jesus's head, not lying with the linen wrappings but rolled up in a place by itself. …

Then the other disciple, who reached the tomb first, also went in, and he saw and believed.

You can tell that this is an elaborate choreography, designed to balance the competing claims to authority of Peter and the Beloved Disciple, who is clearly the favorite apostle of the author, if not the author himself. But what about Mary Magdalene? Jesus next appears to her—his first appearance to anyone—and she goes and tells the disciples, "I have seen the Lord!" Then Jesus appears a few more times to the whole group. In John, you clearly have three major witnesses to the resurrection: Peter, the Beloved Disciple, and Mary Magdalene.

OK, let's stop and notice what all the Gospels have in common: Mary Magdalene, sometimes accompanied by one or more other women, found the empty tomb and brought this amazing news to the male disciples. This is why Mary is often called in Christian tradition "the apostle to the apostles"— because she brought the good news of Easter to the apostles. Even more than this, in two Gospels, Matthew and John, Mary—not Peter—is the first disciple to see the risen Jesus. If we recall that Paul shows that at least some early Christians considered the order in which Jesus appeared to the apostles to be important, you can see that we have the makings here of a real rivalry between Mary and Peter. And that's exactly what you get in early Christian texts that were written later and didn't make it into the New Testament.

As we have seen, in the Gospel According to Thomas, Peter asks Jesus to send Mary away because "females are not worthy of life." But Jesus responds that he will make Mary male so that she will resemble males like Peter. I have suggested that here, Peter and Mary are symbols for the masculine and feminine, and that the reunion of the male and female represents salvation.

The rivalry between Mary and Peter extends to all the apostles in the Gospel According to Philip. One excerpt—which in the manuscript, has a lot of gaps—reads as follows:

> As for the Wisdom who is called the barren one, she is the mother of the angels, and the companion of the—[and here's a gap]— Mary Magdalene—[another gap]—loved her more than all the

disciples and used to kiss her often on her—[and here's a gap]. The rest of the disciples said to him, "Why do you love her more than all of us?"

The Savior answered and said to them, "Why do I not love you like her? When a blind man and one who sees are both together in darkness, they are no different from one another. When the light comes, then the one who sees will see the light, and the one who is blind will remain in darkness."

This is one of the passages that inspired Dan Brown's *The Da Vinci Code*. To Brown, this passage suggests that Jesus and Mary may have had a sexual relationship—or at least, they are a couple. And he presented Mary as the divine female principle, which balances the male divine principle in Jesus. Many people have found Brown's quasi-Valentinian theology of Mary attractive.

But our study of actual Valentinian theology leads us in a different direction. Let's remember that, according to the Valentinians, we all have higher, more divine selves. These are our angelic selves, which Wisdom emitted, along with our human selves. Our higher angelic selves are designated male, and our lower human selves are designated female. And thus the Valentinians talked about salvation as a reunion of male and female selves. They said that in baptism, the female self is made male—that is, baptism elevates our lower female self toward our angelic male self. They used the term bridal chamber to refer symbolically to this process of salvation.

Our passage in the Gospel According to Philip opens by referring to Wisdom producing the angels—our higher male selves. The angels that Wisdom produced form a kind of bodyguard or retinue for Jesus in the Valentinian myth. So I think that this passage does indeed present Jesus and Mary as having a special relationship. But this relationship does not symbolize male and female divine principles. Rather, it symbolizes the relationship between angelic male selves and human female selves. So Mary Magdalene does not stand for the feminine divine. Instead, we are all Mary Magdalene—all of us are called to have a special relationship with our higher angelic self, represented by Jesus.

The Gospel According to Philip accepts the idea that the real people Jesus and Mary had a stronger and closer relationship than Jesus did with Peter and the male disciples. Like the Gospel of Thomas, it depicts the male disciples as questioning this relationship. The Gospel of Philip makes the bond between Jesus and Mary a symbol for true salvation. Consider again the passage I quoted earlier: "There were three who always walked with the Lord: Mary his mother and his sister and the Magdalene, the one who was called his companion. His sister and his mother and his companion were each a Mary."

The name "Mary" has become a symbol for the female in relationship to God. But this is not a female divine being. Rather, we are all female in our relationship to the Lord and to our higher angelic selves. When Peter and the male disciples question the relationship between Jesus and Mary, they reveal that they do not yet understand the higher meaning of this relationship. They are still in darkness, in need of the light that the Valentinian myth can provide.

Conflict between Mary Magdalene and Peter and the other male disciples becomes a primary theme in the Gospel According to Mary—the only early Christian gospel attributed to a woman. Unfortunately, no complete copy of this gospel survives from antiquity. We have two small fragments of the original Greek text. They were found at Oxyrhynchus in Egypt, the same place where the Greek fragments of the Gospel According to Thomas were discovered. The longest surviving fragment is a Coptic translation. It was not part of the Nag Hammadi discoveries. Rather, it was found in the 1890s near Akhmīm, not far from Nag Hammadi in Egypt. The codex in which it appears contains also a copy of the Gnostic Secret Book According to John. The two short Greek fragments overlap with portions of the long Coptic fragment—that's how we know they are from the same text. Scholars agree that the original Greek text must have been written in the 2nd century.

Although the Gospel of Mary has some ideas similar to Gnostic myth, it does not contain any of the distinctive teachings of the Gnostics. There is no Barbēlō, no Ialdabaōth, no talk of a "seed of Seth" or "immovable race." There are more signs of contact with the Gospel According to Thomas and with Valentinian ideas. And in fact, simply having a gospel in which Mary

Magdalene is the primary human character and even the supposed author of the gospel connects this gospel with Thomas and the Valentinians more than with the Gnostics, who did not show any interest in Mary.

At the beginning of our surviving text, Jesus is teaching the disciples after his death and resurrection. When Jesus finishes his discourse, he tells the disciples to go forth and preach the gospel, and then he goes away. Rather than going out to preach, the disciples become distressed and they weep. They fear that people will kill them as they did Jesus. Mary then stands up and basically tells the disciples to stop being such wimps. God's grace will protect them, and so they should be resolute.

Peter than asks Mary to reveal to him and the other apostles any teachings that Jesus gave her that they do not know. Mary then tells how the Savior appeared to her in a vision and told her about how the human soul must ascend past hostile powers to reach its heavenly home.

When she finishes her revelation, Andrew and Peter charge that Mary is lying. Andrew says that the ideas she claims that Jesus taught her are strange, and Peter argues that Jesus would not reveal such things to a woman in private. "Did he choose her over us?" he asks. Mary weeps and says she is not lying. The apostle Levi comes to Mary's defense. He accuses Peter of being prone to anger and says that Jesus did in fact love Mary more than he loved the men because he knew her so well. Levi tells his colleagues that they need to go preach the good news. In the Coptic translation the gospel ends with all the apostles going forth to teach and preach. In the Greek fragment, only Levi does.

From this summary, you can see that there are two issues that cause conflict between Mary and the male disciples: the content of the teaching that she reveals, which Andrew calls "strange," and the very fact that Mary, a woman, is teaching it. Let's look first at the doctrines that the Gospel of Mary teaches.

As I said, when our fragment begins, Jesus is in the middle of teaching all the disciples after his resurrection. Why would a Christian author think that Jesus talked with his disciples after his resurrection? Well, in the New Testament Gospels of Luke and John, Jesus appears to the disciples after the crucifixion and has conversations with them. Luke tells us that Jesus gave the disciples additional teachings about the Scriptures and his mission during these appearances, but he does not tell us what they were. So this left the door open to later Christians to imagine what it was that Jesus taught the disciples after his resurrection and that does not appear in the gospels as we have them. The Secret Book According to John is a great example of this. The Savior reveals the Gnostic myth to the disciple John by himself after the crucifixion and resurrection, and then John shares this teaching with the other apostles.

So that's what's happening in the Gospel According to Mary: The resurrected Jesus gives teachings to the disciples that are not recorded in the New Testament gospels. What he teaches sounds a lot like what we have seen in Valentinianism. First, Jesus says that matter and the material world are ultimately not real. At some point matter will dissolve and cease to exist. Valentinus and his followers also taught that matter is not really real. It originated in ignorance, according to the Gospel of Truth, or in the passions of Wisdom, according to Valentinian myth.

Second, Peter asks the Savior what "sin" is, and the Savior replies that there's no such thing as sin. This may seem surprising, but Jesus goes on to explain that what we call sin is actually what we produce when we fall into ignorance and turn away from the good. So the gospel is not really saying there's no sin from which we need to be saved. Rather, it denies that sin has real existence—sin results from our ignorance and failure to remain faithful to the good. Again, this is reminiscent of Valentinus and his followers.

Third, Jesus condemns passion as arising from matter and ignorance. "Passion" refers to unhealthy emotions like anger, grief, resentment, and so on—the emotions that lead to immoral acts. Instead, Jesus urges his disciples to be content and inwardly peaceful.

Finally, the Savior tells the apostles to go and preach the good news, and he warns them not to add any rules or laws beyond the things that he has commanded.

So the teaching that Jesus gives to all the disciples in the Gospel of Mary sounds vaguely Valentinian—matter and sin are ultimately unreal because they are rooted in ignorance. The gospel should lead people to give up the unhealthy emotions and instead achieve inner peace. Perhaps the most radical thing Jesus says is that his followers are not to add any rules beyond what he taught them. Maybe this refers to such later church rules as no teaching and preaching by women.

The secret teaching that Jesus reveals to Mary looks even more like what we have seen among Valentinians. The Savior tells Mary that the human soul will need to ascend past certain hostile powers, like darkness, desire, and ignorance. These powers try to prevent the soul from ascending to its true home, but the soul tells them about its true nature, and then it can pass them by.

This looks a lot like the Valentinian ritual for the dying that we studied earlier. There, too, the human soul needed to say certain things in order to ascend past the rulers and the Creator God. On the other hand, the Gospel of Mary lacks any of the distinctive vocabulary and characters of Valentinianism.

So I think this gospel teaches a theology very similar to that of the Valentinians, but may not actually come from the Valentinians. Instead, we see that some Valentinian ideas, like the origin of sin in ignorance, were shared by other Christians and not limited to them. And yet some of these ideas, especially the soul's ascent past hostile powers, were controversial among Christians. It's this last concept—the soul's ascent—that Andrew labels as "strange." Andrew must represent critics of this idea among early Christians.

I think what's even more important is that the Gospel According to Mary reveals that Christians were divided over the role of women in the church and over the nature of religious authority in general.

Peter objects to Mary's revelation for two reasons: She is a woman, and she received these teachings in private, without the other disciples knowing. In the text Peter's objections are somewhat strange because Mary shared her revelation only after Peter asked for it. Peter had said: "Sister, we know that the Savior loved you more than all other women. Tell us the words of the Savior that you remember, the things you know that we don't because we haven't heard them." This makes Peter's later charges against Mary seem rather artificial. Doubtless Peter represents Christians who did not believe that women should teach in the Church and who questioned revelations from Christ that are not generally known.

The Gospel According to Mary has Mary deny that she is lying, but it's the male disciple Levi who responds most fully to Peter. Levi makes three points. First, he attacks Peter personally as prone to anger, which is of course one of the passions that the Savior said Christians must renounce. So to some extent the gospel seems to be saying that Christians who see Peter as the leading disciple are mistaken and that they should look beyond him for true apostolic authority.

Second, Levi says that the Savior has true knowledge of Mary and in fact did love her more than the male disciples—not just more than other women, as Peter originally said. So the gospel also defends the primacy of Mary as Jesus's most beloved disciple, and thus as the most reliable source of revelation.

Finally, Levi tells the male apostles that they should follow Jesus's original teachings. As he puts it, the disciples must "clothe ourselves with the perfect human being"—that is, be remade in the image of God as the Savior teaches. The apostles should preach the gospel, and they should not, Levi says, "lay down any other rule or law that differs from what the Savior said." Here Levi repeats what Jesus had said earlier. The gospel is saying that certain other Christians have developed rules and regulations that don't follow the original message of Jesus. They have turned away from that message and the new understanding of God it brings. Most likely the rules that the gospel condemns are those that prohibited female leadership, that restricted Christian truth to official books like the New Testament gospels, and that discounted the revelations that worthy people receive from Jesus. Somewhat like the Gnostic Gospel of Judas, the Gospel According to Mary condemns emerging power structures in the Church that restricted authority to male priests.

Mary Magdalene, the first person to see the empty tomb according to the gospels, becomes a rallying point or mascot for this protest—just as Peter, the first person to see the risen Jesus according to Paul, became a symbol for the emerging church structure of bishops and priests.

In the long run, of course, it looks like Peter won his contest with Mary Magdalene. He became known as the first Pope, the undisputed leader among the apostles. In contrast, Christians began to identify Mary Magdalene with unnamed sinful women in the gospels, eventually turning her into a former prostitute—something for which there is no foundation in the New Testament. Mary has retained her highly sexualized identity in modern pop culture. Dan Brown made her Jesus's lover, and she has added an erotic dimension to Jesus movies, from *The King of Kings* in the 1920s to *Jesus Christ Superstar* in the 1970s. Maybe it's time to go back to the ancient sources and reacquaint ourselves with Mary, the model disciple.

Despite the opposition and skepticism of some Christians, interest in new or hidden revelations from Jesus did not go away. Among the Nag Hammadi codices are multiple books that are called "revelations" or "secret books." We have already met the Gnostic works the Secret Book According to John and the Revelation of Adam. But not only Gnostics produced such new revelations, as the Gospel According to Mary shows.

In the next lecture we'll meet three more works from Nag Hammadi that did not come from the Gnostics, but do present new revelations that challenged emerging orthodoxy. They are revelations to James, Peter, and Paul.

Competing Revelations from Christ
Lecture 16

M any of the writings found at Nag Hammadi call themselves apocalypses or revelations; they contain new religious truth that God has revealed. To some extent, this is no surprise because Christianity began with extraordinary experiences of revelation. The Book of Revelation, for example, records the visionary experience of a Christian named John. But people who wrote such books would later become controversial among Christians, who believed that that the time for revelations had ceased. In this lecture, we'll look at some of the visions and writings that sparked this controversy, including revelations from Nag Hammadi attributed to the apostles Peter, Paul, and James.

Revelatory Experiences in Early Christianity

- Revelatory experiences and writings were central to the origins of Christianity. The Revelation to John stood in a long tradition of Jewish revelatory literature. Jewish apocalypses, such as Daniel in the Old Testament or the books of Enoch, featured symbolic visions that communicated new information from God.

- By the middle of the 2nd century, however, some Christians began to think that the era of visions and revelations had ended. They believed that the earliest gospels of Jesus contained everything that Jesus taught. The task of the church was to pass on what these gospels taught, not to come up with new ideas.

- But not all Christians agreed. In the 170s, three Christians in Asia Minor, Montanus, Priscilla, and Maximilla, claimed to have received the Holy Spirit. These new prophets began to speak new revelations about the return of Jesus and the arrival of the kingdom of God.

- Some Christian congregations accepted the message of these prophets and began to follow their teachings. These supporters called their movement New Prophecy, and it spread from Asia Minor to Rome and North Africa. Other congregations rejected New Prophecy as false, and some Christian communities split over the question.

- New Prophecy Christians agreed that certain Christian teachings were settled, such as the divinity of Christ, but they believed that the Holy Spirit could reveal new things, especially new and more rigorous ethical principles.

The New Testament Revelation to John consists of puzzling visions that reveal the true meaning of current events and forecast what God will do in the future.

  o The followers of New Prophecy did not limit these new revelations to the three original prophets, and they believed that women could be prophets or serve in church leadership roles just as easily as men.

  o These beliefs posed a challenge to developing structures of church authority: If God is still speaking through prophets, why should Christians obey human leaders?

- Members of the New Prophecy movement did not write new books of revelation, but some other Christians did. Several books found at Nag Hammadi present secret or special revelations, including revelations to Paul, Peter, and James. All these works were originally written in Greek, probably in the 2nd or 3rd century, then later translated into Coptic.

The Revelation of Paul

- The Revelation of Paul from Nag Hammadi is a short text in which the apostle Paul goes on a journey to the heavenly spheres, which were often numbered in antiquity from the first to the seventh heaven or more. Paul's journey starts at the third heaven and goes to the tenth. Along the way, he interacts with various spirits and angels, some of which try to prevent him from ascending further.

- Paul has two encounters with divine revealers. At the beginning of the text, a small child—almost certainly Christ—appears to him. This child encourages Paul to awaken his mind and to recognize the cosmic rulers that surround him, especially the one that makes bodies for souls. The child invites Paul to ascend to meet the twelve apostles, which begins Paul's journey upward through the heavens.

- At the seventh heaven, Paul meets an old man seated on a throne— the God of Israel. The old man questions Paul about his identity, his origin, and his destination. Paul is able to give the man the correct answers and to show him a sign that indicates his blessed status. The old man then allows Paul to proceed to the eighth heaven, where Paul meets the twelve apostles. But Paul keeps going, to the ninth and the tenth heavens, where he greets his fellow spirits.

- The revelations here sound similar to what we have seen in Gnostic literature. The God of Israel is not the ultimate God but only the god of this lower cosmos, which extends as far as the seventh heaven. True Christians belong to the realm above this world. The book does not, however, contain all the elements of the Gnostic myth.

The Revelation of Peter

- The Revelation of Peter from Nag Hammadi describes the Savior revealing religious truths to Peter as they sat in the Temple in Jerusalem the night before Jesus's crucifixion. In this discussion, the Savior reveals three important truths: the natures of saved and unsaved human beings, the true identity of the Jesus who will be crucified, and the future of the Christian church.

- The Savior explains to Peter that there are two kinds of human beings: those with mortal souls, who are destined for destruction, and those with immortal souls, who will eventually receive grace. According to this teaching, people do not have free will. They are born with mortal or immortal souls, and their eternal fates are predetermined. It may not be clear at the moment who belongs to which group, but eventually, it will be.

- Peter then has a vision of Jesus being crucified while another figure stands beside the cross, smiling and laughing. The Savior explains that there are actually two Jesuses. The one that Peter saw smiling and laughing is "the living Jesus," and the man on the cross is a fleshly substitute. The Savior explains that when Jesus is arrested, the living Jesus will be set free, and only the fleshly substitute will remain to be tortured and killed. The living Jesus will stand nearby, laughing at the blindness of those crucifying the substitute.

  o Peter then sees yet another divine figure, someone who looks like the living Jesus, but who is clothed with the Holy Spirit, surrounded by a bright light, and praised by a multitude of angels. This is the real Savior, who merely revealed himself in the living Jesus. Even the living Jesus is not the real savior but the "bodiless body" in which the Savior appeared.

  o This is a fascinating way to understand the nature of Jesus and his crucifixion. As early Christians grew to believe that Jesus was divine, they sometimes had difficulty understanding how he could have suffered and died on the cross or, indeed, why he needed to eat or drink like an ordinary human being before his death.

  o Docetic Christians solved this problem by saying that Jesus was not really human at all but only appeared to be human. The Revelation of Peter takes a different approach. The body of Jesus was real, it says, but it was merely a fleshly substitute for the living Jesus. The living Jesus escaped from the fleshly body before he could be tortured and killed. Further, even the living, spiritual Jesus was only a vessel for the truly divine Savior.

- Finally, the Savior tells Peter how the Christian church will develop after his death: At first, people will listen to the truth, but then certain Christians will lead people astray and teach them to worship a dead man—the crucified Christ. These false leaders will set up a false church, and they will tell people that salvation comes only through them and their pseudo-church. Right now, these leaders oppress true believers, "the little ones," but eventually, truth will win out, and the little ones will be vindicated.

The Secret Book of James

- The text known as the Secret Book of James presents itself as a letter written by the apostle James. The author is clear that this writing is not meant to be read by all Christians, much less all people. He tells his recipient to share the book only with those who are capable of being saved through it.

- According to the Secret Book, the revelation occurred 550 days after the resurrection, at a time when the twelve disciples were gathered together. They were remembering everything that the Savior had taught them and writing it down in books. Jesus then appeared and asked to speak only to James and Peter.

- Ironically, when Jesus has Peter and James alone, he reveals to them that the era of prophecy is over; it ended with the beheading of John the Baptist. James and Peter should not seek to prophesy even if they are asked. Christians seeking revelation should look to the books of Jesus's teachings that the disciples wrote, especially the parables of Jesus.
  - The parables that Jesus mentions—"The Shepherds," "The Seed," and others—are found in the New Testament gospels. The true meaning of these parables is not always obvious, which is the point: Zealous Christians will try to decipher what the parables mean. Jesus urges James and Peter to "be eager for the word"—that is, to study the gospels and their parables carefully—but he cautions that this will be hard work.

o Jesus says, "The word is like a grain of wheat. When someone sowed it, he had faith in it, and when it sprouted, he loved it, because he saw many grains instead of just one. And after he worked, he was saved because he prepared it as food, and he still kept some out to sow."

o The meaning of this parable seems to be that the word of God requires effort. First, to benefit from it, we must make it grow. Next, we prepare it as food and plant some more. In other words, we must first study the parables and teachings of Jesus in the books the apostles have written and gain our own salvation. Then, we should offer these teachings to others— prepare some food and plant more seeds.

o Jesus says, "This is also how you can acquire heaven's kingdom for yourselves. Unless you acquire it through *gnōsis*, you will not be able to find it." We gain *gnōsis* and salvation through studying and teaching the word. This is *gnōsis* through books—not just the gospels in the New Testament but also new books, including the Secret Book of James.

o This is a spirituality of education and study of written texts. Salvation comes through teachers and students reading and trying to understand the teachings of Jesus found in Christian literature. And Jesus is the model teacher. He instructs Peter and James, and he patiently answers their questions. Like all good teachers, he hopes that his students will eventually become wiser and more learned than he is.

Suggested Reading

Brakke, "Parables and Plain Speech in the Fourth Gospel and the *Apocryphon of James*."

Lewis, *Introduction to "Gnosticism,"* chapters 17–18.

Meyer, ed., *The Nag Hammadi Scriptures*, "The Secret Book of James," "The Revelation of Paul," and "The Revelation of Peter."

Tabbernee, *Prophets and Gravestones*.

Questions to Consider

1. Why might many early Christian leaders have found the idea of continuing revelation dangerous?

2. Do think that written revelations, such as those of Paul and Peter, reflected genuine religious experiences that someone had, or were they just made up? How might we be able to tell?

Competing Revelations from Christ
Lecture 16—Transcript

Many of the writings found at Nag Hammadi call themselves "apocalypses" in Greek, or "revelations"—they contain new religious truth that God has revealed. Now to some extent this is no surprise because Christianity began with extraordinary experiences of revelation. A man thought to be dead, Jesus of Nazareth, appeared to people, revealing his true divine nature. The apostle Paul first persecuted believers in Jesus, but then he, too, experienced a revelation of Christ, who appointed him apostle to the Gentiles. Christians not only saw and heard revelations, they wrote them. The book of Revelation in the New Testament records the fantastic visionary experience of a Christian named John.

But only decades later, people who had experiences like Paul's or wrote books like John's would become controversial among Christians. It seemed to some that the time for revelations had ceased. So not everybody welcomed the new revelations contained in the Nag Hammadi codices. In this lecture we'll look at some of the new visions and writings that sparked this controversy, including revelations from Nag Hammadi attributed to the apostles Peter, Paul, and James.

Now it's important to remember how central revelatory experiences and writings were to the origins of Christianity. The Revelation to John stood in a long tradition of Jewish apocalyptic—revelatory—literature. Jewish apocalypses, like Daniel in the Old Testament or the books of Enoch, featured symbolic visions that communicated new information from God. Sometimes an angel explains to the recipient of the revelation what it all means, but just as often, the visions remain obscure and enigmatic, open to new interpretations. So, too, the New Testament Revelation to John consists of puzzling visions that reveal the true meaning of current events and forecast what God will do in the future.

Experiences of revelation and the writing of apocalyptic books did not cease when the original apostles passed away. The book of Revelation comes from the 90s, well after the time of the first apostles. And we have met more Christian books that reveal divine secrets in visionary experiences—

the Gnostic Secret Book According to John, for example, and the Gospel According to Mary. Valentinus allegedly had a vision of the Word of God as a newborn baby.

By the middle of the 2nd century, however, some Christians began to think that the era of visions and revelations had come to a close. They believed that the earliest gospels of Jesus contained everything that Jesus taught. The Gospels of Matthew, Mark, Luke, and John—and for some Christians, Thomas—recorded what Jesus had said to the disciples, and there was nothing more to know. The task of the Church was to pass on what these gospels taught, not to come up with new ideas. The era of revelations was over.

But not all Christians agreed. In the 170s, three Christians in Asia Minor, modern-day Turkey, claimed to have received the Holy Spirit. These new prophets began to speak new revelations from Christ. They were Montanus, a man, and Priscilla and Maximilla, two women. When they were filled with the Holy Spirit, God would speak through them in the first person. For example, Montanus said in a state of prophetic ecstasy, "I am the Lord God, the Almighty dwelling in a human being."

Through these three prophets came new revelations about the return of Jesus and the arrival of the kingdom of God. These revelations urged Christians to prepare for the kingdom through fasting, prayer, and sexual purity.

Christians disagreed over whether the new revelations that came through Montanus, Priscilla, and Maximilla were legitimate. Some Christian congregations accepted the message of the prophets and began to follow their teachings. These supporters called their movement New Prophecy, and it spread from Asia Minor to Rome and North Africa. Other congregations rejected New Prophecy as false, and some Christian communities split over the question. Often, lay people enthusiastic about New Prophecy came into conflict with their more skeptical clergy.

Central to New Prophecy was the conviction that the era of revelation was not over. New Prophecy Christians agreed that certain Christian teachings were settled, such as the divinity of Christ. But they believed that the Holy Spirit could reveal new things, especially new and more rigorous ethical principles. For example, the New Testament taught that it was OK for a Christian to get married a second time if their husband or wife dies. But God revealed through the new prophets that those days were over: Now every Christian must marry only once, if he or she got married at all. The Holy Spirit revealed that God now had higher expectations.

The followers of New Prophecy did not limit these new revelations to the three original prophets, and certainly they believed that women could be prophets just as easily as men. As New Prophecy developed its own congregations, they allowed women to serve in leadership roles. At the same time, these Christians resisted the growing power of a formal official clergy. As bishops and priests began to claim the power to forgive Christians who committed grave sins, New Prophecy members objected. Only God could forgive serious sins like adultery or apostasy, not the Church. The Holy Spirit said through one new prophet, "The Church can pardon a sin, but I will not do it, so that people will not commit other offenses."

The New Prophecy belief in continuing revelations posed a challenge to developing structures of church authority. If God is still speaking through prophets, then why should Christians obey human leaders instead? And surely God can speak through women as well as men.

Members of the New Prophecy movement may have received revelations from God, but they did not write new books of revelation like the one in the New Testament. They collected the short oracles that their prophets spoke, but they did not compose lengthy discourses from Jesus. But as we have seen, some Christians did. The Secret Book According to John presents the Gnostic myth as a long revelation from the Savior to the apostle John, and the Gospel According to Mary reveals teachings that Jesus gave to Mary and the other disciples after his resurrection.

Some Christians may have wanted to restrict the teachings of Jesus to what was in the New Testament gospels, but the Gospel of Luke said that Jesus taught more than what was recorded there. Luke says that after his resurrection, Jesus appeared to small and large groups of disciples more than once and taught them. But Luke does not tell us everything that Jesus taught in these post-resurrection meetings. He just says that Jesus opened the disciples' minds so that they could fully understand the scriptures.

Luke opened the door for other Christians so that they could imagine what Jesus taught the disciples after his resurrection and so that they could claim that he shared some secret teachings with only one or a few of his disciples. That's exactly what we saw in the Gospel According to Mary. In that book, after the resurrection, Jesus gives the disciples teachings that are not found in the other gospels, and he also reveals secret teachings to Mary alone.

Several books found at Nag Hammadi also present such secret or special revelations. Let's look at three examples—revelations to Paul, Peter, and James. All of these works were originally written in Greek, probably in the 2nd or 3rd century, and then they were later translated into Coptic, but they are very diverse in their contents.

Let's start with the Revelation of Paul. If you wanted to write a new revelation for an early Christian apostle, Paul was a great candidate because Paul tells us that he had visionary experiences. He became a Christian apostle when Christ appeared to him and told him to preach to the Gentiles. In his Second Letter to the Corinthians, he says that when he was suffering from some chronic physical pain, Christ spoke to him and said, "My grace is sufficient for you, for my power is made perfect in weakness."

But even more dramatically, Paul says that at one time, he was elevated to what he calls "the third heaven," to Paradise, and heard "things that are not to be told, that no mortal is permitted to repeat." Paul says that he is not sure whether he was in his body or not when he had this experience. So it's no surprise that we have at least two Revelations of Paul from antiquity. One of these has long been known. In it, Paul visits both Paradise and Hell, and he sees the punishments of the wicked in hell and the rewards for the righteous in heaven. It's a kind of precursor to Dante's *Inferno*.

The Revelation of Paul from Nag Hammadi is a very short text in which Paul goes on a heavenly journey. Now many ancient people believed that the earth was surrounded by heavenly spheres that could be numbered from the lowest, the first heaven, to the highest, usually the seventh heaven—but sometimes there are more than seven. Paul's journey starts at the third heaven, which we know from the New Testament he had already visited, and he goes all the way to the tenth heaven. Along the way Paul interacts with various spirits and angels, some of which try to prevent him from ascending further.

Paul has two encounters with divine revealers. At the beginning of the text, a small child appears to him. This child is almost certainly Christ. He encourages Paul to awaken his mind and to recognize the cosmic rulers that surround him, especially the one that makes bodies for souls. The child tells Paul that he is standing on the mountain of Jericho—which is fictional, there is no mountain at Jericho—and he invites Paul to ascend to meet the twelve apostles. This begins Paul's journey upward through the heavens.

At the seventh heaven, Paul meets an old man seated on a throne. The man is dressed in white, and his throne shines seven times brighter than the sun. This old man is clearly the God of Israel, for he looks just like visions of God in Jewish apocalypses like Daniel and 1 Enoch. The old man questions Paul about his identity and his origin and about where he is going. Paul is able to give the man the correct answers and to show him a sign that indicates his blessed status. The old man then allows Paul to proceed to the eighth heaven, where Paul meets the twelve apostles. But Paul keeps going, to the ninth and then the tenth heaven, where he greets his fellow spirits.

What's revealed in the Revelation of Paul will not be news to those of us who have explored Gnostic literature: The God of Israel is not the ultimate God, but only the god of this lower cosmos, which extends as far as the seventh heaven. True Christians belong to the realm above this world—the eighth, ninth, and tenth heavens. And yet, this book does not have all the rest of Gnostic myth. For example, the old man is not called Ialdabaōth, and there's no Barbēlō.

It's noteworthy that Paul ascends higher than the twelve apostles. They live in the eighth heaven, but Paul goes all the way to the tenth. According to this book, Paul is by far the most important apostle of all.

The author of the Revelation of Peter from Nag Hammadi would certainly disagree. As in the case of Paul, there is another Revelation of Peter, in which Peter tours hell and sees the wicked punished. It survives in Latin and some other languages. But the Revelation of Peter from Nag Hammadi is not at all like that. Instead, this revelation tells how the Savior revealed religious truths to Peter as they sat in the Temple in Jerusalem the night before Jesus's crucifixion, before Peter famously denied Jesus three times.

In his discussion with Peter, the Savior reveals three important things—the natures of saved and unsaved human beings, the true identity of the Jesus who will be crucified, and the future of the Christian church. On all three of these points, the Revelation of Peter differs dramatically from the teachings of many other Christians.

The Savior explains to Peter that human beings come in two kinds. Some people have mortal souls. These souls are destined for destruction, and they can bear no good fruit. Other people have immortal souls. They look like the people with mortal souls, but they eventually reveal themselves to be immortal and they receive grace. According to this teaching, people really do not have any free will. They are simply born with mortal or immortal souls, and their eternal fates are predetermined. It may not be clear right now who belongs to which group, but eventually it will be.

Many other Christians would have found this teaching alarming. They emphasized that all people have free will and can choose whether or not to have faith in God and live righteous lives. Not so, says the Savior to Peter: "There will be no grace among those who are not immortal."

Peter does not seem particularly disturbed by this teaching, but he becomes upset when he has a premonition that Jesus will be arrested and crucified. Peter not only sees Jesus being crucified on the cross, but he also sees another figure smiling and laughing beside the cross.

The Savior tells Peter that he should not be afraid of his coming crucifixion. He explains that there are actually two Jesuses. The one that Peter saw smiling and laughing is "the living Jesus"—a term we have seen in the Gospel According to Thomas. The man on the cross is simply a fleshly substitute for the living Jesus. The savior explains that when Jesus is arrested, the living Jesus will be set free, and only the fleshly substitute will remain. It's only the fleshly substitute that the evildoers and the demons will be able to torture and kill. The living Jesus will stand nearby, laughing at the blindness of those crucifying him, for they will not see that they are not killing him, only his fleshly substitute.

But that's not all. Peter then sees yet another divine figure, someone who looks like the living Jesus, but who is clothed with the Holy Spirit, surrounded by a bright light, and praised by a multitude of angels. This, it turns out, is the real Savior, who merely revealed himself in the living Jesus. Even the living Jesus is not the real savior, but the "bodiless body" in which the Savior appeared.

This is a fascinating way to understand the nature of Jesus and his crucifixion. As early Christians grew to believe that Jesus was divine, they sometimes had difficulty understanding how Jesus could also have suffered and died on the cross. And besides that, if Jesus was God, did he really need to eat or drink or sleep like an ordinary human being?

Some Christians solved this problem by saying that Jesus was not really human at all. His body was not a human body like that of other human beings. Jesus only appeared to be human, and he did things like eat, drink, and sleep not because he needed to, but to maintain the appearance of a human being. And then surely his death as well was not really real.

Opponents of this view called this teaching "docetism" and the Christians who believed it "docetists." "Docetism" comes from the Greek word *dokein*, which means "to seem" or "to appear." According to docetism, Jesus only seemed to be a human being; he appeared to have a human body, but he really did not. Docetism appears as a danger already in the New Testament. The author of the Second Letter to John condemns Christians who do not believe that Jesus really came in the flesh. No, says this author, Jesus had a real human body, and he really suffered and died.

The Revelation of Peter takes a different approach. The body of Jesus was real, it says, but it was merely a fleshly substitute for the living Jesus. The living Jesus escaped from the fleshly body before he could be tortured and killed. This idea, that a divine Jesus left the human Jesus before the crucifixion, can be found in other Christian texts from the 2nd and 3rd centuries. Proponents of this view often cited the Gospel of Mark, in which Jesus on the cross cries out, "My God, my God, why have you forsaken me?" This would be the human Jesus crying out to the divine or living Jesus who has left him.

The Revelation of Peter does not cite the passage in Mark, but it, too, believes that a living, spiritual Jesus departed from the fleshly, human Jesus and so did not suffer and die on the cross. And it goes even farther—even this living, spiritual Jesus is only a vessel for the truly divine Savior.

The author of this Revelation was well aware that many (and probably most) Christians did not agree with him. They believed that the divine Jesus, somehow, in some mysterious way, really did suffer and die for their sins in a human body on the cross. And so the Savior tells Peter how the Christian church will develop after his death. At first, people will listen to the truth; but then certain Christians will lead people astray and teach them to worship a dead man, that is, the crucified Christ.

According to the Revelation of Peter, these false leaders will set up a false church, and they will tell people that salvation comes only through them and their pseudo-church. Some of them, it says, will "call themselves bishops and deacons, as if they have received authority from God," but they actually serve the ignorant leaders. These people are, says the Savior, "dry canals," not sources of living water. Right now these leaders oppress the true believers, "the little ones," but eventually truth will win out, and the little ones will be vindicated.

In this revelation the Savior is made to criticize sharply the emerging orthodox church and its leaders. Their worship of Christ is worship of a dead man, and their bishops and deacons are false leaders. They claim to be the only source of salvation, but they actually lead people astray. The author even calls out a church leader whose name we know. He criticizes a dead man named Hermas.

We have a text from 2nd-century Roman Christianity called the Shepherd of Hermas. This text is a good example of emerging orthodox Christianity in Rome, with its clergy and claims to offer salvation. The Shepherd of Hermas became one of the most popular books in ancient Christianity, but the Revelation of Peter calls Hermas "the firstborn of unrighteousness."

Ironically, the author of the Revelation accuses his Christian opponents of being "dominated by heresy." Of course, it's now the Revelation of Peter that orthodox Christians call heresy. It's good to be reminded that during the 2nd and 3rd centuries, it was not yet clear what form of Christianity would end up being the dominant form. And it was not only the emerging Orthodox Church that called people heretics. The Christians we are studying, the ones who were the victims of intolerance and heresy-hunting, were often just as eager to accuse their opponents of heresy.

Our final example of a secret revelation from Nag Hammadi is the Secret Book of James. This "secret book" actually has no title in the manuscript. It presents itself as a letter, written by the apostle James to someone whose name is lost in a hole in the manuscript. After greeting his recipient, James writes, "Because you ask that I send you a secret book which was revealed to me and Peter by the Lord, I could not turn you away." Because James refers to the text as a "secret book," we now call it the Secret Book of James. And James is very clear that this book is meant to be secret; it is not meant to be read by all Christians, much less all people. Here's what he says:

> [I have written] it in the Hebrew alphabet and sent it to you, and you alone. But because you are a minister of the salvation of the saints, endeavor earnestly and take care not to rehearse this text to many— this text that the Savior did not wish to tell all of us, his twelve disciples. But blessed will be those who will be saved through the faith of this discourse.

No one believes that the Secret Book of James was originally written in Hebrew; the author wrote it in Greek. But the idea of it being written in Hebrew makes it sound even more esoteric and special. James tells the recipient not to share the book with many people, only with the people who are capable of being saved through it. This, too, is meant to make the book seem very special, for surely the author did hope that it would be widely circulated.

James goes on to say that he had sent the recipient another secret book ten months earlier. That book, he says, was revealed to me. But this book has been revealed more for other people, and James admits that he himself cannot understand everything in it. But he still urges those who read it to try to comprehend it, for that's the path to salvation.

James says that the Savior Jesus revealed the information in this book only to him and Peter. According to James, it was 550 days after the resurrection, and the twelve disciples were gathered together. They were remembering everything that the Savior had taught them and writing it down in books. Jesus then appeared to them and asked to speak only to James and Peter. He told the other ten disciples to keep writing their books.

When Jesus has Peter and James alone, he gives them a revelation that is both new—not contained in the books the disciples are writing—and secret—meant only for the advanced Christians who are capable of receiving it.

Ironically, Jesus reveals to James and Peter that the era of prophecy is over. James asks Jesus, "Lord, how shall we be able to prophesy to those who request us to prophesy to them? For there are many who ask us and they look to us to hear an oracle from us." Jesus answers, "Do you not know that the head of prophecy was cut off with John?" Here, Jesus refers to the beheading of John the Baptist. According to this Secret Book, the death of John the Baptist was the end of the time of prophecy. James and Peter should not seek to prophesy even if they are asked.

It's very likely that the Secret Book is criticizing the New Prophecy movement. Christians should not look to the new prophets for saving knowledge because prophecy came to an end with John the Baptist. Where, then, should Christians look for revelation? According to the Secret Book of James, they should look to the books of Jesus's teachings that the disciples wrote, especially the parables of Jesus.

The Savior points James and Peter to his parables:

> It was enough for some people [to listen] to the teaching and understand "The Shepherds" and "The Seed" and "The Building" and "The Lamps of the Virgins" and "The Wage of the Workmen" and "The Coins" and "The Woman."

Here, Jesus refers to parables that are found in the New Testament gospels. These parables are sometimes puzzling, and their true meaning is not obvious. And that's the whole point—because zealous Christians will try to decipher what these strange parables mean. Jesus urges James and Peter to "be eager for the word"—that is, to study and contemplate the gospels and their parables carefully.

This will be hard work:

> The word is like a grain of wheat. When someone sowed it, he had faith in it, and when it sprouted, he loved it, because he saw many grains instead of just one. And after he worked, he was saved because he prepared it as food, and he still kept some out to sow.

This is a new parable, which sounds like ones in the New Testament, but it's different. The meaning seems to be that the word of God requires effort from people. First, you have to make it grow so that you can benefit from it. Next, you can prepare it as food and plant some more. That is, first you need to study the parables and teachings of Jesus in the books the apostles have written and so gain your own salvation. But then you should go on and offer these teachings to others—prepare some food and plant some more seeds.

Jesus says, "This is also how you can acquire heaven's kingdom for yourselves. Unless you acquire it through *gnōsis*, you will not be able to find it." According to the Secret Book of James, you gain *gnōsis* and salvation through studying and teaching the word. This is *gnōsis* through books—not just the gospels in the New Testament, but also through new books like this one, and the one that James wrote ten months earlier.

This is a spirituality of education in and study of written texts. Salvation comes through teachers and students reading and trying to understand the teachings of Jesus found in Christian literature. Jesus is the model teacher. He instructs Peter and James, and he patiently answers their questions. All of his students have written down his teachings in their books. And like all good teachers, he hopes that his students will become even wiser and more learned than he is. "Be eager to be saved without being urged," he says to Peter and James. "Be fervent on your own, and, if possible, outdo even me, for this is how the Father will love you."

Such study is hard work, and it requires learning and intelligence. And in the ancient Roman Empire, where only about five percent of people could read, it's definitely reserved for the very few. The Secret Book of James is frankly elitist. It's a secret revelation, reserved only for the few who are capable of receiving it. And it presents salvation as an intellectual enterprise of hard work and study that people must do themselves. Jesus says:

> I say this to you so that you may know yourselves. Heaven's kingdom is like a head of grain that sprouted in a field. And when it was ripe, it scattered its seed, and again it filled the field with heads of grain for another year. So with you—be eager to harvest for yourselves a head of the grain of life, so that you may be filled with the kingdom.

You can see from these three revelations from Nag Hammadi that Christians in the 2nd and 3rd centuries looked for *gnōsis* and salvation in very different ways. Some, like the New Prophecy Christians, continued to expect the Holy Spirit to speak through inspired people, both men and women. Others, like the authors of the Revelations of Paul and Peter, presented new teachings as special revelations made to the major apostles. They claimed to make such secret revelations available to everyone.

Others, like the author of the Secret Book of James, worked to find *gnōsis* by studying the teachings of Jesus in a variety of Christian books, but they said such *gnōsis* would be available only to a select few.

As they debated these issues, some Christians accused others of "heresy"—false teaching. In the next lecture we'll see how Christian leaders invented the idea of heresy, precisely in response to the diverse forms of *gnōsis* we have explored so far.

The Invention of Heresy
Lecture 17

So far, we have met a diverse range of Christians, including the Gnostics, the Valentinians, and others. In this lecture and the next, we'll discuss how some Christian leaders responded to these groups and, thus, how they began to create the Christianity that eventually emerged as Catholic orthodoxy. We can divide the opposition to Gnostics and Valentinians into two basic kinds. In this lecture, we'll look at those theologians, such as Justin Martyr and Irenaeus of Lyon, who simply condemned the quest for higher *gnōsis* and developed the idea of heresy to demonize and stigmatize it. In the next lecture, we'll turn to others, such as Clement of Alexandria and Origen, who offered alternative orthodox paths to *gnōsis*.

The Idea of Heresy

- The English word *heresy* comes from the Greek word *hairesis*, which meant "school of thought," "sect," or "faction." It originally did not have negative connotations.

- Early Christians, however, had a strong sense that they should be a single, harmonious group. They considered themselves to be the single body of Christ, and thus, they worried about the constant divisions among them. Even in the New Testament, we find authors who condemned the existence of factions or *haireses* and blamed the devil for Christian teachings that they considered erroneous.

- Historians generally credit Justin Martyr with first developing a full concept of heresy. Justin was a Christian philosopher who taught in Rome in the middle of the 2nd century.

  - Justin argued that he and Christians like him were part of the one true church, but the Gnostics, Marcion, and the Valentinians were merely "schools of thought," which could not be the source of truth. Truth came only from the Word of God, present in Jesus and now in the church. Justin wrote a book, now lost, entitled *Against All the Schools of Thought That Have Arisen.*

○ According to Justin, people who followed Marcion and Valentinus may have called themselves Christians, but they were not members of the church; instead, they were "godless and impious members of a school of thought"—heretics.

○ Again, according to Justin, heresies were instigated by demons that had opposed God's Son, the Word, for centuries. In Justin's time, these demons were inspiring the Romans to persecute the Christians and inspiring such men as Marcion and Valentinus to start heresies.

Irenaeus's Theory of Heresy

- Justin's work had great influence on Irenaeus. At the center of Irenaeus's view of heresy and orthodoxy was the idea of a succession of teachers and students. Irenaeus borrowed the idea of succession from Valentinian teachers—who traced their academic lineage back to the apostles and Jesus—and applied it to both the groups he opposed and the Christians he supported.

- According to Irenaeus, all heretical groups existed in a kind of family tree of teachers and students. For example, Valentinus learned from the Gnostics, and he taught Ptolemy, and so on. However, the Valentinian family tree did not go back to Jesus; instead, it could be traced to Simon Magus, a character in the New Testament Acts of the Apostles.

  ○ In chapter 8 of Acts, Simon appears as a magician who offers the apostles money in exchange for the superior power of the Holy Spirit. Later Christians decided that Simon must have been the first heretic.

  ○ As Irenaeus presented him, Simon was inspired by Satan to become the first teacher of false *gnōsis*, and all heretical teachers were intellectual descendants of Simon.

- As a succession of teachers that go back to Simon, the heretics were, according to Irenaeus, a false mirror image of the bishops—pastors who were emerging as leaders in the governing structure of many Christian groups at the time. True bishops, Irenaeus claimed, could trace their lineage back to at least one of the original apostles, all of whom were taught by Christ.

- Irenaeus also attacked the idea that Jesus taught or revealed certain secret teachings that were not available to everyone.
  - The Valentinians seem to have presented at least part of their apostolic teaching as reserved only for advanced Christians— the spiritual ones. We have seen also that such texts as the Gospel According to Mary, the Revelation of Peter, and the Secret Book of James claimed that Jesus revealed certain special teachings when he appeared to just one or two apostles.

  - Irenaeus, however, denied that the apostles had any secret teachings. If they did, they would surely have shared them with their successors, the bishops. Irenaeus also claimed that Jesus and the apostles would never have adapted their teachings to different audiences. If the apostles withheld certain advanced teachings from beginning Christians, they were effectively lying to those Christians, which of course, the apostles wouldn't do.

  - Instead, Irenaeus asserted that all true apostolic teachings are clearly manifest throughout the world and available to anyone through any true Christian congregation.

- Irenaeus also focused on the Bible in his effort to combat what he called Christian heresies. The Gnostics, we have seen, created new scriptures that retold the stories in Genesis, and Marcion rejected the Old Testament altogether. In response, Irenaeus promoted one of the first versions of what would become a Christian canon of the Bible with the Old and New Testaments.

o   Irenaeus agreed that the Old Testament was inferior to the New Testament, but that was because God was gradually revealing his truth to humanity as it progressed. The New Testament improved upon the Old Testament, but both came from the same God.

o   Irenaeus argued that Christians should use only the four gospels of Matthew, Mark, Luke, and John to understand Jesus and his teachings. He accused heretical groups of relying too much on a single gospel, which tended to skew their views of Jesus. Irenaeus also considered the letters of Paul to be scripture and part of the New Testament.

•   But even Irenaeus's version of the Bible was not sufficient for opposing such alleged heretics as the Valentinians because the Valentinians used basically the same scriptures, although interpreted differently. To judge the truth or falsehood of competing interpretations of the Bible, Irenaeus relied on the "rule of faith," a summary of Christian beliefs that he claimed the church had received from the apostles. The rule of faith stated the basic doctrines of Christianity, and any teachings that violated the rule were clearly false.

Irenaeus's Vision of Christianity

•   As we've seen, the Gnostics and Valentinians both taught that the ultimate God is remote from us and unknowable and that God emanates into a complex structure of multiple aeons. They also taught that the god who created this world is a lower, inferior god. Irenaeus accepted some aspects of this view but rejected most of it.

•   Irenaeus agreed that the ultimate God, whom he called the Father, is unknowable **(see Figure 5)**. But instead of multiple aeons, the Father has two somewhat lower aspects of himself: the Son or Word of God and the Holy Spirit, who is also God's Wisdom.
    o   It is the Son of God who makes the Father known to humans, and through him, humans gain access to the Father. The Son

Figure 5. Irenaeus's View of God

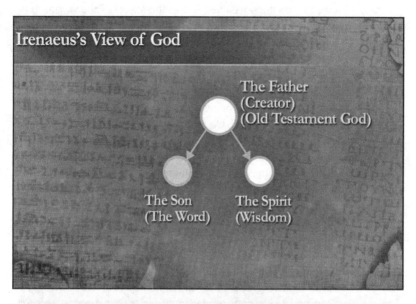

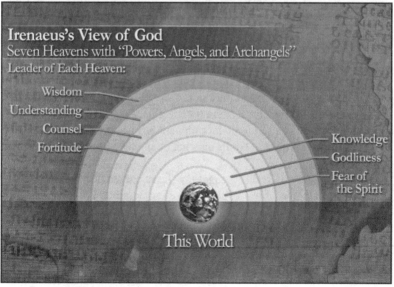

also does the work of organizing and directing the physical cosmos in which we live; he was the maker of the world.

- ○ Meanwhile, the Holy Spirit is in charge of the spiritual powers that serve God, and the Spirit is present among Christians.

- In addition to the Father, Son, and Holy Spirit, Irenaeus taught that many other divine beings exist between God and humanity. The earth is surrounded by seven spheres or heavens, in which multiple powers, angels, and archangels dwell. Each of the seven heavens has a guiding power, which is named. The highest heaven is Wisdom, and the rest are Understanding, Counsel, Fortitude, Knowledge, Godliness, and Fear of the Spirit.

- Irenaeus also developed a view of human salvation in response to other Christians.
  - ○ The Gnostics, Valentinians, and the Gospel According to Thomas all taught that Jesus saves people primarily by revealing true *gnōsis* to us: Christ makes us aware of the higher God and leads us to understand our true natures as spiritual beings in this material world.

  - ○ Irenaeus, in contrast, emphasized that the Son of God became human in order to make human beings holy or sacred. The Word of God became a real human being, and this human—Jesus— was tested by suffering and death. But the Word triumphed over these things in the resurrection. As Irenaeus saw it, human beings had become morally and physically corrupt, and it was the purpose of God's incarnation to make us holy again.

  - ○ In fact, Irenaeus thought that Jesus passed through every stage of human life—childhood, young adulthood, middle age, and old age—so that he could sanctify all human beings, from babies to the elderly.

  - ○ Irenaeus called what Jesus accomplished "recapitulation": Jesus lived like Adam, but he undid all the damage Adam did.

For example, Adam was made from virgin soil, and Jesus was born from a virgin woman. Adam's only father was God, who made him, and Jesus's real father was God. In this way, Jesus was a new Adam. Although the old Adam sinned and brought human beings into corruption and death, the new Adam—Jesus—was sinless and, thus, brought human beings into holiness and life.

- The Gnostics, the Valentinians, and the other Christians we have studied so far considered our true selves to be only our spiritual selves. Our bodies are not part of our real selves, and they will be destroyed or perish into nothingness. Irenaeus, in contrast, believed that our bodies are essential to who we are. The Son of God had to come in a real body of flesh to make us holy, and the resurrection of the dead will be a resurrection of the fleshly body that we now have.

- This resurrection of the flesh is necessary because the kingdom of God itself is not spiritual or immaterial; it will be a physical realm. In fact, it will be this world, miraculously transformed by God.
  - The saved human beings, with real bodies, will live in this earthly kingdom and enjoy its fertility. They will grow in love for God and knowledge of him. They will see God in their bodies.

  - Some special Christians, the holiest of people, will ascend to live in the heavens. But for eternity, many people will dwell in a new city of God on earth. God will be present everywhere, to everyone.

Suggested Reading

Behr, *Irenaeus of Lyons: Identifying Christianity*.

Brakke, *The Gnostics*, chapters 4–5.

Grant, *Irenaeus of Lyons*.

Royalty, *The Origin of Heresy*.

1. Who claimed apostolic succession—and why—among early Christian groups?

2. What are the most important areas of agreement and disagreement between Irenaeus and his Gnostic and Valentinian opponents?

The Invention of Heresy
Lecture 17—Transcript

Since we began this course, we have met an astonishingly diverse range of Christians. The Gnostics taught that the God of the Old Testament, the God who created this world, was the ignorant and hostile Ialdabaōth, and they looked to the Barbēlō aeon for the hope and salvation. Valentinus and his followers argued that the God of the Old Testament was not evil, just inferior to the ultimate God, and they looked forward to being reunited with their male angelic selves in the divine Fullness. The Gospel According to Thomas invited people to discover God through knowledge of themselves, and so to experience the kingdom of God now, not at some future time. The Gospel According to Mary criticized Christians who would exclude women from positions of leadership, and the Revelation of Peter said that the Savior Jesus did not die on the cross, only a fleshly substitute for him did. In addition, we have met Marcion, the New Prophecy movement, and the teachers of *gnōsis* in the Secret Book of James.

As diverse as all these people and texts are, they share one thing—later Christians consider them heretical, false Christians, teachers of erroneous doctrine, even inspired by the devil. They may be different from one another, but they all became known as opponents of orthodox Christianity, the true faith. How did this happen? How did the ideas of orthodoxy and heresy come into being?

The Christianity that eventually dominated the Roman Empire and medieval Europe was created in part precisely in opposition to the kinds of Christianity we have been studying. So the various forms of so-called Gnosticism are worth studying, not just because they are themselves interesting, but also because they help us to understand how orthodox Christianity came to be what it was.

In this next lecture and the next, I'm going to discuss how some Christian leaders responded to the Gnostics, the Valentinians, and other such groups—and thus how they began to create the Christianity that eventually emerged as Catholic orthodoxy. We can divide the opposition to Gnostics and Valentinians into two basic kinds. On the one hand, some leaders and theologians simply condemned the quest for higher *gnōsis*, and they developed the idea of heresy to demonize and stigmatize it. The important people in this effort were Justin Martyr, Irenaeus of Lyons, and other ancient heresiologists. That's what I'm going to talk about in this lecture. On the other hand, other leaders and theologians offered alternative orthodox paths to *gnōsis*, and so they tried to appeal to the desire for higher knowledge of God that attracted people to the Gnostics and Valentinians. The important Christians here were Clement of Alexandria and Origen of Alexandria. That will be the subject of the next lecture.

Both of these strategies—the invention of heresy and the teaching of orthodox *gnōsis*—contributed to the rich traditions that would become Roman Catholicism and Eastern Orthodoxy. We'll discover also that even the Gnostics' most vehement critics, like Irenaeus, did not differ from them completely. They shared some of the same basic ideas about God and this universe.

Let's turn first to the invention of the idea of heresy. The English word "heresy" comes from the Greek word *hairesis*, which meant something like "school of thought," or "sect," or even "faction." It was a common word and did not originally have negative connotations. Ancient teachers of medicine often talked about themselves as dividing up into various "schools of thought" or *haireses*, based on how they understood sickness and disease. There was, for example, "the methodist school of thought" or "the Hippocratic school of thought." A school of thought could take its name from an aspect of its teaching or from its founding scholar.

Likewise, the ancient Jewish historian Josephus used the term *hairesis* to describe differing sects among Jews. Josephus lived in the 1st century and was a younger contemporary of Paul. He said that there were three important *haireses* or sects among the Jews—the Pharisees, the Sadducees, and the Essenes. Certainly Josephus did not mean to call these different groups within Judaism "heresies" in the later negative sense.

Ancient medical doctors argued for the superiority of their particular school of thought over others, but the existence of different schools of thought did not really bother them. They expected differences of opinion and perhaps even valued the debates among them.

Early Christians, however, had a strong sense that they should be a single, harmonious group. They considered themselves to be the single body of Christ, and so they worried about the constant divisions among them. In his letters to the Corinthians, Paul lamented the fact that there were divisions among the Christians in Corinth. But even he thought that there might be some benefits from such quarrels: "There have to be factions—*haireses*— among you," Paul wrote, "for only so will it be clear who among you are genuine." The author of 2 Peter in the New Testament worried about false teachers who "secretly bring in destructive *haireses*"—perhaps meaning "ways of thinking." The author of 1 Timothy attributed false Christian teachings to the devil, and he warned against "what is falsely called *gnōsis*." So already in the New Testament, Christian authors condemned the existence of factions or *haireses* and blamed the devil for Christian teachings that they considered erroneous.

The Christian that historians credit with first developing a full concept of heresy is Justin Martyr. Justin was a Christian philosopher who taught interested students in Rome in the middle of the 2nd century. He is called Justin Martyr because in the 160s the Roman government executed him for his Christian beliefs. Justin either knew personally or knew of Marcion, Valentinus, and their followers, and he considered them to be false Christians because they did not worship the God of the Old Testament as the highest God.

Justin took the idea of a *hairesis* or "school of thought," and he made it an entirely negative term. Justin argued that he and Christians like him were part of the one true Church, but the Gnostics, Marcion, and the Valentinians were merely "schools of thought." No mere school of thought could be the source of truth. Truth came only from the Word of God present in Jesus and now in the Church. Justin wrote a book, now lost, entitled *Against All the Schools of Thought That have Arisen.*

Justin argued that "schools of thought," or as we may now put it, "heresies," were not really Christian, even if their members claimed that they were. People who followed Marcion and Valentinus may have called themselves Christians, but Justin said they were not really Christians, but Marcionites or

Valentinians. They are not members of the Church, but "godless and impious members of a school of thought"—heretics. True Christians, in contrast, are "right-thinking"—in Greek, orthodox.

How did heresies originate? According to Justin, they were instigated by demons. The demons had been opposing God's Son, the Word, for centuries, and now they were doing so by inspiring the Romans to persecute the Christians and by inspiring men like Marcion and Valentinus to start heresies.

Now Justin's rhetoric against the Gnostics and the Valentinians was very harsh and uncompromising, but there was little Justin could do against them in practical terms. Justin did not represent the official Christian church in Rome because there was no official church in Rome, just many small house churches and study groups. Plus, Justin himself was no bishop or priest. He was simply a compelling Christian teacher and preacher, much like Valentinus. All Justin could do was try to persuade people that he was teaching Christian truth and that his rivals were teaching demonic heresy.

Justin's work, however, had a great influence on Irenaeus of Lyons. We have met Irenaeus multiple times, and I hope you will remember that he was the leader of a small group of Christians in Lyons, in Gaul, modern-day France. The Christians in Lyons had gone through a terrible persecution, and their bishop had been martyred, when Irenaeus became their leader.

Irenaeus was alarmed about the activity of Valentinian teachers in his area, and so around the year 180, he wrote his massive book *Detection and Overthrow of Gnōsis, Falsely So-Called* or *Against the Heresies*. In this book he described the teachings of the Gnostics, Marcion, Valentinus, the Valentinians, and other groups that he considered false Christians. All these people, he said, were offering nothing but false *gnōsis*.

I have used Irenaeus's book several times to gather information about the Gnostics and the Valentinians, but now I want to focus on how Irenaeus presented these groups as heretics. What was Irenaeus's theory of heresy and orthodoxy?

At the center of Irenaeus's view was the idea of a succession of teachers and students. You may remember that Valentinian teachers like Ptolemy promoted their authority in part by claiming that they could trace their teaching back to the apostles. According to the Valentinians, Jesus taught the apostles like Paul. Then Paul had a student named Theudas, and Theudas was the teacher of Valentinus. Valentinus then taught Ptolemy, who taught his own students. Irenaeus took this idea of academic (or now, apostolic) succession and applied it both to the teachers and groups he opposed and to himself and the Christians he supported.

According to Irenaeus, all heretical groups existed in a kind of family tree of teachers and students. For example, Valentinus learned from the Gnostics, and he taught Ptolemy, and so on. But this family tree did not go back to Jesus Christ, as the Valentinians claimed, but instead to Simon Magus, a character in the New Testament book, the Acts of the Apostles. In chapter 8 of Acts, Simon appears as a magician who offers the apostles money in exchange for the superior power of the Holy Spirit. Later Christians decided that Simon must have been the first heretic. As Irenaeus presented him, Simon was inspired by Satan to become the first teacher of false *gnōsis*: All heretical teachers are intellectual descendants of him and his students.

And so Simon taught the Gnostics, who taught Valentinus, who of course taught Ptolemy and the other Valentinian teachers. Simon also taught Cerdo, who was the teacher of Marcion. Irenaeus traces these genealogical lines of heresies in order to discredit them and to show that they all originated in the evil Simon Magus.

As a succession of teachers that go back to Simon, the heretics were, according to Irenaeus, a false mirror image of the bishops, the teachers of true Christianity. Starting around the 110s, decades before Irenaeus, many Christian groups developed a specific form of government, led by an ordained clergy. The idea was that in each city there would be a leading pastor, called the bishop, and individual congregations were led by men called *presbyters* in Greek—elders, or later, priests. At this early period the Christians in a city elected their bishop, and the bishop appointed and ordained the elders. This system did not appear everywhere at once, and even in Irenaeus's time there were still several major cities with more than one bishop or no bishop at all. But leaders like Irenaeus promoted the one-bishop system as security against false teachers like the Valentinians.

In his fight against heretics, Irenaeus portrayed the clergy of bishops and elders as the sacred counterpart to the demonic succession of teachers. True bishops, Irenaeus claimed, could trace their lineage back to at least one of the original apostles, all of whom were taught by Christ, not Simon Magus. As an example, he provided a genealogy for the bishops of Rome, a list of Roman bishops that started with Peter and then went down to the current bishop. This succession of bishops back to the apostles and Jesus guaranteed the truth of what the bishops taught. Heretics go back to Simon Magus, but bishops go back to Jesus.

Now modern scholars doubt the historical accuracy of Irenaeus's lists, both his lists of heretics and his list of Roman bishops. Probably parts of these lists are correct—for example, we do not doubt that Valentinus taught his student Ptolemy—but in general, we are not convinced by Irenaeus's lists. But that's not really the point. Irenaeus's idea of the apostolic succession of bishops became hugely important as the Roman Catholic and Eastern Orthodox churches established their authority in later centuries.

Irenaeus also attacked the idea that Jesus taught or revealed certain secret teachings that were not available to everyone. The Valentinians seem to have presented at least part of their apostolic teaching as reserved only for advanced Christians, the spiritual ones, and not for ordinary Christians. Like good teachers, they withheld more difficult concepts until students made adequate progress. We have seen also that texts like the Gospel According to Mary, the Revelation of Peter, and the Secret Book of James claimed that Jesus revealed certain special teachings when he appeared to just one or two apostles. These books made this esoteric teaching available to those deemed worthy of it.

Irenaeus would have none of this. He denied that the apostles had any secret teachings. If they did, they would surely have shared them with their successors, the bishops. But Irenaeus claimed that Jesus and the apostles would never have adapted their teachings to different audiences. If the apostles withheld certain advanced teachings from beginning Christians, Irenaeus said, then they were effectively lying to those beginning Christians—which, of course, the apostles would never do. Instead, he asserted that all true apostolic teachings are clearly manifest throughout the world and available to anyone through any true Christian congregation.

Irenaeus also focused on the Bible in his effort to combat what he called Christian heresies. The Gnostics, we have seen, created new scriptures that retold the stories in Genesis, and Marcion rejected the Old Testament altogether. In response, Irenaeus promoted one of the first versions of what would become a Christian canon of the Bible with an Old and a New Testament. Irenaeus agreed that the Old Testament was inferior to the New Testament, but that's because God was gradually revealing his truth to humanity as it progressed. The New Testament improved upon the Old Testament, but both testaments come from the same God.

Irenaeus argued that Christians should use the four gospels of Matthew, Mark, Luke, and John to understand Jesus and his teaching completely. He accused heretical groups of relying too much on a single gospel. For example, he said that the Valentinians used the Gospel of John too much, and Marcion used only the Gospel of Luke. In this way, their views of Jesus were skewed in one way or another. Instead, Irenaeus, said, Christians should read all four gospels—and no more than those four. Irenaeus also considered the letters of Paul to be scripture and part of the New Testament. He did not have the precise list of 27 New Testament books that eventually Christians would use—that would not come for another 200 years—but Irenaeus represents an early step in the process of creating a Christian Bible with Old and New Testaments.

But even this Bible was not sufficient for opposing alleged heretics like the Valentinians because the Valentinians used pretty much the same scriptures as Irenaeus. I doubt they would have disagreed with much of what Irenaeus said about the contents of the Bible. And yet the Valentinians interpreted those scriptures differently, as we saw in Ptolemy's letter to Flora and other Valentinian works. How could one judge the truth or falsehood of competing interpretations of the Bible? To do this, Irenaeus claimed that the Church has

333

received from the apostles a summary of Christian beliefs called "the rule of faith." This rule of faith stated the basic doctrines of Christianity, and any teachings that violated this rule were clearly false.

Here's an example of Irenaeus giving this rule of faith:

> The Church, which is dispersed throughout the entire world and to the ends of the earth, received from the apostles and their disciples this faith—in one God the Father Almighty, who made heaven and earth and the sea and all that is in them, and in one Christ Jesus, the Son of God, incarnate for our salvation, and in the Holy Spirit, who predicted through the prophets the dispensations of God, the coming, the birth from the Virgin, the passion, the resurrection from the dead, and the ascension of the beloved Jesus Christ our Lord in the flesh into the heavens, and his coming from the heavens in the glory of the Father to recapitulate all things and to raise up all flesh of the human race ... and that he might execute a just judgment on all.

If you are familiar with contemporary Christianity, this may remind you of one of the Christian creeds, like the Apostles' Creed or the Nicene Creed. Creeds are short statements of the Christian faith that Christians often recite at worship services and use for discriminating between true and false doctrines. And in fact, the rule of faith that Irenaeus promoted was an early version of such creeds. Irenaeus wanted bishops and other church leaders to use this rule of faith to test the teachings of other Christians and decide whether they are authentically Christian or heresy, false *gnōsis*.

And what should a bishop do when he detected that someone was teaching something that violated the rule of faith and so was a heretic? Irenaeus encouraged bishops to withdraw fellowship from such Christians, to refuse to give them the Eucharist, and if they were ministers or office-holders, to fire them. During Irenaeus's day, Christians were still very few, and they remained a small and sometimes persecuted minority in the Roman Empire. So really, he and his fellow bishops did not have any genuinely coercive powers at their disposal. Later on, in the 4th century, when Constantine and the other emperors supported Christianity, heretics could be fined or sent into exile or even executed. But in the 2nd and 3rd centuries, bishops could only refuse to have anything to do with Christians they called heretics and they could expel them from their communities. But such so-called heretics could just form their own Christian groups, which is precisely what the Valentinians and Marcion and others did when opposing Christian leaders acted against them.

Still, even if Irenaeus did not have any real coercive powers to stop the teachers and groups he called heretics, he did put into place a new conception of orthodoxy and heresy. Irenaeus's ideas of an orthodox succession of bishops from the apostles and a demonic succession of heretics from Simon Magus, his promotion of a Christian Bible, and his rule of faith—all these became very important parts of emerging Catholic Christianity.

But Irenaeus did even more than this to oppose the Gnostics and Valentinians. He developed and taught his own version of Christian truth, and this, too, proved highly influential in the centuries that followed. Let's look at some of the key features of Irenaeus's vision of Christianity.

First, and most importantly, Irenaeus disagreed with the Gnostic and Valentinian pictures of God. The Gnostics and Valentinians both taught that the ultimate God is very remote from us and unknowable, and that God emanates into a complex structure of multiple aeons. They also taught that the god who created this world, the god of Genesis, is a lower, inferior god, with the Gnostics saying that he is the malicious and ignorant Ialdabaōth.

Irenaeus accepted some aspects of this view, but he rejected most of it. He agreed that the ultimate God, the highest God, is really unknowable and can't actually be named. Irenaeus called this God the Father. But Irenaeus argued that God the Father did not emanate into 24 or 36 aeons. Instead, the Father has two somewhat lower aspects of himself—namely, the Son or Word of God, and the Holy Spirit, who is also God's Wisdom. It is the Son of God who makes the Father known to human beings. Through the Son, human beings gain access to the Father. Irenaeus said that the Son also does the work of organizing and directing the physical cosmos in which we live— he was the maker of the world. Meanwhile, the Holy Spirit is in charge of the spiritual powers that serve God, and the Spirit is present among Christians.

So Irenaeus also has a God that is both one and multiple, but his God is far less multiple than that of the Gnostics. Despite his harsh rhetoric, Irenaeus's view of God is not directly opposed to that of the Gnostics. Instead, the difference between them is a matter of degree. Now, Irenaeus's view is not quite the Trinity because he considers the Son and the Spirit to be lesser than the Father, but it's on the way to the Trinity. Plus, Irenaeus taught that the God of the Old Testament, the god who created this world, is the ultimate Father, not some inferior god—although it was the Son or Word who did the actual work of making things. According to Irenaeus, when God said, "Let us make humanity in our image," this was the Father speaking to the Son and the Holy Spirit.

In addition to the Father, Son, and Holy Spirit, Irenaeus taught that there are many other divine beings that exist between God and humanity. The earth, he said, is surrounded by seven spheres or heavens, in which multiple powers, angels, and archangels dwell. Each of the seven heavens has a guiding power, which is named. The highest heaven is Wisdom, and the rest are Understanding, Counsel, Fortitude, Knowledge, Godliness, and Fear of the Spirit.

Irenaeus's picture of God and the cosmos is less complicated than that of the Gnostics and Valentinians, but it still features an inaccessible highest God and then a lot of divine beings and powers between that God and human beings.

Irenaeus also developed a view of human salvation in response to other Christians. The Gnostics, Valentinians, and the Gospel According to Thomas all taught that Jesus saves people primarily by revealing true *gnōsis* to us— Christ makes us aware of the higher God and leads us to understand our true natures as spiritual beings in this material world.

Irenaeus, in contrast, emphasized that the Son of God became human in order to make human beings holy or sacred. Jesus sanctifies people, both body and soul. The Word of God became a real human being. The man Jesus was tested by affliction, suffering, and death, but the divine Word triumphed over these things in the resurrection. As Irenaeus saw it, human beings had become morally and physically corrupt, and it was the purpose of God's incarnation to make us holy again.

In fact, Irenaeus thought that Jesus passed through every stage of human life—childhood, young adulthood, middle age, and old age—so that he could sanctify all human beings, from babies to old people. Irenaeus considered people old when they are in their 40s, and so he explained that Jesus lived to the age of 49.

Irenaeus called what Jesus accomplished "recapitulation"—Jesus lived like Adam, but he undid all the damage Adam did. For example, Adam was made from virgin soil, and Jesus was born from a virgin woman. Adam's only father was God who made him, and Jesus's real father was God. Adam was associated with a woman, Eve, who disobeyed God, and Jesus was associated with a woman, his mother Mary, who obeyed God. So Jesus was a new Adam. But while the old Adam sinned, and so brought human beings into corruption and death, the new Adam Jesus was sinless, and so brought human beings into holiness and life.

The Gnostics, the Valentinians, and the other Christians we have studied so far considered our true selves to be only our spiritual selves. Our bodies are not part of our real selves, and they will be destroyed or perish into nothingness. Irenaeus, in contrast, believed that our bodies are essential to who we are. The Son of God had to come in a real body of flesh to make us holy. And the resurrection of the dead will definitely be a resurrection of the fleshly body that we now have. This body of flesh will rise from the dead and become glorious and imperishable. Yes, Irenaeus knew that Paul had said in 1 Corinthians that "flesh and blood cannot inherit the kingdom of God." But Irenaeus interpreted this verse symbolically: Paul was not referring to literal flesh and blood, but he was talking about sinful activities that come from the desires of the flesh. Fleshly desires and actions will not inherit the kingdom of God. Flesh and blood bodies certainly will.

And that's because the kingdom of God itself is not spiritual or immaterial— it will be a physical realm. It will, in fact, be this world, miraculously transformed by God. The Gnostics may have considered this world and the cosmos a mistake, and the Valentinians may have seen them as a result of ignorance. But Irenaeus taught that God created this world and the cosmos, and in the future he will transform them into an earthly paradise. The saved human beings, with real bodies, will live in this earthly kingdom and enjoy its fertility. They will grow in love for God and knowledge of him. They will see God, in their bodies.

Some special Christians, the holiest of people, will ascend to live in the heavens. But for eternity many people will dwell in a new city of God on earth. God will be present everywhere, to everyone. Here Irenaeus and the Gnostics were completely opposed.

Irenaeus developed these ideas—God the Father, Son, and Holy Spirit; Jesus Christ as recapitulating and reversing what Adam had done; the resurrection of the body and life in an eternal kingdom here on earth—all these ideas he developed in response to the "false *gnōsis*" that he saw in the Gnostics and the Valentinians. And all this, he said, came from the apostles.

This is true *gnōsis*—Irenaeus wrote—the teaching of the apostles, and the ancient institution of the Church, spread throughout the entire world; the succession of bishops, to whom the apostles entrusted each local church; and the genuine preservation, coming down to us, of the Scriptures, with a complete collection allowing for neither addition nor subtraction.

Irenaeus condemned false *gnōsis* as heresy, and he said that true *gnōsis* was simply the teaching of the Church, handed down from the apostles by the bishops, and present in the Bible.

But what about Christians who aspired to a more mystical and spiritual understanding of the faith? Especially Valentinianism appealed to Christians who sought a deeper, more philosophical understanding of Christian scriptures and teaching. Irenaeus did not have much to offer them, for he condemned the idea that there would be any higher Christian teachings reserved for more advanced Christians.

Other opponents of the Gnostics took a different path, however. In the next lecture we'll meet Christian teachers who joined Irenaeus in condemning the Gnostics and Valentinians as heretics, but who taught their own versions of *gnōsis*—a *gnōsis* that was higher and even secret, and yet orthodox.

Making *Gnōsis* Orthodox
Lecture 18

In the last lecture, we saw that Christian teachers and leaders, such as Justin Martyr and Irenaeus, opposed rival forms of Christianity by inventing the concepts of heresy and orthodoxy. Irenaeus strongly rejected the idea that Jesus or the apostles reserved any kind of special teaching only for advanced Christians. All of what Irenaeus called "true *gnōsis*" was publicly available in the preaching of bishops in apostolic succession. Other Christians joined Irenaeus in calling the Gnostics and Valentinians heretics, but they recognized the appeal of a more advanced understanding of the Christian faith. In this lecture, we'll discuss two ancient Christian intellectuals who were anti-Gnostic yet offered Christians alternative paths to *gnōsis*: Clement of Alexandria and Origen.

Clement of Alexandria

- Clement (150–211 to 215) was a younger contemporary of Irenaeus who taught in Alexandria, Egypt, in the last decades of the 2nd century.

- Clement accepted the basic reality that not all Christians could attain the same level of ethical perfection and intellectual understanding of the faith. But unlike the Valentinians—who had divided Christians into animate and spiritual people—Clement believed that Christians are at different points on a single path leading from ignorance and sin to *gnōsis* and salvation. Every person has the possibility of making this journey, although only a few reach the final stage of perfect *gnōsis* and become true Gnostics.

- In Clement's time, of course, practically no one was born and raised a Christian; thus, everyone started in a state of sin and ignorance. But according to Clement, God's Word led people to Christianity in two ways: through the Bible and Jewish tradition and through Greek philosophy. God's Word speaks through both of these, but the Word is fully present only in Jesus Christ.

- When people become Christian, they begin a process of growth. In the early stages, the Word of God teaches Christians how to achieve ethical improvement. In this process, they acquire what Clement calls "faith," that is, belief in the basic teachings of Christianity that the church proclaims throughout the world. Like Irenaeus, Clement believed that Jesus and the apostles established a kind of rule for what Christians should believe, which Clement called the "ecclesiastical norm."
  - Clement also encouraged Christians to move beyond mere faith to true *gnōsis*, a deeper understanding of the mysteries of Christianity. For Clement, this true *gnōsis* consisted mainly of a more spiritual understanding of the Scriptures.

  - People who have only faith understand the Bible literally and simply, but people who have *gnōsis* learn to read the Bible symbolically and to find multiple meanings in it.

- Clement presented himself as uniquely able to lead interested Christians from simple faith to advanced *gnōsis* because he claimed to have received secret teachings not written in the Scriptures through apostolic succession. But unlike the secret teachings offered by the Gnostics and Valentinians, Clement claimed that the *gnōsis* he offered perfected faith and did not violate the church's ecclesiastical norm. It was orthodox *gnōsis*.

The Life of Origen

- Another resident of Alexandria, Origen (c. 185–c. 254), became one of the most brilliant theologians of the ancient church. Origen developed his theological vision in part to create an alternative to Gnostic and Valentinian myth.

- The young Origen was a charismatic teacher, and he became known for his opposition to the Valentinians in particular. Although he defended so-called orthodox Christianity against Gnostics, Valentinians, and other "heretics," he eventually came into conflict with the bishop of Alexandria and was expelled from the Alexandrian church.

- Origen left Alexandria and settled in Caesarea Maritima on Palestine's Mediterranean coast. There, he opened a new school, and as a priest, he preached almost daily in church. In the 250s, Origen was arrested during a persecution of Christians. He was eventually released from jail, but the harsh treatment he received left him weak, and he died a few years later.

- This account of Origen's life reveals a complicated relationship with the organized church. On the one hand, he was a bit like Irenaeus: faithful to the church, an opponent of heretics, and a member of the clergy. On the other hand, he was also like Clement and even Valentinus: dedicated to advanced learning, eager to help people advance to higher *gnōsis*, and unwilling to close off conversation about difficult ideas.

Origen's Christian Myth

- Origen appealed to Christians who wanted a more intellectual, less close-minded approach to Christian truth, but he also understood that some people found the myths of the Gnostics and Valentinians attractive. In response, he attempted to provide a better myth for so-called orthodox Christianity—a better story of creation, fall, and salvation. In an amazing book called *On First Principles*, he laid out his comprehensive vision of Christian truth.

- Origen's story of salvation resembles that of the Gnostics in that it's a story of a fall from a blessed existence somewhere else into life in this world, then a return to union with God. But Origen's story emphasizes the abundance of God's love and the freedom of human beings—God wants everyone to be saved, and it seems that everybody will be. And Origen's story does not make this universe a mistake, nor does an inferior or hostile god rule it; instead, this universe is a good creation, made by God to help us to return to him.

- Like others we've met so far in this course, Origen believed that God is both one and multiple. There is only one God, but the unknowable, inaccessible Father makes himself known through his Word or Son, who exists with him eternally. Likewise, there is God's Holy Spirit, which is God's immediate presence among Christians. Origen insisted that the Son and the Spirit are not emanations like the Gnostic aeons. Instead, they are integral aspects of God and have eternally existed with God.

- Long before this universe came into existence, God created and ruled over a multitude of rational beings. These were pure intellects, who contemplated God through his Word. Their very reason to exist was to be educated by God's Word. Yet these rational beings had free will and could choose to turn away from God, which they did; they began to neglect contemplation of God. This was the origin of sin: the fall of the rational beings away from *gnōsis* of God.

- Because God loves all the intellects, he wanted to bring them back to contemplation of him. And for that reason, he created this material universe through his Word. By placing the fallen intellects in material bodies, God would teach them how to overcome their physical desires, such as greed and lust. The rational beings would morally improve, advance in knowledge of philosophical and religious truth, and gradually return to contemplation of God.

- The rational beings fell away from their original communion with God to varying degrees, and thus, they needed to be healed and educated in different ways. God assigned each fallen intellect to the body and place in the universe that would be best for it pedagogically.
  - The intellects that fell away the least became archangels, angels, and other good spirits. Those that fell away to a moderate degree became heavenly bodies, such as the sun, moon, planets, and stars. The rational beings that fell away the farthest are now Satan and his demons.

  - Human beings fell away from God less than the demons but more than the angels and the heavenly beings. God has assigned each of us to be born in just the right body and at just the right time and place so that we can begin the process of improving ourselves morally and learning about God intellectually.

- One intellect, however, did not fall away from contemplating God through his Word. In fact, this one intellect loved and studied the Word so intensely that the two became fused. This intellect became the soul of Jesus. United with this intellect, the Word of God could enter a human body and live and die as Jesus. The Son of God died for the sins of all fallen beings; he showed them how to live a moral life; and he taught them about the Father. In this way, he made it possible for the fallen beings to reform their lives and return to *gnōsis* of God.

- Origen was well aware that few people actually became Christian and started their return to God. And few, if any, Christians reached the level of contemplation of God that they had experienced so long ago when they were purely intellects. The reason for this is that people have free will, and they can choose whether to live righteously and to pursue *gnōsis*. But God loves all rational beings and does not give up on them. Like a good teacher, God can lead people to love and knowledge of him, but he does not force them.

- Thus, Origen argued that after this universe comes to an end, there will be future worlds, in which the fallen intellects will continue their journey back to God. In these future worlds, the experiences that intellects have will reflect how they have performed so far in their re-education.
  - People who were wicked in this universe will have bad experiences that we call hell, and better people will have more pleasant experiences that we call heaven. But neither of these experiences is eternal.

  - Because God does not compel rational beings to love him, it will take him many ages to bring them all back to him. But he will do it. The end result will be what Origen called the *apokatastasis*—the return of all rational beings to eternal contemplation of God.

- Origen's vision was a beautiful story of a fall from God and a return to him. It explained why we suffer and why this material world exists—for our long-term benefit. And it reassures people that God loves them and wants them to love him. It preserves both human free will and God's love for all his creatures.

○ But Origen's grand scheme raised some unsettling questions for other Christians. For example, does the *apokatastasis* mean the return of all fallen intellects to God—even Satan and the demons? Where does the resurrection of the body fit into Origen's cosmic vision of multiple worlds? And after the *apokatastasis*, could we fall away again?

○ Origen seems to have thought that the situation at the *apokatastasis* will be similar to the original condition in which the intellects contemplated God but not precisely the same. The intellects will have both bodies and a hierarchical arrangement that will provide stability. Thus, they will love God forever—freely but without fear of falling away.

Suggested Reading

Dawson, *Allegorical Readers and Cultural Revision in Ancient Alexandria*, chapter 4.

Heine, *Origen: Scholarship in the Service of the Church*.

Origen, *On First Principles*.

Trigg, *Origen*.

Questions to Consider

1. Irenaeus, Clement, and Origen are all considered "proto-orthodox," defenders of emerging orthodox Christianity. What do these three share in common? In what ways do they differ?

2. According to Origen, why are some people good and some bad, some people highly spiritual and others less so?

Making *Gnōsis* Orthodox
Lecture 18—Transcript

Ironically, the first early Christian who claims in his own writings that he's a Gnostic was not a Gnostic. He was Clement of Alexandria, a Christian author who, like Irenaeus of Lyons, opposed the Gnostics and the Valentinians. But unlike Irenaeus, Clement did not deny the existence of secret Christian *gnōsis*. Instead, he himself taught such secret *gnōsis*—but *gnōsis* that he said was orthodox, faithful to the teachings of the emerging Church.

In the last lecture, we saw how Christian teachers and leaders like Justin Martyr and Irenaeus opposed rival forms of Christianity by inventing the concepts of heresy and orthodoxy. Irenaeus strongly rejected the idea that Jesus or the apostles reserved any kind of special teaching for only advanced Christians. All of what Irenaeus called "true *gnōsis*" was publically available in the preaching of bishops in apostolic succession.

Clement and other Christians joined Irenaeus in calling the Gnostics and Valentinians heretics, but they recognized the appeal of a more advanced understanding of the Christian faith, one that could be shared only with those Christians who wanted to study sacred texts and traditions more deeply. In this lecture, I discuss two ancient Christian intellectuals who were anti-Gnostic and yet offered Christians alternative, more "orthodox" paths to *gnōsis*— Clement and Origen, both residents of that remarkable city, Alexandria.

Clement was a younger contemporary of Irenaeus, and he taught small groups of people in Alexandria, Egypt, in the last decades of the 2nd century. As I have mentioned before, Alexandria was one of the leading centers of intellectual life in the ancient world. Two important institutions supported serious scholarship in the city, the Museum and the Library. The Museum was not a place to see exhibits, as we might think. Instead, it was a kind of think-tank, where scholars, usually supported by the government, carried out research, led seminars, and gave lectures. And the famous library contained a huge collection of scrolls, filled with the accumulated wisdom of Greek culture, including works of philosophy, history, drama, and poetry. Young people came to Alexandria from all over the Roman Empire to study with the best-known scholars, some of whom were Jews or Christians.

We have already met the great Jewish philosopher Philo, who lived in Alexandria and died around the year 45. We'll come back to him in the next lecture. And most historians believe that Valentinus spent his early years in Alexandria before he moved to Rome around 140. It seems very likely that the Gnostic school of thought originated in Alexandria as well. All of these teachers and groups used Greek wisdom, including philosophy, mathematics, and astronomy, to deepen their understanding of the Bible. And Christians like Valentinus believed that their teachings about Jesus continued in this great tradition of Greek learning.

This is the environment in which Clement worked. Unlike Irenaeus, he did not have any ordained position in a church. Rather, he was an independent teacher, as Justin Martyr had been in Rome. Christians who had the intellectual talents and financial resources for advanced study of philosophy could meet with Clement. Clement would guide them in reading sacred texts and works of philosophy, and he would help them improve their ethical lives. Clement was something like a Christian guru, a spiritual guide, who helped his students become as wise and virtuous as they could be. They could become perfect Christians—or, as Clement put it, true Gnostics.

You'll remember that the Valentinians divided Christians into two groups. The "animate people" were oriented to or dominated by soul, and they were ordinary, non-Valentinian Christians. The "spiritual people" were oriented to or dominated by spirit, and they were the Valentinians. We found that a great deal of ambiguity surrounded Valentinian teachings on whether people were predestined to be animate or spiritual or whether people had the free will to move between these categories. Valentinians seemed to disagree about whether animate people, non-Valentinian Christians, would enjoy the same full salvation that they did.

All of this reflected a basic reality: that some Christians were interested in and capable of the advanced study and reflection that Valentinian teachers offered, but most were not. Clement also accepted this basic reality: Not all Christians attained the same level of ethical perfection and of intellectual understanding of the faith. But rather than divide Christians into two categories with two different names—animate people versus spiritual people—Clement said that Christians are at different points on a single path leading from ignorance and sin to *gnōsis* and salvation. Every person has the possibility of making this journey, although only very few reach the final stage of perfect *gnōsis* and become true Gnostics.

In Clement's day, of course, practically no one was born and raised a Christian, and so everybody started in a state of sin and ignorance. But, according to Clement, God's Logos or Word was leading people to Christianity in two ways: on the one hand, through the Bible and Jewish tradition, and on the other hand, through Greek philosophy. God's Word speaks through both of these, but God's Word is fully present only in Jesus Christ.

When people become Christian, they begin a process of growth. In the early stages, the Word of God teaches Christians how to become better people ethically. Clement took this stage of the Christian life very seriously. One of his books gives Christians detailed instructions on how to live properly, including what kinds of clothing, jewelry, and shoes they should wear; how they should behave at dinner parties; and even how and when they should have sex with their spouses. It's clear from Clement's directions that he expects most of his followers to be fairly well-off and educated.

Meanwhile, as they are improving morally, Christians acquire what Clement calls "faith"—belief in the basic teachings of Christianity that the Church proclaims throughout the world. Like Irenaeus, Clement believed that Jesus and the apostles established a kind of rule for what Christians should believe, which Clement called "the ecclesiastical norm."

But unlike Irenaeus, Clement did not think that Christians should be satisfied with simple faith in the basic teachings of the Church. He expressed frustration with certain Christians who he said "are called orthodox" and want "only the bare faith." Instead, Clement encouraged Christians to move beyond mere faith, to true *gnōsis*—a deeper understanding of the mysteries of Christianity. For Clement, this true *gnōsis* consisted mainly of a more spiritual understanding of the Scriptures. People who have only faith understand the Bible literally and simply; but people who have *gnōsis* learn to read the Bible symbolically and to find in it multiple meanings.

Clement presented himself as uniquely able to lead interested Christians from simple faith to advanced *gnōsis*. That's because he claimed to have received through apostolic succession secret teachings, not written in the Scriptures. Jesus taught this true *gnōsis* to the apostles, Clement said, and the apostles taught this unwritten knowledge to their students, and Clement received it from them. But unlike the secret teachings offered by the Gnostics and Valentinians, Clement claimed that the *gnōsis* he offered perfected faith and did not violate the Church's ecclesiastical norm. It was orthodox *gnōsis*. Clement invited Christians to advance beyond simple faith and to learn from him how to become true Gnostics—not like the falsely named Gnostics who worshiped the Barbēlō or followed Valentinus.

It seems that a persecution of Christians broke out in Alexandria shortly after the year 200. During that turmoil, Clement left the city and resettled in Asia Minor. Another intellectually gifted Alexandrian Christian, a teenager named Origen, lost his father during that persecution, for he was executed as a Christian. According to one story, the young Origen wanted to join his father in martyrdom, but his hopes were dashed when his mother hid his clothes and he was too modest to leave the house naked.

Christianity was fortunate that Origen did not die for the faith so young because he ended up becoming one of the most brilliant theologians of the ancient church. Origen's theology was always very controversial, but it set the agenda for Christian thought for centuries to come. And Origen was a determined foe of both Gnostics and Valentinians: He developed his theological vision in part precisely to create an alternative to Gnostic and Valentinian myth.

Even when he had not yet reached the age of 20, Origen attracted students who wanted to study Christianity with him. Origen led a highly ascetic life. He remained celibate until his death, and he ate, drank, and slept very little. He devoted himself to scholarly pursuits, especially studying and writing about the Bible. Historians are not sure whether to believe a report that he even had himself castrated, so that no one would suspect him of impropriety when he taught women.

The young Origen was clearly a charismatic teacher, and he became known for his opposition to the Valentinians in particular. Valentinian Christianity had become very popular among educated and wealthy Christians in Alexandria. Origen worked to change that. Upper-class Christians would throw dinner parties, where the after-dinner entertainment would be a debate between Origen and a Valentinian teacher. One prominent Valentinian Christian whom Origen persuaded to give up Valentinianism was named Ambrose. Ambrose was so taken with Origen's intelligence and faith that he financially supported the scholar for decades. For example, Ambrose paid for a team of scribes to record Origen's theological works as he dictated them.

Although Origen defended so-called orthodox Christianity against Gnostics, Valentinians, and other so-called heretics, he eventually came into conflict with the bishop of Alexandria, Demetrius. At first, the bishop supported Origen and even put him in charge of training new converts. But Demetrius became angry as Origen gained a worldwide reputation and traveled to places like Arabia, Palestine, and Athens to teach and preach at the request of other bishops. When Demetrius heard that a bishop in Palestine had ordained Origen a priest without his permission, he had Origen expelled from the Alexandrian church. The basis for the expulsion was the charge that Origen had said that even Satan would eventually repent and be saved. As we'll see, that may be true.

In any case, Origen left Alexandria and settled in Caesarea Maritima on Palestine's Mediterranean coast. There he opened a new school, which attracted many students, including pagans. And as a priest, he preached almost daily in church. In the 250s, Origen was arrested during a persecution of Christians. He was eventually released from jail, but the harsh treatment left him very weak, and he died a few years later. He left behind an enormous set of writings, of which only a small part survives today.

You can tell from this account of Origen's life that his relationship with the organized Church was a little complicated. On the one hand, he fought against Christians identified as heretics, he tried to serve the Church, and he became a priest. On the other hand, the bishop of Alexandria considered him disobedient and too much of a freethinker. And this captures well who Origen was. He was a little bit like Irenaeus—faithful to the Church, an opponent of heretics, a member of the clergy—but also a lot like Clement and even Valentinus—dedicated to advanced learning, eager to help people advance to higher *gnōsis*, unwilling to close off conversation about difficult ideas.

Like Clement, Origen believed that different Christians are at different stages on a path to higher contemplation of God, and he too wanted to help them move from a simple faith in the literal meaning of the Bible to a deeper *gnōsis* of the Bible's symbolic meanings. Origen agreed with Irenaeus that Jesus and the apostles had passed on to the Church a rule of faith, a basic set of teachings that all Christians must believe. And he agreed, too, that this rule of faith showed that Christians like the Gnostics, Marcion, and Valentinus were not true Christians, but heretics.

Unlike Irenaeus, however, Origen said that there's more to Christianity than the rule of faith. He pointed out that the apostles did not explain how the doctrines in the rule of faith were true. For example, the rule of faith teaches that the Son or Word of God became incarnate in Jesus, but the apostles did not explain how that worked. How is the Son divine? How could he unite with a human being? Moreover, there are other questions that the rule of faith did not cover at all. For example, the rule of faith teaches that God created the universe in which we live, and that at some point this universe will come to an end. But the apostles did not say whether this is the only universe that has ever existed or will ever exist. Were there created worlds before this one? Will there be worlds after this one ends? Inquiring minds want to know, but the rule of faith does not say.

Origen claimed that the apostles left these questions open precisely so that intellectually gifted Christians—"lovers of wisdom," he called them—would have stuff to study, think about, speculate on, and debate. In other words, Origen believed that the rule of faith was not just the limit to Christian thought—it was also the starting point for an intellectual journey into the mysteries of God, the universe, and our lives. Origen believed that the answers to all these questions were hidden within the Scriptures, which are filled with clues from God. There's no guarantee that, even after a lifetime of study, anyone would find all the answers—but Christians should try!

You can see why Origen made some bishops like Demetrius nervous. Just like Valentinian teachers, Origen wanted Christians to search for deeper, more esoteric teachings than what they would hear in a regular church service. The only difference was that, in Origen's view, the Valentinians found false teachings, the wrong answers. Still, that wasn't very reassuring to someone like Demetrius. On the other hand, the bishop of Caesarea was more open-minded: He welcomed Origen and authorized him to preach.

So Origen appealed to Christians who wanted a more intellectual, less close-minded approach to Christian truth. But Origen understood also that some people found the myths of the Gnostics and Valentinians fascinating and attractive. The stories that they told explained how God emanated into the aeons, how and why this world came to be, and where we human beings come from and where we're going. The Gnostic myth was a compelling response to alienation from this world of suffering, oppression, and death, and it offered hope for an existence of serenity, equality, and life.

So Origen realized that so-called orthodox Christianity needed a better myth—a better story of creation, fall, and salvation to compete with that of the Gnostics and Valentinians. And that's what he tried to provide. In an amazing book called *On First Principles*, Origen laid out his comprehensive vision of Christian truth, and in his countless sermons and biblical commentaries, he refined and elaborated on that vision for the Christians who flocked to hear him preach or who read his books with enthusiasm.

Origen's story of salvation resembles that of the Gnostics in that it's a story of a fall from a blessed existence somewhere else into life in this world, and then a return to union with God. But Origen's story emphasizes the abundance of God's love and the freedom of human beings—God wants everyone to be saved, and it seems that everybody will be. And Origen's story does not make this universe a mistake, nor does an inferior or hostile God rule it; instead, this universe is a good creation, made by God to help us to return to him.

Like everyone we've met so far in this course, Origen believed that God is both one and multiple. There's only one God, but the unknowable, inaccessible Father makes himself known through his Word or Son, who exists with him eternally. Likewise, there's God's Holy Spirit, which is

God's immediate presence among Christians. Origen insisted that the Son and the Spirit are not emanations like the Gnostic aeons. Instead, they are integral aspects of God, which have eternally existed with God.

Long before this universe came into existence, God created and ruled over a multitude of rational beings. These were pure intellects, who contemplated God through his Son or Word. Their very reason to exist was to be educated by God's Word. And yet these rational beings had free will, and they could choose to turn away from God—and this they did. For whatever reason, the intellects became bored or started to neglect contemplation of God. They were like students in a classroom who get distracted and stop paying attention. This was the origin of sin—the fall of the rational beings away from *gnōsis* of God.

Because God loves all the intellects, he wanted to bring them back to contemplation of him. And for that reason God created this material universe through his Word. By placing the fallen intellects in material bodies, God would teach the intellects how to overcome their physical desires, like greed and sex. The rational beings would morally improve, and then they could advance in knowledge of philosophical and religious truth and gradually return to contemplation of God.

Now, the rational beings fell away from their original communion with God to varying degrees—some very little, some a great deal, and some in between—and so they needed to be healed and educated in different ways. So God decided to assign each fallen intellect to the body and place in the universe that would be best for it pedagogically. The intellects who fell away the least became archangels, angels, and other good spirits—they don't need much re-education, and so they have the least difficult bodies to manage. Next are the intellects that God made into heavenly bodies, like the sun, moon, the planets, and the stars. The rational beings that fell away the farthest are now Satan and his demons.

And between the heavenly beings and the demons are human beings. We fell away from God less than the demons, but more than the angels and the heavenly beings. God has assigned each of us to be born in just the right body and at just the right time and place, so that we can begin the process of improving ourselves morally and learning about God intellectually.

So Origen agreed with the Gnostics and Valentinians that our bodies are secondary parts of who we are. But our bodies are not prisons from which we need to be liberated, nor are they the means by which evil cosmic rulers enslave us. Instead, they are gifts to us from God, to help us return to him. They are like training wheels for the bicycle of the soul. If we can master our bodies, then we can train and educate our souls as well.

And why are some people born to wealthy parents in comfortable lives in the 21st century and other people are born to poor families in difficult conditions during the Middle Ages? Again, these differences are all part of God's plan—each of us has been born in precisely the best situation for us to use our free will rightly and to obey and love God.

It turns out, however, that one intellect did not fall away from contemplating God through his Logos or Word. In fact, this one intellect loved and studied the Word so intensely that it became filled with or fused with God's Word, just as iron you put in a fire becomes infused and red-hot with the fire's heat. This intellect became the soul of Jesus. United with this created but unfallen intellect, the Word of God could enter a human body and live and die as Jesus. The Son of God died for the sins of all fallen beings; he showed them how to live a moral life; and he taught them about the Father. In this way, he made it possible for the fallen beings to reform their lives and return to gnōsis of God.

Origen was well aware that few people actually became Christian and started their return to God. And he knew that, during their lifetimes, very few, if any, Christians reached the level of contemplation of God that they had experienced so long ago when they were purely intellects. That's because people have free will, and they can choose whether to live righteously and whether to pursue gnōsis. But God loves all the rational beings, and so he does not give up on them. Like a good teacher, God can lead people to love and knowledge of him, but he does not force them. And he wants everyone to get an A eventually.

So Origen argued that, after this universe comes to an end, there will be future worlds, ages to come, in which the fallen intellects will continue their journey back to God. In these future worlds the experiences that intellects have will reflect how they have performed so far in their process or re-education. This is not reincarnation because you aren't reborn in this universe—instead, it's like going to a new school after finishing at your old one. People who were wicked in this universe will have bad experiences that we call hell, and better people will have more pleasant experiences that we call heaven. But both of these experiences—heaven and hell—are not eternal, just a really, really long time. Because God does not compel the rational beings to love him, it will take him ages and ages to bring them all back to him. But he will do it. The end result will be what Origen called the *apokatastasis*—the return of all rational beings to eternal contemplation of God.

Origen's vision was a beautiful and awesome story of a fall from God and a return to him. It explained why we suffer and why this material world exists—it's all for our long-term benefit. And it reassures people that God loves them and wants them to love him. It preserves both human free will and God's love for all his creatures.

But Origen's grand scheme raised some unsettling questions for other Christians. For example, does the *apokatastasis* really mean the return of all fallen intellects to God? Does this mean that even Satan and the demons will be saved? You'll remember that Bishop Demetrius accused Origen of teaching this and got him expelled from the church in Alexandria for it.

Modern scholars debate what Origen really taught on this point. Some historians point to passages in Origen's writings where he says that some rational beings may get so used to sinning—they sin so bad and for so long—that their very nature changes and they are incapable of choosing the good any longer. Such passages suggest that Satan and the demons may have gone beyond God's help. Other historians point to passages in which Origen speaks about salvation in fully inclusive terms. Quoting Paul's First Letter to the Corinthians, Origen often says that, in the end, God will be "all in all." Still other historians suggest that Origen changed his mind on this point. The youthful Origen, fighting against Valentinians in Alexandria, taught that all beings would be saved, but the older Origen, preaching daily from the Bible in Caesarea, eventually excluded demons and truly wicked people from salvation. In the spirit of Origen, I'm going to leave that question unanswered.

Another problem that Origen's thought raised was the idea of the resurrection of the body. Where does that fit into Origen's cosmic vision of multiple worlds and a return of intellects to contemplating God?

This, too, is a matter that historians argue about because Origen's writings are difficult to pin down on this point. But you'll recall that in an earlier lecture I suggested that Christians have tended to waver between emphasizing that the resurrected body will be spiritual and a transformed version of our present body and saying that the resurrected body will be fleshly and very similar to our present body. Origen is clearly on the spiritual and transformative end of the spectrum. He tends to say that we'll have spiritual bodies quite different from what we have now—not at all flesh and blood—but that these spiritual bodies will have the same form or pattern as our present bodies. Our individual identities will survive, but not our current materials.

If Origen were alive today, I think he would say that what will rise from the dead and live forever is our individual DNA, not the actual physical genes, but the abstract pattern or code that the DNA represents. That code will be the basis for a new body, but one not made of the stuff we now consist of, rather one that is entirely spiritual and suited to eternal existence in intellectual *gnōsis* of God.

This insight leads us to the final question that Origen's thought posed to ancient Christians. If free will is essential to who we are, and God never forces us to love him or contemplate him, does that mean that, after the *apokatastasis*, we could fall away again and start this all over? What's to guarantee that we won't get bored again and once again neglect contemplation of God and fall into sin?

Origen seems to have thought that the situation at the *apokatastasis* will be like the original condition in which the intellects contemplated God, but not precisely the same. For one thing, the intellects will now have bodies—spiritual bodies, to be sure, but bodies nonetheless. And Origen seems to suggest that at the end, all the intellects will not be equal—there will be some hierarchy among the returned rational beings, although all will experience full blessedness. It seems that bodies and the hierarchical arrangement of the intellects will give them a stability that they did not have at first. And so they will love God forever—completely freely, but without the fear of falling away.

Together the two Alexandrian theologians, Clement and Origen, created an orthodox version of *gnōsis* and even an orthodox myth that could compete with what the Gnostics and Valentinians taught. They made major contributions to the theology and spirituality of what would become orthodox Christianity. And yet both were and remain controversial figures. Neither is an official saint of the Roman Catholic Church—although Clement is in other branches of Christianity, like Eastern Orthodoxy. In fact, a church council tragically and unjustly declared Origen a heretic three centuries after his death.

Still, the orthodox *gnōsis* that Origen taught immensely influenced later Christianity. His theology set the agenda for Christian thought for the next several centuries. Origen's vision of God's transformation of humanity through free will remains at the heart of Eastern Orthodox Christianity. And if it weren't for the Gnostics and Valentinians, he would not have developed his theology as he did.

Indeed, the story that I have told thus far about so-called Gnosticism has been very much a Christian story—a story of competing ideas about the new revelation and salvation that Jesus brought. It's time now to widen our focus and start looking at the importance of Gnosticism for religions other than Christianity. And in the next lecture we'll start with Christianity's closest relative, Judaism.

Gnosticism and Judaism
Lecture 19

C hristian bishops and teachers were not the only religious leaders who worried about so-called heretics in late antiquity. In the 2nd century, just when Irenaeus and Clement were criticizing Gnostics and Valentinians, Jewish rabbis also complained about "sectarians" or even "heretics" who claimed that there were "two powers in heaven"—not one God but two. Based on these complaints and other evidence, many historians have argued that the first Gnostics were Jews. That is, these historians claim that the Gnostic school of thought started out as a Jewish religious movement and only later included Jesus in its teachings and began to seem Christian. In this lecture, we'll explore why many scholars believe in the Jewish origins of Gnosticism.

Multiple Divine Powers
- We have already met ancient Jews who, like the Gnostics, imagined that God is both one and multiple at the same time.
  - For example, the Jewish philosopher Philo of Alexandria anticipated the Gnostics by depicting God as consisting of multiple powers and aspects and by saying that a lower, second God created this universe **(Figure 6)**. Philo died well before the Gnostic school of thought began, but it's almost certain that Gnostics read some of Philo's works, and it's quite certain that Valentinus and his followers did.

  - We have also seen that the Aramaic Targum Pseudo-Jonathan, a text that is later than the time of the Gnostics, presented God as having a lower manifestation or aspect called his *Memra*, or "Word." It was the Word, says this targum, that walked around in the Garden of Eden and that caused the flood.

- What inspired Jews, such as Philo and the author of the targum, to divide God into multiple powers, rather than conceiving of a single God? In Philo's case, Greek philosophy played an important role.

Figure 6. Philo of Alexandria's View of God

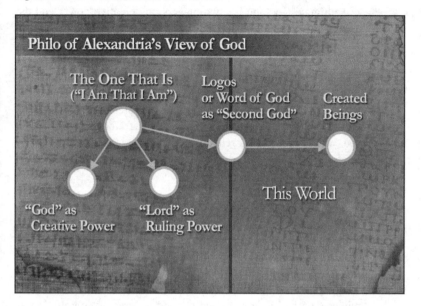

- Philo had learned from reading Plato that the most perfect God and source of all being should be highly spiritual and remote from us and, therefore, that a lower craftsman god created this world. Philo assumed that Moses taught the same thing in Genesis.

- The author of the targum probably had not read much Greek philosophy, but he was clearly worried that a God who walks in a garden and destroys humanity with a flood could not be the ultimate perfect God; surely, this must be a less divine aspect of God.

- The Jewish Bible also provided material for thinking of God as multiple powers. Consider, for example, a story found in Genesis 18. Here, the biblical author tells us that the Lord appeared to Abraham, but Abraham actually sees three men.

Philo concluded that these three men must represent the ultimate God and his two powers, the creative power and the ruling power. There are also other passages in the Bible in which people see God in some human form or forms.

- Ancient Jews came up with numerous explanations for such visions in the Bible. Human characters may have seen an angel; or perhaps the multiple figures of God are simply different forms of the one God; or perhaps there are lower aspects of God that people can see, while God himself remains invisible. This last idea is not too far from the Gnostic idea of an ultimate Invisible Spirit and aeons emanating from God.

Hypothesizing the Jewish Origins of Gnosticism

- As we know, the religions that eventually became Christianity and Judaism both started among Jews in the 1st century. The Jews whom we call the first Christians—Peter, Paul, James, Mary Magdalene, and others—heard the message of Jesus and saw him after his death. They concluded that he was the Messiah (Greek: "the Christ"), whom God had long promised to send to Israel. Certainly, in this sense, all Christian groups originated in Judaism.

- The proponents of the Jewish origins of Gnosticism argue that Jews developed the Gnostic myth without having had any encounter with, or knowledge of, Jesus. Jews came up with the story of the Invisible Spirit, the Barbēlō, Wisdom, Ialdabaōth, and the seed of Seth apart from knowledge of Jesus, and only later did Gnostics learn about Jesus and incorporate him into their mythology. The Gnostic school of thought, then, started out Jewish and subsequently became Christian.

- Among the arguments for this position is the fact that much Gnostic literature, such as the Secret Book According to John, the Revelation of Adam, and so on, is intensely engaged with the Jewish Bible, especially Genesis. Gnostic texts retell the story of Genesis multiple times. To be sure, they often "correct" the errors that Moses made, but they clearly believed that this is where religious truth could be found. Jews are probably the best candidates for people who would be focused on the book of Genesis.

- Further, several of these same Gnostic works don't have many Christian features, or their Christian features are suspiciously marginal.
  - ○ The Secret Book According to John, for example, presents itself as a revelation from the Savior to the apostle John after the death and resurrection of Christ. But only at the beginning and end of the book is the Savior who speaks explicitly identified as Jesus and the recipient of the revelation identified as the apostle John. The long discourse in between has few, if any, explicitly Christian elements.

  - ○ Scholars have argued that the revelation itself was first composed by one or more Gnostic Jews, and later, someone made it Christian by creating a frame story around the Gnostic myth.

- Scholars have also noted that many ideas and incidents in Gnostic texts have parallels in Jewish literature, especially rabbinic literature. We have already seen similarities between the Reality of the Rulers and the Jewish Targum Pseudo-Jonathan. But there are other examples, in which, for example, Gnostic retellings of the creation of humanity or of the flood story resemble ideas found in Jewish texts.

- Of course, the most remarkable feature of Gnostic literature in relation to Judaism is that the Gnostics identified the God of Genesis—the God worshipped by the Jews—as the ignorant and malicious Ialdabaōth. Why would Jews have decided that the God of their ancestors was not the true God but a flawed divinity that was hostile to human beings?
  - ○ Platonism would have convinced some Greek-speaking Jews, such as Philo, that any true God must be remote, extremely spiritual, and not subject to such emotions as anger or regret. The God of Genesis is neither remote nor particularly spiritual, and he gets angry at humans and destroys many of them in a

flood. Some Jews may have concluded, therefore, that the God of Genesis was an imperfect deity, and they may have looked for a higher God.

- o Scholars also point to the devastating history of the Jews in the 1st and 2nd centuries—with multiple rebellions against Roman rule and the second destruction of the Temple—as an explanation for the tendency to turn away from their ancestral God. Thanks to Platonism, Jews were already inclined to question the divinity of the biblical God, and they now saw that God as a deluded, arrogant failure.

© sedmak/iStock/Thinkstock.

God had promised King David that one of his sons would always reign in Jerusalem, but the long history of foreign rule in Judaea may have led some Jews to question God's ability to fulfill his promises.

- • Eventually, the Gnostics encountered the Christian message about Jesus and introduced Jesus into the Gnostic myth. They also added Christian elements to the beginning and end of some of their revelatory books. Christian leaders, such as Irenaeus, saw this teaching as a threat to true Christianity and attacked it. Valentinus, in contrast, found the myth fascinating, but he revised it to make it even more explicitly Christian. Thus, the Gnostic myth was originally Jewish and was later rendered Christian.

Countering the Hypothesis

- This theory of how Gnosticism originated is compelling. One of its advantages is that it sets aside Irenaeus's picture of the Gnostics as Christian heretics. Instead, they were Jews whose understandable response to contemporary events was to create a new religious movement. Despite this advantage, many historians are skeptical of the Jewish hypothesis.

- One reason for this skepticism is that many of the passages in Jewish literature that resemble elements in Gnostic texts are from Jewish texts that date well after the Gnostic writings. In addition, we can't be sure that such texts as the Secret Book According to John were originally Jewish and later made Christian. Moreover, the Gospel of Judas is one of the earliest Gnostic texts, and it is mostly Christian; the majority of the text consists of conversations between Jesus and the disciples or Jesus and Judas.

- As we discussed, those who claim that the first Gnostics were non-Christian Jews argue that Jews became so disappointed in their fate that they lost confidence in their God and concluded that he was inferior and malicious. But this claim does not seem completely plausible.
  - From antiquity to today, the history of the people of Israel has been replete with catastrophic events. Through all their pain and suffering, Jews have complained to God, but they have not concluded that he was evil.

  - Instead, the Jews have considered their suffering to be punishment for their sins, and they have repented and asked God for forgiveness. Or they have concluded that God will keep his promises to his people in the future, when the Messiah comes and God establishes his kingdom.

- It seems likely that the first Gnostics were Jews or a mix of Jews and Gentiles. The interest in Genesis in Gnostic texts points to Jewish authors. But those Jews must have heard about or had some encounter with Jesus.

o As we have seen, early Christians disagreed about almost everything, but they all agreed that Jesus represented something new—a new revelation, a new intervention by God in history, a new means of salvation. This something new called into question everything that had gone before.

o Jesus may have come from the biblical tradition and his teachings may have made complete sense within Judaism, but his followers believed that his appearance necessitated rethinking the Bible and the history of Israel.

o Some scholars believe that Jewish intellectuals of the late 1st or early 2nd century had reasons to doubt the God of Genesis. The teachings of Platonism made him seem like a lower, inferior god, and Jewish hopes for a land and a king had been frequently crushed. However, these factors appear to be necessary but not sufficient causes for the appearance of the Gnostic myth and the transformation of the God of Genesis into Ialdabaōth.

o What the Jews really needed was a new revelation that would explain and confirm their doubts and give them new hope. The most likely catalyst was the proclamation of Jesus, and the teachings of Paul and the Gospel of John were the steps that led from doubts about the God of Israel to the creation of the Gnostic myth.

Suggested Reading

Pearson, *Gnosticism, Judaism, and Egyptian Christianity*.

Scholem, *Major Trends in Jewish Mysticism*.

Segal, *Two Powers in Heaven*.

Smith, *No Longer Jews*.

1. Do you find the arguments for a purely Jewish origin for Gnosticism persuasive? Why or why not?

2. In what ways does the Hebrew Bible or Old Testament itself suggest that there is not simply one God?

Gnosticism and Judaism
Lecture 19—Transcript

Christian bishops and [teachers] were not the only religious leaders who worried about so-called heretics in late antiquity. In the 2nd century, just when Irenaeus of Lyons and Clement of Alexandria were criticizing Gnostics and Valentinians, Jewish teachers—the rabbis—started to complain about "sectarians" or even "heretics" who claimed that there were "two powers in heaven"—not one God, but two.

Who were these heretics who believed in two heavenly powers? Most likely they were simply Christians, for they believed in the divinity of Jesus as God's Son, as well as believing in God the Father. But it seems that some of the "two powers" believers that concerned the rabbis also saw one of the two powers as inferior or even evil and opposed to the one God. Could these have been Gnostics? Were there Jewish Gnostics, or maybe Gnostic Jews?

Many historians not only have answered yes to these questions, but they have also argued that the first Gnostics were Jews and not Christians at all. That is, these historians claim that the Gnostic school of thought started out among Jews as a Jewish religious movement, and only later did it include Jesus in its teachings and start to look Christian. I find this argument unlikely, but in this lecture I want to explain why many scholars believe in the Jewish origins of Gnosticism and how emerging Judaism is part of the story of Gnosticism and emerging Christianity.

We have already met ancient Jews who, like the Gnostics, believed that it was too simple to think of God as simply one and who instead imagined that God is both one and multiple at the same time. For example, the great Jewish philosopher Philo of Alexandria lived during the time of Jesus and Paul, although he did not know about either of them. Philo died well before the Gnostic school of thought began, but it's almost certain that Gnostics read some of Philo's works and it's definitely certain that Valentinus and his followers did.

Philo believed that the ultimate God is beyond all specific names and should be understood simply as "The One That Is." He pointed out that in the book of Exodus, when Moses encounters God in a burning bush, God identifies himself as simply "I am that I am." Philo concluded that the names of God in the Greek Bible, such as "God" and "Lord," must refer not to the ultimate God himself, but to powers or aspects of God. The name "God," Philo said, refers to God's creative power, and "Lord" refers to his ruling power. God is therefore not just one, but also three. Most people can perceive only these lower powers of God, but the purest and most learned human intellect might be able to apprehend "The One That Is" alone by itself.

According to Philo, "God" and "Lord" are not the only powers of God, just the most senior ones. According to Genesis, God created the universe by speaking: "Then God said, 'Let there be light'; and there was light." It's God's speech that brought the world into existence. And so Philo designates as the Logos or Word of God the divine principle that mediates between the ultimate God and the creation. The Word is God's "chief messenger," standing "on the border and separating the creature from the Creator." Philo could call the Logos "a second God." So Philo anticipated the Gnostics by depicting God as consisting of multiple powers and aspects and by saying that a lower, second God created this universe.

We have also looked at the Aramaic Targum Pseudo-Jonathan, a text that is later than the time of the Gnostics. We saw that it, too, retold stories from Genesis. Like Philo, the targum presented God as having a lower manifestation or aspect called his *Memra*, or "Word." It was the Word, says the targum, that walked around in the Garden of Eden and that caused the flood.

What inspired Jews like Philo and the author of the targum to divide God up and not just have a simple single God? In Philo's case, Greek philosophy played an important role. He had learned from reading Plato that the most perfect God and source of all being should be highly spiritual and remote from us and that therefore a lower craftsman god created this world. Philo assumed that Moses taught the same thing in Genesis. The author of the targum probably had not read much Greek philosophy, but he too was clearly worried that a God who walks in a garden and destroys humanity with a flood could not be the ultimate perfect God—surely he must be a somewhat less divine aspect of God.

But the Jewish Bible itself also provided material for thinking in this way. Consider, for example, a story in chapter 18 of Genesis. The biblical author says that the Lord appeared to the patriarch Abraham by the oaks of Mamre as Abraham sat at the entrance to his tent. But what does Abraham see? He sees three men. These men talk with Abraham and predict to him that his wife Sarah will become pregnant. What does it mean that the Lord appeared to Abraham and he saw three men? Philo concluded that this must represent the ultimate God and his two powers, the creative power and the ruling power.

This, of course, is not the only passage in the Bible in which people see God in some human form or some other form. In chapter 7 of the book of Daniel, the hero Daniel sees a figure called an Ancient One, seated on a throne, dressed in white clothing, and having hair like wool. That would seem to be God. But then there's a second figure—"one like a son of man," who is presented to the Ancient One and is given glory and dominion, so that all peoples and nations shall serve him. Here's a second power. There seem to be two powers in heaven—just as the rabbis said people thought.

Ancient Jews came up with all sorts of explanations for visions like this in the Bible. Perhaps what Daniel saw was an angel. Maybe the multiple figures are just different forms of the one God. Or maybe God is not simply one, but maybe he has lower aspects of himself that people can see, while he himself remains invisible, beyond what human beings can know. This last idea is certainly not too far from the Gnostic idea of an ultimate Invisible Spirit and then a bunch of aeons emanating from God.

And, as I said, some historians conclude that it was Jews who first conceived of the Gnostic myth. The Gnostic school of thought, they say, originated in Judaism! This is a very important hypothesis, and so let's look at why many scholars believe it to be true, and then I'll explain why I'm skeptical about it.

First, we should be clear about what these historians are arguing. As you know, all of the first Christians were Jews, so Christianity itself came from Judaism. Or, better, the religions that eventually became Christianity and Judaism both started out among Jews in the 1st century. The Jews whom we call the first Christians—men like Peter and Paul and James, and women like Mary Magdalene—they heard the message of Jesus and then saw him after his death. They concluded that he was the Messiah—in Greek, the Christ— whom God had long promised to send to Israel. So certainly in this sense, all Christian groups originated in Judaism.

But the proponents of the Jewish origins of Gnosticism argue that Jews developed the Gnostic myth without having had any encounter with Jesus and before they may have heard about Jesus through the preaching of early Christians. Jews came up with the story of the Invisible Spirit, the Barbēlō, the mistake of Wisdom and the generation of Ialdabaōth, and the seed of Seth apart from any exposure to Jesus or preaching about Jesus. Only later did Gnostics learn about Jesus and incorporate him into their mythology. The Gnostic school of thought started out non-Christian—Jewish, in fact—and then subsequently Christianized, or became Christian.

Let me explain the arguments for this position. First, we have seen that the original Gnostic literature—the Secret Book According to John, the Revelation of Adam, and so on—these texts are intensely engaged with the Jewish Bible, especially Genesis, pretty much to the exclusion of lots of other sacred literature. Gnostic texts retell the story of Genesis multiple times. To be sure, they often "correct" the errors that Moses made, but they clearly believed that this is where religious truth is to be found. Jews seem like the best candidates for people who would be this obsessed with the book of Genesis.

Moreover, several of these same Gnostic works don't have a lot of Christian features, or the Christian features are suspiciously marginal. The Secret Book According to John, you may remember, presents itself as a revelation from the Savior to the apostle John after the death and resurrection of Christ. But only at the beginning and end of the book is the Savior who speaks explicitly identified as Jesus and the recipient of the revelation identified as the apostle John. The long discourse that the Savior speaks has few if any explicitly

Christian elements, although the aeon named the Divine Self-Originate is also called "the anointed one" or "Christ." And yet figures called "anointed ones" appear in non-Christian Jewish literature as well as in Christian literature.

So basically, the Secret Book seems Christian only at the beginning and the end, in the so-called frame story that sets up the long revelation of the Gnostic myth. And so scholars argue that the revelation itself was composed first by one or more Gnostic Jews. Only later did someone make it Christian by creating the frame story about Jesus and the apostle John.

Similarly, the Reality of the Rulers starts out with a quotation from the New Testament Letter to the Ephesians, but then it simply retells stories from Genesis. The Christian opening could have been added later to an originally Jewish Gnostic text. And the Revelation of Adam does not have any clear references to Jesus, the New Testament, or anything Christian.

Moreover, scholars have discovered that many ideas and incidents in Gnostic texts have parallels in Jewish literature, especially rabbinic literature. We have already seen similarities between the Reality of the Rulers and the Jewish Targum Pseudo-Jonathan. But there are other examples where, say, Gnostic retellings of the creation of humanity or of the flood story resemble ideas found in Jewish texts.

Of course, the most remarkable feature of Gnostic literature in relation to Judaism is that the Gnostics identified the God of Genesis—the God of Israel, the God Jews worship—as not really God, but as the ignorant and malicious Ialdabaōth. The true God is the higher God, the Invisible Virgin Spirit, who saves humanity through Forethought, the Barbēlō. Why would Jews have decided that the God of their ancestors was not really the true God, but instead a flawed divinity hostile to human beings?

Well, some historians point to the influence of Platonism and the example of Philo. Philo demonstrates that some Greek-speaking Jews were highly influenced by Greek philosophy, especially Platonism. Platonism would have convinced them that any true God must be very remote from us, extremely spiritual, and not at all subject to emotions like anger or regret. The God of Genesis not only is not remote or very spiritual, but he also gets angry at human beings and changes his mind about having made them and destroys many of them with a flood. Jews may have concluded, therefore, that the God of Genesis was an imperfect deity, and they may have looked for a higher God.

But even more than that, historians point to Jewish history in the 1st and 2nd centuries. Except for a brief period in the 100s B.C., Jews had not had an independent country of their own in the land of Israel for centuries. In 587 B.C., the Babylonians conquered Judea, destroyed Solomon's Temple, and exiled many Jews. From that time on, most Jews lived outside the land of Israel. And those who did live there lived under the rule of various foreign powers.

Eventually, in 63 B.C., the Romans conquered Judaea and governed it. Some Jews resented being under Roman rule; after all, God had promised the land of Israel to Abraham and his descendants, and God had promised King David that one of his sons would always reign as a king in Jerusalem. And now none of this was true—and it had not been true for a long time.

Some Jews in Palestine started a revolt against the Romans around 66 A.D. At first, the Jews found some success in taking over the country, but eventually, more Roman legions arrived and crushed the rebellion. The Roman armies conquered Jerusalem in the year 70 and destroyed the second Temple that had been built there. A group of Jews at the fortress of Masada committed suicide rather than surrender to the Romans.

If that experience was not bad enough, the Jews revolted again in the 130s, this time under the leadership of a rebel named Simon bar Kokhba. We don't know much about bar Kokhba's background, but some Jews considered bar Kokhba the messiah, and looked to him to free Israel and establish a Jewish kingdom. But once again, the Romans prevailed. Once again, they destroyed Jerusalem, and this time the Romans expelled Jews from that city. They renamed it Aelia Capitolina, and Jews were no longer allowed to enter it.

Between these two wars in Palestine, Jews in Alexandria and elsewhere in Egypt rebelled in the 110s. These Jews were tired of discrimination and harassment, and they believed that the Romans were not protecting their civil rights. Here, too, the Roman army put down the rebellion with great force, and the thriving community of Jews in Alexandria seems to have disappeared from history.

Many historians believe that after these devastating experiences, some Jewish intellectuals turned against the God who had promised them so much. Thanks to Platonism, they were already inclined to question the divinity of the biblical God, but now they saw that God as a hopeless failure, deluded, arrogant. That God may have proclaimed, "There is no God besides me," but recent events showed that that claim was bogus. There were other gods—the Roman gods, for example—and they had demonstrated their power over this pretender to divinity.

And so, historians argue, the teachings of Philo show that some of the basic ideas of the Gnostic myth already existed among educated Jews in the 1st century. Platonism led some of these Jews to become skeptical about the divine nature of the biblical God, and then the misfortunes that the Jews experienced in the 1st and 2nd centuries led some of them to see the God that their ancestors worshiped as really Ialdabaōth.

Eventually, the Gnostics encountered the Christian message about Jesus, and they or certain Christians introduced Jesus into the Gnostic myth. And they took some of their revelatory books and made them Christian by adding Christian stuff to them at the beginning and the end. At this point, Christian leaders like Irenaeus saw this teaching as a threat to true Christianity, and they attacked it. The Christian Valentinus, on the other hand, found the myth fascinating, but he revised it to make it even more explicitly Christian. And so the Gnostic myth was originally Jewish and was later rendered Christian.

This is a compelling theory of how Gnosticism originated. One of its great advantages is that it sees beyond what Irenaeus and other Christian heresiologists would like us to believe. According to Irenaeus, the Gnostics were Christian heretics; there was an original Christian message, taught by Jesus to the apostles, and the Gnostics deviated from that. Instead of learning from apostles like Peter, they listened to the demonically inspired Simon Magus.

I have pointed out multiple times that Irenaeus's picture of early Christian history is more fantasy than reality. Christians disagreed with one another from the very start, and his depiction of the Gnostics and Valentinians as heretics is meant to disparage them as demonic and derivative—in no way an authentic expression of religious truth.

The hypothesis of a Jewish origin of Gnosticism sets aside Irenaeus's picture. The Gnostics were not heretics, at least not Christian heretics. Instead, they were Jews who responded in understandable ways to contemporary events and so created a new religious movement.

Despite these advantages, I and many other historians are skeptical of the Jewish hypothesis. Here are our reasons. First, many of the passages in Jewish literature that resemble things in Gnostic texts come from Jewish texts that date well after the Gnostic writings. The earliest works from the Jewish rabbis date to the 200s, but most of them were organized and written down centuries later. To be sure, Philo is earlier than the Gnostics, and so are some Jewish apocalyptic texts. And later rabbinic texts do contain traditions that go back to the period of the Gnostics. But most Jewish literature that has things that sound Gnostic was written during the centuries after the Nag Hammadi codices were buried. So this does not suggest that Gnostics got all of their major ideas from Judaism. Instead, there's a good chance that some Jews got their ideas about multiple gods and others things in Genesis from the Gnostics—and that's what alarmed the rabbis. I'll say more about that in a bit.

Second, we can't really be sure that texts like the Secret Book According to John went through the literary stages of being originally Jewish and then later made Christian. It is true that in the Secret Book, the most obviously Christian elements, such as references to Jesus and the apostle John, occur only at the beginning and the end, in the frame story. But especially at the beginning, it's very hard to pinpoint where the frame story ends and the originally non-Christian discourse begins. And, as I noted earlier, the discourse does prominently feature an aeon called Christ—namely, the Divine Self-Originate, the son in the father-mother-son triad. Plus, the whole point of the revelation discourse is to talk about the godhead and the events of Genesis, which don't give many opportunities to talk about distinctively

Christian things. And besides, what are distinctively Christian things? At this period, what "Christianity" would be was up for grabs. It wasn't clear yet what it would mean to think and write in a Christian way. Just because a text does not feel very Christian to us now does not mean it wasn't Christianity for people in the 2nd century.

Third, the Gospel of Judas became available only in 2006, and it's a significant new piece of data. We know that it's an early Gnostic text because Irenaeus named it when he wrote in 180. Along with the Secret Book, it's the earliest Gnostic text that we can date with some certainty. In the Gospel of Judas, too, Jesus's revelation discourse sticks to talking about God, the creation, and Adam and Eve, and doesn't have much so-called Christian stuff in it. But unlike the Secret Book, the Gospel of Judas is mostly Christian: The majority of the text consists of conversations between Jesus and the disciples or between Jesus and Judas. At least these Gnostics were very much a part of what we call Christianity.

Finally, the question of why Jews would turn against the God of the Bible and call him the evil Ialdabaōth is a problem. Those who claim that the first Gnostics were non-Christian Jews argue that Jews became so disappointed in how things were going for the Jews that they lost confidence in their God and concluded that he was inferior and malicious. Is this really plausible?

From antiquity until today, the people of Israel, the Jews, have had their ups and downs, and to be frank, that history has seen several catastrophic events. Through all their pain and suffering, Jews have complained to God, argued with him, and bewailed their fate, but they have not concluded that the God they worshiped was evil. Instead, they have considered their sufferings to be punishments for their sins, and so they have repented and asked God for forgiveness. Or, they have concluded that God will keep his promises to his people, but in the future, when the Messiah comes and God establishes his kingdom.

In my view, it does seem very likely that the first Gnostics were Jews, or a mix of Jews and Gentiles. The knowledge of and interest in Genesis in Gnostic texts points to Jewish authors. But I think that these Jews must have heard about or had some encounter with Jesus or preaching about Jesus. As we have seen, Christians disagreed about almost everything from the very beginning, but they all agreed that Jesus represented something new—a new revelation, a new intervention by God in history, a new means of salvation. This something new called into question everything that had gone before. Jesus may have come from the biblical tradition and his teachings may have made complete sense within Judaism, but his followers believed that they had to rethink the Bible and the history of Israel.

Some Jews, like Paul, concluded that people no longer needed to follow the Law of the Old Testament; they only had to have faith in Jesus. Paul sometimes sharply contrasted the Law, which brought sin and death, with the Gospel, which brought righteousness and life. The author of the Gospel of John, who must also have been a Jew, likewise set Moses and Jesus in opposition and depicted Jesus telling a group of Jews that their father was the devil.

To my mind, Jewish intellectuals of the late 1st or early 2nd century did indeed have reasons to have doubts about the God of Genesis. The teachings of Platonism made him seem like a lower, inferior god, and Jewish hopes for a land and a king had been frequently crushed. But I think that these factors were necessary, but not sufficient causes for the appearance of the Gnostic myth and the transformation of the God of Genesis into Ialdabaōth. What they really needed was the proclamation of something new, a new revelation that would explain and confirm their doubts and give them a new hope. The most likely catalyst, then, was the proclamation of Jesus, and the teachings of Paul and the Gospel of John were the steps that led from doubts about the God of Israel to the creation of the Gnostic myth.

But even if Gnosticism did not spring from disaffected Jews who had never heard of Jesus, that does not end the story of Gnostic myth and Judaism. For one thing, the religions or movements that we call "Christianity," "Judaism," or "the Gnostic school of thought" were not clearly separate from each other in the first three or four centuries A.D. Instead, Judaism and Christianity were both emerging and gradually becoming the kinds of religions we would recognize. But that was a slow process, and much of it took place in dialogue—what became Judaism was in part a function of what Christianity was not, and vice versa.

At the heart of the debate among these evolving traditions was how to make sense of passages in the Bible that suggested multiple divine powers or in which people seemed to see God, who, of course, should not really be seen. Gnostics divided God into aeons and created Ialdabaōth, but other Christians used the ideas of God's Son or Word and the Holy Spirit to explain why the Bible seems to speak of multiple gods and what people like Daniel saw when they saw God in a human form. The so-called Son of Man that Daniel saw, Christians said, was really Christ, the Word of God, before he became incarnate in Jesus.

The emerging Jewish leaders, the rabbis, rejected these ideas as not monotheistic enough—these ideas divided God up and created two powers in heaven. Instead, the rabbis suggested that the biblical visions were of the only God or were of angels—servants of God. For example, the Son of Man that Daniel saw could be a symbolic representation of the entire people of God, or he could be an angelic being, like the archangel Michael. But he was not a second god. In any case, the rabbis defined Orthodox Judaism in opposition to Gnosticism and Christianity.

Moreover, Jews were not immune to the appeal of mysticism, myth-making, and secret *gnōsis* that inspired the Gnostics and the Valentinians. Jews developed their own traditions of cosmic speculation and esotericism.

From the late ancient into the medieval period, learned Jews discussed how to understand the vision of a heavenly chariot and four living creatures that appears in the first chapter of the biblical book of Ezekiel, which dates to the 500s B.C. That vision did not play a prominent role in Gnostic and Valentinian myths, but other early Christians did try to figure out what it means. Irenaeus, for example, said that the four creatures represent the four gospels of the New Testament. Jewish mystics used the vision and its imagery to describe their own mystical encounters with God and his divine powers, aspects, and angels. This is known as Ma'aseh Merkavah, the work of the chariot, or merkavah mysticism.

In the 12ᵗʰ and 13ᵗʰ centuries, a new form of Jewish secret *gnōsis* emerged in Europe—now called Kabbalah. I'll return to this tradition in a later lecture because, strangely enough, it developed at about the same time as a new form of *gnōsis* among Christians—the Cathars.

It's unlikely that we can trace any direct links between our Gnostics and Kabbalah, but it's certainly possible that some of the cosmological and mystical speculations of the Gnostics influenced the development of merkavah mysticism. The evidence, however, is scarce and ambiguous. Nonetheless, these Jewish movements demonstrate that interest in the secrets of God and the cosmos and in direct knowledge of God was not limited to Jews and Christians of the 2ⁿᵈ and 3ʳᵈ centuries.

Indeed, to talk about *gnōsis*, secret knowledge, and mysticism only in terms of Jews and Christians is also misleading. Other philosophical movements that were neither Jewish nor Christian also knew about and responded to the ideas of the Gnostics. In the next lecture we will meet two of them: Hermeticism and Neoplatonism.

Gnōsis without Christ
Lecture 20

During the 2nd and 3rd centuries, the search for *gnōsis* of a remote and perfect God became popular among educated, spiritually inclined people in the Roman Empire. The Gnostics and Valentinians appealed to this desire for *gnōsis*, as did the Gospel According to Thomas and other Christians, such as Clement and Origen. But non-Christians were part of this trend, as well. In this lecture, we'll look at two non-Jewish, non-Christian forms of *gnōsis*: Neoplatonism and Hermeticism. In each case, we will see real overlaps with Gnostic and Valentinian thought and spirituality, as well as some important differences.

Hermeticism

- *Hermeticism* refers to a body of literature associated with a divine revealer named Hermes Trismegistus. Hermes was the Greek messenger god, who brought communications among the gods and between the gods and lower entities, such as human beings. Greeks living in Egypt identified Hermes with the Egyptian god Thoth, the scribe of the gods. Egyptians praised Thoth as "thrice great," or in Greek, *trismegistus*. Thus, the combined deity of Thoth and Hermes became known as Hermes Trismegistus.

- Hermetic literature is a set of texts that attributes its teachings to revelations from Hermes Trismegistus or one of his divine disciples. Hermetic texts can be divided into two categories: pseudo-scientific technical works about astrology, alchemy, and similar topics and teachings about God, the cosmos, and human salvation.

- The basic features of the Hermetic view are remarkably similar to the views of the Gnostics and the Valentinians.
  - According to the Hermetists, our true self is our soul or intellect, which is a fragment of the divine. Our true existence is immaterial and unchanging. Nonetheless, we are imprisoned

in this world of material change, dwelling in bodies that impede our knowledge of God and matters of eternal truth.

- ○ Because we are divine in our true selves, God wants us to know him, just as he wants to know us. But this communion between God and human beings cannot take place as long as we live in ignorance—thinking that the material world is our true home and our bodies are our true selves.

- The first step in overcoming ignorance is philosophical study. Later, the Hermetic initiate must have an experience of enlightenment (a rebirth)—a vision of or contact with God. Through this rebirth, the Hermetist becomes divine and gains immortality. Obviously, he or she is still a composite of body and soul, still tied to this changing world of matter, but the initiate has become a god by achieving *gnōsis* of God and of the true divine self.

- In some respects, this path is not very different from what we see in Gnostic and Valentinian mysticism, which also encouraged people to turn away from the body and the material world and to engage in religious and philosophical study. The Gnostics and Valentinians, like the Hermetists, suggested that it's possible to have experiences of acquaintance with God in the present life.

- There are some differences, however, between Hermetic *gnōsis* and that of the Gnostics and Valentinians. The Hermetists did not have an elaborate myth and were not as interested in the Jewish tradition as the Gnostics and Valentinians. The Hermetists also claimed that Hermes Trismegistus revealed the truth through Egyptian gods, such as Ammon and Isis. Jesus Christ had no role in Hermeticism.

Poimandres

- The Hermetic tractate Poimandres relates the story of creation. The author of this text tells of his encounter with a divine being, who announces, "I am the Poimandres, the intellect of the realm of absolute power." Later, Poimandres says that he is the author's intellect, as well. Thus, Poimandres embodies the connection between human beings and God; that connection is intellect.

- In the creation story told by Poimandres, the ultimate God engendered a second intellect to be the demiurge or craftsman of the material world **(Figure 7)**. This craftsman then created seven heavenly rulers to assist him, and together, the craftsman god and his rulers created the other heavenly beings and the irrational animals, meaning all living creatures except human beings.

- Poimandres then tells how humanity came into being: "Then the intellect that is parent of all by being life and light engendered a human being equal to itself." Humanity is equal to the ultimate God! God loved the human being and handed over to it all of creation.

- This archetypal divine human saw the created material world and felt attracted to it. He entered it and combined with it; in this way,

Figure 7. Hermetic View of God in Poimandres

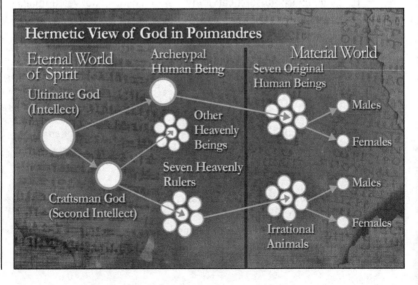

humanity is both immortal—because of its divine origin—and mortal—because of its union with the material world.

- Next, seven earthly human beings came into existence. At first, these seven human beings, as well as the animals, were androgynous, but then God separated them into males and females so that they could multiply and fill the world.
  - Poimandres explains that human beings have divided into two kinds. Some people love the body. Entangled in their physical desires, they remain in the darkness of ignorance. But other people recognize themselves as truly divine intellects, and they devote themselves to self-improvement and contemplation of God.

  - The good people will leave behind their bodies when they die, and their true intellectual selves will ascend through the seven spheres of this cosmos. As Poimandres says, "They ascend to the parent and personally hand themselves over to become powers, and by becoming powers, they come to be within God. Such is the good end of those who possess *gnōsis*: to become God."

Plotinus
- The 3rd-century philosopher Plotinus initiated a new chapter in philosophical history known as *Neoplatonism*. Like the Gnostics and Valentinians, Plotinus sought to achieve *gnōsis* of the ultimate God, but his new approach emphasized our essential connection to God rather than our state of alienation from God.
  - Like the Gnostics, Plotinus believed in a remote and ineffable source of all that is, which he called The One **(Figure 8)**. The One thinks, and his thinking produces the first emanation from him—Intellect. In turn, Intellect generates Soul, the principle that gives life to all that is.

  - From this divine triad—The One, Intellect, and Soul—all of reality emanates. It's not quite right to say that The One exists; rather, The One is Being itself. And from The One, all being emanates through Intellect and Soul, creating new levels of

Figure 8. Plotinus's View of God

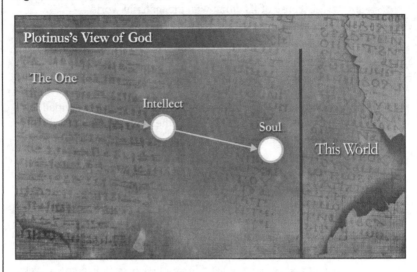

reality that are both lower than and contained in The One. Everything that exists is an emanation from or a level of reality within The One.

○ Plotinus agreed with the Gnostics that the material world is not true being, but he did not believe that there was a clear separation between spiritual reality and the material world. Rather, everything exists on a continuum.

• Plotinus said that the body is not the true self, but he did not set the soul and the body in opposition. Instead, the unity and beauty of the body indicates the presence of the soul, which gives life to the body. The material world is not a flawed imitation of the spiritual forms but the visible manifestation of the world of spiritual forms. The cosmos gets its unity and beauty from the divine Soul that animates it. So, too, the body is not the true self but a manifestation of the true self.

- Further, the true self is not separated from its source. Rather, the self consists of layers of being, and the deepest or most central layer remains in The One. Even now, we exist both in heaven and on earth, both in The One and apart from it.
  - Of course, we are seldom conscious of our connection to The One. Rather than attending to our higher selves, we become distracted by lower, less real concerns. Instead, we should cultivate awareness of the true being at the center of our selves.

  - In practical terms, we should study philosophy and live disciplined lives that are not focused on material needs and concerns. We should practice contemplation and try to heighten our consciousness of our presence within The One. If we do so, Plotinus says, we can have fleeting experiences of true *gnōsis*, moments of union with The One. We do not need to wait for some future moment to return to The One: We can do so now.

- According to Plotinus's model, The One is Being itself, and The One is also The Beautiful and The Good. To be is good; thus, as absolute Being, The One is absolute Goodness.
  - Everything that is has its being from The One. Things exist because they participate in The One and receive life from The One. They are more or less real depending on how close they are to The One or how deeply they participate in The One.

  - This means that all things that exist are also good because they participate in The One's Goodness and receive goodness from The One. They are more or less good depending on how close they are to The One or how deeply they participate in The One. Thus, evil does not really exist; it is simply a deficit of goodness.

Iamblichus
- In the ancient world, Neoplatonism took an important turn with the thought of Iamblichus (c. 250–330). Iamblichus disagreed with Plotinus that the soul remains always connected with The One. For Plotinus, even though it may seem that the soul is far away from

God, it has not fallen away completely. For Iamblichus, the soul is completely fallen.

- Iamblichus distinguished between the soul and the intellect. We might be able to say that our intellect, because it's rational, still maintains a connection with God, but it's not fully within God. But the soul is an intermediary between the intellect and the spiritual world, on the one hand, and the body and the material world, on the other. The soul is fully descended from God, and it leads a kind of double life: It participates in both the higher spiritual reality and the lower material world.

- According to Iamblichus, because the soul has fallen away from The One, it must be purified and restored to its previous condition. As a method of doing this, Iamblichus promoted *theurgy*, that is, the performance of rituals involving material elements that can make the soul more divine.
  ○ Iamblichus taught that material objects, such as animals, plants, and stones, and immaterial things, such as numbers and sacred names, can serve as symbols that draw divine power to the soul. Because the soul is embodied, God has provided material means for the soul to experience the divine.

  ○ In this way, Iamblichus sought to bring actual religion as practiced by pagans into the philosophical life.

Suggested Reading

Copenhaver, *Hermetica*.

Fowden, *The Egyptian Hermes*.

Hadot, *Plotinus, or The Simplicity of Vision*.

Iamblichus, *On the Mysteries*.

Layton, *The Gnostic Scriptures*, "The Hermetic Corpus (Excerpts)."

Meyer, ed., *The Nag Hammadi Scriptures*, "The Discourse of the Eighth and Ninth," "The Prayer of Thanksgiving," and "Excerpt from the Perfect Discourse."

Plotinus, *The Enneads*.

Shaw, *Theurgy and the Soul*.

Questions to Consider

1. What do Hermeticism and Neoplatonism share with Gnosticism and Valentinianism?

2. How does Plotinus's view of our relationship with God differ from that of the Gnostics?

Gnōsis without Christ

Lecture 20—Transcript

During the 250s and 260s, Plotinus was probably the most famous and important philosopher in the Mediterranean world. Plotinus did not like to talk about his biographical details, and so he's somewhat mysterious. One of his students tells us that Plotinus was born in Egypt, and he studied in—where else?—Alexandria. Eventually he settled in Rome to teach his version of Platonist philosophy, and students came to Rome from all over the Mediterranean world to study with him. A wide variety of people attended his seminars—not only academically inclined students, but also literate wealthy people, including politicians. And other philosophers interacted with Plotinus and debated ideas with him. Among these were Gnostic Christians.

Plotinus found the teachings of the Gnostics horrifying. The Gnostics seemed to be following Plato, and some of Plotinus's students found their insights into the origin and nature of this universe compelling. But in his view, the Gnostic myth distorted Platonic views and ultimately opposed Plato. Plotinus wrote an entire treatise *Against the Gnostics* in order to refute them.

Of course, like the Jewish and Christian opponents of the Gnostics we have already met, Plotinus hated the Gnostics not simply because their ideas were so different from his. He hated them also because their ideas were so similar to his. If Irenaeus complained that the Gnostics say they are Christians but really are not, Plotinus complained that the Gnostics say they are Platonists but really are not. Like the Gnostics and the Valentinians, Plotinus taught that our true selves do not belong to this world and that we should seek *gnōsis*—acquaintance—with God. Plotinus offered his own brand of Gnosis, which was not Jewish or Christian, simply Platonist—or, as we now call it, Neoplatonist.

During the 2nd and 3rd centuries, seeking *gnōsis* of a remote and perfect God became very popular among educated, spiritually inclined people in the Roman Empire. The Gnostics and Valentinians appealed to this desire for *gnōsis*, and so did the Gospel According to Thomas and other Christians like Clement and Origen. But non-Christians were part of this trend as well, and in this lecture, I want to look at two non-Jewish, non-Christian forms of Gnosis—Neoplatonism and Hermeticism. In each case, we'll see some real overlaps with Gnostic and Valentinian thought and spirituality, but also some important differences.

Let's start with what's called Hermeticism because it originated centuries before Plotinus lived. *Hermeticism* refers to a body of literature associated with a divine revealer named Hermes Trismegistus. Hermes was, as you may know, the Greek messenger god. He would bring communications between and among the gods and between the gods and lower entities such as human beings.

Greeks living in Egypt identified Hermes with the Egyptian god Thoth. Thoth was the god of the moon and of the calendar. He was also the scribe of the gods—the one who wrote down what the gods had to say—and in this way he was like Hermes. Egyptians praised Thoth as "thrice great," or in Greek, *trismegistus*. And thus the combined deity of Thoth and Hermes became known as Hermes Trismegistus.

This combination of Greek and Egyptian deities suggests that the people who produced Hermetic books were Greek-speaking residents of Egypt. They wanted to combine the philosophical and religious wisdom of Greece and Egypt.

Hermetic literature is a set of texts that attributes its teachings to revelations from Hermes Trismegistus or from one of his divine disciples, such as the Greek god Asclepius and the Egyptian gods Isis, Ammon, and Tat. So all of this is revealed knowledge, purportedly hidden for centuries—just like some of the Gnostic revelations that we have studied.

The Hermetic texts offer two kinds of knowledge. In one category are pseudo-scientific technical works about astrology and the powers of gemstones and plants. Some of these teach alchemy, the art of transforming ordinary minerals into precious metals like silver and gold. Some of these technical Hermetic works may originate as much as two centuries before Christ.

We are more interested in the second category of Hermetic texts—those that offer teachings about God, the cosmos, and human salvation. These works come from the 2nd and 3rd centuries A.D.—precisely the period of the Gnostics, the Valentinians, and Origen. The Hermetists competed with Christians like the Gnostics, Valentinians, and Origen, as well as with Neoplatonists like Plotinus, in offering people a path to *gnōsis* of God.

What was the Hermetic path to *gnōsis*? In its basic features, it was remarkably similar to those of the Gnostics and the Valentinians. According to the Hermetists, our true self is our soul or intellect, which is itself a fragment of the divine or at least of the same nature as the divine. Our true existence is immaterial and unchanging. We are nonetheless imprisoned in this world of material change, dwelling in bodies that impede our knowledge of God and matters of eternal truth.

Because we are divine in our true selves, God wants us to know him, just as he wants to know us. But this communion between God and human beings cannot take place as long as we live in ignorance of our true selves, thinking that the material world in which we live is our true home and the bodies in which we exist are our true selves.

The first step in overcoming our ignorance is philosophical study. Hermetic texts vary greatly in their difficulty, ranging from the rather simple and accessible, to the rather complex and obscure. The Hermetist must travel on an intellectual journey of reading and study, which gets progressively more difficult as he or she learns more. Many Hermetic texts are written in a dialogue format. The revealing deity engages in questions and answers with a human or divine student, and we expect that these dialogues replicate conversations that would have taken place between Hermetic teachers and their disciples. Eventually, however, the disciple must move on from having a teacher, and his or her intellect must travel upward on its own. At some point, the Hermetic initiate must have an experience of enlightenment, which is often called a rebirth. In this rebirth, the initiate has a vision of or contact with God. This rebirth is, as you can imagine, basically indescribable, beyond words, but it seems that the enlightened person both sees something—most frequently light—and hears something—hymns and praises to God.

This rebirth divinizes the Hermetist. The Hermetist becomes divine and gains immortality. Obviously, he or she is still a composite of body and soul, still tied to this changing world of matter, but the initiate has become a god by achieving *gnōsis* of God and of the true divine self. All of this is not very different from what we see in Gnostic and Valentinian mysticism. The Gnostics and Valentinians also encouraged people to turn away from the body and the material world and to engage in religious and philosophical study. They, too, suggested that it's possible to have experiences of acquaintance with God in the present life. The Gnostics believed that ultimate salvation, the final return of divine fragments to the Entirety, would happen only at the end of this universe. But the Valentinians resemble the Hermetists in claiming that in some sense a person can have full salvation now. As one Valentinian teacher told his student, "Leave the state of dispersion and bondage, and then you already have resurrection!"

How, then, did Hermetic *gnōsis* differ from that of the Gnostics and Valentinians? First of all, the Hermetists did not have an elaborate myth like those of the Gnostics and Valentinians, and they were not nearly as interested in the Jewish tradition. The Hermetists claimed that Hermes Trismegistus revealed the truth, and that truth comes to us through such Egyptian gods as Ammon and Isis. Jesus Christ has no role to play in Hermeticism.

One important Hermetic tractate does tell a story of creation and draws from Genesis to do so. This work is called Poimandres because the divine figure who reveals its teachings calls himself Poimandres. This name appears nowhere else in ancient literature, and scholars are not sure what it means. The best guess is something like "Shepherd of Men" because parts of the word sound like the Greek words for "shepherd" and "man."

In any case, the anonymous author of the text says that one day he was contemplating eternal truths but feeling weighed down by the materiality of his body. Suddenly, a huge divine being appeared to him and said, "I am the Poimandres, the intellect of the realm of absolute power." Later, Poimandres says that he is the author's intellect as well. And so Poimandres embodies the connection between us human beings and God—that connection is intellect. He has appeared in order to reveal the origin of the cosmos and the salvation of human beings.

The creation story that Poimandres tells draws some of its language and imagery from Genesis. For example, the first thing that happens is a separation of light from darkness. But here, that separation indicates the division between the eternal world of spirit and the changeable world of matter.

As Poimandres tells it, the ultimate God engendered a second intellect to be the demiurge or craftsman of the material world. This craftsman then created seven heavenly rulers to assist him, and together, the craftsman god and his rulers created the other heavenly beings and the irrational animals, meaning all living creatures except human beings.

So, like Gnostic and Valentinian myth, the Hermetic story has a creator god who is lower than the ultimate source of everything. But this creator god is not arrogant and malicious like Ialdabaōth, nor is he simply ignorant, like the Valentinian creator god. Instead, he's more like Plato's craftsman, an intellect similar to but lower than the ultimate God. Moreover, the Hermetists don't multiply God into a series of aeons, and so none of these aeons falls, like Wisdom. Instead, everything happens according to the Highest Intellect's plan.

And this is how humanity came into being:

> Then the intellect that is parent of all [that is, the highest God] by being life and light engendered a human being equal to itself; and the intellect had a burning desire for it, since it was its own offspring. For the offspring was very beautiful, having its parent's image. For truly, even God had a burning desire for its own form. And God handed over to its offspring all its own crafted products.

You can see here that humanity is divine in origin—equal to the ultimate God. God loved the human being, and handed over to the human being all of creation. And in fact, this archetypal divine human being saw the created material world and felt attracted to it. He entered it and combined with it, and in this way humanity is both immortal—because of its divine origin— and mortal—because of its union with the material world.

What happened next is that seven earthly human beings came into existence. At first these seven human beings—as well as the animals—were androgynous, but then God separated them into males and females, so that they could multiply and fill the world. Once again there are parts of this story that probably come from Genesis—humanity is in the image of God, and the male and female are separated by God, who wants human beings and animals to multiply. But there is no Adam, no Eve, and no Garden of Eden.

Now Poimandres explains that human beings have divided into two kinds. Some people love the body. Entangled in their physical desires, they remain in the darkness of ignorance. But other people recognize themselves as truly divine intellects, and they devote themselves to self-improvement and contemplation of God. The good people will leave behind their bodies when they die, and their true intellectual selves will ascend through the seven spheres of this cosmos—you may recall that ancient people, even Irenaeus, believed that the earth was surrounded by heavenly spheres, usually, but not always, seven. In any event, Poimandres says this: "They ascend to the parent and personally hand themselves over to become powers, and by becoming powers, they come to be within God. Such is the good end of those who possess *gnōsis*: to become God."

The author of this treatise then begins to preach to people, exhorting them to give up physical pleasures and ignorance and turn to the light of immortality. If they do, then the readers of Poimandres can themselves become divine powers. This is the goal of Hermetic *gnōsis*: to cast off the mortality of the body and the material world, and to become divine through knowledge of the self and God.

Now here's an ancient person describing an experience much like what the Hermetists sought:

> Often I reawaken from my body to myself: I come to be outside other things, and inside myself. What an extraordinarily wonderful beauty I then see! It is then, above all, that I belong to the greater portion. I then realize the best form of life; I become one with the Divine, and I establish myself in it.

This speaker, like the Gnostics and the Hermetists, differentiates between himself and his body. He needs to wake up to his true self, and when he does, he has an experience of true beauty. And he becomes one with God. But this speaker was no Gnostic or Hermetist. He was, in fact, a determined enemy of the Gnostics. This speaker was Plotinus, the greatest philosopher of the 3rd century.

Plotinus represents an important turning point in the history of Platonism. Scholars call *Neoplatonism* the new chapter in philosophical history that Plotinus initiates. We think of the Gnostics and Valentinians, by contrast, as belonging to the preceding era of "Middle Platonism." Like his predecessors, Plotinus sought to achieve *gnōsis* of the ultimate God and source of all being, but his new approach to that *gnōsis* emphasized our essential connection to God rather than our state of alienation from God.

Like the Gnostics, Plotinus believed in a remote and ineffable source of all that is, which he called The One. In contrast to the Gnostics, however, Plotinus had a much simpler model for how everything comes forth from The One. In a way that should be familiar to us, Plotinus taught that The One thinks, and his thinking produces the first emanation from him—Intellect—in Greek, *Nous*. In turn Intellect generates Soul, the principle that gives life to all that is.

From this simple divine triad—The One, Intellect, and Soul—all of reality emanates. It's not quite right to say that The One exists; rather, The One is Being itself—he simply is. And from The One all being emanates through Intellect and Soul, creating new levels of reality that are both lower than and contained in The One. Everything that is, is an emanation from or a level of reality within The One.

To visualize this, imagine a perfectly still pool of water. Then imagine a kind of eruption in the center of the pool—perhaps caused by a stone that has been dropped, but better, by some force of life within the pool. What happens is that the eruption in the center of the pool generates waves in concentric circles that emanate out from the center. As each wave moves outward, it retains the original circled shape of the center, but it also gradually diminishes, to the point that it eventually dissipates.

This is how reality is. Being emanates from The One in gradually diminishing levels. To think of this spatially is not right, of course, but levels of reality that are closer to The One have a higher level of being, while those farther away, less so. But each level of reality is contained within The One and maintains a connection with it—just as all the waves in the pool are within the pool and retain the shape of the center.

For Plotinus, brute matter, like rocks and dirt, is where being or reality peters out. That's where the waves dissipate. And so Plotinus agreed with the Gnostics that the material world is not true being, but he did not believe that there was some vast chasm or clear separation between spiritual reality and the material world. Rather, everything exists on a continuum.

This means that Plotinus vigorously objected to the idea that one of the divine aeons went astray and fell into the material world, as happens with Wisdom in different ways in the Gnostic and Valentinian myths. According to Plotinus, there is no "mistake" or "error" within God. God does not fall into the material world. Instead, God gradually unfolds or emanates, and matter is the end result of that divine process.

Let's apply this to ourselves. Both the Gnostics and the Valentinians pictured humanity as consisting of fragments of divine substance imprisoned or trapped in our material bodies. Salvation is the eventual return of this divine substance to the Entirety or Fullness.

Plotinus could speak equally negatively about the body. The body, he said, is not our true selves. Plotinus's biographer, Porphyry, said that Plotinus seemed ashamed even to have a body. But Plotinus did not set the soul and body in direct opposition. Instead, the unity and beauty of the body indicate or display the presence of the soul, which gives life to the body. In general, the material world is not a flawed imitation of the spiritual forms created by an ignorant deity like Ialdabaōth. Instead, the material world is the visible manifestation of the world of spiritual forms. The cosmos gets its unity and beauty from the divine Soul that animates it. So, too, the body is not our true self, but it is a manifestation of our true self.

Even more, our true self is not separated from its source, The One. Rather, our self consists of layers of being, just like the waves of the pool, and at the heart of our self is The One, just as the waves in the pool are always part of the pool and connected to its center. The highest or deepest or most central level of our self remains in The One. It's still with God. Even now, we exist both in heaven and on earth, both in The One and apart from it.

The problem is, of course, that we are seldom conscious of our connection to The One. Rather than thinking about and attending to our higher self, we get distracted by lower, less real things and concerns. We worry about food and shelter and money and sex and so on—the diminished, nearly non-existent waves in the pool, so to speak. Instead, we should cultivate awareness of what's really real, the true being at the center of our selves.

In practical terms, we ought to study philosophy and live disciplined lives that are not focused on material needs and concerns. We should practice contemplation and try to heighten our consciousness of our presence within The One. If we do so, Plotinus said, we can have fleeting experiences of true *gnōsis*, moments of union with The One, times in which we see Beauty itself and stand fully within the divine. We don't need to wait for some future moment to return to The One—we can do so now.

It must be said, of course, that, like every spiritual path we have encountered in this course, what Plotinus recommended was possible only to wealthy, educated individuals with the time and money to devote to philosophy and self-improvement. Plotinus himself led a very ascetic life: He didn't eat a lot and he wore only simple clothes—all this so that he could concentrate on spiritual matters, not material ones. But even giving up earning money required money—and certainly all this reading and study required a first-class education. You get the feeling that, like the gradually diminishing waves of the pool, some people are farther away from The One and so less real than others.

In any event, we should notice one more thing about Plotinus's teaching that will become important in a later lecture. According to Plotinus's model, The One is Being itself, and The One is also The Beautiful and The Good. To be is good, and so as absolute Being, The One is absolute Goodness.

Everything that is, has its being from The One. Things that exist, exist because they participate in The One and receive life from The One. They are more or less real depending on how close they are to The One or how deeply they participate in The One. This means that everything that is, is also good. Things that exist are good because they participate in The One's Goodness and receive goodness from The One. They are more or less good depending on how close they are to The One or how deeply they participate in The One.

And so evil does not really exist. Rather, evil is simply a lack of good or a deficit of goodness. So every person is good because every person exists and has life in The One, but we call some people "bad" or "evil" because they have a deficit of goodness, not as much good as other people. You can see that Plotinus had a quite different sensibility or outlook on the world than the Gnostics had. The Gnostics looked at the world around them and saw hostile rulers trying to enslave them through fate and the counterfeit spirit. Plotinus, however, saw a world that reflected the goodness of The One— the only source of evil was being distant from The One, something that we often bring on ourselves by turning to material pleasures rather than spiritual reality. Plotinus's doctrine of evil's non-existence would have a profound effect on the Christian theologian Augustine of Hippo, as we'll see later in the course.

Now, Neoplatonism did not end with Plotinus. In fact, scholars tend to see all of subsequent Platonist philosophy in the West as Neoplatonism stemming from Plotinus. But in the ancient world, Neoplatonism took an important turn with the thought of Iamblichus. Iamblichus was from Syria and lived from about 250 to 330 A.D. He was not Plotinus's student directly. He studied with Porphyry, who was Plotinus's student and biographer. Although Iamblichus learned about Plotinus's philosophy from Porphyry, he eventually broke with Plotinus and Porphyry on an important point.

Plotinus, you may recall, taught that our soul remains always connected with The One, even as it is distant from The One. In spatial terms, our soul has not fallen away completely from The One. It may seem that your soul is far away from God—and in a sense it is—but, even when you feel this most acutely, the heart of your soul has not fallen away from him; it continues to be within The One, and you just need to intensify your awareness of your presence within God.

Iamblichus disagreed. He argued that the soul is completely fallen. Iamblichus carefully distinguished between the soul and the intellect. You might be able to say that our intellect, because it's rational, still maintains a connection with God, but it's not fully within God. But the soul is an intermediary between the intellect and the spiritual world on the one hand, and the body and the material world on the other hand. The soul is fully descended from God, and it leads a kind of double life: It participates in both the higher spiritual reality and the lower material world.

In this respect, Iamblichus sounds a lot like the Valentinians, who saw the soul as a substance between spirit and matter, able to choose between good and evil. Iamblichus also sounds more like the Gnostics than like Plotinus when he says that the soul has completely fallen away from God. And in fact, in his book entitled *On the Soul*, Iamblichus noted that the Gnostics attribute the soul's fall to what he called "derangement and deviation." It seems that Iamblichus did not agree with the Gnostics on the cause for the soul's descent.

In any case, Iamblichus believed that because the soul has fallen away from The One, it must be purified and restored to its previous condition. As a method of doing this, Iamblichus promoted a kind of theurgy; he advocated rituals involving material elements that can make the soul more divine. Iamblichus taught that a range of ritual activities can help the soul get closer to God. Material things like animals, plants, and stones, and immaterial objects like numbers and sacred names can serve as symbols that draw divine power to the soul. Like the Hermetists, Iamblichus drew on traditional Egyptian religion to support his ideas, and he integrated Egyptian gods and rituals into his philosophy.

Plotinus had not opposed religious rituals like sacrifices to the gods, but he did not consider them nearly as important as studying philosophy and practicing forms of meditation and contemplation. His student Porphyry, Iamblichus's teacher, criticized Iamblichus's interest in theurgy. He did not think that all theurgy was wrong, but he thought it was not really necessary, and he was skeptical that material things can bring the divine to human beings.

Iamblichus, however, argued that God had placed certain rational ideas in symbolic forms throughout the natural world. Names, numbers, plants, animals, stones—they all form a kind of code through which divine beings communicate with human beings and help the human soul to return to its true nature. Because the soul is embodied, God has provided material means for the soul to experience the divine. In this way, Iamblichus sought to bring actual religion as pagans practiced it into the philosophical life. His teachings had a strong influence on the Roman emperor Julian, who later in the 360s tried to revive paganism just as Christianity was beginning to dominate the empire.

Even though Plotinus and Iamblichus disagreed with the Gnostics in important ways, just like the proto-orthodox Christians we have met, they developed their philosophies in dialogue with Gnostic thought. When Plotinus encouraged people to become aware of the presence of God within them through self-contemplation, he echoed Gnostic mystical texts like the Foreigner and Zōstrianos, which I discussed in Lecture 7. And when Iamblichus taught that the soul had fallen completely away from God, he brought Neoplatonist thought closer to that of the Gnostics.

Plotinus, however, thought that the Gnostics went too far from Plato on important points, and he found them to be arrogant—thinking that only they can be saved. *Gnōsis*, Plotinus argued, is available to everyone. Iamblichus believed this as well, and he attempted to formulate a way to salvation that would appeal to a wide range of people.

In our next lecture, however, we'll meet a religious teacher who made a much more thorough attempt to create a single religion from all existing religions—Mani.

The Mythology of Manichaeism
Lecture 21

Historians have frequently depicted Manichaeism as the culmination of ancient Gnosticism. It was a Gnostic myth that went global and became the basis for a highly organized international religion. As we will see, Manichaeism shares several characteristics with Gnosticism, but the salvation described by its founder, Mani (216–274), was not found primarily in *gnōsis*, that is, in direct acquaintance with the ultimate God. Instead, Mani enlisted people in an ongoing war between Good and Evil, Light and Darkness, in which the disciplined use of the body played a central role. In this way, Manichaeism differed greatly from the Gnostic school of thought.

Revelation to Mani
- In the year 228, a 12-year-old Christian boy named Mani, who lived in a village near Babylon, received a startling vision. An angel called al-Tawm ("the Twin") appeared to Mani to bring a revelation from God—the king of the Paradise of Light. From this meeting, the religion of Manichaeism was born, which would eventually challenge Christianity for supremacy in the late ancient world.

- The Christian sect to which Mani belonged was known as the Mughtasila, which means, "the ones who wash themselves." They were also known as Elchasaite Christians because they followed the teachings of a book attributed to a man named Elchasai.
  - The Elchasaites worshipped Jesus as the Messiah and Son of God, and they placed great emphasis on ritual purity. They followed many of the precepts of the Jewish Law, including circumcision and a calendar of festivals and other observances. They also put a high value on baptism, which brought forgiveness of sins, purified the body of evil spirits, and offered protection from illness and impurity.

  - The Elchasaite Christians endeavored to keep themselves in a pure and sacred state, even to the point of regulating the food that they ate. They would not eat any food that they themselves did not plant, harvest, and prepare, and even this food required ritual cleansing in water before it could be eaten. That is, they baptized their food.

- ○ Notice here the close connections among the body, food, and salvation. For the Elchasaites, the body was where good and evil came into conflict. By baptizing the body, they expelled the demons of Satan, and by baptizing their food, they kept themselves pure from pagan uncleanness. Mani's religion would have similar features.

- After his vision of his divine Twin, Mani began to doubt some of the teachings and practices of his Christian community. As the years went by, he gradually understood the full implications of the revelation he had received, and he came into greater conflict with Christian leaders.

- Finally, after 12 years, at the age of 24, Mani received a new revelation from his divine Twin: God was calling Mani to be his apostle and prophet. It was Mani's mission to bring the gospel of truth to all people—in fact, to show that all previous religions were leading to the new gospel that Mani would proclaim.
  - ○ Mani learned that he was the Comforter, or Paraclete, that Jesus had promised he would send to his followers. In the Gospel of John, Jesus explains that the Paraclete would teach people all things and remind them of everything that Jesus said. The Paraclete would chastise the world for its sin, teach it about righteousness, and bring it judgment.

  - ○ Not only was Mani the Paraclete, but he was also the seal—or completion—of all prophecy **(Figure 9)**. God had sent the entire human race prophets, beginning with Adam, Seth, and Noah, but prophecy had then taken different paths in different areas of the world. In the Mediterranean world, God spoke through Jesus, but in Asia, India, and China, he spoke through the Buddha. In Persia and Babylonia, God's prophet was

Figure 9. Mani as the Seal of the Prophets

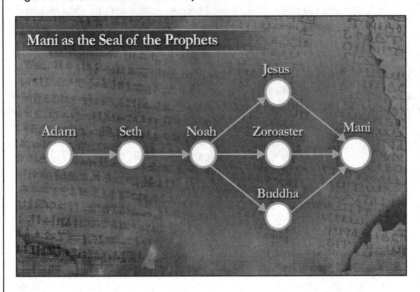

Zoroaster. Mani was sent to unite all these religions into one Gospel of Truth.

- Mani traveled to bring his Gospel of Truth to central Eurasia and India. In Iran, he at first found sympathy from the Sassanian rulers, even if they did not convert to his new religion. Later, however, Mani ran afoul of the Zoroastrian priests and was imprisoned and tortured. He died in 274 at the age of 58.

Mani's Teachings

- Like the Gnostics and Valentinians, Mani presented his teachings in the form of a myth about the structure of God and the origin of the universe in which we live. The Manichaean myth **(Figure 10)** is extremely complex, but its central theme is the struggle between Good and Evil or between Light and Dark. We are still engaged in this struggle today.

Figure 10. Manichaean Pantheon (Simplified!)

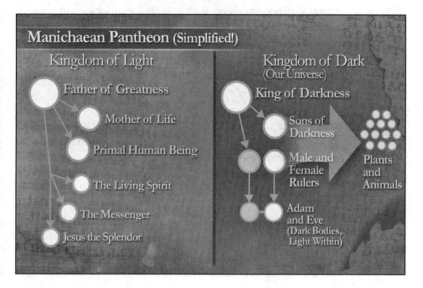

- We can see why the Manichaean myth might have appeal: It provides a clear explanation for the existence of evil and suffering.
  - According to Mani, evil is real because it has existed from the beginning. God—the true God, the Father of Greatness—did not create evil or let it come into being. Instead, Evil or the Dark has always been, and we now find ourselves in the realm of evil.

  - Pain and suffering are equally real because there are many particles of light trapped in the realm of Dark that is this universe. According to Mani, all living beings, including plants and animals, contain fragments of light. When we hurt another living being, we are causing pain to the light contained within it.

- Manichaeism also explains why we are attracted to both good and evil. Our evil impulses arise from the body, which is composed of the dark and draws us to do evil acts. At the same time, our souls are composed of light and draw us to do good.

- In Mani's view, Paul captured this problem in Romans 7: "I know that nothing good dwells within me. I can will what is right, but I cannot do it. ... I find it to be a law that when I want to do what is good, evil lies close at hand. For I delight in the law of God in my inmost self, but I see in my members another law at war with the law of my mind, making me captive to the law of sin that dwells in my members" (18–23).

- Indeed, Mani says that there is a war within each of us and all around us—a war between Good and Evil, Light and Dark. Our own selves are the battlefields of that war, as the light of our true selves battles with the dark of our bodies.

- In Romans, Paul laments, "Wretched man that I am! Who will rescue me from the body of death?" (24). Mani claimed to have the answer to Paul's question. He organized his church precisely so that it could win the war between Good and Evil and rescue the light from the dark.

Manichaean Church Organization

- The Manichaean church was an international organization with a well-organized hierarchy **(Figure 11)**. The supreme leader was considered Mani's successor, and he was called The Guide. Below The Guide, Manichaeans were organized into five ranks, but these five ranks were placed within two larger, more significant groups: the Elect and the Hearers. The distinction between the Elect and the Hearers and the interactions between them are at the heart of how Manichaeism worked.

- The Elect comprised the top four ranks. The first three of these ranks formed the church hierarchy and were limited in number. The fourth rank consisted of monks who filled a variety of roles in local congregations: preachers, choirmasters, scribes, and the like. Local members of the Elect lived together in monastic communities and committed themselves to live in absolute purity. If they did so, their souls of light would escape their bodies of darkness at death, and the light would return to the realm of Light.

Figure 11. Manichaean Church

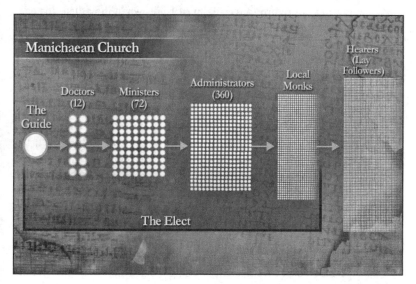

- Most Manichaeans, however, were Hearers, not the Elect. The Hearers practiced a less rigorous version of the Elect's lifestyle. In general, they were expected to lead a conventional moral life by avoiding sin, but they could get married and have sex with their spouses. The Hearers had a less restricted diet than the Elect, but they still had to refrain from alcohol and meat. They were expected to give 10 percent of their income as alms to the church in support of the Elect and of poor Hearers.

- Both the Elect and the Hearers participated in a regular schedule of fasting—not eating or drinking until after the sun went down on Sundays and at other times. There was also an annual 30-day fast that led to the holiest Manichaean festival, the Bema. The Bema commemorated Mani's death and return to heaven. By sharing periods of fasting, the Elect and the Hearers expressed their solidarity with each other.

- Because the Hearers did not live a life of complete purity, their light did not return to the realm of Light when they died. Instead, their light fragments were reincarnated in new human bodies. In their next lives, they might be Elect and, thus, could escape this realm of darkness.

- Nonetheless, the Hearers had a crucial role to play in the liberation of light from the darkness. First, by supporting the Elect, they enabled the Elect to live completely purely and free their souls of light. Second, by bringing fruits and vegetables to the Elect, the Hearers helped the Elect to liberate the light in those plants.
  - The Elect had rendered their bodies so pure that when they ate the food brought by the Hearers, their digestive systems would separate the light from the dark and enable the light to escape upward toward the realm of Light.

  - During the current period of war with the realm of Darkness, the rulers of Dark are oppressing the fragments of light. But the Manichaean church and its rituals continually liberate light and send it back to the realm of Light.

  - In fact, the Manichaeans believed that they could actually see this process taking place in the waxing and waning of the moon. As light leaves the earth, it travels upward and gathers at the moon, and the moon's light gradually grows as more light arrives there.

  - When the moon's light gets full, the light heads to the next stop, which is the sun, and the moon's light slowly diminishes. The changing patterns of the sun's path and of daylight are also functions of liberated light traveling from here to the realm of Light.

  - In the sky, Manichaeans believed that they could see their religion at work—a dramatic confirmation of the truth of their message.

Suggested Reading

BeDuhn, *The Manichaean Body*.

Gardner and Lieu, *Manichaean Texts from the Roman Empire*.

Tardieu, *Manichaeism*.

Questions to Consider

1. How did Mani's explanation of evil differ from that of the Gnostics, Origen, and Plotinus?

2. How would a Manichaean Hearer have lived his or her religious life?

The Mythology of Manichaeism
Lecture 21—Transcript

In the year 228, a 12-year-old Christian boy received a startling vision. He lived in a village near Seleucia and Ctesiphon—twin cities on either side of the Tigris River, not far from the ancient city of Babylon. It was now part of the Sassanian Empire. The Sassanians ruled an empire that was based in Iran and extended into modern-day Iraq, and then to the borders of its great rival empire—that of the Romans.

Our 12-year-old probably was not thinking about imperial politics when an angel appeared to him claiming to bring a revelation from God, who was named the King of the Paradise of Light. The boy's name was Mani, and the angel who appeared to him was called al-Tawm—the Twin or the Companion. Mani had met his divine twin or double. From this meeting, a new religion was born—a religion that would eventually extend from Britain and Europe in the West to China in the East, a religion that would challenge Christianity for supremacy in the late ancient world. This was the religion of Mani, or Manichaeism.

Historians have frequently depicted Manichaeism as the culmination of ancient Gnosticism. It was a Gnostic myth that went global and became the basis for a highly organized international religion. As we'll see, Manichaeism does share several characteristics with the Gnostics: above all, a complicated myth that explains the origin of evil and suffering and offers a path of salvation from this world of darkness. But the salvation that Mani offered was not found primarily in *gnōsis*—that is, in direct acquaintance with the ultimate God. Instead, Mani enlisted people in an ongoing war between good and evil, light and darkness, in which the disciplined use of the body played a central role. In this way, Manichaeism differed greatly from the Gnostic school of thought.

Like the Gnostics and Valentinians, however, Manichaeism had a major impact on the history of Christianity, thanks to the most famous Manichaean who ever lived, St. Augustine of Hippo. But we'll come to that part of our story in the next lecture. For now, let's return to the early 3rd century and to the revelation of the King of the Paradise of Light to the young Mani.

As I said, when Mani received his first revelation at the age of 12, he was a Christian. The sect to which he belonged was known as the Mughtasila, which means, "the ones who wash themselves." They were also known as Elchasaite Christians because they followed the teachings of a book attributed to a man named Elchasai. Most modern scholars do not think that Elchasai really existed, but that does not matter for our purposes.

The Mughtasila or Elchasaites worshiped Jesus as the Messiah and Son of God, and they placed a great deal of emphasis on ritual purity. They followed many of the precepts of the Jewish Law, including circumcision and a clear calendar of festivals and other observances. As the name "the ones who wash themselves" suggests, they put a high value on baptism. The washing of baptism brought forgiveness of sins, but it also purified the body of evil spirits and offered protection from illness and impurity. Baptism was only the first of many ritual cleansings with water that a member might undergo during his or her lifetime.

The Elchasaite Christians endeavored to keep themselves in a pure and sacred state, even to the point of regulating the food that they ate. They would not eat any food that they themselves did not plant, harvest, and prepare. "Pagan" food they considered entirely impure and taboo. But even their own food required ritual cleansing in water before it could be eaten—that is, they baptized their food.

We want to notice here the close connections between the body, food, and salvation. For the Elchasaites, the body was where good and evil came into conflict. By baptizing the body, they expelled the demons of Satan, and by baptizing their food, they kept themselves pure from pagan uncleanness. Mani's religion would have similar features.

After his vision of his divine twin, however, the teenage Mani began to doubt some of the teachings and practices of his Christian community. For example, he questioned the practice of baptizing food and avoiding foods that the Elchasaites had not produced. It seemed to Mani that people's health did not vary whether they ate baptized or unbaptized food, and he observed that all foods produce the same excrement.

As the years went by, Mani gradually understood the full implications of the revelation that he had received, and he came into greater conflict with Christian leaders. Mani's father was asked to explain the rebellious behavior of his son, and he could not do so.

Finally, after 12 years, in the year 240, at the age of 24, Mani received a new revelation from his divine Twin. The angel announced to him, "The time has now come for you to manifest yourself in order to announce your power." The Twin told Mani that God was calling him to be his apostle and prophet. It was Mani's mission to bring the gospel of truth to all peoples—in fact, to show that all previous religions were leading to the new gospel that Mani would proclaim.

Mani learned that he was the Comforter or Paraclete that Jesus promised he would send to his followers. In the Gospel of John, Jesus delivers a farewell speech to his disciples. He tells them that he will soon return to his Father, but he promises to send them a Comforter (in Greek, *paraklētos*) or Paraclete—the Holy Spirit. The Paraclete would teach people all things and remind them of everything Jesus had said. And this Paraclete would chastise the world for its sin, teach it about righteousness, and bring it judgment. Mani learned that he was in fact that Paraclete, the final messenger of God that Jesus promised.

Not only this, but Mani was the Seal—or completion—of All Prophecy. God had sent the entire human race prophets beginning with Adam, Seth, and Noah, but then prophecy had taken different paths in different areas of the world. In the Mediterranean world God spoke through Jesus, but in Asia (India and China) he spoke through the Buddha. And in Persia and Babylonia, God's prophet was Zoroaster. Mani was the culmination or seal of all these lines of prophecy. He was sent to unite all these religions into one Gospel of Truth.

And that's what Mani set out to do. Mani himself did not take his message to the West and into the Roman Empire. His disciples and successors would do that. Instead, he traveled east, bringing his Gospel of Truth to central Eurasia and as far as India.

Within Iran, Mani at first found sympathy from the Sassanian rulers, even if they did not convert to his new religion. Eventually, however, the priests of the official Zoroastrian religion became alarmed at the spread of Manichaeism, and they sought to turn the King, Bahram, against the religion and its founder. They found their chance when Mani managed to convert a prince named Bat. Bahram did not want one of the empire's rulers to abandon the official religion of the state, and so he imprisoned Mani and had him tortured. In 274, at the age of 58, Mani died from his sufferings. Like his predecessor Jesus, Mani had died for his message.

Mani's message did not die with him, however. Mani knew that Jesus had not left any written works, nor had Jesus given his disciples strict instructions as to how to organize and run a church. Mani believed that this is why Christianity did not truly reflect what Jesus had taught. Mani was determined not to make the same mistake that Jesus had. So he wrote several religious treatises, including an account of his own life, and multiple letters. Only fragments of these writings survive today, but in antiquity they formed the core of a canon of Manichaean scriptures.

In addition to his writings, Mani organized his followers into an international church that could continue to spread his message after his death. Let's look first at the teachings of Mani and then turn to the organization and practices of the Manichaean church.

Like the Gnostics and Valentinians, Mani presented his teachings in the form of a myth about the structure of God and the origin of the universe in which we live. From what we can tell, Mani and his followers did read and borrow from Gnostic literature, but they also used the New Testament and a lot of other early Christian writings, including the Gospel of Thomas. As we'll see, his followers also incorporated literature and ideas from other religious traditions, like Zoroastrianism and Buddhism.

The Manichaean myth is far more complex than any of the myths we have encountered thus far, and so I will leave out many characters and instead focus on its most important theme—the struggle between good and evil or between light and dark.

Unlike everyone we have met thus far in the course, Mani was a strict dualist. That is, he believed at the heart of reality are two eternal principles: good and evil, light and dark. Sometimes modern people call the Gnostics dualists because they sharply divided reality into twos—the Entirety versus this universe, the immaterial world versus the material world, the soul versus the body, the Gnostics versus everybody else. But Gnostic myth is not fundamentally dualistic because it posits one single principle that is the source of all true being—the Invisible Virgin Spirit.

Mani, in contrast, believed that from the beginning there have been two natures or realms—the Kingdom of Light ruled by the Father of Greatness and the Kingdom of Dark led by the King of Darkness. These two realms were roughly equal in power, and it was good for both natures that they were divided and separated from one another.

The universe that we live in came into being when the King of Darkness saw the beauty of the realm of light and decided to attack it and try to take possession of it. He was assisted by his Sons of Darkness and other rulers, both male and female. To defend his realm, the Father of Greatness called forth or emanated a series of powers, most importantly the Mother of Life and the Primal Human Being. The Father sent the Primal Human Being out to defend the light against the dark.

Notice that the Father of Light only emanates new divine beings in response to the threat from the dark. This contrasts with the Invisible Spirit of Gnostic myth, whose very nature as a thinking intellect leads it to emanate the Barbēlō and the other aeons.

The Primal Human Being decided to defeat the Sons of Darkness and its other rulers by submitting to them. He allowed the rulers of darkness to consume part of his light substance. He knew that the light would be like poison to the dark. The presence of the light would gradually weaken the dark, so that the dark would be rendered unable to attack or harm the Kingdom of Light.

The defeated Primal Human Being then prayed to the Father of Greatness that he might be rescued from the realm of dark. In response, the Father generated a second set of divine beings, most importantly the Living Spirit.

The Living Spirit rescued the Primal Human Being and brought him back to the realm of light, where the Mother of Life welcomed him. This ended the first war between the light and the dark.

With the war over, the Mother of Life and the Living Spirit set about trying to recover the light substance that was still trapped in the realm of dark. Together with a new divine being named the Messenger, they organized the dark realm into the universe in which we live. They began to gather the light together out of the darkness, so that it could return to the realm of light. The sun, the moon, and the stars are made up of light, on its way out of darkness back to its true home.

The Messenger appeared to the King of Darkness and his other rulers in male and female forms. The rulers developed a great desire for what they saw—the male rulers desired the female form, the female rulers the male form. And their desire resulted in them ejaculating out the light that they had consumed—mixed, however, with their own sin. These mixtures of light and sin became the seeds for plants and animals, which are composites of living light and deadly dark. And so the world in which we live came into being as a mixture of light and dark. This universe is basically the realm of dark, but whatever in it is alive and beautiful is due to the presence of the light trapped within it.

The creation of this world by the divine beings of light led the rulers of darkness to start a second war between good and evil, light and dark. This war began with the creation of humanity, and it continues to this day.

The King of Darkness and his fellow rulers created Adam and Eve so that they might continue to possess the light and disperse it into the human race. They created Adam and Eve in the image of the Messenger's male and female forms, which they had seen earlier. And thus humanity was created in the image of a divine being. But Adam and Eve were ignorant of their true nature; they did not know that they were fragments of light trapped in the realm of dark.

At this point, yet another divine being of light enters the story: Jesus the Splendor. Jesus the Splendor came to Adam and Eve and woke them up from their ignorance. He encouraged them to eat from the tree of knowledge of good and evil. When they did, they realized that they belonged to the realm of light and were trapped in this realm of dark. Adam cried out, "Woe! Woe upon the maker of my body, and upon the one who has shackled my soul, and upon the rebels that have enslaved me!" Adam became determined to extricate his soul, his essence of light, from the realm of dark and return it to its true home.

And thus began the second war between light and dark, good and evil—the effort to rescue all the remaining particles of light from this realm of evil and send them back to the realm of light. And that's the battle in which we are all engaged—or we should be engaged in it!

The Manichaean myth is quite complicated, and I have given you a very simplified version. But I hope that you can see why the myth might have appeal. It provides a very clear explanation for the existence of evil and suffering—and for why people often feel torn between good and evil.

According to Mani, evil is real because it has existed from the beginning. God—the true God, the Father of Greatness—did not create evil or let it come into being. Instead, evil or the dark has always been, and we now find ourselves in the realm of evil.

Pain and suffering are equally real because there are so many particles of light trapped in this dark realm. Mani was deeply aware of the damage and pain that even we cause other living beings, even when we don't mean to. According to one story, when Mani walked on grass, he could hear the cries of pain coming from the souls of light within the individual blades of grass. All living beings—including plants and animals—contain fragments of light. When we hurt another living being, we are causing pain to the light contained within it.

And Manichaeism explains why we are attracted to both good and evil. My evil impulses arise from my body, which is composed of the dark. My body of darkness draws me to do evil acts. At the same time, however, my soul is composed of light, and thus I want to do the good as well.

In Mani's view, Saint Paul captured this problem very well in his Letter to the Romans. In chapter 7 Paul writes,

> I know that nothing good dwells within me, that is, in my flesh. I can will what is right, but I cannot do it. ... I find it to be a law that when I want to do what is good, evil lies close at hand. For I delight in the law of God in my inmost self, but I see in my members another law at war with the law of my mind, making me captive to the law of sin that dwells in my members.

Indeed, says Mani, there is a war within each of us—and a war all around us—a war between good and evil, light and dark. Our own selves are the battlefields of that war, as the light of our true selves battles with the dark of our bodies.

In Romans, Paul laments, "Wretched man that I am! Who will rescue me from this body of death?" Mani claimed to have the answer to Paul's question. Mani organized his church precisely so that it could win the war between good and evil and rescue the light from the dark.

The Manichaean Church was an international organization with a well-organized hierarchy. As with all ancient religious movements, we cannot say how many Manichaeans there were, but they were certainly spread far and wide. The supreme leader was considered Mani's successor, and he was called The Guide. He lived in Babylon. Below The Guide, Manichaeans were organized into five ranks, but these five ranks were placed within two larger, more significant groups: the Elect and the Hearers. The distinction between the Elect and the Hearers and the interactions between them are at the heart of how Manichaeism worked.

The Elect comprised the top four ranks. The first three of these ranks formed the church hierarchy and were limited in number. At the top, just below the Guide, were 12 Doctors or Teachers, below them 72 Ministers, and then in third place 360 Administrators. These officers were in charge of assigned geographical territories. The fourth rank consisted of monks who filled a variety of roles in local congregations: They were preachers, choirmasters, scribes, and the like.

These local members of the Elect lived together in monastic communities. The Elect committed themselves to live in absolute purity. If they did so, their souls of light would escape their bodies of darkness at their death, and the light would return to the realm of light.

The purity of the Elect had five aspects. First: truth. The Elect pledged never to lie and to be faithful to the truth that Mani taught. In practical terms, this meant that the Elect promised to be obedient to church doctrine and leaders.

Second: nonviolence. This principle meant, of course, that the Elect should not harm other people, but it also meant that they must not harm animals and plants because the Manichaeans believed that fragments of light existed in all living beings. Therefore, the Elect could not participate in raising animals for food or in agriculture because killing animals and harvesting plants would do violence to the light within those animals and plants.

Third: religious behavior. In general, the Elect had to live completely moral lives and avoid bodily pleasure. But specifically, they were required to be celibate. Sex and reproduction were the means by which fragments of light were trapped in new bodies of darkness, and so the Elect were forbidden to engage in sex.

Fourth: purity of mouth. The Elect were strict vegetarians—vegans by our definition. They consumed no animal products, including dairy products, nor did they drink any alcoholic beverages. Their diet was designed to do as little harm as possible to fragments of light, and as we shall see, it was designed to liberate light.

Fifth: poverty. The Elect did not make money. Instead, they relied on the Hearers for their financial support.

This lifestyle sounds a lot like Christian monasticism, which developed about the same time or somewhat later. Christians who did not like monks sometimes accused them of being Manichaeans.

Most Manichaeans, however, were Hearers, not the Elect. The Elect formed an exclusive group, limited to those who wanted to make such an intense commitment. The Hearers practiced a less rigorous version of this lifestyle. In general, they were expected to lead a conventional moral life by avoiding such sins as idolatry, lying, theft, and so on. The Hearers could get married and have sex only with their spouses. They abstained from sex during certain periods of fasting. They had a less restricted diet than the Elect, but they still had to refrain from alcohol and meat.

The Hearers lived in their own households, and they had regular jobs. They were expected to give 10 percent of their income as alms to the church in support of the Elect and of poor Hearers. These contributions came not only as money, but also in the form of fruits and vegetables, for the Hearers were permitted to engage in agriculture.

Both the Elect and the Hearers participated in a regular schedule of fasting. Fasts meant not eating or drinking until after the sun went down. They fasted once a week, on Sundays, and there was an annual 30-day fast, which led to the holiest Manichaean festival, the Bema. The Bema commemorated Mani's death and return to heaven. By sharing periods of fasting, the Elect and the Hearers expressed their solidarity with each other.

The Hearers also confessed their sins to the Elect weekly, on Mondays—and the Elect confessed their sins to each other as well. And the annual 30-day fast was also a period for confession and forgiveness of sins.

Because the Hearers did not live a life of complete purity, their light did not return to the realm of light when they died. Instead, their light fragments reincarnated in new human bodies, and perhaps in their next lives they would be Elect and so escape this realm of darkness completely.

Nonetheless, the Hearers had a crucial role to play in the liberation of light from the darkness. First, of course, by supporting the Elect, they enabled the Elect to live completely purely and so free their souls of light. Second, by bringing fruits and vegetables to the Elect, the Hearers helped the Elect to liberate the light in those plants. Let me explain.

Manichaean worship took place on a calendar much like those of Judaism and Christianity: It was both weekly and annual. When Manichaeans gathered, they prayed and sang hymns. Much of the Manichaean literature that survives consists of lengthy hymns and prayers to divine beings of light. But at the heart of their worship was a sacred meal.

The Hearers would bring to the Elect bread, fruits, and vegetables for them to eat. The Elect had rendered their bodies so pure that, when they ate these food offerings, their digestive system would separate the light from the dark and enable the light to escape upward toward the realm of light. In other words, Manichaean ritual was a rescue operation—the Hearers and the Elect worked together to liberate the light that was present in the food that the Elect consumed. The Hearers did the problematic but necessary work of harvesting and preparing the food, something that caused pain to the light within. But when they brought the food to the Elect, they made it possible for the Elect to liberate the light through their pure bodies.

During this period of the second war, the rulers of dark are oppressing the fragments of light. But the Manichaean church and its rituals are continually liberating light and sending it back to the realm of light. The Manichaeans believed that they could see this happening. They attributed the waxing and waning of the moon to this process. As light leaves the earth, it travels upward and gathers at the moon, and the moon's light gradually grows as more light arrives there. When the moon's light gets full, then the light heads onward to the next stop, which is the sun, and so the moon's light slowly diminishes. So, too, the changing patterns of the sun's path and of daylight are a function of liberated light traveling from here to the realm of light. In the sky, Manichaeans could see their religion at work—this was a dramatic confirmation of the truth of their message.

Now as you can imagine, Christian bishops, Zoroastrian priests, and other religious leaders ridiculed Manichaean teaching and practice. They said it was ludicrous to think that, when a Manichaean Elect belched or farted, he was sending liberated light to the eternal realm. But even they recognized the appeal of Manichaeism and so its danger to their religions.

As I have said, Manichaean myth offered a clear explanation for the problem of evil and a systematic program of salvation from it. Wherever they went, Manichaean missionaries claimed that their religion was the culmination or true meaning of the local religion. In Christian areas, Manichaean literature drew heavily on Christian scriptures and texts, but in Buddhist areas, it featured Buddhist characters and ideas. In late antiquity as today, people found very attractive the idea of a single religion that would unite all previous religions and overcome religious divisions.

Just as the Sassanian king had tortured Mani, the Roman emperors found Manichaeism to be a grave danger. It drew people away from the traditional worship of the Roman gods, and it came from Persia, the great enemy of the Romans. And so in the 290s, the Roman emperor Diocletian outlawed the Manichaean religion as a threat to the Roman state.

But just as Roman persecution failed to stop the spread of Christianity, so, too, Manichaeism continued to grow in the Roman Empire—it even spread as far as China, where Marco Polo met a group of Manichaeans in 1292. When Christianity became legal in the Roman Empire in the early 300s, this helped the Manichaeans because it was sometimes hard to tell the difference between a community of Manichaean Elect and a monastery of Christian monks.

Manichaeism did eventually fade away, thanks to the rise of Christianity and Islam—but its influence did not fade away. In our next lecture, we'll meet Saint Augustine of Hippo. Augustine spent a decade as a Manichaean Hearer, and when he converted to Christianity, he brought that long experience of Mani's Gospel of Truth with him.

Augustine on Manichaeism and Original Sin
Lecture 22

S aint Augustine (354–430) is one of the most important figures in the history of Christianity. He was the bishop of the North African city of Hippo and a brilliant theologian, yet he was once a heretic—a Manichaean. He later became a Christian, but Manichaeism did not leave his life and thought. Augustine developed many of his teachings about Christianity in opposition to Manichaeism, but even in his own lifetime, his critics said that he never really escaped his Manichaean past: His doctrines of predestination and original sin might as well have been Manichaean. Whether that's true or not, there is no doubt that Manichaeism, a religion that no longer exists, profoundly shaped important elements of Western Christianity.

Augustine's Search for Wisdom

- Augustine's mother, Monica, was a devout Christian, but his father was not. His mother prayed that Augustine would become a Christian, but Augustine had a mind of his own. As a student in his late teens, he was influenced by Cicero, who had argued that people find true happiness only in the pursuit of wisdom—philosophy. Augustine was inspired to seek true wisdom, but he immediately ran into two problems.

  o First, according to Monica, Christianity was the highest form of wisdom, but when Augustine turned to the Bible, he found that it was not particularly well written and that many of its characters engaged in acts that were clearly immoral.

  o Second, Augustine may have been inspired by Cicero's claim that true happiness comes from philosophy, but he found it difficult to give up other forms of happiness, such as sex and other sensual pleasures.

- Manichaeism provided solutions to both of these problems.

- Recall that Mani presented his religion as a higher form of Christianity. He agreed that the Old Testament and its view of God are problematic, and he called his followers to a deeper understanding of the message brought by Jesus and Paul. With this perspective, Augustine saw some connection to Christianity but without the difficulties he had identified earlier.

- Recall, too, that Manichaeism had two kinds of adherents: the Elect, who led celibate and morally pure lives, and the Hearers, who led normal married lives. In Manichaeism, Augustine found a group that valued celibacy and moral purity but made a place for those who wanted to have sex and lead less demanding ethical lives.

- In addition, Manichaeism explained why Augustine wanted to pursue philosophy yet not give up certain physical pleasures. On the one hand, Augustine is a fragment of the Light, which makes him aspire to the Good. On the other hand, he is enmeshed in the Dark, particularly his body, which draws him away from the Good. The conflict between Light and Dark at the heart of Manichaeism explained Augustine's own conflicting desires.

- For all these reasons, Augustine became a Hearer. After a few years, however, he began to have doubts about Manichaean teachings. In 384, he moved to Milan and discovered new perspectives that furthered his break with Manichaeism.
  - First, he encountered the writings of Plotinus, which gave him a new way to think about good and evil.

  - Second, Augustine heard the preaching of the Christian bishop of Milan, Ambrose (339–397). Ambrose interpreted some of the morally dubious activities of characters in the Old Testament symbolically and, in this way, helped Augustine see that Christianity could be philosophically sophisticated.

- In 386, Augustine declared his conversion to Christianity. He later returned to North Africa and ultimately became the bishop of Hippo, although Manichaeism continued to shape his thought.

Augustine on God, Evil, and Sin

- Augustine devoted many of his early writings to refuting Manichaean ideas, particularly those related to God, evil, and sin.
  - The Manichaeans taught that Good, represented by God, and Evil, led by Satan, are both eternal principles. They were originally completely separate, but when Evil attacked the Good, fragments of the good Light became trapped in the Darkness of evil.

  - Human beings experience this mixture of good and evil in their very persons. Our true selves are fragments of the good Light, but our bodies are composed of the evil Darkness. For this reason, we feel torn between good and evil.

  Manichaeism shaped the theology of Saint Augustine, which in turn dominated Western Christianity for centuries—and remains highly influential today.

  - Our goal should be to live our lives so that Light will eventually be liberated from the darkness and return to the Light realm, enabling Light and Darkness—Good and Evil—to be fully separate once again.

- In response to these teachings, Augustine argued that the Manichaeans' God could not truly be God because he was vulnerable to evil. Any true God should be omnipotent and almighty, and the Manichaean God was not because Evil had been able to seize and trap some of the Light. The only God worthy of worship, Augustine said, would be all-powerful and not vulnerable to evil.

- What, then, is the origin of evil? The Manichaeans argued that Evil had always existed, alongside the Good. It was an active, independent force, present in our bodies and other things in the world. But Augustine learned from Plotinus that evil is simply a lack of good. Everything that exists—animals, plants, our bodies, and even Satan—is good by virtue of its existence. The evil in these things is their lack of good—their failure to be fully and completely good.

- And why do humans want to do both good and evil? The Manichaeans explained that we are a mix of the good and evil elements that are at war with each other, but Augustine said that was far too simplistic.
  - People do not find themselves torn between two alternatives, good and evil. Rather, we have multiple, complex, and ambiguous desires. Our will is divided among many things that we want, only some of which are good.

  - For true happiness and goodness, we should desire and love only one thing—the ultimate good, God. If we did that, all the things we desire would sort themselves out in a proper order, and we would reject the bad things.

  - Instead, our will, our center of desire and loving, has turned away from God. We may want to love God wholeheartedly, but we cannot; we still have persistent desires for lesser good things and for bad things.

  - This turning away from God results in a lack or deficit in our love for God—the definition of evil.

- Thus, in opposition to the Manichaean teaching that evil and sin come from an enduring principle of evil, Augustine argued that they arise from a lack of good and from the human will turning away from God.

Augustine on Original Sin and Predestination

- One objection to Augustine's view of evil is that none of us remembers a time when we loved God completely but then began to desire other things. Augustine would respond that we didn't turn away from God as individuals; rather, we turned away at the beginning of creation—in Adam!

- In Augustine's interpretation of Genesis, God made Adam and Eve completely good. They loved God completely and were without sin. But they also had free will. They could freely love God forever and live forever, or they could choose to turn away from God, which as we saw, is evil.

- In response to their turning away from him, God justly and rightly sentenced Adam and Eve to death—but not only Adam and Eve. Somehow, in a spiritual way that Augustine never quite explains, all the human beings that would ever live were present in Adam and Eve; we also turned away from God, and we, too, were justly condemned. Thus, when we are born, we are already sinful; we inherit the original sin of Adam.

- If Augustine had stopped there, probably few would say that the idea of original sin is Manichaean. But when Augustine was pressed by his critics to explain how and why original sin is transmitted, he focused on sex.
  - In the Garden of Eden, before they committed sin, Adam and Eve could have had sex, but for them, sex would have been perfectly rational and controlled.

  - But when Adam and Eve turned away from God, their wills became divided, and they lost control of their bodies. For Augustine, the fact that we lose control of ourselves in sex—

that our desires seem to take over—shows precisely how sin has damaged our nature. Sex is dominated now by what Augustine called *concupiscence*, which is love or desire that has gone astray. Because sex is clouded by concupiscence, the conception that results is clouded by sin.

- The Manichaeans had a negative view of sex because conception entangled more fragments of Light with the evil Darkness of bodies. Augustine seemed to be tying sinfulness directly to sex and the body, just as the Manichaeans did. We can see from Augustine's view that he had to explain in some way how it is that everyone ends up turning away from God: Once he decided that all humanity turned away from God in Adam and Eve, then sexual reproduction became the means by which we are all connected to these earliest humans.

- If original sin explains how we ended up with our perverse and divided will, how can we escape from sin and be saved?
  - Augustine's answer is that we can do nothing to help ourselves. Our will is hopelessly divided, and as much as we may want to, we cannot learn to love God wholeheartedly on our own. We will always have competing desires that will distract us and pull us away from God and the Good.

  - The only solution is for God to give us the grace to be saved. God must choose to heal a person's divided will and bring him or her back to loving God. This means that God must choose which human beings he will save and which he will not. This is predestination—the idea that God decides which people will be saved and that people can do nothing on their own to give up evil and love God completely.

- For Augustine, predestination was good news; it was a blessing to believe that his salvation depended fully on God. Augustine had found it difficult to give up sex and other pleasures and devote his life to God. Only when he felt God empowering him could he do so. Predestination is also a logical result of the belief that God is omnipotent. If God is almighty, then nothing can happen without God willing it to happen, including human beings giving up evil and turning back to God.

Suggested Reading

Augustine, *Confessions*.

Brown, *Augustine of Hippo*.

Fredriksen, *Sin*.

O'Donnell, *Augustine*.

Questions to Consider

1. How did the Neoplatonism of Plotinus turn Augustine away from the Manichaeans and shape his view of evil and sin?

2. Augustine believed that his own experience confirmed that human beings cannot turn away from sin on their own but must have grace from God. Is Augustine's story idiosyncratic, or does it seem universal?

Augustine on Manichaeism and Original Sin
Lecture 22—Transcript

When Christians refer to the Immaculate Conception, what do they mean? If you asked people on the street, they would probably say that the Immaculate Conception is Jesus being conceived by a virgin, without any sex. But that's not it. Rather, the Immaculate Conception refers to Mary, Jesus's mother, being conceived by her parents without the stain of original sin.

The Catholic Church teaches that, through sexual intercourse, every human being inherits the guilt of Adam and Eve's sin. Even before we are born, all of us are unclean in the sight of God—all of us, that is, except Mary. Her parents did conceive her through sex, but God did not allow Mary to inherit original sin. Her conception was immaculate—totally clean.

Christians got the idea of original sin from St. Augustine, one of the most important figures in the history of Christianity. Augustine lived in the 4th and 5th centuries. He died in 430 A.D. He was the bishop of the North African city of Hippo in present day Algeria. Hippo was not one of the leading cities in the Roman Empire, but Augustine was such a brilliant theologian and politician that he became one of the dominant figures of his time. His ideas deeply shaped the beliefs of the Roman Catholic and Protestant churches even today.

And yet Augustine was once a heretic. From the age of 20 to about when he was 30, Augustine was a Manichaean. For 10 years, Augustine learned the teachings that we discussed in the last lecture: that good and evil, light and dark, are two fairly equal and opposed principles; that the world in which we live and we ourselves are a mixture of these two substances; that evil is located in the substance of our bodies; and that a lifestyle of celibacy and moral purity can liberate the light that is trapped in this world of darkness.

Eventually, Augustine left the Manichaeans and became a Christian, but Manichaeism did not leave Augustine's life and thought. Augustine developed many of his teachings about Christianity in opposition to Manichaeism, but already in his own lifetime critics of Augustine said that he never really escaped his Manichaean past. His doctrines of predestination and original sin might as well have been Manichaean, some say. Whether that's true or not, there is no doubt that Manichaeism, a religion that no longer exists, profoundly shaped important elements of Western Christianity.

How did Augustine end up becoming a Manichaean in the first place? Well, the young Augustine was what we could call a "seeker"—someone looking for the meaning of life and the answers to big questions. And for a while, he thought Manichaeism offered him what he had been searching for.

Augustine was born in 354. His mother was a devout Christian, but his father was not. Like most children of his day, Augustine was not baptized. His mother Monica prayed that Augustine would become a Christian, but Augustine had a mind of his own. In his late teens, when he was a student in Carthage, he read a book by Cicero, the great philosopher. Cicero's book argued that people find true happiness only in the pursuit of wisdom—that is, in philosophy. Augustine was inspired in the way that young people can be, and he decided to seek true wisdom. But right away he ran into two problems.

First, Monica had always said that Christianity was the highest form of wisdom, and so Augustine turned to the Bible. He did not find what he was looking for. Rather, he found that the Bible was not very well written— at least in comparison to the beautiful prose of Cicero. Plus, many of the characters in the Bible did clearly immoral things: The patriarchs of the Old Testament had multiple wives and concubines, and characters like Jacob engaged in all sorts of morally dubious acts. How could the Bible be the source of wisdom? So Christianity did not appear very promising.

Second, Augustine may have been inspired by Cicero's claim that true happiness comes from philosophy, but he found it difficult to give up other forms of happiness, like sex. Augustine was not what we would call a player—that is, he did not have multiple girlfriends or casual hook-ups—but around this time he did begin a long-term relationship with a woman who became his concubine, and eventually the two of them had a son. Augustine found sexual and emotional satisfaction in this relationship, and he feared that the serious pursuit of philosophy meant that he would have to give it up. In general, Augustine enjoyed the sensual pleasures that philosophy seemed to condemn—sex, food, and so on.

So Augustine wanted to seek wisdom, but Christianity appeared flawed to him, and he did not want to live the more austere life of the true philosopher. Manichaeism provided solutions to both of these problems. Let's remember that Mani presented his religion as the culmination of Christianity—or a higher form of it. He agreed that the Old Testament and its view of God are problematic, and he called his followers to a deeper understanding of the message brought by Jesus and Paul. And so Augustine could see some connection to Christianity, but without all the difficult stuff that he didn't like.

Recall, too, that Manichaeism had two kinds of adherents: the Elect, who led celibate and morally pure lives, and the Hearers, who could live normal married lives. So Augustine could join a group that valued celibacy and moral purity, but that also made a place for someone like him, someone who wanted to have sex and a less demanding ethical life.

In addition to all of this, Manichaeism explained what Augustine was experiencing. Why did Augustine want to pursue philosophy completely and yet at the same not want to give up certain physical pleasures? Because, said the Manichaeans, he was a mix of the light and the dark. On the one hand, Augustine is a fragment of the light, which makes him aspire to the good. On the other hand, he is enmeshed in the dark, particularly his body, which draws him away from the good. The conflict between light and dark at the heart of Manichaeism explained Augustine's own conflicting desires.

And so Augustine became a Manichaean Hearer. His mother was horrified, but she continued to support Augustine's career ambitions. Augustine was studying rhetoric, so that he could become a teacher and then a government bureaucrat and speechwriter. The Manichaeans may have been a shadowy, even illegal religious group, but they were spread across the empire, and they were loyal to one another. Manichaeism actually provided Augustine with connections that could help him professionally.

After a few years, however, Augustine began to have doubts about Manichaean teachings. You will remember that the Manichaeans did not just make claims that we would call religious—that God is a certain way and that salvation comes through certain rituals—but their teachings verged also on what we would call science. That is, they explained such things as

427

the behavior of the sun, moon, and stars through their idea of the return of liberated light to the light realm. Augustine began to question Manichaean assertions about such matters, and even the most highly praised Manichaean leaders could not answer his questions.

For a time, Augustine kept to himself just how serious his doubts were, and he remained a part of the Manichaean community even after he had given up believing in its teaching. As I mentioned, the Manichaeans were proving to be helpful to Augustine's career, and he had not found a real alternative to Manichaeism in his quest for wisdom.

A new job caused Augustine to relocate to Milan in Italy in 384, and there, he found new perspectives that helped him to break with the Manichaeans. First, he encountered the writings of Plotinus in Latin. We met Plotinus a few lectures ago and learned about his mystical teachings and how they reflect his knowledge of the Gnostics. Plotinus, as I'll explain in a moment, gave Augustine a new way to think about good and evil, a way that he found superior to that of the Manichaeans.

Second, Augustine heard the preaching of the Christian bishop of Milan, Ambrose. Ambrose combined the kind of Platonism you find in Plotinus with Christianity, and he interpreted the strange stories of the Old Testament symbolically. That is, Ambrose explained that the morally dubious activities of biblical characters could be understood as not being literally true, but as communicating higher truths through allegories. So Ambrose helped Augustine to see that Christianity could be philosophically sophisticated.

In 386, Augustine declared his conversion to Christianity and received baptism. The works of Plotinus and the preaching of Ambrose prepared him to take this step intellectually. Spiritually, Augustine had a religious experience in which he felt empowered to give up sex and other pleasures to devote himself fully to God. He hoped to lead a life of religious seclusion and study.

When he returned to North Africa, however, Christians quickly realized that Augustine was a natural leader. One day in 391, Augustine was visiting the city of Hippo, and when the Christians saw him worshiping in their church, they wanted to make him one of their priests—and eventually their bishop. Augustine resisted this, but the Christians of Hippo literally grabbed him and forced him to be ordained a priest. Four years later he became their bishop. At the age of 40, Augustine was known internationally as one of Christianity's rising theological stars.

And yet, Augustine had been a Manichaean throughout his 20s, a very formative period in any person's life. And so he couldn't just leave Manichaeism behind or forget it. Manichaeism continued to shape Augustine's thought in two ways. On the one hand, Augustine developed his teachings on God, evil, and sin precisely in response to what he had learned in Manichaeism. Just as we have seen earlier Christians like Irenaeus and Origen develop Christian theology in order to refute Gnostic teachings, so, too, Augustine's theology was thoroughly anti-Manichaean. On the other hand, critics of Augustine's teachings on predestination and original sin argue that Manichaean ideas about the evils of the body and sex lingered in Augustine's thought, even if he would deny that. That is, Manichaeism lives on in Western Christianity in the doctrine of original sin.

Let's turn now to each of these ways that Manichaeism shaped Augustine's theology. This is important because Augustine's thought dominated Western Christianity for centuries—and remains highly influential today. First, Augustine devoted many of his early writings to refuting Manichaean ideas. Certainly he did this because Manichaeism remained popular, especially among young, philosophically inclined people like he had been. But another reason Augustine criticized the Manichaeans so much was to show skeptical Christians that he was not a Manichaean anymore and that he could be trusted as a Christian leader. Few people are as eager to criticize a religion as someone who was a member but then rejected it!

Now many of Augustine's anti-Manichaean writings address questions of how to interpret the Bible, especially the Old Testament. Here, Augustine applied what he had learned from Ambrose to show that Old Testament stories that seem to show characters like Abraham or even the God of Israel behaving badly can be understood in more positive ways. He also refuted Manichaean claims that passages in the New Testament supported their teachings. But we want to focus here on the bigger ideas of God, good, and evil. How did Augustine respond to Manichaean views on these crucial topics?

Recall that the Manichaeans taught that good, represented by God, and evil, led by Satan, are both eternal principles and even substances. They were originally completely separate, but when evil attacked the good, some of the good ended up mixed up in evil. Or, fragments of the good light ended up trapped in the darkness of evil. Human beings experience this mixture of good and evil in their very persons. Our true selves are fragments of the good light, but our bodies are composed of the evil darkness. For this reason, we feel torn between good and evil. These opposing inclinations result from the mix of light and dark within ourselves. Our goal is to live our lives so that that light will eventually be liberated from the darkness and return to the light realm, so that light and darkness, good and evil, will be fully separate once again. Augustine developed a Christian theology of God, good, and evil that opposed Manichaeism on all these points.

Augustine argued that the Manichaean's God could not truly be God because their God was vulnerable to evil. That is, any true God should be omnipotent, almighty, and the Manichaean good God surely was not this because evil was able to seize and trap some of the light. The only God worthy of worship, Augustine said, would be all-powerful and not vulnerable to evil. And so the first principle that Augustine laid down against the Manichaeans is that God is almighty and more powerful than any evil principle.

If that's so, then where did evil come from? Remember: The Manichaeans had a very clear answer to the origin of evil. Evil has just always existed alongside the good. But Augustine posited that there is a single, all-powerful God, and this God is the source of all that is and more powerful than anything else. This makes the problem of evil much more difficult because we don't want to imagine an all-good and all-powerful God creating evil.

This is where Plotinus helped Augustine. Plotinus agreed that there is simply one ultimate principle, God, and God is entirely good. What, then, is evil? Plotinus answered that evil is not anything of its own—it's simply the absence of good, or the lack of good, or a deficit of good. For Plotinus, everything that exists is good; simply to exist is good. So evil is a lack of existence—it really is nothing.

Here are a couple of analogies. Imagine a healthy body, which is good. Now imagine a wound on that body. "Woundedness" is not a thing of its own. There is no wound out in the world, planning to attack a body. Rather, the wound is a lack of health, a deficit in the goodness of the body. Likewise, consider rust on a car. Again, rust is not an independent thing, something that exists apart from the car. Rather, rust is a decline in the car, a lack, a deficit.

The Manichaeans saw evil as an active independent force, present in our bodies and other materials in the world. But Augustine learned from Plotinus that evil is a lack of good. For Augustine, everything that exists is good—not only animals and trees, but also our bodies, and even the devil. All these things are good to the extent they exist. Their evil is their lack of good—their failure to be fully and completely good. Satan certainly is evil, but his evil is a lack of good.

So how does this work at the level of the individual human being? Let's recall that one thing that attracted Augustine to Manichaeism is that it could explain his contradictory desires for both good and evil. Why do we want both to do good and to do evil? Because, the Manichaeans explained, we are a mix of the good and evil elements that are at war with one another. We may be fragments of the light and so inclined to the good, but we have bodies of darkness, which pull us toward evil.

Augustine now said that this is far too simplistic. People don't find themselves torn simply between two alternatives, good and evil. Rather, we find that we have multiple, complex, and ambiguous desires. We do not simply think, "Shall I do good or evil?" Instead, Augustine said, we want to do a variety of things that are not all good or all bad. I may want to help at a homeless shelter, go to a church service, have some ice cream, take a nap, tell a lie, and so on, all at the same time. The problem is, then, not that I have two substances at war within me, the light and the dark or the good and the evil—the problem is that my will is divided among too many things that I want, only some of which are good.

For true happiness and true goodness, I should desire and love only one thing—the ultimate good, God. If I did, all these other good and desirable things would sort themselves out in a proper order of priority, and I would reject the bad things. But instead, my will, my center of desire and loving, has turned away from God. I may want to love God whole-heartedly, but I cannot—I still have persistent desires for other lesser good things and for bad things.

This turning away from God is what's evil about me. Remember, evil is a lack or deficit of good, and here what has happened is that my will has turned away from God, and there is now a lack or deficit in my love for God—that's what's evil. And that's why my will now desires a lot of different things—good, bad, and in-between—rather than desiring the one good thing, God.

So, in opposition to the Manichaean teaching that evil and sin come from an enduring principle of evil, Augustine argued that they arise from a lack of good and from the human will turning away from God. In this way, he formulated his teachings about God, good, and evil in direct opposition to Manichaeism.

Now what about the idea that some of Augustine's views continued to reflect Manichaeism? Here we come to his very controversial teachings about original sin and predestination. As we've just seen, Augustine believes that each of us is sinful because our will has turned away from God, and rather than loving God with our whole hearts, we instead find ourselves loving and desiring a whole bunch of different things, and our will is divided. This raises two questions: First, how did I get this way? Second, what can I do to solve this problem and devote myself fully to God? The doctrine of original sin answers the first question—how I got into this condition—and the doctrine of predestination answers the second—how I can be fixed.

So as to the first question, you may object to Augustine's view by saying that you never remember actually turning away from God. You don't remember a time when you loved God fully and completely, but then began to desire other things. Well, Augustine says, that's because you did not turn away from God as an individual in your own life. Rather, you did it at the beginning of creation—in Adam.

Let me explain. As Augustine interprets Genesis, God made Adam and Eve completely good. They loved God completely and were without sin. But God also made Adam and Eve with free will. They could freely love God forever, and also live forever. But they could also choose to turn away from God, and that's what they did. When Eve took from the forbidden fruit, and Adam accepted it from her, they turned away from God, and, as we have seen, this turning away of the will was evil. They did not have to do this. The serpent did not force them to do so. They just did. Without any mitigating circumstances, this crime deserved death—after all, God had told Adam and Eve that the penalty for disobeying him would be death.

This turning away from God was a catastrophe. Adam and Eve now had the perverse and divided will that I just described. God justly and rightly sentenced Adam and Eve to death. But not only Adam and Eve—somehow, in a spiritual way that Augustine never quite explains, all humanity, all the human beings that would ever live, were present in Adam and Eve, and so we, too, turned away from God, and we, too, were justly condemned. And so when we're born, we're already sinful, we're already guilty—we inherit the original sin of Adam.

So no human being is born good and then goes bad. Rather, we all went bad in the Garden of Eden, and now all our wills are evil and hopelessly divided among many desires. No human being fails to do something sinful—we may find that idea pretty reasonable—but in Augustine's view, no human can ever hope to be sinless. We're born sinful.

Now if Augustine had stopped there, probably few would say that the idea of original sin is Manichaean. But he did not stop there. Rather, when Augustine was pressed by his critics to explain precisely how and why original sin is transmitted to new people, he focused on sex. How do we know that our wills are disordered and not in line with God? Just look at sex, Augustine said.

In the Garden of Eden, before they committed sin, Adam and Eve could have had sex, Augustine said. But sex for them would have been perfectly controlled. They would have moved their sexual organs at will, and sexual intercourse would have been as rational and controlled as shaking hands. But when Adam and Eve turned away from God, their wills became divided, and they lost control of their own bodies. Our sexual organs no longer obey us. They get aroused when we don't want them to, and they fail to do their job at times when we do want them to. This is, of course, a very male-oriented way of looking things. But for Augustine, the fact that we lose control of ourselves in sex, that our desires seem to take over, shows precisely how sin has damaged our nature. Sex is dominated now by what Augustine called concupiscence, which is love or desire that has gone astray. Because sex is clouded by concupiscence, the conception that results is clouded by sin.

As the author of Psalm 51 wrote, "Behold, I was brought forth in iniquity, and in sin did my mother conceive me." Here is where Augustine seemed to go Manichaean in the eyes of his critics. The Manichaeans, too, had a negative view of sex because conception simply entangled more fragments of light with the evil darkness of bodies. And now Augustine seemed to be tying sinfulness directly to sex and the body, just as the Manichaeans did. You can see from Augustine's view that he had to explain in some way how it is that everyone ends up in this position of turning away from God: Once he decided that all humanity turned away from God in Adam and Eve, then sexual reproduction seemed to be the means by which we are all connected to these earliest human beings.

You can see now why Christians who believe in original sin came up with the idea of Mary's Immaculate Conception. God had to intervene miraculously to prevent the sexual intercourse of Mary's parents from transmitting the guilt of sin to Mary, the future mother of Jesus, who had to be without sin.

So if original sin explains how we ended up with our perverse and divided will, how can we escape from sin and be saved? What we can do about our situation? Augustine's answer is that we can do nothing to help ourselves. My will is hopelessly divided, and as much as I may want to, I cannot learn to love God with all my heart on my own. I will always continue to have competing desires and interests that will distract me and pull me away from God and the good. The only solution is for God to give me the grace to be saved. God must choose to heal a person's divided will and bring him or her back to loving him. And this means that God must choose which human beings he will save in this way and which not. This is predestination—the idea that God decides which people will be saved, and that people can do nothing on their own to give up evil and love God completely.

It's important to understand that Augustine does not deny that people decide whether to do good or bad things. I myself decide whether to help a poor person or to tell a lie—no one, not even God or Satan, forces me to do one or the other. People are fully responsible for the evil deeds that they commit. What I cannot do is change my overall orientation that is away from God. I cannot by myself choose to give up loving myself and other things more than God. I cannot by myself heal my divided and perverse will. Only the gift of God's grace can do that—and God must choose to give me that grace.

You can see why some people found Augustine to be still somewhat of a Manichaean. Manichaeans had a very pessimistic view of the world in which we live: It's the realm of darkness in which we fragments of light are trapped. Likewise, Augustine has a very pessimistic view of human nature as it now exists: We can do nothing good unless God gives us the grace to do so.

But it's important to remember that for Augustine, this idea was good news, a relief. It was a blessing to him to believe that his salvation depended fully on God. Augustine had found it very difficult to give up sex and other pleasures to devote his life to God. Only when he felt God empowering him could he do it. Also, for Augustine, predestination is a logical result of believing that God is omnipotent. If God is almighty, he says, then nothing can happen without God willing it to happen—and that includes human beings giving up evil and turning back to God.

We've come a long way in this lecture, just as Augustine did. He started out looking for true wisdom, which he had learned from Cicero was the only path to true happiness. But his desire for sex and other physical pleasures prevented him from devoting himself fully to God and the good. Manichaeism seemed to offer a good explanation for his situation: He was a fragment of light, trapped in a body of darkness.

But Augustine eventually found this teaching far too simple, inadequate to explain the complexity and ambiguity of his diverse desires and loves. For decades Augustine struggled to come up with a new theological understanding of how sin and salvation works. He needed answers that explained his own experience, but he also worked out his ideas through dealing with Manichaeism. The result is the theology of original sin and predestination that dominated Western Christianity for centuries. In this way, the Gnostic ideas of Manichaeism shaped how Western Christians have believed.

But Manichaeism was not the last manifestation of *gnōsis*. In the next lecture we'll meet the Mandaeans, the Cathars, and other groups that promoted views remarkably similar to those of the ancient Gnostics.

Gnostic Traces in Western Religions
Lecture 23

W hat happened to the ancient Gnostics and their ideas? Did they simply disappear until Gnostic texts in Coptic were discovered in the 20th century? We have already seen that Gnostic ideas influenced orthodox Christianity, ancient Judaism, Platonism, and the development of Manichaeism. Although the classic period of "Gnosticism" was over by 450, key themes and ideas from ancient Gnosticism persisted into the Middle Ages and beyond. In this lecture, we'll look at three primary facets of Gnostic and Valentinian thought, myth making, *gnōsis*, and dualism, that emerged in the later religious history of Europe and the Near East.

Myth Making
- The Gnostics and Valentinians created complex myths that explained who God is and how this universe came into being. Unlike Greek or Roman myths, Gnostic and Valentinian myths do not feature human-like gods with personalities or traditional stories. Instead, they are highly philosophical. Gnostic and Valentinian myths may appear to be overly complicated, but that complexity may have been part of their appeal. As believers learned more about the myth, they gained a sense of personal knowledge of divine secrets.

- The Mandaeans, a religious and ethnic community in modern Iraq and Iran, carry on this tradition of myth making to the present day. The Mandaeans may have originated in the 4th or 5th century, and today, they probably number around 10,000 to 15,000.

- Because they are so few in number and have lived in relative isolation, Western scholars did not know much about the Mandaeans until the 20th century. A deeper understanding of the Mandaean religion came with the work of an English scholar named Ethel Stevens (Lady Drower), who lived in Iraq and brought many Mandaean manuscripts to Great Britain.

- The myths of the Mandaeans resemble those of the Gnostics, Valentinians, and Manichaeans. Like that of the Manichaeans, Mandaean myth distinguishes between a realm of light and a realm of darkness. Supreme deities and lower emanations rule both realms. For example, the Lord of Greatness or King of Light rules the world of light, along with numerous lower beings. The lowest divine being is Ptahil, the god who created the cosmos in which we live.

- The Mandaeans achieve contact with the world of light through rituals involving water. A Mandaean temple must have a pool, called a Jordan after the Jordan River in Palestine. Baptism in this pool connects a person with the realm of light.

- John the Baptist plays an important role in Mandaean mythology and ritual as a teacher and priest. Because the Mandaeans came into conflict with Christians, Jesus Christ sometimes plays a negative role in their mythology; at other times, he's a good character.

- The Mandaeans have existed for nearly all of their history under Muslim rule, and for the most part, they have enjoyed the freedom to practice their faith as a "religion of the book," similar to Judaism, Christianity, and Islam itself. The Mandaean community provides a living link with the ancient period of Gnosticism.

Gnōsis

- A second key feature of ancient Gnosticism was, of course, *gnōsis*, firsthand acquaintance with God. The quest for *gnōsis* continued in the Christian tradition apart from the groups that became known as heretics. Already in the 2nd century, Clement of Alexandria taught that Christians should aspire to transcend mere faith in the doctrines of the church and to achieve *gnōsis* with God. The ideal Christian, Clement said, was the true Gnostic.

- One of Clement's greatest admirers was the Christian monk Evagrius of Pontus (c. 345–399). After a brief career as a church official, Evagrius became a monk in the Egyptian desert, where he attracted many disciples and became the greatest teacher of spirituality in early monasticism.

○ Evagrius taught that the monk goes through two stages in his spiritual life. For the first and longer period, he is an ascetic practitioner. Through fasting, celibacy, prayer, and scripture reading, the practitioner seeks to overcome his sinful desires and to achieve freedom from negative emotions. Then, the monk can become a Gnostic, someone who engages in higher contemplation of the Bible, the universe, and ultimately, God himself.

○ For Evagrius, the goal of the monastic life was to achieve a vision of God that was beyond all concepts or images. Evagrius believed that the ideas and pictures that fill our minds are sometimes good, but ultimately, they distract us from God, who is beyond anything we can say or imagine. Evagrius described the experience of *gnōsis* as seeing one's mind as a sapphire-blue sky. The goal is to rid the mind of everything so that it's a blank screen on which God can project himself, somehow without any images at all.

○ After his death, Evagrius's teaching became an object of controversy, and he was condemned at the Council of Constantinople in 553. Nonetheless, his teachings lived on because monks considered them too profoundly helpful to be lost.

• Another milestone figure in the history of mystical knowledge of God in Christianity is the mysterious Pseudo-Dionysius the Areopagite. This author combined the Bible with Neoplatonist philosophy and monastic traditions; in so doing, he created a new tradition of mystical theology for Christians.

○ Pseudo-Dionysius believed that we know God in two ways. First, because God pours himself into the creation and because everything emanates from God, we learn about God through images and names that are drawn from the creation and that appear in the Bible. This is called *kataphatic theology*, in which assertions are made about God to achieve growth in understanding him.

o The second way of knowing God is by negating everything we assert about him. Because God is beyond all our names and images, through this *apophatic theology*, we un-know everything we have asserted about God.

o The Christian mystic must engage in both kataphatic and apophatic ways of knowing God, oscillating between saying things about God, then denying those things. This creates a space within us, a place of un-knowing, that God's divine energy can fill.

o In this form of *gnōsis*, believers negate their own minds and selves so that God can take over. Ultimately, they gain *gnōsis*—knowledge—of God through *a-gnōsis*—non-knowledge.

Dualism

- As we learned earlier, dualism is the division of reality into sharply distinguished pairs—Good versus Evil, Light versus Dark, and so on. Dualism appears in both moderate and strict forms, and both forms could be found among the Cathars, a movement that spread in Western Europe in the 12th century.

  o The Cathars took their name from the Greek word meaning "pure ones" and claimed to represent a higher form of Christianity, purer than what they saw as the corrupt and polluted Roman Catholic Church.

  o The Cathars believed in two gods: a good and loving God of the New Testament and an evil and vengeful god of the Old Testament. They also believed that this material world is evil and that Christ came to free our spiritual selves from imprisonment.

  o The Cathars organized themselves as the Manichaeans did, into two levels of membership. The Perfect gave up sex and private property, and they abstained from meat and dairy products. When they died, their souls would escape this world. Ordinary believers supported the Perfect and lived less ascetically. When they died, their souls would be reincarnated in new bodies.

- ○ By around 1200, the Cathars had gained many followers in southern France and northern Italy. People found Catharism attractive because, like Manichaeism, it offered a clear explanation for the existence of evil and suffering, and it provided a systematic plan for gaining salvation. The Cathars also allowed women to preach and serve as leaders and criticized the corruption of Catholic bishops and priests.

- ○ Not surprisingly, the Catholic Church saw Catharism as a threat. In 1209, Pope Innocent III called for a military campaign to wipe out the Cathars in southern France. This campaign is known as the Albigensian Crusade, and it persisted for 20 years. By the early 1300s, Catharism had disappeared.

- At precisely the same time that Catharism arose in Western Europe, a Jewish form of esoteric religion appeared in Provence and northern Spain—Kabbalah. Kabbalah shows some remarkable similarities to Gnosticism.
  - ○ Kabbalah teaches that the ultimate God is completely unknowable. He is Ein Sof ("No End"), and he emanates into lower manifestations called *sefirot*. Much of Kabbalistic literature is devoted to speculation about the *sefirot*—what their characteristics are and how they relate to one another. The *sefirot* also serve as a ladder of contemplation: That is, the Kabbalist gains greater *gnōsis* of God by contemplating each of the *sefirot*.

  - ○ Kabbalah is not dualistic in the way Manichaeism or some Cathars were. Everything comes from the Ein Sof. But the Kabbalists do take evil seriously. There are a series of negative emanations from God that form an evil counterpart to the divine *sefirot*.

    o   Kabbalists devoted themselves to speculation and mysticism based on folklore and learned study. They claimed to find many of their teachings in the Bible, which they did not interpret literally but as pointing to higher, deeper meanings.

The Survival of Gnostic Teachings

- Kabbalah resembles Gnostic myth in several important ways, which might prompt us to ask whether Gnostic teachings somehow survived "underground" for centuries. But no one has been able to show any continuous line of tradition from the ancient Gnostics to the Kabbalists of the 12th century.

- In fact, there seems little need to posit underground streams of tradition to account for the emergence of mythological speculation, dualism, or interest in *gnōsis* at different times and places in Western religious history. The biblical tradition itself invites and encourages such responses.

- The Bible, especially Genesis, is filled with stories that raise questions for curious readers. Why is humanity created twice? Who are the "sons of God" we met earlier who mate with human women? And why did God command Adam and Eve not to eat from the tree of knowledge of good and evil?
  - o Although many Jews and Christians may have been content with simply accepting these stories, others have questioned them. This questioning has led to new stories—myths that try to explain the true nature of God and the origins of ourselves, our world, and the evil that causes pain and suffering.

  - o In addition, there have always been people who have not been satisfied with the basic teachings of their religious tradition, whatever it may be. These people have yearned for a closer, more intimate connection with the ultimate source of all being. In other words, they have sought *gnōsis*.

- It's unlikely that these impulses to question tradition, to tell new stories about human existence and our world, and to seek *gnōsis* of God will ever disappear.

Suggested Reading

Barber, *The Cathars*.

Evagrius of Pontus, *The Greek Ascetic Corpus*.

Harmless, *Desert Christians*, chapters 10–11.

Louth, *The Origins of the Christian Mystical Tradition*.

Lupieri, *The Mandaeans*.

Pseudo-Dionysius, *The Complete Works*.

Scholem, *Major Trends in Jewish Mysticism*.

Tishby, *The Wisdom of the Zohar*.

Questions to Consider

1. What elements of Gnostic and Valentinian teaching have persisted in Western religious history?

2. How might we explain the appearance of similar religious ideas and stories in very different times and places?

Gnostic Traces in Western Religions
Lecture 23—Transcript

What happened to the ancient Gnostics and their ideas? Did they just disappear until Gnostic texts in Coptic were discovered in the 20th century? We have already seen how Gnostic ideas influenced orthodox Christianity, ancient Judaism, and Platonism. And we have met the religion of Mani, who incorporated elements of Gnostic myth into his new universal religion.

As for the Gnostics themselves, however, the last compelling evidence for their existence comes from the late 4th century and the early 5th century. Around 375, the Christian bishop of Konstantia on Cyprus, Epiphanius, wrote a massive work called the *Panarion* or *Cure-All*. Epiphanius described all the bad ideas people have had about God, starting with Adam, along with remedies against them. According to Epiphanius, Gnostics still existed during his lifetime. He claimed to have met some, including a group of Gnostic women who tried to seduce him.

Scholars aren't really sure whether to trust Epiphanius. On the one hand, he describes mythological teachings that do sound a lot like what we find in Gnostic texts, and he does say that he met Gnostics. On the other hand, Epiphanius reports that the Gnostics engaged in a variety of horrifying acts, including ritualized sex, infanticide, and cannibalism. There's no basis in Gnostic writings for such behaviors, and so it seems that Epiphanius's report is mostly slander.

Seemingly better evidence is provided by the Nag Hammadi codices themselves. Some person or group of people wanted these texts copied in the 4th or 5th century, and then later buried them. But were these people Gnostics or Valentinians or just people interested in mythology and *gnōsis*? We have no way to be certain.

As for the Valentinians, we know that in the late 380s a Christian mob attacked and damaged a church that belonged to them in the eastern Roman Empire. So there were certainly Valentinians in the late 4th century.

After this period Christian writers and church councils often listed Gnostics and Valentinians among the heretical groups that they condemned, but it's likely that they were just repeating what others had said before them. It became traditional to include Gnostics and Valentinians in lists of Christians to be rejected, long after any of them were around. My own interpretation of the evidence is that the Gnostics dwindled to very few people by the 300s, and the same is true of the Valentinians by the 400s. I think that the Gnostics lost adherents to the Valentinians, who provided a more explicitly Christian version of Gnostic myth, and to general Platonism, which offered *gnōsis* without all the mythology. Eventually Valentinian Christianity also faded in competition with other forms of Christian *gnōsis* like the teachings of Origen and Clement. Then, desert monasticism offered an opportunity to pursue the mystical life at a higher level, and maybe others joined Manichaean communities.

So I think by, say, 450 A.D., the classic period of Gnosticism was certainly over. Knowledge about Gnostic and Valentinian teachings did not completely go away thanks to the writings of their enemies, like Irenaeus and Epiphanius. But of course, these were biased accounts, and so not until the 20th century would the voices of Gnostics and Valentinians really be heard again. But is that all that we can say? Did the religious questions and attitudes that the Gnostics addressed go away? Surely that cannot be the case—indeed it was not. Key themes and ideas from ancient Gnosticism persisted into the Middle Ages and beyond.

Let's look at three primary facets of Gnostic and Valentinian thought. First, myth-making: the invention of elaborate mythology to explain the nature of God, the origin of the cosmos, and the creation of humanity. Second, *gnōsis*: the quest to experience first-hand acquaintance with God. And third, dualism: the strong separation of good from evil, and the ultimate God from this world and its creator. All three of these themes emerged in the later religious history of Europe and the Near East.

First, myth-making: The Gnostics and Valentinians created and elaborated on complex myths that explained who God is and how this universe came into being. Now these myths differed from the well-known pagan myths. Unlike what you see in Greek or Roman mythology, Gnostic and Valentinian myths did not feature human-like gods with personalities. Greek and Roman gods participated in stories that did explain things, like how people got wine, but they are often something like soap operas. They were good stories to share, and people could appreciate the quirky characters of certain gods and goddesses, relate to their emotions, and worship them.

In contrast, the Gnostic and Valentinian myths are highly philosophical; their entire purpose was to explore the nature of God, the origin of the cosmos, and other philosophical ideas. They were not meant to provide stories to share and enjoy. Only when the Gnostic myth turns to biblical events from Genesis do we get real characters. The Gnostic and Valentinian myths may appear to be overly complicated to us, but I have suggested that complexity may have been part of the appeal. As you learned more about the myth, you gained a greater sense of your personal knowledge of divine secrets.

Mani also developed an elaborate myth, which his followers augmented in later centuries. Manichaean myth continued the Gnostic tradition of philosophical myth-making, but its divine beings started to look more like the characters of more popular myths, with human-like motivations.

The Mandaeans carried on this tradition of myth-making—even to the present day. The Mandaeans are a religious and ethnic community. Their traditional home is along the Tigris and Euphrates rivers in modern-day Iraq and Iran. The Mandaeans may have originated in the 4th or 5th century A.D., and they have endured ever since. They developed their own dialect of the Aramaic language, called Mandaic. Today the Mandaeans may be as few as 10 or 15 thousand. Because of the political turmoil and warfare that have troubled Iraq and Iran in recent decades, many Mandaeans have perished, and others have immigrated to countries like the United States and Australia.

Because they have become so few in number and because they have lived in relative isolation, Western scholars did not know much about the Mandaeans until the 20th century. A remarkable English scholar named Ethel Stevens— better known as Lady Drower—lived in Iraq during the 1920s, '30s, and '40s. She got to know the Mandaeans very well, and she brought many of their manuscripts to Great Britain. In this way, Western scholars learned about one of the oldest still-existing religions of the Middle East.

People sometimes say that the Mandaeans simply are Gnostics. They say this not only because the Mandaeans have a myth much like that of the Gnostics, but also because their name might come from the Mandaic word for "knowledge." Other scholars, however, dispute this idea. They suggest that the name refers to the *bit manda*, the small temple in which the Mandaeans worship. So, in fact, there is not a strong reason to identify the Mandaeans as Gnostics. Nonetheless, the myths of the Mandaeans resemble the myths of the Gnostics, Valentinians, and Manichaeans. I say "myths of the Mandaeans" because there is a great deal of Mandaean literature, and it does not all have the same stories. The *Ginzā* or *Treasure* is the most important Mandaean book.

Like that of the Manichaeans, Mandaean myth distinguishes between a realm of light and a realm of darkness. Supreme deities as well as lower emanations rule both realms. For example, the Lord of Greatness or King of Light rules the world of light, along with numerous lower beings. The lowest divine being is Ptahil—he is the god who created the cosmos in which we live.

So just as Gnostic and Valentinian myths have a spiritual Entirety or Fullness populated by multiple aeons, the Mandaeans have a world of light populated by many *malki* or rulers. And just as the Gnostics and Valentinians attributed the creation of the world we live in to a lower craftsman god, so, too, the Mandaeans believe that Ptahil made this universe. And just as the Gnostics and Valentinians asserted that the first human being, Adam, had a share of the divine life placed within him, so, too, the Mandaeans tell how Ptahil created Adam and placed within him a soul or spirit derived from the light world. The Mandaeans achieve contact with the world of light through rituals involving water. A Mandaean temple must have a pool called a Jordan, after the Jordan River in Palestine. This pool must have flowing water, and so Mandaean temples are located near rivers or channels. Baptism in this pool connects a person with the realm of light.

John the Baptist from the New Testament plays an important role in Mandaean mythology and ritual. They don't see him as the founder of their religion, but as one of their most important teachers and priests. Because the Mandaeans came into conflict with Christians, Jesus Christ sometimes plays a negative role in their mythology, but at other times, he's a good character.

The Mandaeans have existed for nearly all of their history under Muslim rule, and for the most part they have enjoyed the freedom to practice their faith as a "religion of the book," like Judaism, Christianity, and Islam itself. Some of the most interesting new scholarship on Mandaeism shows how Mandaean myth developed in dialogue with Islam. The Mandaean community provides a living link with the ancient period of Gnosticism, and its recent difficulties are heartbreaking.

A second key feature of ancient Gnosticism was, of course, *gnōsis*, first-hand acquaintance with God. You'll recall that some Gnostic texts described practices of contemplation that could lead to mystic knowledge of the Barbēlō aeon. And in the Gospel of Truth, Valentinus invited Christians to experience intimate knowledge of the Father through communion with the Son. This quest for *gnōsis* continued in the Christian tradition, apart from these groups that became known as heretics. Already in the 2nd century, Clement of Alexandria taught that Christians should aspire to transcend mere faith in the doctrines of the Church and to achieve *gnōsis* with God. The ideal Christian, Clement said, was the true Gnostic.

One of Clement's greatest later admirers was the Christian monk Evagrius of Pontus, who lived from about 345 to 399. As his name implies, Evagrius came from Pontus, a city in Asia Minor or modern-day Turkey. But after a brief, but tumultuous career as a church official, Evagrius became a monk in the Egyptian desert. When Christianity became a legal religion in the early 4th century, thousands of men and women chose to seek a closer relationship with God by living alone or in communities in or near desert areas. Evagrius was one of these seekers. After he moved into the desert in northern Egypt, he attracted many disciples, for he was truly the greatest teacher of spirituality in early monasticism.

Evagrius taught that the monk goes through two stages in his spiritual life. For the first and longer period, he is an ascetic practitioner—through spiritual disciplines like fasting, celibacy, prayer, and scripture reading, the practitioner seeks to overcome his sinful desires and to achieve freedom from negative emotions. Then the monk can become a Gnostic—someone who engages in higher contemplation of the Bible, the universe, and ultimately

God himself. Probably by the late 300s, the so-called Gnostic heresy had faded away, and so Evagrius could once again use the name "Gnostic" in a positive sense, for the ideal Christian—indeed, the ideal monk.

For Evagrius, the goal of the monastic life was to achieve a vision of God that was beyond all concepts or images. The monk needed to learn that the ideas and pictures that fill our minds are sometimes good, but ultimately they distract us from God, who is beyond anything we can say or imagine. Evagrius described the experience of *gnōsis* as seeing one's mind as a sapphire blue sky—I like to think of it as a pure blue screen. Your goal is to rid the mind of everything so that it's a blank screen—a screen on which God can project himself, somehow without any images at all.

Although Evagrius lived alone in a desert hut, monks came from all over to learn from him, and he wrote a bunch of fascinating, but very obscure works to help monks become Gnostics. Unfortunately, after his death, Evagrius's teaching became an object of controversy. Some monks objected to his idea of prayer without images. They believed that humanity was in God's image, so that it's perfectly OK to imagine God as something like a human being. You can use that mental picture of God to focus during prayer.

But even more, Evagrius had adapted some of the most controversial ideas of the great theologian, Origen. For example, Evagrius seemed to suggest that all rational beings, including demons, would eventually be saved and return to God. For these reasons and for unrelated political reasons, Evagrius was condemned at the Council of Constantinople in 553. His writings became illegal in the Byzantine Empire.

Nonetheless, Evagrius's teachings lived on because monks considered them too profoundly helpful to be lost. His works, which he wrote in Greek, survived in languages like Syriac outside the Byzantine Empire, and some of his writings in Greek survived because monastic copyists just changed the name of the author to someone else. During the last 100 years, scholars have rediscovered and published many of Evagrius's writings. So once again, people can learn about his spirituality for the Gnostic monk.

Another milestone figure in the history of mystical knowledge of God in Christianity is the mysterious Pseudo-Dionysius the Areopagite. In the 500s, a Greek-speaking Christian living in Syria published a set of works about God, the church, and even angels. The author claimed to be Dionysius, a resident of Athens whom the apostle Paul converts to Christianity in the book of Acts. In other words, the author said that he was a disciple of Paul and that he wrote his books in the 1st century A.D. For centuries, Christians believed this to be true. But in the modern period, scholars revealed that the author had borrowed liberally from Proclus, a Neoplatonist philosopher of the 5th century. And so now we call the author *Pseudo*-Dionysius.

Pseudo-Dionysius combined the Bible with Neoplatonist philosophy and monastic traditions, including Evagrius, and in so doing he created a new tradition of mystical theology for Christians. Like the ancient Gnostics, Pseudo-Dionysius asked, How do we know God? His answer was that we do so in two basic ways. First, because God pours himself out into the creation, because everything emanates from God as Plotinus taught, we learn about God through images and names that are drawn from the creation and that appear in the Bible. So we understand God better through names like "King" and "Shepherd" and "Father," and through images like "rock" and "light" and "mind." This is called *kataphatic theology*—from the Greek word meaning "to grasp." Through kataphatic theology we make assertions about God and grow in our understanding of him.

And yet there is another way of knowing God: by negating everything we say about God. God is beyond all our names and images, and so through *apophatic theology*—from the Greek, "to say No"—we un-know everything we have asserted about God.

The Christian mystic must engage in both kataphatic and apophatic ways of knowing God; he or she must oscillate between saying things about God and then denying those very things. Ultimately, you have to even negate your negations about God. All of this creates a space within you, a place of unknowing, which God's divine energy can fill. In this form of *gnōsis*, you end up negating your own mind and self so that God can take you over. Ultimately you get *gnōsis*—knowledge—of God through *a-gnōsis*—non-knowledge.

In Lecture 7, we saw in works like Zōstrianos and the Foreigner how the Gnostics tried to achieve mystical knowledge of God. Only in recent years have scholars begun to explore how we can draw a line from the mysticism we see in Gnostic writings to the works of Plotinus and the other Neoplatonists and ultimately to the mysticism of Pseudo-Dionysius.

In the later Middle Ages, the works of Pseudo-Dionysius were translated from Greek into Latin. Then they helped inspire a new flowering of mysticism in Western Europe—a new flourishing of *gnōsis* in the heart of Roman Catholic Christianity.

Beginning with Constantine in the early 300s, the Roman emperors helped the Christian bishops to establish a single orthodox catholic church out of the diverse groups we saw earlier in the course. In Western Europe, the Pope emerged as the most powerful religious leader, and eventually he led a vast church that dominated medieval Europe. But medieval Europe was also the scene for a revival of our third feature of Gnosticism: dualism. As we learned earlier, dualism is the division of reality into sharply distinguished twos— good versus evil, light versus dark, spirit versus matter. Dualism appears in both moderate and strict forms. The Gnostics and Valentinians were moderate dualists: They made a strong distinction between the spiritual existence of God and the material universe of Ialdabaōth or the creator, but they believed that ultimately the good God, whether the Invisible Spirit or the Deep, is in charge. Everything relies on and comes from the ultimate God.

The Manichaeans, in contrast, were strict dualists. In their view, good and evil, light and dark are equally eternal and exist as opposed independent principles. Eventually, light will triumph over dark, but dark had its own origin and existence.

Both strict and moderate dualism could be found among the Cathars, a movement that spread in Western Europe in the 12th century. The Cathars took their name from the Greek word meaning "pure ones". the Cathars claimed to represent a higher form of Christianity, purer than what they saw as the corrupt and polluted Roman Catholic Church. The Cathars may have gotten some of their ideas from an earlier movement called the Bogomils, who were active in Bulgaria starting in the 10th century.

The Cathars believed in two gods: a good and loving God of the New Testament, and an evil and vengeful God of the Old Testament. The Old Testament God created the world in which we live. Some Cathars were strict dualists—they believed that these two gods existed independently of one another and were eternally opposed. Others were moderate dualists— they believed that the evil creator god had fallen away from goodness, something like the Gnostic Ialdabaōth. Either way, the Cathars agreed that this material world is evil and that Christ came to free our spiritual selves from our imprisonment.

The Cathars organized themselves as the Manichaeans did, into two levels of membership. The Perfect gave up sex and private property, and they abstained from meat and dairy products. When they died, their souls would escape this world. Ordinary believers supported these Perfect and lived less ascetically. When they died, their souls would be reincarnated in new bodies.

Because they considered the material world evil, the Cathars did not celebrate sacraments with material objects like water, bread, and wine. Their baptism was a laying on of hands, which transmitted the Holy Spirit. They formed their own hierarchy of bishops and priests.

By around 1200, the Cathars had gained many followers in southern France and northern Italy, and several local rulers either joined the group or allowed them the freedom to practice their religion. Why did people find Catharism attractive? Well, like Manichaeism, it offered a clear explanation for the existence of evil and suffering, and it provided a systematic plan for how to gain salvation. Moreover, the Cathars allowed women to preach and serve as leaders—after all, our gendered bodies are not our true selves. And finally, the Cathars criticized the corruption and luxurious lifestyle of Catholic bishops and priests. They offered an alternative hierarchy of leaders, who were conspicuously poor and strictly ascetic. Local nobles probably welcomed an opportunity to undermine the power of bishops and ultimately of the Pope. In other words, Catharism not only offered a clear and compelling religious life, but it also was an outlet for protest against the wealth and power of the Catholic Church.

As you can imagine, the Church took the Cathar threat very seriously. At first the Pope sent out preachers to argue against the Cathars and explain why their teaching was heretical. But in 1208, one of these preachers was murdered in southern France. Pope Innocent III suspected that local nobles sympathetic to the Cathars were responsible. So in 1209, the Pope called for a military campaign to wipe out the Cathars in southern France. This campaign is known as the Albigensian Crusade because the French city of Albi was a center of Cathar activity.

Warfare between crusading forces and local armies persisted for 20 years, and tens of thousands of Christians were killed—not only suspected Cathars. The goal was to make the local nobles fully submit to church authority. The crusade came to an end when the nobility agreed to establish an organization to investigate and punish heresy in their regions. Here we see one of the early forms of what became the Inquisition—a central organization designed to detect and eliminate heresy. By the early 1300s Catharism had disappeared.

Now, it's fascinating to realize that it was also during the 12th century, precisely when Catharism arose in Western Europe, that another form of esoteric religion appeared in Provence and northern Spain: Kabbalah. Kabbalah is a form of Jewish esoteric mysticism. It's probably the most famous form of Jewish mysticism. Many people know about its central text, the *Zohar*. But Jewish mysticism is a much larger and more diverse phenomenon. Kabbalah is just one kind of it—and it's of interest to us because it shows some remarkable similarities to Gnosticism.

Like the Gnostics and Valentinians, Kabbalah teaches that the ultimate God is completely unknowable. He is Ein Sof—literally, "No End." That is, God is completely infinite and beyond any concept we may have of him, just like the Gnostics' Invisible Spirit. Some Kabbalists believed that mystical knowledge of the Ein Sof itself is possible, but most said that no human being could ever contemplate this ultimate source of all being.

And just like the Gnostics and Valentinians, Kabbalah teaches that the Ein Sof emanates into lower manifestations of itself called *sefirot*. There are 10 *sefirot*, which are very much like the Gnostic aeons. These *sefirot* have names like Wisdom, Understanding, and Love—clearly aspects or attributes of God. The last of the *sefirot* is the Shekinah, or presence of God. The Shekinah is that aspect of God that can dwell among the people of Israel and that human beings can know.

A lot of Kabbalistic literature is devoted to speculation about the divine emanations, the *sefirot*—what their characteristics are and how they relate to one another. The *sefirot* also serve as a ladder of contemplation—that is, the Kabbalist gains greater and greater *gnōsis* of God by contemplating each of the *sefirot*, starting with the lowest one. Again, we might remember how in the Gnostic works the Foreigner and Zōstrianos, heroes with those names mentally ascended through the aeons to reach the Barbēlō and possibly to have a fleeting experience of the Invisible Spirit.

Not only this, but the Kabbalists used gender to imagine the unity and stability of God. The last *sefirah*, the Shekinah, is feminine, and the unity of the godhead finds expression in the female Shekinah's unity with the sixth *sefirah*, which is gendered male. Humanity is in the image of God because we too exist in male and female. Both by ascending through the *sefirot* through contemplation and by practicing the divine commandments, human beings can participate in the life of the godhead.

Kabbalah is not dualistic in the way Manichaeism or some Cathars were. Everything comes from the Ein Sof. But the Kabbalists do take evil seriously. There are a series of negative emanations from God that form an evil counterpart to the divine *sefirot*. These include Lilith, the evil feminine parallel to the Shekinah, and her consort Samael.

Kabbalists devoted themselves to speculation and mysticism based on folklore and learned study. They claimed to find many of their teachings in the Bible, which they did not interpret literally, but as pointing to higher, deeper meanings.

So Kabbalah resembles Gnostic myth in several important ways: It claimed that an unknowable God unfolded in a series of emanations, some of which are male or female; it encouraged people to ascend mystically through these emanations to contemplation of God; it speculated upon a multitude of divine beings and evil rulers; and it interpreted the Bible symbolically. How are we to understand these similarities? Did Gnostic teachings somehow survive "underground," so to speak, for centuries? Most scholars don't think so. No one has been able to show any continuous line of tradition from our ancient Gnostics to the Kabbalists of 12th-century Provence and Spain.

In addition, one has to ask, why did this kind of religious and philosophical movement appear among Jewish scholars at this time and place? Is it a coincidence that this is the same time when Catharism became popular among Christians in nearby areas? No one has satisfactorily answered these questions, either. We can attribute the rise of the Cathars in part to dissatisfaction with the church hierarchy and to desires for a more austere form of Christianity. But it's difficult to make that same argument for the rise of Kabbalah, which we must remember was and remains a movement primarily of intellectual Jews. Did the violence of the Crusades and the persecution of Jews in Europe encourage interest in the transcendent realm? Historians aren't sure.

In my view, there's little need to posit underground streams of tradition to account for the emergence of mythological speculation, dualism, or interest in *gnōsis* at different times and places in Western religious history. The biblical tradition itself invites and encourages such responses. The Bible, especially Genesis, is filled with stories that raise questions for those who want to ask them. Can a God who walks around in a garden and asks where Adam is truly be the highest and most perfect God? Why is humanity created twice—once in Genesis chapter 1 and then again in chapter 2? Who are the "sons of God" who mate with human women in Genesis 6? And perhaps above all, why did God command Adam and Eve not to eat from the tree of the knowledge of good and evil? Why shouldn't human beings know what good is and what evil is? Why should their eyes remain closed?

Although many Jews and Christians may have been content with simply accepting these stories and figuring that whoever wrote them knows best, others have asked these questions and tried to answer them. This has led them to tell new stories, with new divine and human characters—myths that try to explain the true nature of God and the origins of ourselves, our world, and the evil that causes such pain and suffering.

And there have always been people who have not been satisfied with the basic teachings of their religious tradition, whatever it may be. Some people have yearned for a closer, more intimate connection with the ultimate source of all being. They have not wanted simply information about God. They have not been content with assenting to the knowledge that their priests and rabbis and teachers have offered them. Instead, they have sought first-hand knowledge of the divine, true acquaintance with God. They have sought *gnōsis*.

It's unlikely that these impulses to question tradition, to tell new stories about human existence and our world, and to seek *gnōsis* of God will ever go away. In our next lecture, we'll explore how fascination with *gnōsis* and ancient Gnosticism has manifested itself in our own time—both among religious scholars and in popular culture.

"Gnosticism" in the Modern Imagination
Lecture 24

After the discovery of the Nag Hammadi codices in 1945, translations of these sources appeared throughout the 1960s and 1970s and struck a chord with many people. During this period of questioning, people were drawn to Gnosticism's suggestion of rebellion against orthodox Christianity and its new ways of thinking about God. In the last decades of the 20th century, somewhat darker Gnostic ideas have resonated in popular culture, including the possibilities that the existence we know is not real, the powers that rule this world are malevolent, and our own identities are uncertain. In this lecture, we'll explore how fascination with *gnōsis* and ancient Gnosticism has manifested itself in our own time.

Some modern fiction expands on the Gnostic idea of the hostile powers of this world; thanks to technology, the evil rulers can now watch us more closely and control events more fully than ever before.

Gnosticism in Popular Culture

- The science fiction novels of Philip K. Dick (1928–1982) are an excellent example of the appeal of Gnostic ideas in popular culture. Dick's novels feature mega-corporations that exert great power over our lives and authoritarian governments that limit our freedom. He was also interested in altered states of consciousness and esoteric philosophy, and the Gnostic texts from Nag Hammadi gave him new ways to think about these themes.

  o *VALIS* was one of Dick's last and most popular novels. It appeared in 1980, well after Dick had read the Nag Hammadi writings. The central character of the book is a man named

Horselover Fat, who suffers a series of disappointments and losses in his life. But just as the world seems to him increasingly meaningless and hostile, Fat begins to receive revelatory messages.

o The novel suggests that Horselover Fat may not be who we think he is—or who he thinks he is. This introduces an important theme from the Gospel According to Thomas and Valentinian Christianity: Until we gain *gnōsis*, we are divided from our true selves. We live an alienated existence, in which our surface self is not our true self. Only *gnōsis* or, in Horselover Fat's terminology, *plásmate* can end this self-alienation and make us whole again.

- The psychologist Carl Jung (1875–1961) was another source of inspiration for Dick and other modern thinkers. Jung posited that each individual has his or her own consciousness, made up of that person's specific experiences. But beyond or beneath each individual consciousness is what Jung called the *collective unconscious*.

o The collective unconscious is a repository of patterns, forms, and symbols that enable us to make sense of our experience through the collective wisdom of humanity. Certain key symbols, called *archetypes*, recur in human culture because they carry with them healing messages from beyond our own selves.

o Dick and other 20th-century thinkers considered the central ideas of Gnosticism to exemplify mythologically what Jung taught. Each of us may have individual experiences, but there is a higher or deeper wisdom that is seeking to communicate with us. This wisdom transcends any specific individual, yet we all participate in it. Like Jung's collective unconscious, the Barbēlō wants to communicate spiritual truth to us; she can because we have spiritual power within us and, thus, can participate in the Barbēlō.

- We can also see themes of the collective unconscious in the 1982 film *Blade Runner*, which was based on one of Dick's short novels, *Do Androids Dream of Electric Sheep?* Androids—robots that seem to be human—work well with Gnostic themes because they raise the question of what it means to be truly human: What makes a human being human? Is a soul necessary? Is it possible to think that you're a human being when you're not?
  - Gnostic myth raises the possibility that some people lack the spiritual element that makes us part of the divine Entirety. Such people may think they are real, but they are doomed to perish into nothingness. Indeed, before they are saved, even the saved people don't know who they really are. They think they are people who belong to this universe, but they are actually spiritual beings who belong to the Entirety.

  - In *Blade Runner*, people who seem to be human may actually be "replicants," bioengineered beings who are designed to last only four years. The main characters are Rick Deckard, whose job is to track down rebellious replicants but who may be one himself, and Rachel, a replicant who realizes her true nature during the course of the film. The Gnosticism of *Blade Runner* lies in the theme of knowing or not knowing who you really are.

- A movie that has an even clearer relationship to Gnosticism is *The Matrix* (1999). In this film, the main character is named Neo, an anagram for One. Neo is the One who is called to save people.
  - People in the story do not live in the real world but in the matrix, a computer program designed by robotic life forms to trap human beings. Rulers police this world to keep human beings in their place. Human beings are, in fact, in a kind of coma state, with their brains plugged into the virtual world that they think is real.

  - But Neo and his friends have come out of their comas, unplugged from the matrix, and learned that they live in a bleak, post-apocalyptic world controlled by machines. This knowledge enables Neo and his companions to reenter the matrix and act with new freedom within it. They can literally bend this world to their will because they have gained the *gnōsis* that this world is not real.

Gnosticism and Modern Religion

- The discovery of the Nag Hammadi codices inspired not only novels and movies in pop culture but also new religious movements. In fact, there is now a Gnostic Christian church, known as the Ecclesia Gnostica.

- Although this church calls itself Gnostic, in its theology and practice, it more closely resembles Valentinian Christianity. The religion is highly liturgical and, following the Valentinian Gospel According to Philip, believes in five basic sacraments, or mysteries: baptism, chrism, eucharist, redemption, and bridal chamber.

- The Valentinian character of the church appears in its devotion to Sophia, or Wisdom. These Christians believe that Sophia fell into this lower created world and continues to be active in it, caring for human beings and helping them return to the Fullness from which they came.

- The scriptures of the Ecclesia Gnostica include the canonical Bible; the Nag Hammadi texts; and Manichaean, Mandaean, and Hermetic literature. The church combines formal, traditional Christian ritual with a passion for seeking *gnōsis* wherever it may be found.

Ongoing Debates about Gnosticism

- Once historians read the Nag Hammadi texts, they were impressed by the great variety of ideas, stories, and genres found. And they noticed that few of the texts matched the reports about so-called Gnostic groups in the church fathers. Rather than clarifying Gnosticism, the Nag Hammadi codices vastly increased the diversity of thinking about the religion. This great diversity animates the most important debate today among scholars of ancient Gnosticism: Is there a real category of "Gnosticism," and if so, what is it?

- In 1966, an international group of scholars met to discuss the problem of Gnosticism. They decided that we should distinguish carefully between *gnōsis*, the claim to have divine knowledge, and *Gnosticism*, a system of belief.
  - Gnosticism, according to these scholars, has two primary ideas. First, there is a divine spark in human beings that comes from the spiritual world and that we must become aware of. Second, some aspect of the divine has moved into this world to recover lost divine energy.

  - According to this definition, Gnosticism is not to be identified with such religions as Judaism or Christianity, although it interacts with them.

- More recently, some scholars have argued that the single category Gnosticism includes too many different texts and groups. It gives the mistaken impression that all of these instances of Gnosticism formed a single religious community, which they did not. These scholars also argue that the idea of Gnosticism distorts our understanding of the texts and traditions we include in it. People tend to have certain preconceived notions of what Gnosticism is, and they impose those ideas on everything that's called Gnostic.

- Another group of scholars believes that Gnosticism is still a useful category of analysis. It brings together religious groups and texts that share certain features, even if they did not all make up a single religion.

- Still other scholars believe that there really was a religion called Gnosticism, and almost everyone we have studied in this course belonged to it. There were many varieties of Gnosticism, but there are also many varieties of Christianity or Islam, yet we still speak of them as a single religion.

- Finally, there is a small group of scholars who agree that there never was a single religion called Gnosticism and find it problematic to lump together so many different texts and traditions in a single category. Yet these scholars also believe that there was an original group called the Gnostics—those who produced certain texts and who developed the myth of the Invisible Spirit, the Barbēlō, and Ialdabaōth.

- According to this view, the other people and movements that we have studied share certain themes and ideas with the original Gnostics: the idea of saving *gnōsis*, the power of myth to express where we came from and where we're going, and the hope of achieving union with the divine, both within ourselves and with the realm above us.

- Yet these later groups and movements—the Valentinians, Manichaeans, Cathars, and so on—were not part of one religion called Gnosticism; instead, they were new attempts to express religious insight using the sacred books, philosophies, and rituals of the past.

- It's important to note that the texts and groups that we have studied do not belong to a religious tradition that's lost or that is different from Judaism, Christianity, Islam, or other religions.
  - Instead, we need to recognize that the quest for *gnōsis*, the creation of mythology, and the desire for mystical union with God have been present in Western religious history since ancient times. Setting these elements apart as a separate thing called Gnosticism helps us to see that this tradition exists, but the danger is that we will fail to see that it's part of the Jewish and Christian traditions, as well.

  - What the people we have studied in this course would want us to do is to read their texts, to consider with open minds what they teach us, and to pursue our own quests for the truth about God and ourselves—that is, to seek our own *gnōsis*.

Suggested Reading

Brakke, *The Gnostics*, chapter 1.

Dick, *VALIS*.

Ecclesia Gnostica, http://gnosis.org/eghome.htm.

Flannery-Dailey and Wagner, "'Wake Up!' Gnosticism and Buddhism in *The Matrix*."

King, *What Is Gnosticism?*

Markschies, *Gnosis*.

Williams, *Rethinking Gnosticism*.

Questions to Consider

1. Can you think of other recent novels, television programs, or movies that feature Gnostic themes?

2. What are the advantages and disadvantages of considering so many different teachers, writings, and groups in the single category of Gnosticism?

"Gnosticism" in the Modern Imagination
Lecture 24—Transcript

Even after the Inquisition and a military crusade crushed the Cathars in the 13th century, there were a few moments when the themes of Gnosis re-surfaced in Western religious history. For example, in the 15th century, Marsilio Ficino translated a manuscript of Hermetic texts from Greek into Latin, and this set off a wave of interest in Hermetic thought among European intellectuals. Later in the 18th and 19th centuries, you can find in the works of the poet and illustrator William Blake, and in Theosophic movements, ideas like the divine nature of humanity and the quest for a higher and hidden wisdom.

But the specific teachings of the ancient Gnostics—the Barbēlō aeon, the error of Wisdom, the creator god Ialdabaōth—these became the subjects mostly for church historians and theologians. And all they had to read were the accounts of the heresiologists like Irenaeus. The voices of the Gnostics and the Valentinians themselves seemed lost forever.

All that changed definitively in 1945, with the discovery of the Nag Hammadi codices. As texts and translations of these new sources appeared through the 1960s and into the 1970s, they struck a chord with many thoughtful people. This was a period of great social change, in which people were questioning traditional religious doctrines and seeking new rights for women and minority groups of all kinds. Gnosticism suggested rebellion against orthodox Christianity and new ways of thinking about God, which included a feminine aspect to the divine. The message of the Gospel According to Thomas was especially appealing: "Know God and you will know yourself," Jesus says in this gospel—and people heard a Christian version of the 1960s' call to self-realization and fulfillment.

But there's an even deeper and darker side to Gnosticism's appeal in the last decades of the 20th century. I think that few would deny that the 20th century was one of the worst centuries in the history of Western civilization. To be sure, it brought lots of wonderful advances in areas like healthcare and education and travel, but it also brought two world wars with an unprecedented number of deaths, the horrific evil of the Holocaust, and the possibility that we could end all human life as we know it with nuclear weapons.

Plus, advances in technology have obviously improved our lives in many ways, but they have also raised profound questions about what it means to be human. If robots can perform our tasks, if computers can beat us at games, and if we can talk to our cell phones, who's real and who's not? If we can create virtual worlds and live and work in them as avatars of ourselves, how can we be sure that the world we know is the true one? It's no surprise, then, that the ideas from Gnosticism that have resonated in popular culture are those that consider the possibility that the existence we know is not real, that the powers that rule this world are malevolent not good, and that we cannot be sure of our own identities.

The science-fiction novels of Philip K. Dick are an excellent example. Dick was born in Chicago in 1928 and died of a stroke in 1982 at the age of only 53. Despite his premature death, Dick published over 40 novels and 120 short stories. Several popular movies have been based on his works, including *Total Recall*, *Minority Report*, *The Adjustment Bureau*, and *Blade Runner*, which I'll return to. Dick's novels feature mega-corporations that exert great power over our lives and authoritarian governments that limit our freedom. He was always interested in altered states of consciousness and esoteric philosophy, but the Gnostic texts from Nag Hammadi gave him new ways to think about these themes.

VALIS was one of Dick's last and most popular novels. It appeared in 1980, well after Dick had read the Nag Hammadi writings, and you can see the impact that they had on his thinking. The central character of the book is a man named Horselover Fat, who suffers a series of disappointments and painful losses in his life. And yet in 1974, just as the world seems to him increasingly meaningless and hostile, Fat begins to receive revelatory messages. One of these messages informs him that his son has an unknown illness, and thanks to the message, Fat's son is saved. Fat comes to believe that the world in which we live is completely irrational, but there is a higher existence that is rational and that sometimes breaks into this world. That is, we do indeed live in the dark cosmos of Ialdabaōth, but the spiritual rationality of the Entirety, the voice of the Barbēlō, is speaking to him. Or is it? Maybe, the narrator suggests, Horselover Fat is just mentally ill, schizophrenic, hearing things.

Fat composes a series of 52 thoughts that express his philosophy. Among these is the idea that "The Empire never ended." That is, the oppressive world structures that the Roman Empire embodied persist until the 1970s, and in fact, the growth of technology means that the hostile powers that rule this world can watch us even more closely, and they can control events even more fully.

And yet, just as the Gnostics believed that the spiritual power that Ialdabaōth took from his mother Wisdom persisted among human beings, so, too, Horselover Fat believes that a divine energy he called *plásmate* can unite with a human being and give that person the information about truth and reality. This *plásmate*, Fat says, was present in Jesus, but then it lay dormant until 1945, when the Nag Hammadi codices were discovered. The divine information has become available once more.

Now, as I have already suggested, the novel mentions that Horselover Fat, its main character, may not be who we think he is—or who he thinks he is. And it's not clear at times how Fat and the book's narrator relate to one another. Here, Dick introduces an important theme from the Gospel According to Thomas and Valentinian Christianity—that is, until we gain *gnōsis*, we are divided from our true selves. We live an alienated existence, in which we our surface self, the self we think we know, is not our true self. Only *gnōsis*—or, in the novel *VALIS*, *plásmate*—can end this self-alienation and make us whole again. As Jesus says in the Gospel of Thomas, we must make the two one.

Of course, Dick did not draw only on Gnosticism for his novels and stories. The psychologist Carl Jung was another source of inspiration for him, and in fact, Jung's analytic psychology prepared the way for many thinkers like Dick to adapt Gnosticism. Jung, who died in 1961, posited that each individual has his or her own consciousness, made up of that person's specific experiences. But beyond each individual consciousness or, perhaps better, lying beneath it, is what he called the collective unconscious. The collective unconscious is a repository of patterns, forms, and symbols that enable us to make sense of our experience through the collective wisdom of humanity. Certain key symbols, called *archetypes*, recur in human culture because they carry within them healing messages from beyond our own selves.

Dick and other 20th-century thinkers considered the central ideas of Gnosticism to exemplify mythologically what Jung had taught. Each of us may have individual experiences, but there is a higher or deeper wisdom that's seeking to communicate with us. This wisdom transcends any specific individual, and yet we all participate in it. Like Jung's collective unconscious, Forethought or the Barbēlō wants to communicate religious and spiritual truth to us, and she can because we have spiritual power within us, and thus we participate in the Barbēlō. And notice that this is not just formless spiritual energy that we need to tap into—no, it's a message; it's information; it's knowledge. What VALIS (V-A-L-I-S) stands for is Vast Active Living Intelligence System—a mind that can connect us with reality and thus with ourselves.

You can see these same themes in the 1982 film *Blade Runner*. Ridley Scott directed this movie, which is based on one of Dick's short novels, *Do Androids Dream of Electric Sheep?* Androids, robots that seem to be human, work well with Gnostic themes because they raise the question of what it means to be truly human: What makes a human being a human being? Is a soul, whatever that is, necessary? Is it possible to think that you're a human being when you're really not one?

Gnostic myth raises the possibility that some people lack the spiritual element that makes us really part of the divine Entirety. Such people may think they are real, but they are doomed to perish into nothingness. As the Gospel of Truth says, a person without *gnōsis* is "a modeled form of forgetfulness" and will dissipate once knowledge removes ignorance. And even the saved people, before they are saved, don't really know who they are. They think they are people who belong to this universe, when they are really spiritual beings who belong to the Entirety.

In *Blade Runner*, people who seem to be human may actually be "replicants"—bioengineered beings who are designed to last only four years. They appear to be human beings—they even bleed—but they don't have feelings, or at least that's the idea. The replicants were sent away from earth to serve as slaves on another planet, but some have returned to try to get their maker to extend their lives. The hero of the movie, Rick Deckard, is a "blade runner." His job is to track down replicants and destroy them—or, as the corporation that made them puts it, "retire" them.

Certainly the environment in which the story takes place—Los Angeles in 2019—is bleak enough to have been created by someone like Ialdabaōth. It's dark, it rains all the time, and no one seems happy at all. But, unlike in *VALIS*, there doesn't seem to be much hope of a higher, alternative reality from which salvation might come. What people seem to need to wake up to is the fact that they're going to die—if they're a replicant, fairly soon, but all the rest of us, in due time.

Instead, the Gnosticism of *Blade Runner* lies in the theme of knowing or not knowing who you really are. The rebellious replicants that Deckard hunts know that they are replicants, and they seek their original creator, hoping that he can extend their lives. It turns out that he can't. But Deckard also meets Rachael. Rachael at first does not know that she's a replicant—after all, she has memories of her childhood. But she and Deckard learn that these memories do not belong to her; rather, they belong to the niece of the creator and have been implanted in Rachael. Rachael's moment of *gnōsis*, so to speak, is when she realizes her true nature as a replicant—news that portends her imminent, rather than distant, death. Although this would seem to be bad news—perhaps Rachael would have preferred not to know this—the movie suggests in several ways that knowing one's true self is liberating.

The unresolved mystery in the story is whether Deckard himself might be a replicant. There are a couple of clues that he is. For example, blade runners have developed a test to determine whether someone is a replicant. When Rachael asks Deckard whether he has taken the test, he doesn't reply. And Deckard, at least as the star Harrison Ford portrays him, does not display a very wide emotional range. My own view is that Deckard suspects that he might be a replicant, but doesn't know for sure—and that he has chosen not to find out. For him at least, maybe ignorance is better than *gnōsis*.

One movie that has an even clearer relationship to Gnosticism is *The Matrix*, which came out in 1999 and stars Keanu Reeves and Laurence Fishburne. The writers and directors, Larry—now Lana—Wachowski and her brother Andy, had read some of the Nag Hammadi treatises, but they drew on several religious and philosophical traditions in crafting this film. The Christian references are pretty obvious. One positive character is named Trinity, and our hero's real name is Neo—an anagram for One. Neo is the One who is called to save people.

But from what will Neo save them? From ignorance. From mistakenly thinking that the world they live in is the real world. People are not living in the real world. Rather, they are living in the matrix, a fake world, a computer program designed by robotic life forms to trap human beings. Rulers police this world to keep human beings in their place. Human beings are, in fact, in a kind of coma state, with their brains plugged into the virtual world that they think is real.

But Neo and his friends have woken up—literally. They have come out of their comas, unplugged from the matrix, and learned that they in fact live in a bleak, post-apocalyptic world controlled by machines. This knowledge enables Neo, Trinity, Morpheus, and others to re-enter the matrix and to act with new freedom within it. They can literally bend this world to their will— because they have gained the *gnōsis* that this world is not real.

Now all of this is very Gnostic—living in a world that's ultimately not real and that's controlled by forces hostile to human beings; the need to gain *gnōsis*, understood as waking up to reality and to one's true self; and the freedom from the rulers and their control that *gnōsis* brings. But there's at least one huge difference between *The Matrix* and ancient Gnostic myth: In *The Matrix*, the real world is the material world and the fake world is all in our heads. In Gnostic myth, it's the exact reverse: The real world is the purely spiritual world of the intellect and the fake world is the material world. Here we see a crucial difference between the Gnostics and most modern people.

If I were to ask you what's more real, the idea of a table or an actual table that I can use as a desk and set a lamp on, you would almost certainly say the material table that I can use is more real. I can touch it, and if I try to walk through it, I can't. It's very real. That's the view of *The Matrix* as well.

But if I were to ask an ancient Gnostic that same question, she would answer just as any ancient Platonist would—the idea of a table is more real because it's eternal, unchanging, always accessible to me through my intellect. The material table came into being at a certain time, and at some point it will be discarded and destroyed. The real world of Gnosticism is the spiritual world of the Entirety, not the world of flesh, blood, and bodies. That's why *The Matrix* ultimately is not really Gnostic, even though it takes some of its central themes and plot elements from Gnostic myth.

The discovery of the Nag Hammadi codices inspired not only novels and movies in pop culture, but also new religious movements. Many Christians began quietly integrating works like the Gospel of Thomas into their spiritual lives. But some went further. You can now join a Gnostic Christian Church—the Ecclesia Gnostica.

The Ecclesia Gnostica, or Gnostic Church, originated in Gnostic revival movements in France and England that go back into the 19th century. But it really took off and developed its distinctive theology and rituals in the post–Nag Hammadi era. The main congregation is located in Los Angeles and, at the time of this taping, is led by a bishop, Dr. Stephan A. Hoeller. You can find many of Dr. Hoeller's writings and sermons on the church's website. In 2014 there were parishes also in Portland, Oregon, and Seattle, Washington. At one time, there were congregations in Salt Lake City, Utah, and Oslo, Norway. There are a few other separate Gnostic churches in the United States and Europe with which the Ecclesia Gnostica has fellowship.

Although the church calls itself "Gnostic," in its theology and practice, it more closely resembles Valentinian Christianity. The church is highly liturgical in character. That is, like Roman Catholic, Eastern Orthodox, and Anglican Christians, the Ecclesia Gnostica organizes its worship life according to a yearly calendar of festivals and seasons, and it celebrates the Eucharist as the Mass. Following the Valentinian Gospel According to Philip, the church believes in five basic sacraments or mysteries: baptism, chrism, eucharist, redemption, and bridal chamber. The church considers redemption and bridal chamber—the two distinctively Valentinian sacraments—as the greatest ones. The church says, however, that it does not perform bridal chamber as a physical ceremony.

The Valentinian character of the church appears in its devotion to Sophia or Wisdom. These Christians believe that Sophia fell into this lower created world and continues to be active in it, caring for human beings and helping them return to the Fullness from which they came. This picture of Wisdom derives from Valentinian myth rather than from the original Gnostic myth. Today it provides the Ecclesia Gnostica with a feminine supplement to their worship of the Father, Son, and Holy Spirit.

Their scriptures include the canonical Bible, but also the Nag Hammadi texts, as well as Manichaean, Mandaean, and Hermetic literature. The Ecclesia Gnostica combines formal, traditional Christian ritual with a passion for seeking *gnōsis* wherever it may be found. Of course, they celebrate Jesus at Christmas and Easter, but they also commemorate Valentinus and Carl Jung.

Now, while the Nag Hammadi texts have been inspiring people to write novels, make movies, and establish churches, historians have also been hard at work. For centuries, historians of religion had little evidence for Gnosticism other than the hostile reports of orthodox Christian theologians. Suddenly they had all sorts of new data to look at. Obviously, the first order of business was to edit, translate, and publish the Coptic texts. That project involved scholars from all over the world and lasted well into the 1970s and 1980s. That may seem like a long time, but compared to the fate of the equally famous Dead Sea Scrolls, the Nag Hammadi codices became available fairly quickly.

Once historians could read the Nag Hammadi texts, they could see the variety of groups and traditions they came from. We have seen that there are Valentinian works, Hermetic works, classic Gnostic works, and texts that don't sort into any previously known ancient religious community. Historians were impressed by the great variety of ideas and stories and kinds of texts in the Nag Hammadi codices. And they noticed that there were very few texts that matched the reports about so-called Gnostic groups in the church fathers. In other words, rather than clarifying exactly what Gnosticism was or showing us one dominant Gnostic group, the Nag Hammadi codices vastly increased the diversity of what we call Gnosticism. That great diversity animates the most important debate going on today among scholars of ancient Gnosticism: Is there even such a thing as "Gnosticism"? And if so, what is it?

You may think it's kind of odd to raise this question in the final lecture of a course on Gnosticism, but it's hard to think about this question without having looked at all the diverse people, texts, and traditions that scholars have considered part of Gnosticism. The so-called original Gnostics of Barbēlō and Ialdabaōth, the Valentinians, the Gospel According to Thomas, the Gospel of Mary, the Hermetic texts, Mani and Manichaeism, the Mandaeans, even the Cathars—all these and more have been included in the category "Gnosticism." But is that really a category? Or is it just our version of Irenaeus's "false *gnōsis*"? What makes all these different teachings and groups the same thing—"Gnosticism"?

How to define Gnosticism has perplexed scholars for decades, if not centuries. Let me give you an example from the late 20th century. In 1966, an international group of scholars met at Messina on the island of Sicily to discuss the problem of Gnosticism. The scholars decided that we should distinguish carefully between *gnōsis*, the claim to have divine knowledge, and *Gnosticism*, a system of belief. Lots of religious people claim to have *gnōsis*, but Gnosticism is found most clearly in books like the Secret Book According to John, and in systems like the Valentinian myth.

Gnosticism, the scholars at Messina said, has two primary ideas. First, there is a divine spark in human beings that comes from the spiritual world and that we must wake up to and become aware of. And second, some aspect of the divine, like the aeon Wisdom, has moved downward into this world in order to recover the lost divine energy. According to the Messina definition, Gnosticism is not to be identified with religions like Judaism or Christianity, although it interacts with them. You can see that this is a very basic definition, and it doesn't get really into the specifics of so-called Gnostic myths. The original Gnostic myth and the Mandaean myth are very different, but according to this definition, they are both Gnosticism.

Most scholars have been unhappy with such a simple definition, and so they often add other elements like extreme negativity about this world and our physical body, or dualism—a sharp distinction between spirit and matter.

More recently some historians have argued that such definitions of Gnosticism don't get us anywhere. The most prominent scholars making this argument are Michael Williams and Karen King. In their view, a single category "Gnosticism" includes too many different texts and groups. It gives the mistaken impression that all of these instances of Gnosticism formed a single religious community, when in fact the Manichaeans and the Mandaeans, for example, are two different groups.

And even more, these scholars argue, the idea of Gnosticism" distorts our understanding of the texts and traditions that we include in it. People tend to have certain preconceived notions of what Gnosticism is and what Gnostics say and do, and they impose these ideas on everything that's called Gnostic. So, for example, we tend to think all Gnostics hate the body or think that the divine savior Jesus wasn't really human. When we read a text that we say is from Gnosticism, then we impose these preconceived ideas on the text— even if they are not there, or even if the text contradicts those ideas.

When we put all these texts and groups in the same category, we are basically doing what Bishop Irenaeus did back in the 2nd century. You'll remember that Irenaeus argued that all the teachers and groups that he considered heretical were manifestations of a single error, false *gnōsis*, and he said that they all could be traced back to a single evil teacher, Simon Magus. Scholars like King and Williams fear that we are doing the same thing when we say that all the movements that we have studied make up a single thing called Gnosticism. In their view, there may have been Valentinianism and Manichaeism and Hermeticism in the ancient world, but there was no single Gnosticism. We should stop talking about Gnosticism, and we should not call people or texts "Gnostic."

Another group of scholars believes that Gnosticism is still a useful category of analysis. It brings together religious groups and texts that share certain features, even if they did not all make up a single religion. These historians might define Gnosticism simply as belief that a lower god created this world and that our soul or spirit comes from the divine realm. We can collect these religious groups and texts into a single category, "Gnosticism," just as we might group different religions into a category, "monotheism."

Other scholars continue to take the next step and argue that there really was a religion called Gnosticism, and pretty much everyone that we have studied in this course belongs to it. There was, and remains today, a Gnostic religion, in which *gnōsis* is what saves people. Yes, there are a lot of varieties of Gnosticism, but there are also lots of varieties of Christianity or Islam. And yet we still speak of them as a single religion.

Finally, there's a smaller group of scholars who agree that there is not and never was a single religion called Gnosticism, and who agree that it's problematic to lump together so many different texts and traditions in a single category. And yet we—because I'm one of these scholars—we believe that there was an original group called the Gnostics. These are the Christians who produced the Secret Book According to John, the Gospel of Judas, and other similar texts. And they are the ones who developed the myth of the Invisible Spirit, the Barbēlō, and Ialdabaōth. They identified themselves as "the immovable race" or "the seed of Seth," and they celebrated the baptism of the five seals.

According to this view, the other people and movements that we have studied share certain themes and ideas with the original Gnostics—the idea of saving *gnōsis*, the power of myth to express where we came from and where we're going, and the hope of achieving union with the divine, both within ourselves and the realm above us. And yet these later groups and movements—the Valentinians, the Manichaeans, the Cathars, and so on—were not part of the same religion, Gnosticism, but they were new attempts to express religious insight using the sacred books, philosophies, and rituals of the past.

I think that more is at stake in this scholarly debate than mere labels—you may ask, what does it matter whether we call a particular text or group Gnostic or talk about Gnosticism? I think what matters is to recognize that the texts and groups that we have studied do not belong to some other religious tradition, one that's foreign and lost and different from Judaism or Christianity or Islam or whatever. Instead, we need to recognize that the quest for *gnōsis*, the creation of mythology, and mystical union with God have been present in Western religious history since ancient times—and that at times they have been parts of Judaism and Christianity, and sometimes they have been separate.

Setting all this stuff apart as a separate thing called Gnosticism does help us to see that this tradition of *gnōsis*, mythmaking, and mystical contemplation really exists—but the danger is that we'll fail to see how it's part of the Jewish and Christian traditions as well. What the people we have studied in this course would want us to do is to read their texts, to consider with open minds what they teach us, and—just possibly—to pursue our own quests for the truth about God and ourselves—that is, to seek our own *gnōsis*.

Bibliography

Augustine. *Confessions*. Translated by Henry Chadwick. Oxford: Oxford University Press, 1992.

Baker-Brian, Nicholas J. *Manichaeism: An Ancient Faith Rediscovered.* London: T. & T. Clark, 2011.

Barber, Malcolm. *The Cathars: Dualistic Heretics in Languedoc in the High Middle Ages*. New York: Longman, 2000.

BeDuhn, Jason David. *The Manichaean Body: In Discipline and Ritual.* Baltimore, MD: Johns Hopkins University Press, 2000.

Behr, John. *Irenaeus of Lyons: Identifying Christianity*. Oxford: Oxford University Press, 2013.

Brakke, David. *The Gnostics: Myth, Ritual, and Diversity in Early Christianity*. Cambridge, MA: Harvard University Press, 2010.

———. "Parables and Plain Speech in the Fourth Gospel and the *Apocryphon of James.*" *Journal of Early Christian Studies* 7, no. 2 (1999): 187–218.

———. "The Seed of Seth at the Flood: Biblical Interpretation and Gnostic Theological Reflection." In *Reading in Christian Communities: Essays on Interpretation in the Early Church*, edited by Charles A. Bobertz and David Brakke, pp. 41–62. Notre Dame, IN: University of Notre Dame Press, 2002.

Brown, Peter. *Augustine of Hippo: A Biography*. New ed. Berkeley: University of California Press, 2000.

Copenhaver, Brian. *Heremetica: The Greek Corpus Hermeticum and the Latin Asclepius in a New Translation*. New York: Cambridge University Press, 1992.

Davies, Stevan L. *The Gospel of Thomas and Christian Wisdom*. 2nd ed. Dublin: Bardic Press, 2004.

Dawson, David. *Allegorical Readers and Cultural Revision in Ancient Alexandria*. Berkeley, CA: University of California Press, 1992.

Dick, Philip K. *VALIS*. Boston: Mariner Books, 2011 (1981).

Dunderberg, Ismo. *Beyond Gnosticism: Myth, Lifestyle, and Society in the School of Valentinus*. New York: Columbia University Press, 2008.

Ecclesia Gnostica. http://gnosis.org/eghome.htm.

Ehrman, Bart D. *Lost Christianities: The Battles for Scripture and the Faiths We Never Knew*. New York: Oxford University Press, 2003.

Evagrius of Pontus. *The Greek Ascetic Corpus*. Translated by Robert E. Sinkewicz. Oxford: Oxford University Press, 2003.

Flannery-Dailey, Frances, and Rachel Wagner. "'Wake Up!' Gnosticism and Buddhism in *The Matrix*." *Journal of Religion and Film* 5, no. 2 (2001). http://www.unomaha.edu/jrf/gnostic.htm.

Foerster, Werner. *Gnosis: A Selection of Gnostic Texts*. Vol. I: *Patristic Evidence*. Oxford: Clarendon Press, 1972.

Fowden, Garth. *The Egyptian Hermes: A Historical Approach to the Late Pagan Mind*. Princeton: Princeton University Press, 1988.

Fredriksen, Paula. *Sin: The Early History of an Idea*. Princeton: Princeton University Press, 2012.

Gardner, Iain, and Samuel N. C. Lieu. *Manichaean Texts from the Roman Empire*. Cambridge: Cambridge University Press, 2004.

Grant, Robert M. *Irenaeus of Lyons*. London: Routledge, 1997.

Hadot, Pierre. *Plotinus, or The Simplicity of Vision*. Translated by Michael Chase. Chicago: University of Chicago Press, 1993.

Harmless, William, S.J. *Desert Christians: An Introduction to the Literature of Early Monasticism*. New York: Oxford University Press, 2004.

Heine, Ronald E. *Origen: Scholarship in the Service of the Church*. Oxford: Oxford University Press, 2010.

Iamblichus. *On the Mysteries*. Translated by Emma C. Clarke, John M. Dillon, and Jackson P. Hershbell. Atlanta: Society of Biblical Literature, 2003.

Jenott, Lance. *The "Gospel of Judas": Coptic Text, Translation, and Historical Interpretation of the "Betraye's Gospel."* Tübingen: Mohr Siebeck, 2011.

Kasser, Rodolphe, Marvin Meryer, and Gregor Wurst, eds. *The Gospel of Judas from Codex Tchacos*. Washington, DC: National Geographic, 2006.

King, Karen L. *The Gospel of Mary of Magdala: Jesus and the First Woman Apostle*. Santa Rosa, CA: Polebridge, 2003.

———, ed. *Images of the Feminine in Gnosticism*. Philadelphia: Fortress Press, 1988.

———. "Reading Sex and Gender in the *Secret Revelation of John*." *Journal of Early Christian Studies* 19, no. 4 (2011): 519–538.

———. *The Secret Revelation of John*. Cambridge, MA: Harvard University Press, 2006.

———. *What Is Gnosticism?* Cambridge, MA: Harvard University Press, 2005.

Krosney, Herbert. *The Lost Gospel: The Quest for the Gospel of Judas Iscariot*. Washington, DC: National Geographic, 2006.

Layton, Bentley. *The Gnostic Scriptures: A New Translation with Annotations and Introductions.* New Haven: Yale University Press, 1995.

———. "The Riddle of the Thunder (NHC VI,2): The Function of Paradox in a Gnostic Text from Nag Hammadi." In *Nag Hammadi, Gnosticism, and Early Christianity*, edited by Charles W. Hedrick, Jr., and Robert Hodgson, pp. 37–54. Peabody, MA: Hendrickson, 1986.

Lewis, Nicola Denzey. "*Apolytrosis* as Ritual and Sacrament: Determining a Ritual Context for Death in Second-Century Marcosian Valentinianism." *Journal of Early Christian Studies* 17, no. 4 (2009): 525–561.

———. *Introduction to "Gnosticism": Ancient Voices, Christian Worlds.* New York: Oxford University Press, 2013.

Louth, Andrew. *The Origins of the Christian Mystical Tradition: From Plato to Denys.* 2nd ed. Oxford: Oxford University Press, 2007.

Luittikhuizen, Gerard. *Gnostic Revisions of Genesis Stories and Early Jesus Traditions.* Leiden: Brill, 2006.

Lupieri, Edmondo. *The Mandaeans: The Last Gnostics.* Translated by Charles Hindley. Grand Rapids, MI: William B. Eerdmans, 2002.

Marjanen, Antti, and Petri Luomanen, eds. *A Companion to Second-Century "Heretics."* Leiden: Brill, 2005.

Markschies, Christoph. *Gnosis: An Introduction.* Translated by John Bowden. London: T. & T. Clark, 2003.

McGinn, Bernard M. *The Foundations of Mysticism.* Vol. 1 of *The Presence of God: A History of Western Christian Mysticism.* New York: Crossroad, 1991.

McGuire, Anne. "Women, Gender, and Gnosis in Gnostic Texts and Traditions." In *Women and Christian Origins*, edited by Ross Shepard

Kraemer and Mary Rose D'Angelo, pp. 257–299. New York: Oxford University Press, 1999.

Meyer, Marvin. *The Gnostic Discoveries: The Impact of the Nag Hammadi Library*. San Francisco: HarperSanFrancisco, 2005.

―――.*The Gnostic Gospels of Jesus: The Definitive Collection of Mystical Gospels and Secret Books about Jesus of Nazareth*. New York: HarperOne, 2005.

―――, ed. *The Nag Hammadi Scriptures: The International Version*. New York: HarperOne, 2007.

Miller, Robert J. *The Complete Gospels*. Salem, OR: Polebridge Press, 2010.

O'Donnell, James J. *Augustine: A New Biography*. New York: HarperCollins, 2005.

Origen. *On First Principles*. Translated by G. W. Butterworth. Gloucester, MA: Peter Smith, 1973.

Pagels, Elaine. *Beyond Belief: The Secret Gospel of Thomas*. New York: Random House, 2003.

―――. *The Gnostic Gospels*. New York: Random House, 1979.

Pearson, Birger A. *Gnosticism, Judaism, and Egyptian Christianity*. Minneapolis: Fortress, 1990.

Plotinus. *The Enneads*. Translated by Stephen MacKenna. London: Penguin, 1991.

Pseudo-Dionysius. *The Complete Works*. Translated by Colm Luibheid. New York: Paulist Press, 1987.

Räisänen, Heikki. "Marcion." In *A Companion to Second-Century "Heretics,"* edited by Antti Marjanen and Petri Luomanen. Leiden: Brill, 2005.

Robinson, James M. *The Nag Hammadi Library.* New York: HarperOne, 1990.

Royalty, Robert M. *The Origin of Heresy: A History of Discourse in Second Temple Judaism and Early Christianity.* London: Routledge, 2012.

Rudolph, Kurt. *Gnosis: The Nature and History of Gnosticism.* San Francisco: HarperOne, 1987.

Scholem, Gershom. *Major Trends in Jewish Mysticism.* New York: Schocken, 1946.

Segal, Alan F. *Two Powers in Heaven: Early Rabbinic Reports about Christianity and Gnosticism.* Leiden: Brill, 1977.

Shaw, Gregory. *Theurgy and the Soul: The Neoplatonism of Iamblichus.* University Park, PA: Pennsylvania State University Press, 1995.

Smith, Carl B. *No Longer Jews: The Search for Gnostic Origins.* Peabody, MA: Hendrickson, 2004.

Tabbernee, William. *Prophets and Gravestones: An Imaginative History of Montanists and Other Early Christians.* Peabody, MA: Hendrickson, 2009.

Tardieu, Michel. *Manichaeism.* Translated by M. B. DeBevoise. Urbana: University of Illinois Press, 2008.

Thomassen, Einar. *The Spiritual Seed: The Church of the Valentinians.* Leiden: Brill, 2008.

Tishby, Isaiah, et al. *The Wisdom of the Zohar.* 3 vols. New York: Oxford University Press, 1989.

Trigg, Joseph W. *Origen*. Atlanta: John Knox Press, 1983.

Tuckett, Christopher. *The Gospel of Mary*. Oxford: Oxford University Press, 2007.

Turner, John D. "Ritual in Gnosticism." In *Gnosticism and Later Platonism: Themes, Figures, and Texts*, edited by John D. Turner and Ruth Majercik, pp. 83–139. Atlanta: Society of Biblical Literature, 2000.

Williams, Michael Allen. *Rethinking Gnosticism: An Argument for Dismantling a Dubious Category*. Princeton: Princeton University Press, 1996.

Notes

Notes

Notes

Notes

Notes

Notes